The Gambler King of Clark Street

The Elmer H. Johnson and Carol Holmes Johnson Series in Criminology

The Gambler King of Clark Street

Michael C. McDonald and the Rise of Chicago's Democratic Machine

~

Richard C. Lindberg

With a Foreword by John Miya

Southern Illinois University Press
Carbondale

Southern Illinois University Press
www.siupress.com

20 19 18 17   4 3 2 1

Publication of this book has been underwritten by the Elmer H.
Johnson and Carol Holmes Johnson Series in Criminology fund.

Cover illustrations: Mike McDonald as treasurer of the Cook County
Democratic Party (Chicago History Museum); Chicago skyline
(cropped; Library of Congress, Prints and Photographs Division)
Cover design: Ashley O'Brien

The Library of Congress has cataloged the hardcover edition as follows:

Lindberg, Richard, 1953–
The gambler king of Clark Street : Michael C. McDonald and the
rise of Chicago's Democratic machine / Richard C. Lindberg
p. cm. — (The Elmer H. Johnson and Carol Holmes Johnson series in criminology)
Includes bibliographical references and index.
ISBN-13: 978-0-8093-2893-2 (alk. paper)
ISBN-10: 0-8093-2893-3 (alk. paper)

1. McDonald, Michael C. (Michael Cassius), 1839–1907. 2. Chicago (Ill.)—Biography.
3. Politicians—Illinois—Chicago—Biography. 4. Democratic Party (Chicago, Ill.)
—History—19th century. 5. Businessmen—Illinois—Chicago—Biography.
6. Gamblers—Illinois—Chicago—Biography. 7. Irish American criminals
—Illinois—Chicago—Biography. 8. Chicago (Ill.)—Politics and government
—19th century. 9. Political culture—Illinois—Chicago—History—19th century.
10. Political corruption—Illinois—Chicago—History—19th century. I. Title.

F548.45.M45L56 2009
977.3'041092—dc22
[B]   2008037830

ISBN-13: 978-0-8093-3583-1 (pbk.)
ISBN-13: 978-0-8093-8654-3 (e-book)

*For the late Paul Newey, who saw corruption
and tried to do something about it*

If Gabriel himself came to Chicago he would lose his character before he had been here six weeks.
—Evangelist Dwight Lyman Moody, speaking to his Chicago Avenue Church congregation, April 5, 1889

There will be gambling in Chicago when we are all dead!
—Captain Luke Colleran, Chicago Police Department, March 12, 1898, following a raid on an illegal poker game held across the street from City Hall

From all they say Chicago is in a terrible situation, being completely in the hands of gamblers and crooks. You may have heard the name of our gaming overlord, Mike McDonald. His fame, I am sorry to say, is widespread. [They] say he is a most influential man in politics here at this time. At Clark and Monroe Streets he owns a faro bank where all sorts of terrible things go on.
—Letter from Martha Freeman Esmond to her friend Julia Boyd in New York, July 17, 1874

Contents

Illustrations

Foreword

John Miya

It's said that history is simply a fiction written by the winners. The whitewashed versions of history rarely reveal more than the intentions of the authors or their patrons. The world that was familiar to the people of the past in their daily press is buried below the polished surfaces of museums and textbooks. But if someone is willing to dig deeper into the vast archive of the past and follow the odd and complicated threads of fact, sometimes a fuller picture emerges. It may be more than we dreamt of or more than we want to know. From this more thorough and nuanced but very real history, we begin to learn about ourselves and the true path that lead us to where we are.

I am a dedicated, fifth-generation Chicagoan who currently resides with my family in what is affectionately known as "The People's Republic of Evanston," a Democratic stronghold but also a city famous for the leaders of the Temperance Movement who were political polar opposites of the nineteenth-century Chicago Democrats. Although my father taught history and my mother's family has lived in the city for generations, I knew only a little of Chicago's story and that of my own family, mostly from oral history.

My maternal grandmother was born at the turn of the twentieth century in a house on the North Side, and I grew up in that house with her. When she was born, our neighborhood still had vegetable farms, but it quickly grew into a tightly knit residential community fed by new transportation options built by the city's titans and scoundrels. Chicago's sprawl of ethnic neighborhoods were often defined by the local Catholic church. Our parish was named for the sixth-century Irish nun and educator Saint Ita. It reflected the Irish Catholic neighborhood that still existed when I was very young. We displayed our culture by wearing green on Saint Patrick's Day. I knew that I had some Irish lineage because my grandmother said that her father (the only Republican in many generations of my family) exclaimed every Saint Patrick's Day that if he only knew what drop of blood in his arm was Irish, he would cut the vein. Being half-Irish, this might have proved fatal.

I eventually learned that my great-grandfather's disdain for the lineage was a reference to his uncle Michael ("Mike") McDonald. As I grew old enough to understand more of the story, my grandmother gave me small snippets. Perhaps in the voice of her father, she said that Mike was "the first Irishman to own his own mayor in the City of Chicago," that his second wife had "shot her piano student," and that when he died, he had to renounce his marriage to a Jewish woman so that he could "die a good Catholic." Grandma also kept, in a dresser drawer, a derringer pistol that Mike had given to his sister (or possibly a niece) when she moved to Chicago to "keep under her pillow, because Chicago was a dangerous place." As far as I know, there was never a bullet with this pistol.

One Saint Patrick's Day when my colleagues at the Chicago Board of Trade doubted the authenticity of my "wearing of the green," I decided to do a quick Internet search for my known Irish relative. The first result to come up was Richard Lindberg's recently published book. I immediately recognized that the Gambler King of Clark Street was indeed our Mike McDonald. I ordered a copy of the book and was soon lost in one jaw-dropping story after another. I learned more about how Chicago went from a swamp to the Windy City in this book than I had from any other source of local history. I knew Mike was our black sheep, but I had no idea that he had been the "chief ram" of Cook County as well. This discovery helped me better understand a complicated duality that Americans face: we desire to know about our roots but fear acknowledging what lies in those tangled depths. But to deny this story is to pretend that its legacy doesn't still exist. It's a story about alliances and organization, and organized crime. It's also the story of a man who made an empire out of confidence, intrigue, and deception, but who in his personal life was repeatedly deceived by his own wives in dramatic fashion, perhaps to the point that it finally broke him.

Although I came to understand the careful editing of oral tradition done by grandparents, as they decide what they want to be passed down, I couldn't reject this real narrative of my family history. I introduced myself to Richard as, apparently, the only known strain of blood relatives to Mike in Chicago. And I began to do a little of my own research in the family archive that my mother keeps and shared it with Richard. There isn't much mention of Mike, just his sister (known as Jenny in my family but referred to as Mary Jane in this book) and her many children, including my great-grandfather. In a nod to this legacy, the wedding rings that my wife and I wear are family heirlooms that are engraved "Louis and Jenny 1867" on the inside, but I scarcely know the person she was. One letter to her from a relative written on the bloody morning of a Civil War battle tells her to wait until after the war to get married, as all the good men are in combat. I can't help but think this is a dig at her brother Mike. Louis, her husband and my great-great-grandfather, was said to have never completely recovered from his war wounds.

If not for this book, the story of Mike McDonald's role in the history of Chicago would be just a few loose threads like the stories from my grandmother, though most of her accounts have developed into fact. I did learn, for example, that the pistol she kept was manufactured in Brooklyn in the 1840s. It is a classic example of a nineteenth-century gambler's pistol. Although it's not easy for my large hands to pull the trigger and it's small enough to fit up one's sleeve or into a vest pocket, the bore of the single shot is oversized, so that it would make a lot of noise and smoke but apparently not put a lot of power behind the lead. It's as likely to leave a nasty bruise at point-blank range or bounce back at the shooter off any surface as to do any real damage to the target. So it's a bluffer's weapon and has more leverage if not used. Perhaps it's the perfect metaphor for this small Irishman, who, with bluster and threats and the skillful use of a bluff and a gamble, became a king and kingmaker. The men who might have that role now are likely more hidden by the state of the current press than Mike was in his day. Luckily, we have a record and writers like Richard Lindberg to show us "warts and all" how the system was wrought, and perhaps how it may linger today. How we use this real history then is a real measure of our free will, as compared to the consumption of the pabulum of whitewashed history. It is a cautionary tale, not a user's manual, and helps us to have some humility about our place in the world. Hopefully there is enough good in it to be proud of the spirit and gumption that forged the future we inherited. In between the good and the bad, the sin and the virtue, is where we live and where we know the characters and the history are real.

Acknowledgments

Because there has never been a published biography of Michael C. McDonald, what has been told about the Gaslight Era gambler over the years has been told anecdotally: snippets of information found here and there, daily transcriptions in the press, and the published memories of veteran reporters and contemporaries. Stories were retold and handed down through the generations. It was the anthologies of early Chicago history written by Herbert Asbury, Bessie Louise Pierce, Henry Justin Smith, Finis Farr, Lloyd Wendt and Herman Kogan, and Frederick Francis Cook, among others, that created the image of McDonald left to us today.

My personal interest in Mike McDonald and his era dates back to 1983, when I began gathering resources for my third book, *Chicago Ragtime*. And so began a fascinating two-decade research project. I am fortunate to live in Chicago and work with a community of exceptionally talented local historians and genealogists who share an interest in the era's politics and aspects of the notorious. Rick Kogan, eminent author, WGN radio talk-show host, and *Chicago Tribune Magazine* editor, provided help with certain aspects of information retrieval. I tapped author Dick Bales's deep understanding of the methodology of tracking down historical Chicago property records. And Dorman Nelson of Granada Hills, California, and Brenda Mason of Kincardine, Ontario, supplied useful clues in the early and later phases of genealogical research into the McDonald family tree.

The librarians at the National Archives in Washington, D.C., and the Newberry Library and Robert Medina of the Chicago History Museum were of great service. Rose Keefe, one of the best of a new generation of historical crime writers, dug into Ancestry.com on my behalf. Chicago-area genealogist Mike Karsen helped solve some of the lingering mysteries surrounding Dora Feldman McDonald and her family roots. In addition to serving as my graduate thesis adviser many years ago, Steven Reiss of the Northeastern Illinois University history department faculty has worked with me on several notable projects over the years. Mark Dunn, also of NEIU, has closely studied the careers of "Parson" Davies and "Oyster Joe" Mackin, both integral figures in the life of

Mike McDonald. His willingness to exchange information is most appreciated. Additional thanks and appreciation go to my old friend and academic mentor, Bernard Brommel, professor emeritus at NEIU; James Durney of Irish Public Television; Christopher J. Carlin, author and retired chief deputy of the Niagara County Sheriff's Office and a former chief of police for the City of Niagara Falls; former Chicago alderman Dick Simpson, who read the manuscript and offered helpful suggestions; Bob Kostoff, Niagara Falls historian, who followed up on a research request; Carol Jean Carlson, for formatting assistance; Mary Claire Hersh; Denise Lindberg; Karl Kageff of Southern Illinois University Press; John Wilson, for his fine copyediting; James J. Conway; Kay Henderson; Robert Remer; Dan Kelley; and R. Craig Sautter. I am grateful to all of you.

The Gambler King of Clark Street

Introduction: The Dark City on the Edge of Civilization

A CHICAGOAN, WRITING ON THE EVE OF THE WORLD'S FAIR OF 1893, a portentous event that opened the city to the eyes of the world, nostalgically looked back on a simpler age, a time before the Civil War and the remarkable period of industrial expansion following the Great Chicago Fire that doomed the pastoral village life they had once enjoyed to a collection of fragmented and distant memories. They remembered an earlier era when antebellum Chicago seemed to move at a slower, gentler pace; when the spires of churches soared above the roofline of commercial buildings on Lake Street, and the town seemed more of a summer holiday resort basking under clean, cloudless skies, buffeted by gentle winds blowing off of Lake Michigan, than the polluted city of reeking tenements and smokestacks, with its uncollected horse dung and discarded waste moldering on the cinder-block streets of the so-called modern age.

"I wish I could picture to you what to me, was a veritable paradise," wrote Abby Farwell, the eldest daughter John V. Farwell, dry-goods merchant, silk-stocking business leader, city official, and one of Chicago's most prominent early builders. "Not even New York in the 1870s with her brownstone fronts could equal Chicago's marble fronts built of white limestone. There was no smoke to discolor them. Around each house was a flower garden and trees also. Oh those marble fronts! How they glistened in the sunshine and in the moonlight shone resplendent in their pale glory. More like a New England village was early Chicago."[1]

Late in life, these old settlers who had ventured westward toward the prairie settlement in the 1830s, '40s, and '50s looked back upon forgotten places and little-known incidents stirring nostalgic longing, but they were saddened by the relentless grind of urbanization, the push of industry and commerce, and the slums, municipal graft, and escalating street crime that consumed the city.

John L. Wilson remembered there was "good fishing in the river and far within the present city limits the prairie chicken shooting began, and there were plenty of them. We were almost all young men from 20 to 30, unmarried and full of goshheaditiveness [*sic*] and all pulled together when anything was up. In short it was more like a large family out here on the edge of civilization and men were virtuous and women happy—what few of them, 28 according to my list, of sweet 16 and over, all unmarried."[2]

Unrefined and increasingly bifurcated, Chicago in the antebellum period was a city of puzzling contradictions. On the one hand, its great commercial houses, its halls of justice, and its municipal offices were filled with Northern men and abolitionists scheming and contriving to deliver the state's favorite son, Abraham Lincoln, to the White House to protect the Union from the Southern hotheads threatening war; but at the same time, the city was awash in "Copperhead" sentiment and rumblings of sedition.

Destined to organize a political-criminal enterprise whose underpinnings extended far into the twentieth century, Michael Cassius McDonald drifted into Chicago during the early years of the Civil War in order to strike his fortune as a "sporting man." The city was full of "bummers" (drifters, cardsharps, bunko operators) and Southern refugees formerly engaged in the Mississippi riverboat trade, until the outbreak of war forced them to flee north to escape conscription in the Confederate Army.

In a twenty-five-year period spanning some of the worst era of political chicanery and wholesale graft and plunder in the Windy City, McDonald was tarred by Republicans, Protestant clergymen, and the reform press as the unelected ruler of Chicago, dictating to the Democratic Central Committee the nominations of boodlers (elected politicians plundering public monies), cardsharps, and saloon owners personally known to him that could do him some favors—his hand-picked coterie anointed for the county and municipal offices—while threatening political reprisals and ruin to reform independents who dared to defy him. As his reputation grew, McDonald was aptly described as "King Mike." He was clever and cunning and a symbol of "wide open" Chicago, with its reputation as a free-and-easy kind of place: tolerant of newcomers and their imported vices and peccadilloes, less genteel in attitude than the older cities of the East, and more Southern in character and outlook than any other comparably sized metropolis above the Mason-Dixon line.

Reports of "gambling hells" cropping up along the lakefront shoreline, escalating street crime, and the pervasiveness of open vice on the fringe of the commercial district filled the pages of the alarmist newspapers of the day. The rock-solid Yankee blue bloods and the churchgoing Protestants, who had grown up with Chicago in the simpler times, shuddered in horror as the leading journals of opinion—the *Chicago Tribune,* the *Inter-Ocean* and the *Chicago Herald*—all Republican in their sympathies, echoed the concerns of the business and mercantile classes they served with lurid accounts of thievery, prostitution, crooked games, and danger.

Squalid conditions in the tenement neighborhoods surrounding downtown and along "Poverty Flats," the West Side immigrant Italian quarter "teeming with Italian children that crawl through the hallways black as Egypt's darkness and pervaded by the smell of rotten fruits," aroused suspicion and nativist prejudices against the dangerous "foreign element" and the "threat" to the public safety the newcomers posed.[3]

In their pro-business advocacy and ministrations for the "common good," editorialists traced the responsibility for deteriorating social conditions, public drunkenness, and the alarming rise in crime to the immigrant people, the liquor interests, the Democratic Party, and their respective party "bosses"; they were all seen as intertwined and held accountable for the attendant problems of labor unrest and lawlessness that threatened to destabilize communities. Nationally, after 1884, the Democrats were tarred as the party of "Rum, Romanism and Rebellion," galvanizing words coming from Dr. Samuel D. Burchard when he addressed a gathering of worried Republicans and the Religious Bureau of the Republican National Committee a week before the 1884 national election.

In his ruminations on the state of the Democracy, Burchard echoed the sentiments of newspaper publisher and former Chicago mayor Joseph Medill, who, in a blistering March 26, 1879, *Tribune* editorial condemning the character of mayoral candidate Carter Harrison, warned all "good citizens" of the coming rapacity and plunder if the popular Bourbon politician were to be elected. "The Party of Revolution and Robbery" the headline read, preceding the Medill editorial.[4]

The *Chicago Times,* a liberal Democratic sheet, played up crime and scandal in clever, alliterative headlines. Under the direction of publisher Wilbur Fisk Storey, the sensationalistic *Times* roasted its powerful rival and lesser imitators as tools of the moneyed class while espousing provocative viewpoints in defense of those on the fringes of society: atheists, socialists, pimps, and in particular, the gambling fraternity and the street demimonde.

Speaking up for the Chicago streetwalkers and the houses of ill repute that sheltered them, Storey, a notorious ideologue, expressed the solemn belief that "in a majority of cases the owners of premises occupied for purposes of prostitution are large property owners and men of recognized wealth and high standing in the community. In a few instances indeed, the landlords are millionaires and the amount realized from this source is not sufficient to pay their 'pew-rent' not to mention contributions to missionary funds and all that sort of thing, and yet this pittance is squeezed out in just as matter-of-fact a way as if prostitution was one of the Cardinal virtues of the Christian religion."[5] The Chicago Board of Trade men and the State Street magnates were aghast and of a mind to lynch Wilbur Storey, if only they could have gotten away with it.

While the two principal parties paid fealty to the highest ideals of their forebears and bitterly castigated each other in the press, in fact they served their respective self-interests, agreeing only on one thing: the necessity for their parties to control appointments and political patronage at the local, state, and federal levels.

"Politicians genuflected to the concept of public good," wrote presidential biographer Zachary Karabell. "But they didn't seem to hold either very dear. Their careers did not depend on bold acts of legislation, stunning moments of oratory, or fighting for an ideal. Every city had its machine, and counties did as well. National politics was simply the apex of a pyramid that rested on local bosses and layers of graft. It was a system of patronage, first and last."[6]

Before the Progressives of the early 1900s addressed the cry for social justice by society's have-nots and greater honesty in government in a meaningful way, the Democratic Party took a less than proactive stance on behalf of trade unionism, the advancement of the eight-hour workday, universal suffrage, or improved educational opportunities for the poor and indigent. The social welfare question, civil service initiatives, and sporadic anticorruption crusades were subordinated to private reform groups like the Civic Federation, the Anti-Saloon League, the Municipal Voters' League (MVL), various third-party interlopers such as the Labor-Greenback movement, settlement houses, the Knights of Labor, the Socialist Party (enjoying strong citywide support in the 1880s), and more militant worker associations taking root in the city at this time.

By the 1870s, the party of Jackson had deteriorated into a tool of clout-heavy "saloon bosses" from the large urban areas wedded to protecting the taverns from Sunday-closing legislation, the brothel keeper from the sermonizing crusades of the Salvationists and blue bloods, and the faro dealer from taking up space in the city bridewell.

An examination of big-city Democratic machines in Baltimore, New York City, Trenton, New Jersey, and San Francisco during this time reveals highly organized syndicates for plunder and graft that grew rich by holding office through firm control of patronage, the withholding of taxes and revenue, the contracting of new loans to pay current municipal expenses, and the protection of the whiskey sellers and gambling interests that brought them to power. In 1883, the Democratic governor of Maryland, William T. Hamilton, denounced the corruptive tactics of the Arthur Pue Gorman machine in Baltimore; a ring of elected thieves from his own party that had held a lock on power since the end of the Civil War. "Julius Caesar never exercised more absolute power on the great election days in Rome, through his election machinery, than did this. Every branch of public service was held, used and conducted with a Praetorian discipline, vigor and cupidity."[7]

The urban saloon was where the working men went to socialize, cash their paychecks, feast on free sandwiches, and lobby for job appointments. Very often the proprietor of the establishment was an alderman, county commissioner, or some other functionary who "had in right" with the administration. Muckraking journalist Lincoln Steffens, author of *The Shame of the Cities,* his 1902 exposé of big-city political corruption, wryly observed: "The quickest way to clear the city council was to stand at the door and yell 'your saloon's on fire!'"

Journalist Bruce Grant and Washington, D.C., radio commentator Earl Godwin, looking back on a century of temperance agitation, correctly noted in 1936 that "the revulsion of public feeling against the saloon was the result of the persistent villainy of the lower element in the liquor trade, which attempted to control politics and to mix the drink trade with commercialized prostitution and other immoralities."[8]

A Gilded Age "liberal" generally opposed the imposition of blue laws. The liberal subscribed to the pragmatic belief that it was not government's place to legislate morality or deny workers the right to gamble or socialize in the manner they had become accustomed to in the Old World. "No Blue Laws for Chicago!" remained the constant refrain of the Carter Harrison Democrats—the political "Bourbons"—around election time as they pandered to these attitudes in order to maintain and perpetuate local control of patronage.

Thus, an antitemperance, antireformist zeal was championed by McDonald and a rising tide of Irish Roman Catholics, German immigrants, and day laborers who enjoyed their "continental" Sundays in the city's beer gardens and after-hours visits to the downtown gambling resorts. The young roughs living elbow to elbow with gamblers and the purveyors of the vice trade in the poverty and squalor of economically depressed neighborhoods acquired the necessary survival skills by cultivating important political connections with key operatives in the saloon trade opposed to notions of "good government" and civic reform. The embryo of modern Chicago organized crime and its various subbranches was spawned in the decades these men rose to power.

Endorsed and supported by the powerful liquor lobby and ethnic fraternal societies organized to defend the saloon trade against Prohibition and blue laws, McDonald's "ward heelers" were deployed across the city to organize the voters and seize control of the courts, the offices of city hall, the bail bondsmen, the police and fire departments, the Cook County Hospital, the sheriff, and wherever else opportunity lurked to plunder the city treasury and acquire "boodle." How had this political-criminal compact succeeded in delivering the city of Chicago into the hands of a ring of grafters, gamblers, and boodlers?

Far from being unique to Chicago during its formative years, *boodle* was a commonly understood nineteenth-century expression in the decades following the imprisonment of New York City's disgraced William Marcy Tweed, in 1871, which symbolized big-city "boss rule" throughout the land.[9]

Mayor Joseph Medill, an insider among the Protestant elites of the city, recognized the symptoms of contagion in Chicago's own backyard upon taking the oath of office December 4, 1871, less than two months after the Great Chicago Fire.

> For several years past good men have witnessed with grave apprehension the alarming deterioration of integrity in municipal administration, and a feeling of despondency and almost despair came over them. Honesty seemed to have departed from the majority of those holding places of trust and honor. In some cities knavish combinations of unscrupulous partisans had seized upon the municipal government by foul and corrupt means, and then rioted in profligate expenditure. Taxes increased alarmingly. Municipal indebtedness swelled frightfully. The disperate [sic], vicious and criminal classes were placed on the city payrolls and sinecure offices for satellites were created by the thousand. The evil example of the New York municipal rule infected, to greater of less degree, all the municipal governments in the union. Did Chicago wholly escape from the contamination? Can it be shown by the increase of our taxation or funded debt? I fear not.[10]

By the time of the Civil War, the city of white picket fences, clean skies, and the comforting appearance of downtown church spires held sacred was forever lost. Uncollected garbage and stagnant pools of brackish water in the tenement streets and back alleys raised fears of the next cholera epidemic. Small boys rolled dice on the muddy wooden blocks of Ewing Street on the West Side, the poorest of the three geographic divisions (west, south, and north). The dust of soft coal and the carcasses of dead horses awaiting the arrival of the rendering company created an unendurable stench permeating both the slums of Chicago and fashionable State Street. Irish prostitutes born and reared in the misery of "Conley's Patch" in the South Loop wandered up and down the length of Randolph Street ("Gambler's Row"). Nearby, on the east side of "Biler Avenue" (a rough stretch of concert saloons and bagnios lining Pacific Avenue between Harrison and Polk Street), stabbing affrays in the rookeries—the "vilest of the vile"—accompanied nightly robberies and "all other sorts of wickedness."[11]

This particular no-man's land had no Midwestern parallel in the 1870s. On the shoreline of Lake Michigan and along the banks of the Chicago River, the weatherbeaten "bumboats" advertising crooked games of chance and the company of dance-hall slatterns clogged the noisy, dimly lit wharves.

Surveying conditions and the gullibility of the patrons of his resort, Mike McDonald provided American folklorists one of their most novel and enduring quotes by allegedly coining the now famous utterance, "There's a sucker born every minute." The *Police Gazette,* that famous chronicle of criminal mischief and misdeeds, once wryly observed: "As Mike McDonald might have expressed it himself—a sucker has to die every minute to make room for the one that is born."[12]

At McDonald's death, the obituary writers reviewed the essential incidents of his life; the highlights, lowlights, and sidelights to a man of persistent energy but misdirected talents and ability. Mike's friends and supporters were generous in their expression of admiration, unshakeable in the belief that his terrible reputation as an underworld czar was a cruel and undeserved one. The eldest sons, the two ex-wives, and those still loyal to him at the end of his checkered life pitied Mike as one of life's tragic victims—while the heirs to the fortune bickered, clawed, and quarreled with one another over the division of the spoils.

Throughout his extraordinary life, he was viewed as a rogue criminal. The *Chicago Herald* minced few words when it called McDonald "a protector of criminals [who] is the recognized 'King of the Tigers.' He is a little god among the thieves, safe blowers, garroters and crooked classes. He is in every way detestable; to be feared for his dangerous powers and to be despised for this brutality, cowardice and braggadocio. Do the people of Cook County want such a character for a ruler?"[13]

McDonald shrewdly recognized that, like any other commodity, politicians could be bought, sold (often cheaply), and forced to heel with the proper inducement of cash incentives. The invincible Democratic machine of the late twentieth century had its roots in the saloons and backroom gambling dens controlled by McDonald in the nineteenth century. The parallels between his era and the corruption scandals of modern-day Chicago are striking.

Succeeding generations of political "bosses" profited by Mike McDonald's example. He was as clever and flamboyant a character the city has ever known. In many respects, he was the perfect symbol of lusty, rollicking, wicked old Chicago—as the world has come to view us.

A Train Butcher Raising the Wind

THE FATHER—LIKE THE SON—WAS A WHISKEY MAN AND A LOYAL Democrat down to the bone. At the end of old Ed McDonald's life, his many friends and neighbors from the Near West Side of Chicago who knew him in better days gathered by his bedside, recalling the throngs of little children tugging on his coat sleeves in the summer months. The youngest of the neighborhood waifs affectionately called him "Gampa," as they pulled on his flowing white beard to see if it was real or not—the beard extended all the way down to his chest. Ed might have easily been mistaken for Santa Claus as he dispensed candy, trinkets, and a mischievous wink to the little ones.

Along Ashland Boulevard, in this luxuriant neighborhood where the rich and wellborn lived side by side with the self-made Irish American politicians of Chicago, who elevated themselves up from hardscrabble, "Gampa" McDonald was regarded as a "good-hearted" man, free of malice and always quick with a joke. In wintertime, when the snow piled high outside the spacious family mansion Michael Cassius McDonald had acquired just a few blocks south from the estate of Carter Harrison Sr., the five-term mayor of Chicago whom old Ed's famous and clever son had elevated to the pinnacle of political power, "Gampa" McDonald could be observed from the street sitting quietly next to the big bay window, observing the promenade as it passed before him.[1]

In the early winter months of 1895, Ed's physical energy drained away. Death was near for the much-beloved eighty-nine-year-old patriarch, and he had only this last wish to convey. He summoned Mike to his chamber and asked if his son would be so kind as to invite his oldest and dearest friend, Danny O'Connor of Niagara Falls, New York, down to Chicago. Danny and Ed had known each other for seventy-five years. They were two of the old settlers of Niagara County; living portraits of age and wisdom. Upon receiving Mike's urgent dispatch, Danny caught the first train out of New York and presented himself at Ed McDonald's bedside for one last reunion, offering comfort and friendship up until the moment when the old man breathed his last and went out smiling.

In those last few weeks of his life, Ed and Danny recalled the struggles of their early lives in County Cork and subsequent adventures in America. Ed McDonald reflected on the curious circumstances of his passage. His father was a tanner, but Ed didn't have much use for the trade, so instead he stowed away on a vessel captained by an older brother and bound for Quebec. When the anchor dropped and the gangplank was lowered, Ed disappeared into the city. Ireland, and whatever attendant economic or family hardships he had endured, were relegated to the past. He was a full-bodied young man of thirty-three, looking to establish himself in North America.

Ed briefly lingered north of the border, before crossing over into western New York, landing in Niagara County about 1837. Not far away, Irish laborers had dug the Erie Canal. The scattered settlement of farmers and homesteaders living in Niagara Falls lay adjacent to a military outpost guarding the doorway into western New York and Pennsylvania. Fort Niagara protected the waterway from the few remaining Seneca and Iroquois tribesmen skirmishing with the white men for control of the fur trade and the more omnipresent threat posed by Canadian separatists. Relations along the border were often strained, particularly during the Patriot War of December 1837, when French Catholics were in open revolt against the British colonial power, the expansion of English rectories, and the movement to unite Lower and Upper Canada.[2]

It was during these troublesome times when New York State helped elevate the Democratic Party, a popular political movement appealing to the small freeholders, immigrant Irish, and rural yeomanry, to national importance. Historians credit Martin Van Buren, "the Little Magician" from the Hudson Valley region, with fusing together an effective coalition of Jeffersonian Democrats, Southern landholders, and Western frontiersmen already loyal to Andrew Jackson into a cohesive party organization that gained its power and prestige through grassroots campaigning, the formation of local "clubs," and ballot-box manipulation. The diminutive Dutchman was mostly a failure as president but an imposing figure in state politics for four decades and much loved by the working man for his advocacy of democratic principles, his sympathy for the Catholic Church, and his principled opposition to the money changers of Wall Street represented by the newly formed Whig Party. American "nativism," based on Protestant suspicion of "popery," emerged as a potent force in American political life among the Whigs during the late 1830s. This bitter factionalism and anti-immigrant sentiment crafted along social and political lines remained a constant theme of urban life through the late Gilded Age.

Ed McDonald embraced Van Buren and the tenets of the Democratic Party as most consistent with his own beliefs in personal liberty and a man's right to get along in life as he pleased. Only once in his eighty-nine years did "Gampa" Ed go against his conscience and cast his vote for a Republican, and that unhappy event occurred at the insistence of his eldest son during the Chicago mayoral election of 1887, when Mike told his followers that he could not stomach a Swedish socialist named Robert S. Nelson occupying city hall for the next two years. The third candidate on the ballot was an even worse alternative: Prohibitionist John Whitlock.

Mike was the Democratic boss of Chicago, old Ed reasoned, so it wasn't a very good idea to go against his quick-tempered son who looked after him and provided him with the care of servants. But a socialist, a teetotaler, and a Republican were the unhappy choices confronting the McDonalds and the county Democracy after Carter Harrison announced his intention not to run for reelection. They were living in dangerous times, Mike McDonald reasoned, and a socialist mayor would be bad for business, coming on the heels of the 1886 Haymarket Riot, in which seven Chicago police officers were blown to bits by an anarchist's bomb during a labor rally.

The Democrat-gambler Mike was still a capitalist after all, and the times demanded pragmatic thinking. With some trepidation, he crossed party lines to support John Roche, a reform-minded businessman running against Nelson. In the strongest terms, Mike urged his father to do the same; understanding, of course, the likely repercussions to his former business associates in the green cloth trade clocking bets along "Gambler's Alley" once the blue blood Roche was installed as the twenty-fifth mayor of Chicago.

On election day, the father and son went to the polls together, voting the Democratic county ticket, while casting their city ballots for the lone Republican. "I done as ye wanted me to," the old man sighed. "I hope to the Lord that he abate."[3]

Ed McDonald had traveled down many roads in life and had known all classes of men. He resented the rich, praised the poor, and conveyed a sunny disposition and eternal optimism throughout. It was his nature. He was a loyal husband and had never strayed far from his marital obligations after being joined in wedlock to Mary Guy, the immigrant daughter of a Limerick shopkeeper who made the dangerous transatlantic crossing in 1830. Unlike Ed, who was less of a believer in the spirit world, Mary was a devout Roman Catholic who repeated from memory the catechism to her three offspring, although the McDonalds lacked formal education. The census taker reported in 1850 that neither Edward nor Mary were able to read or write.

In 1842, six hundred souls lived in Niagara Falls year-round, although two large hotels accommodated a portion of the estimated twelve thousand tourists who came to view the pristine beauty of nature's attractions each year. Billiard rooms and bowling alleys, byproducts of the seasonal tourist trade, opened in 1851, appealing to the young sports of the town.

Ed supported his family as a common laborer in the Irish section located on the north end of Niagara Falls in the working-class parish of Saint Rafael.[4] The Irish were mostly employed in the sawmills, the paper mill, and machine shops—principal industries for the immigrant poor in this tourist town before the Civil War. The McDonalds survived hardscrabble and launched their family with the arrival of their first child, Michael, born September 2, 1839, followed three years later by a daughter named Mary (otherwise known as Jennie), and the youngest son, Ed Junior, sired in 1845. They were a quarrelsome, dirt-poor Irish Catholic immigrant family just trying to get along.

A bright, nimble-minded lad, Mike attended school sporadically. He attended classes at White's Academy before leaving home at age fifteen in 1854.[5] He learned from his mother to respect the teachings of the faith and always "be foursquare" with his friends and family. Although his chosen avocation led him far afield of Mary's religious devotions, McDonald would occasionally flash a charitable side accompanying the attainment of his wealth and power. He was a generous benefactor to his West Side Chicago parish in later years, and his sizeable bankroll spared many a Cook County grafter and down-and-outer a one-way ticket to the Joliet Penitentiary.

The descriptions of his early life inspired by the moral and political inclinations of the newspapers against the "sporting men" paint an unflattering picture of the gambler as a young man. "Mike McDonald was a rascal when a boy," hissed one *Chicago Herald* reporter who charged that "[his] father came around once in a while to help his precious scion on, but that ungrateful person, instead of appreciating the kindness, was wont to give his father terrible beatings; knocking him down and kicking him brutally in the presence of whoever happened along."[6] McDonald's character thus assailed, the writer recalled that, "He ran on trains when quite small and practiced all kinds of disreputable and dishonest tricks known to the 'candy butcher.'"[7]

The early difficulties between father and son stemmed from Mike's adamant refusal to consent to becoming a local boot maker's apprentice; the drudgery of the profession held no special appeal to him. Railroad life, on the other hand, was exciting and a source of endless fascination to the young man. The train yards in Niagara Falls were located not far from the McDonald home, and that was where young Mike saw the chance to escape the drudgery of the town.

Many resourceful nineteenth-century men began their working lives employed as "candy butchers," or "train butchers"—peddling newspapers to the businessman, poetry and works of fiction to the ladies, and popcorn, apples, confections, and various other sundries to rail passengers traveling between cities. Before the advent of child labor laws and the comforts of the Pullman dining car, it was not uncommon in this country to see boys as young as ten hustling for tips and free meals in the nation's ever-expanding rail system.[8] Until the dining car became a regular feature of passenger railroading, the train butcher filled an immediate and critical need.

A successful train butcher was three parts hustler and one-quarter psychologist, possessing a quick eye, keen wit, and a knack for knowing how to unloosen the passenger's purse string. "Study your man," said one veteran of the long haul. "Watch him get weary of the journey and of looking out the window. Most people want something to do. My game is to look people in the eye and sell them what they want when they want it. Sell gum drops to people without teeth and peppermints to the old lady suffering a cold."[9]

Most were the sons of immigrant Irish, penniless orphans, or juvenile runaways fleeing impoverished households. It is conceivable that McDonald began his enterprise when the Great Western Railway Company initiated service in 1853 from the foot of the newly built suspension bridge in Niagara Falls. The line continued to Windsor, a 229-mile trek across southwestern Ontario. Passengers desirous of connecting to Chicago boarded the state-owned Michigan Central road in Detroit to complete the last leg of the journey. Many of them were Irish immigrants winding their way west.

It was less than an ideal run; farmers who lost their livestock to the onrushing trains slicing through the lower forty committed frequent acts of sabotage against the line, tearing up track or firing their weapons at the locomotive from concealed locations in the woods. In the summertime, the stench of burning coal intermingled with the humid air made passenger accommodations almost unbearable.

William E. Tunis, a former schoolmate of McDonald's, established a news agency along the line that employed local boys to sell papers, magazines, and books to the passengers. In the fall of 1854, Mike took a run to Chicago, his fare paid by the Central in return for his agreement to sell candies and papers. The fifteen-year-old lad lingered for two weeks. What he did during this time can only be surmised, but the city left enough of a favorable impression on him that he returned a year later in the company of four school chums from the Falls—Henry Marvin, Jimmy Fehan, and Joseph and John Maronel.[10]

Sociable and mature beyond his years, Mike McDonald frequented the city firehouse at LaSalle and Washington, a crude twelve- by twenty-four-foot shed, with a cistern made of pine lumber barely large enough to hold two hogsheads of water and attended by volunteers. During off-hours from the railroad, the teenage train butcher with comrades John R. Walsh, Gil Baldwin, and Johnny Main loitered inside the shed, soaking up the ribald stories told by the volunteer company, their utterances of profanity, and a devil-may-care attitude that helped shape behavioral patterns. McDonald harbored a lifelong fascination with the city fire department and received a royal welcome from the men in every firehouse he visited.[11]

Meanwhile, he mastered the skills of the train butcher and transferred his business from the Michigan Central to the Chicago, Burlington, and Quincy line. Just ten years earlier, the CB&Q initiated passenger service after building a thirteen-mile track from Aurora to West Chicago before extending it westward to the Mississippi River. The route flourished in the central Midwest, bringing agricultural goods up from southern Illinois, Iowa, Missouri, and Nebraska to Chicago with a score of wealthy farmers and wheat speculators known to the big-city gamblers as the "Granger element"—easy marks for the gamblers, as the Central rolled across the flat Midwestern plain. He caught on quickly to the rhythms of train life, adding decks of cards and dice and other items to a tray already laden with snacks and beverages, thus helping passengers to relieve the tedium of a long ride to Chicago's Grand Central Depot.

McDonald is believed to be the inventor of the "prize package" swindle, a con game emulated by train butchers on every major rail line in the country. It was simple, deceptive, and quite an ingenious little system he devised. Mike guaranteed the passengers that they would be rewarded with cash prizes in every box of candy they purchased from him. The amount of the prize ranged from one penny to five dollars, but of course there were precious few five-dollar payouts. The average prize was less than three cents—the candy and the box cost him a cent and a half.

In order for the sleight-of-hand trick to return a profit, he had to be persuasive and cunning; capitalizing on the victim's greed, naïveté, and love of speculation. "He had a provoking way of leading on his victims to speculate by sympathizing with them when after three luckless grabs they failed to draw a bill, and he himself would apparently select three boxes at random from his basket, open them and take from them great wads of greenbacks," a *Chicago Times* reporter later wrote. "He would close them, toss them back into the basket, mix them up and invite his victim to try again. But Mike knew how to prevent the cash boxes from turning up again. It was his experience in this line that led him to utter the celebrated assertion that "there is a sucker born every minute."[12]

Before long he was dealing a fine hand of cards and sharing cigars with the older, flashier-looking traveling men he came to know on a first-name basis. For two years, McDonald played poker and whist like a champion against men twice his age, fleecing the unsuspecting through his prize-box scam while slowly building a cash reserve that allowed him to expand his future operations. Years later, many of these same men would continue to patronize "Sure Thing" Mike after the former train butcher emerged as the biggest man in town and satisfy their urge to wager at 176 Clark Street, his usual place of business, where liquor flowed till dawn and vast sums of money changed hands minute to minute.

Since earliest Colonial times, gambling has been interwoven with the fabric of American culture. At various intervals in our nation's history, the public's fascination with games of chance sparked feverish interest and heightened levels of participation. In *Gambling and the Law*, I. Nelson Rose of the Whittier Law School in Costa Mesa, California, author and expert on gambling law, has identified three distinct periods in U.S. history when the gambling craze consumed American culture: the early National Period, from the administration of George Washington up through the 1830s, dominated mostly by sweepstakes, keno, faro, three-card monte, euchre, and national lotteries; the spectacular rise in horse-racing popularity witnessed in the 1890s; and the introduction of legalized riverboat gambling following the debut of the first land-based casinos outside of Las Vegas in the late 1970s. Although President Andrew Jackson clamped down on the gambling menace in the 1830s, the popularity of gaming never waned, and the influence of the syndicates only grew stronger in the big cities after 1840.

From the time of Van Buren up to the Civil War, the nation was awash in lotteries and "gambling hells." Caught up in a gambling frenzy, the slow pace of river travel provided the men of means the opportunity to test their skills in games of chance, but the odds of success were rigged in favor of the Southern "blackleg."[13] Gambling along the banks of the river towns fronting the great Mississippi and Ohio waterways evolved into a sophisticated enterprise, one that was not easily put down by the local authorities. The railroad boom provided yet another means of wagering for the mobile, ever-elusive professional gambler.

Recalling McDonald's shady dealings as a railroad cardsharp and candy butcher, the *Chicago Herald* minced few words when it reported that he "ran on Chicago roads until his reputation became so very bad that he could not obtain employment. He then went to New Orleans, where he plied his crooked vocation as long as his presence could be tolerated."[14] McDonald quit train butchering in 1860, after a brief stint selling souvenir booklets to passengers commuting from Hamilton, Ontario, to Toronto during the royal visit of eighteen-year-old Albert Edward, the Prince of Wales, that September. Thereafter, he returned to Chicago, supposedly to cast his vote for Stephen A. Douglas for president before moving south to New Orleans with one Roger Sherman to launch another get-rich-quick scheme. The plan was to open an "agency" inside the posh St. Charles Hotel along Canal Street selling stereoscopic viewing devices, then the rage all across the country.[15] The Sherman-McDonald alliance was a "blind" for a crooked gambling operation the two men concocted in the anterooms of the hotel.

Wagering on horse races and games of chance was not simply a leisurely pastime but a highly stratified business in the Cotton South teetering on the brink of civil war. Poker, invented in New Orleans, was by far the most popular table game of the 1850s, but euchre, faro, brag, and three-card monte were practiced by "no fewer than 2,000 professional gamblers . . . actively engaged in trimming the traveling sucker from Louisville to the Gulf of Mexico." The professional card cheat was easily recognizable by his distinct, perfumed appearance, typically a "black slouch hat, black broadcloth coat and trousers, black flowing tie, high-heeled boots, and a white shirt with low neck and a loose collar. The white shirt was unbelievably frilled, ruffled and frizzled and amidst its billowing folds gleamed a diamond as large as he could afford and popularly known as 'the headlight.'"[16] Add to that a "Shakespeare" collar, a passion for drink, and the company of a similarly situated woman to "raise the wind" for him until her savings were dissipated and she was of no further use.

After observing firsthand the rituals and stylish fastidiousness of the riverboat gamblers, McDonald acquainted himself with the patrons and sponsors of the lush parlors of Canal Street where billiards, card games, horse racing, and cockfighting were conducted without interference from the police and magistrates. New Orleans, with its sublime glamour, reputation for extravagant living, and air of wickedness left a lasting impression on Mike, affording him a privileged glimpse into a world that stirred his feverish imagination. Here, before him, stretched America's first "wide open" city; a raucous, sweltering cesspool where vice reigned supreme and alliances with sympathetic politicians made it possible for smart fellows to come out ahead. In a world such as this, crime and violence, of course, were endemic. "If there is any city in the civilized world which can offer a bloodier and more revolting record, we are not aware of its existence," groused a writer for the *New Orleans Bee* in 1860.[17]

In 1823, city officials in New Orleans had taken the unusual step of legalizing gambling in the belief that they "should compel the devil to pay tribute to virtue."[18] Six palaces of chance, each of them paying out $5,000 as a means of underwriting the city's Charity Hospital and the College of Orleans presaged similar schemes that gained currency among cash-strapped municipalities in late-twentieth-century America.

As McDonald emulated the gambler's manner of dress, studied the organizational structure of the New Orleans underworld, and observed the shocking police indifference to the nightly saturnalia, an idea began to germinate. Was it not true that liberal Southern "attitudes" toward the traditional vices among the freethinkers of the French Quarter were favorably received by the keno players and faro dealers whose friendship he had cultivated in the Great Lakes frontier town?

He might have remained in this gambler's paradise for the duration of the war if not for the impudent Mr. Sherman, who, according to McDonald's published recollections, was a "hothead Abolitionist" who made his pro-Northern sympathies known to spite the wrong people. The night after the fall of Fort Sumter, a contingent of Confederate regulars raided the hotel to arrest Sherman and interrogate McDonald. They asked what business he had in New Orleans. Thinking fast, McDonald said he was a "New York Democrat who voted for Douglas." It helped him escape imprisonment or possible execution as a Yankee spy. The Federals never knew that he had cast his vote for Douglas in Natchez, Mississippi—illegally. Without so much as inquiring after Sherman, he packed his valise and fled north aboard a Memphis-bound steamer. McDonald managed to remain a step ahead of the Rebel patrols and made his connections to Chicago and then to the safety of his father's Niagara Falls home, where he took a few months off to review his situation.[19]

His thoughts kept returning to Chicago and the gamblers he had observed in their familiar haunts carrying on at all hours: the well-dressed youngbloods in the saloons and gambling dens lining the north side of Randolph Street between State and Dearborn, throwing dice and pulling cards from the green layouts of the faro box in the hazy glow of the gaslight; the hoarse cry of the keno seller heard above all else as he shouts out the number of the card he has just sold and reminds the unwitting patrons ranging in age from sixteen to sixty, men coming from the squalor of the impoverished classes and the opulence of the upper world, "There is luck in odd numbers!"[20]

Chicago was a comparatively young city, but it had much in common with New Orleans. Both locales attracted a fair number of Southern blacklegs who opened for business with minimal opposition. From the earliest times, gambling and vice were entangled on the shores of Lake Michigan, with very little municipal oversight. George C. Rhodes, John Sears, "Colonel" Wat Cameron, George "One Lung" Smith, and Cole Martin struck it rich in Chicago in the 1840s sponsoring backroom keno and card games.

The genteel thieving of the cardsharps carried on up and down the "Hair-trigger Block," that stretch of Randolph Street so-named for the pistol play of George Trussell and Samuel H. "Cap" Hyman, two undisciplined roughs growing rich by gambling who struggled to gain a competitive edge over each other. Street brawls, garroting, and nightly shootings were common in the nocturnal drama of Randolph Street, where Trussell was its most famous and well-adorned citizen blackleg. He had come up from Caledonia, Virginia, about 1839, to take a job as bookkeeper in the banking firm of George Smith and Company. His habits were regular, and he was praised as an exceptional businessman with a good future ahead of him. While attached to Richmond and Company, a large commission house in the city, Trussell's regimen suddenly became quite irregular; he had acquired a yen for fast horses, the faro table, and the company of the fallen women of Fourth Avenue and began neglecting his official duties.

Abandoning the world of commerce and industry, Trussell rented rooms from a notorious Southern "Copperhead" in the Larmon Block at Clark and Washington Streets and ran his own game—a real "gambling hell." Trussell was also instrumental in the evolution of the "turf" sports in Chicago. He was an astute horseman who backed winners and grew rich. One of the horses in his stable, a prized trotter named Dexter, became so famous that a South Side racing oval was named after him.[21] Dexter was the pride of the West, but his owner garnered little respect running crooked faro banks all over Chicago, New Orleans, Buffalo, St. Louis, and New York.

Trussell took as his lover one Mary A. "Mollie" Cosgriff, a callow, fourteen-year-old chambermaid he had met at the American House hostelry in Chicago during one of his afternoon romps. He kept the girl under his wing for a number of years, before the couple sired a child out of wedlock. After she was back on her feet and caring for her baby, Mollie was compelled to become the "madam" of an elegantly furnished, aristocratic-appearing brothel at 178 Fourth Avenue controlled by Trussell so that she could pay for the baby's upkeep. The promised vow of marriage never materialized, and Trussell eventually threw her off after tiring of her maudlin harangues for his sympathy and affection. Typical of the embarrassing notoriety that earned Chicago its reputation as an ungovernable "Wild West" kind of town was the deadly gunplay of the jilted Mollie .

On a September evening in 1866, hours after jockey Budd Doble drove Dexter to victory over the California stallion George M. Patchen Jr., Trussell was toasting his good fortune inside Seneca Wright's Randolph Street concert saloon with a drink in hand, when the angry, lovelorn Mollie suddenly burst through the doors. "Come here George, I want you!" she demanded. Trussell, who had spurned the footman's demand to come out onto the street and hear Mollie's latest complaint just moments earlier, turned away in disgust. The aggrieved woman pushed her way past the horde of drinkers and their consorts. She grabbed him by the collar, spun him around, and drawing a concealed handgun from her purse, fired a shot that pierced his heart. George Trussell, thirty-two years of age, was dead the second he hit the floor.

The coroner and the police arrived within minutes to survey the awful scene and escort the murderess off to the Cook County jail. "Oh don't take me away! I want to kiss George once more. Oh let me kiss George once more!" the woman wailed. "I gave up all for him—all hopes, friends, relatives, everything for him."[22]

Mollie Trussell, as she was known, who had an influential backer footing her legal bills throughout the ordeal, served only a few months' imprisonment before receiving a formal pardon, prompting the bemused *Chicago Times* publisher Wilbur Storey to pen these few lines of wry sarcasm in an editorial vent against the Good Templars and Chicago clergy: "It is well that she had been pardoned. She had *only* killed a man, shot him to the heart in a saloon. Shooting a man in a saloon was good—a *very good* work. If Mollie Trussell had been hung for performing so great a service to mankind and to the temperance reform, a judicial murder would have been committed."[23] The alluring Mollie was never forgotten in Chicago. She eventually migrated to California where, oddly enough, a horse was named after her.

"Cap" Hyman, who underwent a religious conversion soon after the Chicago Fire laid the city of Chicago to waste, was more of a gamesman than an underworld overseer, despite frequent run-ins with Trussell over who would control the take from cassino, a popular card game Cap imported from New York in 1861. "Success generally attended his playing both at this game and at faro, and he soon became known as the oldest and wealthiest gambler in Chicago. In his palmiest days he is said to have been the possessor of $80,000 in clear cash, besides an excellent outfit of jewelry and diamonds. In a single evening in the year 1867, he lost at one sitting $19,000."[24]

And while he dressed "in the most elegant fashion" and "moved among the best members of the profession," Cap spent lavishly and sunk vast sums into a doomed horse-racing venture to keep up with Trussell. His Sunnyside Track in what is now the Lakeview neighborhood of Chicago was a bust, and his choice of female companionship was nearly as regrettable as his principal Randolph Street rival. Cap ran with "Gentle" Annie Stafford, the notorious brothel keeper operating down the street from Mollie Cosgriff at 119 Fourth Avenue in the Cheyenne District, west of downtown. Annie, a rotund procuress, was anything but a gentle fawn. She flailed away at Cap with a horse whip whenever he was suspected of stepping out with the bawds of Little Cheyenne.

The racetrack at Sunnyside ultimately bankrupted the good captain. Then the Great Fire destroyed the small confectionary store he had opened on Randolph Street in a failed attempt to go straight and forsake his past associations. With nothing left of value that might help him to get started again, Cap turned to Jesus for salvation and to the charity of strangers who purchased his "tintype" photographs taken of the fire destruction. He peddled the humble images on street corners until consumption, complicated by venereal disease, laid him low. The Sisters of Mercy took him in, but their charity went only so far. His faculties gone, Cap Hyman ended his days a penniless vagrant in the Johnstown House, a seedy lodging house at the corner of Madison and Des Plaines. The *Chicago Times* noted: "At times he imagined himself a poet, again a candidate for some honored position, and some of the strange hallucinations which sometimes filled his brain would have been amusing had it not been for the feeling of pity which his senseless mutterings aroused in the minds of those who were familiar with his past life."[25]

The lessons learned from the poor examples set by Trussell, Hyman, and other well-known Southern blacklegs taught McDonald that if the Chicago gambling fraternity and sporting world had any hope of surviving adverse public opinion and the attacks of zealous church reformers, what was needed most was sober, evenhanded leadership, a master plan of organization with proper distancing between commercial vice and public gaming, popular support from elected officials, and immunity from police raiding parties. He realized that it might require years of careful planning and trial and error to import the New Orleans method to Chicago, but McDonald shrewdly recognized (as would many big-city Irish American bosses in the coming decades) that the prostitution racket was not only distasteful and an affront to his ingrained Roman Catholic catechism, it was also bad business and potentially ruinous to the lifeblood of the gambling syndicates.[26]

Control of the segregated brothel districts proliferating in urban America in the second half of the nineteenth century gradually shifted away from Southerners and men and women with Anglo-Saxon surnames. Prostitution was mostly abandoned and left to the Russian Jews, Italians, and various Eastern Europeans arriving later in the squalid tenement districts of the big cities. The economically depressed and squalid immigrant ghettos became natural incubators for violent crime, street gangs, and moral turpitude.

At the same time Mike McDonald was racing northward with a plan to "organize" Chicago, his sister Jennie was being trained as a dressmaker, while brother Ed was at sea. Trained as a railroad machinist, the younger McDonald devoted some attention to marine engineering and signed on as a fireman with the *Niles,* a steamship traversing the Great Lakes from Buffalo to Chicago. Later he joined the crew of the *Powhatan,* one of the Black Star Line of tramp steamers sailing down the Atlantic Coast from New York to New Orleans. He was next an assistant engineer on the *Cleopatra,* part of the New York and Mexican Mail Line.[27]

There was no scarcity of jobs aboard the merchant and passenger ships in the "Age of Sail," but the work was hard, and the sea was a lonely place for an introspective man like Ed McDonald who dreamed of a stable and productive home life. Ed's nautical career was filled with many adventures, but he could never quite manage to separate from Mike's baleful influence. His future misfortunes were irreversibly tied to the schemes of his older brother. Lacking Mike's charisma, guile, and knack for self-promotion, Ed was thus compelled to live a life in the shadow and accept the best political patronage plum his brother, the gambler, could dole out—patronage that would ultimately land him a berth in the Cook County jail.

~ 2 ~

Brace Games and Bunko Men

THE OUTBREAK OF THE CIVIL WAR AND LOUISIANA'S SECESSION from the Union in January 1861 temporarily halted casino operations in New Orleans. Martial law was imposed, and the great paddlewheel riverboats were pressed into wartime service. A leisurely way of life was slowly disappearing in the fog of war.

The Confederate states demanded that all able-bodied Southern men join the cause, and the cardsharps, pimps, and grifters (confidence men; tricksters) of New Orleans and Natchez were not exempt from duty. In April 1862, with Admiral David Farragut's fleet pummeling Confederate forts on the Mississippi, the gamblers formed their own volunteer company, the Wilson Rangers, or "Blackleg Cavalry," and served the cause unenthusiastically for less than three weeks before turning and running in the face of superior firepower.

With the arrival of the marauding Union Army and the subsequent oc-cupation of New Orleans, the Rangers slipped back into the city, where their commanding officer, a gambler, supposedly ordered them to "Dismount! Hitch horse! March! Hunt shade! Begin playing!" George Devol, a wizened riverboat gambler who had marked time inside the Chicago bridewell, recalled it differ-ently: "When we got back to the city we dismounted without orders, cut the buttons off of our coats, buried our sabers and tried to make ourselves look as much like peaceful citizens as possible for we had enough of military glory and were tired of war."[1]

Their services voluntarily ended, a faction of the Rangers and sporting men of New Orleans made convenient alliances with the occupying Federals, paid a stiff "street tax" for the privilege of operating, and took in the brother of Union general Benjamin F. Butler as a full salaried partner.[2] Many more refugee black-legs filtered north to avoid conscription, imprisonment, or harassment by the

Union occupiers. Mike McDonald's flight from New Orleans and his decision to permanently settle in Chicago, however, had more to do with the smell of money than an overriding fear of military impressment.

In the first year of the war, McDonald was making mischief in Chicago "playing short cards for a business until he got broke," the *Chicago Herald* reported. "He then engaged in the bounty jumping brokerage business. He used to run bounty jumping confidence men and thieves and crooks of every description to Indianapolis, Buffalo, Cincinnati and other cities on commission, making considerable money robbing the government."[3]

Bounty jumping was a chronic nuisance to the military authorities and the Chicago police, who were pressed into emergency duty to check the menace. In the large cities of the North, state and municipal governments offered the powerful inducement of $300 to $400 cash "incentives" to encourage enlistment. The bounty jumper would seize the first opportunity to desert camp and then reenlist somewhere else in the country where he was not known, and thus secure another government payout. McDonald organized the jumpers into a "ring" that became a flourishing wartime racket and provided resourceful criminals the means to get rich.

In his 1910 volume of city history, *Bygone Days in Chicago,* author Frederick Francis Cook paints a heroic, albeit fictional, account of McDonald valiantly answering President Lincoln's call for volunteers by affixing his signature alongside those of Alderman John Comiskey and a select group of powerful Democratic ward leaders who desire to organize the 23rd Illinois Infantry Brigade—"For the honor of the old land!"—and (more important) to dispel the rising hostility and anger in the North that the party of Jackson and Van Buren was not foursquare behind the defense of the Union. The Irish Brigade of Chicago was mustered in during a stirring, open-air, torchlight rally in Market Hall on April 20, 1861, just seven days after the fall of Fort Sumter. Commanded by Colonel James A. Mulligan, a popular Chicago Irish politician turned soldier, thirty-two sons of the *auld sod* living in the poorest West and South Side immigrant enclaves answered the call that night. Another one thousand were outfitted in Union blue over the next three days and given their marching orders. To be sure, Michael C. McDonald, just twenty-one years of age at the time, was not counted among the enlistees as they prepared to push on to Missouri to engage a Confederate garrison in a disastrous skirmish that resulted in Mulligan's surrender and prison camp internment for most of the green Chicago recruits.[4]

Crime historian Herbert Asbury and Chicago journalist Henry Justin Smith repeated Cook's dubious assertion in their own published volumes, but the truth is McDonald did not return to Chicago until the fall of 1861. He signed no petitions, made no pledges or guarantees, and swore no oaths of allegiance to any particular cause, save his own. He chose instead to ride out the conflict as a war profiteer, trading paid deserters with the government in association with

"Tip" Farrell, Charley Miller, John Sutton, and Matt Duffy, four veteran Chicago confidence men who had taken him under their wing, mentored him, and split the government bounty received for each "repeater" returned to active duty.

"That there is some rascality afoot we are bound to believe," the *Chicago Tribune* reported after two police officers were arrested and charged with receiving bribes from deserters. "The public will join with us in the desire that the guilty offender, who ever they may be, receive punishment."[5] The bluecoats refused to reveal the names of their cohorts, and the case was dismissed for want of evidence, leading the paper to ask, "What guarantee have we that our persons and property will be safe when trusted officials share with thieves the wages of crime?"[6] The officers of the demoralized and understaffed eighty-eight-member city police force (earning just $75.00 a month in 1864) were susceptible to cash bribes and other forms of compensation.

The ring was active in the years 1861–64, the time frame in which McDonald is known to have established his first Chicago residence in Bridgeport, a neighborhood in the old Fifth Ward where the poorest of the famine Irish contended with outbreaks of cholera and smallpox, and where deadly altercations played out at the notorious Garden Saloon at Halsted Street and Archer Avenue, and amid the squalor of wooden lean-to flats, built two to the city lot. The scale of human misery, poverty, and violence earned Bridgeport the nickname "Hardscrabble." In many respects it was the Chicago equivalent of the Five Points section of Manhattan up through the end of the nineteenth century. The police called Bridgeport the "Terror District."

Lumberyards and massive grain elevators dotted the banks of the South Branch of the Chicago River. The distant stench of the Union Stockyards wafted through the tenements, and Camp Douglas, the Confederate prisoner-of-war camp lying directly east of Ward Five, became the focal point of a foiled secessionist plot to free the detainees, unhinge the Federal Armies of the West, and occupy Chicago. The loyalty and courage shown by the 23rd Illinois Infantry Brigade did little to assuage popular feeling among Chicagoans that the Irish of Bridgeport were treacherous to the bone and would side with the Confederacy at their earliest possible opportunity.

Joseph Medill's *Chicago Tribune* whipped up dangerous ethnic, religious, and class demagoguery in those tense, uncertain days; as the paper routinely published the names of "alien voters"—Irishmen and Germans from Bridgeport and the adjacent Sixth and Seventh Wards of the South Side—"sneaks and Copperheads who on the day of the last charter election voted for [Democratic mayoral candidate Francis Cornwall] Sherman. These are the chaps who have loudly prated in years gone by, of their regard for the Constitution and laws. The Irish element of course largely predominates."[7]

Michael C. McDonald's name appears in print in an 1864 listing of Democrats and Copperheads the *Tribune* counted along with the many Sullivans,

O'Briens, Ryans, Kellys, Murrays, Doyles, and Donohues of the South Side suspected of being in league with the Rebellion.[8] Later that year his name was included in a list of five hundred Chicago men shamed and castigated for taking out "foreign protection papers" in order to escape the draft. "Let our ward vigilance committees watch and protect the ballot boxes from their polluting touch," the *Tribune* cautioned its readers on the eve of the national election.[9]

McDonald's underworld ascendance and reputation as the principal supplier of dice, cards, and political patronage in Chicago began on the passenger rail lines and was nurtured by his avoidance of the draft and the success of his bounty jumping ring. His escapades helped establish important connections and provided him the financial means to move up in the underworld while he cleverly avoided arrest and prosecution.

With the backing of whiskey salesman and professional gambler Calvin P. Paige, who sponsored card games in the rear of his Madison Street saloon (where the notorious confidence man Johnny Sutton met his maker during a rapid exchange of gunfire one night in 1864), McDonald and his cohorts achieved business legitimacy by purchasing the rights to own and operate a bar inside the Richmond House at the foot of South Water Street and Michigan Avenue.[10] The fashionable, sixty-room hostelry was a favorite overnight rendezvous for travelers making connections in Chicago because of its economical rate ($1.50 per night), its close proximity to the Illinois Central Depot, and ease of access to the major east-west rail lines stretching along the city lakefront. King Edward, as the Prince of Wales, was its most famous guest during his celebrated Stateside royal tour of 1860.

Before the building was consumed in flames during the Great Chicago Fire of 1871, the Richmond House acquired a reputation as a place where one could go to experience "down-home Southern hospitality" in a semi-exclusive setting. Significantly, it was the principal outpost of gamblers, bookies, confidence men, bunko artists, and suspicious individuals desirous of keeping a low profile while fleecing wealthy patrons inside the hotel.[11] Before the Great Fire, during the summertime racing season, it was customary for the keeper of the Richmond House and other hostelries to sponsor fifty-dollar "trotting sweepstakes," half forfeit (half the admission price) for colts and fillies foaled the year prior that were scheduled to race at the Dexter Park course. As a matter of practice, wealthy and respected hotel men like John B. Drake, owner of the Tremont House where Abraham Lincoln was a guest, sanctioned pool selling in their establishments on the premise that it was good for business.

The "Sport of Kings," integrating the denizens of the underworld with the better element in a leisurely setting given the stamp of legitimacy, was not McDonald's special fixation. He wasn't especially interested in the art and science of horse breeding and was uncomfortable in the company of the big-name "turf men" from around the nation, like Edward Corrigan, who were attempting to monopolize the East and West Coast jockey clubs, but he smelled money in it nevertheless. By the early 1880s, McDonald and his henchmen were said to be in "control" of a syndicate that pulled down a cool $800,000 in one season.[12]

The agreement to purchase the Richmond House bar privilege, launching the Paige and McDonald business partnership and Mike's future road to prominence, was consummated in the fall of 1861.[13] Paige, a well-known raconteur and prosperous gambler, supplied the upfront cash to close the deal, while McDonald busied himself behind the bar stocking the finest wines and spirits, clocking bets on the sulkies, and making important connections with local politicians stopping by for the noon-hour victuals and arriving hotel guests from the Illinois Central Depot flush with green. "Every hotel had its bar, and song and jest and story made the evening reunions memorable," wrote Paul Gilbert in his civic history of Chicago. "There after the day of business, gathered the city's builders from court room and office, from shop and store, to relax and enjoy the society of their fellows. There visiting celebrities were entertained and there were staged many grand events of the social world."[14]

Although McDonald listed his principal wartime occupation as "travel agent" with offices at 219 West Polk Street, the hotel was the real "clearing house" for the nightly "snooker" run by McDonald and his gang of handpicked confidence men, bunko steerers, card cheats, and "cracksmen," whose task was to canvass the train stations and hotel lobbies for the purpose of luring the unsuspecting into games of chance staged in the private rooms of the Richmond House, Paige's saloon, or nearby commercial buildings where accommodations could be made with the property owner.[15]

McDonald's beloved mother Mary passed away in Niagara Falls at age fifty-three on April 11, 1863, and his father, Ed, although a robust man in his fifties and quite capable of supporting himself, was left alone. Against his better judgment, Mike decided to bring his father down to Chicago to live under his roof and at his personal expense—a situation fraught with tension that contributed to years of bruised feelings and open animosity between the two. The son's famous temper must have taken a toll on the *paterfamilias,* but loyalties and obligations to kin were sacrosanct in the tight-knit Irish Catholic culture. Regardless of differences, McDonald was determined to hold his little family together against his growing impatience with the old man's infernal "ways."

However, the arrangement proved most unsatisfactory, and the escalating domestic difficulties eventually forced the gambler to change his living accommodations. The fetching Isabella "Belle" Jewel, a young actress dancing in the chorus line at the McVicker's Theater (where the immortal Sarah Bernhardt would make a glorious and unforgettable Chicago debut in 1880), caught McDonald's attention and soon, with his new paramour by his side, he took up residence at 1433 Wabash Avenue, a more upscale Fifth Ward abode east of the grime, the stench, and the violence of Bridgeport that were so unbecoming to a young man aspiring to achieve sophistication and move in higher social circles.[16]

Having become something of an "uptown swell" by virtue of keeping company with a pretty chorine prominent in the show world, McDonald exhibited his flashy charm by making the rounds with the performers and stage managers at the Grand Opera House, Hooley's Theater, Jack Haverly's theatrical palace at Monroe and Dearborn, and the nearby restaurants forming the nexus of Chicago's emerging "rialto" of the pre-Fire period.[17] Belle Jewel accepted her role as the common-law wife of Michael C. McDonald, but there were no children.

Their decision not to exchange vows remained an open secret during the entire seven years the couple kept house on fashionable Wabash Avenue. Escorting his love mate around to all of the famous show spots, ranging from Kinsley's Opera House Restaurant to Chapin and Gore's Restaurant on Monroe, he introduced Belle to his associates as "Mrs. McDonald." She was accepted "by the boys" as his lawful soul mate, and no one among the inner circle dared to utter a snide remark or spread malicious gossip.

McDonald volunteered no further details of his relationship with Belle. Vanquished from the public record, her name does not appear in any of the sanitized biographical accounts appearing in the published directories of Cook County politicians of the 1880s and 1890s. Hoping to polish his image for the sake of his sons and posterity, McDonald went to great lengths in the twilight of life to blot out this woman's name. It wasn't until after his death that the cloak of secrecy surrounding the private life of the public man was unveiled to reporters.

Following Belle's inevitable split with McDonald—their separation occurring on the eve of the Great Fire, after Mike kindled a new romance with Mary Noonan Goudy, a vivacious Ohio divorcée he met on a business junket to Cleveland—the actress quit Chicago and the theatrical world to become a Sister of Charity of the Blessed Virgin Mary in a St. Louis convent.[18]

Late in the war, while Mike was busy with his romancing, his brother Ed was engaged by the U.S. Government Transfer Service to run a transport ship ferrying Confederate POWs to a station in Lake Erie and eventually down the Atlantic coast. Later, after a few years of marginal living aboard a succession of tramp steamers, Ed accepted a two-year appointment as chief engineer in the *New York Herald* office of publisher James Gordon Bennett. However, relations between Ed McDonald and Bennett soured, and his contract was not renewed.

Depressed, unsure of his future calling, and lacking rudimentary schooling, Ed was adrift and looking to establish himself for much of the decade following the surrender at Appomattox. He resumed his nautical career aboard the steamer *Knickerbocker,* until being summoned back to Chicago in 1876 with a furnace manufacturer's promise of a full partnership in the startup of a new business venture. The company went bankrupt, forcing Ed to accept a menial position in Mike's gambling house as a cashier and bouncer. Now, the youngest, sister Jennie, was the only McDonald family member not beholden to her brother for her daily bread and board. She had wisely gone west to marry a man named Louis Miller, forsaking offers to settle in Chicago.

Mike McDonald devoted much of his time and energy to managing his hotel bar, where he made a few important business contacts of his own, picking up useful bits of information here and there and dealing cards on the side. But as the tide of war slowly turned, Southern desperation mounted. The city was full of disquieting wartime rumors of a pending Confederate intrigue—much of the loose talk emanated from the public houses and hotel bars—the usual places to go to gain intelligence. Ten trunk railroads coursed in and out of Chicago every day of the Civil War, accelerating commerce and bringing to the city a mix of foreign travelers, business agents, westward homesteaders, Southern sympathizers, and *agents provocateurs*. From the latter group came many Confederate exiles who lodged in the Richmond House, considered a rebel haven, quite possibly because of its name.

A secret plan was hatched among the Copperhead leaders in the North and scores of Canadian expatriates to liberate eight thousand POWs from Camp Douglas, disrupt the coming 1864 Democratic Convention, and commence the first armed insurrection above the Mason-Dixon Line. The Sons of Liberty, a cabal of Confederate firebrands directed by Jacob Thompson, former secretary of war under President James Buchanan, hatched the ill-fated plot behind locked doors of a nondescript building overlooking the northwest corner of Clark and Monroe Streets—by strange coincidence, the future location of "the Store," Mike McDonald's deluxe gambling emporium.

Among the rebel plotters were a handful of men who would go on to become standard-bearers of the Cook County Democratic Party in the postwar Reconstruction era: Congressman Bernard G. Caulfield for one, and Dr. Swayne Wickersham, a McDonald man elected First Ward alderman in 1879 and elevated to the chairmanship of the powerful Finance Committee and then city health commissioner. He was an important behind-the-scenes operative appointed by McDonald to numerous party caucuses and state nominating conventions in the 1870s–90s. They were to become important political allies and powerful party spokesmen when the Democrats challenged Ulysses S. Grant in 1868 with a candidate championing the saloon interests, espousing a segregationist point of view, and rebuking any president "who is not in favor of a white man's government; know-nothings who will pass a law requiring that a foreigner shall live in this country twenty-one years before he is entitled to vote . . . and place it [the vote] in the hands of the negro."[19]

McDonald had a knack for remaining one step ahead of trouble and made a wise decision to fold his liquor business at the Richmond House late in 1863 or early 1864—likely due to an extensive remodeling of the lower floors of the hostelry and the installation of a manager from New York City who engaged new concessionaires—and not as a result of wartime intrigues. The building renovation occurred six months ahead of the Camp Douglas Conspiracy.

The full story of McDonald's involvement in the plot may never be known. That he took an active role in its design and execution cannot be positively ascertained nor can it be completely ruled out, although his close association with Caulfield, Wickersham, and James Geary, a gun-running merchant doing business in a used clothing store at the corner of Wells and Madison Streets, is reliably reported in the political pages and accounts of the Chicago underworld in the 1870s. Geary, who provided clothing to escaped rebel prisoners, was the designated middleman for the distribution of arms to the sixty bushwhackers and guerillas who had arrived in Chicago by train the day before the start of the Democratic Convention.

The Sons of Liberty and the many Canadian exiles sneaking past U.S. border patrols in Windsor, Ontario, conducted their clandestine meetings at several downtown locations including the Richmond House, where two hundred members of the Sons of Liberty gathered on July 20, 1864, for the express purpose of "uniting Illinois, Kentucky, Missouri, Ohio and Indiana with the Confederate States of America" by seizing control of the Court House, breaking down the high-boarded enclosure of Camp Douglas, thus freeing up the prisoners to commandeer the polling stations of Chicago and raise havoc in the streets. Two million CSA dollars were transferred to the brigands to purchase arms and recruit new men into the ranks as a result of this meeting.

The Sons of Liberty were the guests of the hotel. They swelled the lobby, puffing cigars, speaking glowingly of Union general George McClellan's prospects as the Democratic "peace candidate" in 1864 as they drew down pints of gin behind the potted palms. As a result of the rumor mill, word began to leak out of a pending intrigue; whispered tales of spies and saboteurs bringing the war to the doorstep of the city were rampant.

It was entirely unreasonable to expect that such a far-flung scheme involving Copperheads from the Border States, Illinois, Indiana, and the provinces of eastern Canada could keep a secret very long. Intelligence about the impending attack was quickly conveyed to Colonel Benjamin J. Sweet, Camp Douglas's commander, by a pair of double agents two days before the planned date of execution. The 196th Pennsylvania Infantry, supported by the 24th Ohio Battery, rushed to Chicago to reinforce Camp Douglas and quash the insurrection before it had the chance to escalate into full-flown combat.

Private homes, including the residence of Charles Walsh, an unsuccessful candidate for Cook County sheriff and brigadier general of the Sons of Liberty, were searched, and stockpiles of ammunition and cavalry carbines seized. The conspirators who failed to escape southward amid the uproar accompanying the first published dispatches of the treachery afoot were imprisoned at Camp

Douglas and later put on trial in Cincinnati. However, only three of the one hundred Illinois men identified with the Sons of Liberty were convicted, despite compelling evidence that the cabal had "put up" a $50,000 bounty on the life of President Lincoln at a meeting in the Richmond House in 1864.[20]

Whatever seditious antics McDonald may have committed on behalf of the plotters escaped detection when he resumed his old trade with a renewed flourish. In the 1860s Chicago was "wide open" as a result of a poorly conceived decision early in the decade to transfer the power to enforce gambling statutes in the city of Chicago from the mayor and common council to a three-member police commission. Patterned after a similar plan in Baltimore, the intent was to diminish and weaken the mayor's hand. The result was wholesale bribery of police officers and unchecked municipal graft.

The police commission was a toothless, impotent political entity frequently deadlocked over trivialities and embroiled in partisan bickering during the course of its fifteen-year run (1861–75). Very little was done to strengthen the commission, professionalize it, and insulate its officers from the pernicious influence of saloon politicians over them. "Until the present law, the Common Council had full jurisdiction over the subject of gambling, [now] taken away from the Council in whose hands it had so creditably existed since its first creation," wrote former mayor John Wentworth. It was under his watch in 1861 that the ill-conceived statute was first enacted.[21]

The mayor, who was elected by and responsible to the people, was reduced to a sinecure—an office without duties or real authority. The Board of Public Works, with its power to appropriate city revenues to civic projects, was transferred to the aldermen, thus foreshadowing decades of scandal and plunder that were to follow. It was during the unhappy mayoralty of John B. Rice (1865–69) when McDonald forged his earliest and most opportune alliances with the ruling cabal of aldermen who tapped their greatest strength in the saloons, pool halls, and gambling dens of the wards. Rice, a Republican who operated downtown theaters and was ill-prepared to administer the affairs of the growing city, was more concerned with thwarting the rising influence of the dreaded labor unions and so-called anarchists, while graft, prostitution, and gambling were largely ignored. Lawlessness prevailed, and the "Gambling Hells" of the city ran all night without the interference of the police.

After severing ties with the Richmond House, McDonald opened a billiard hall and bar at 61–63 Randolph and the first of several satellite gambling rooms in the downtown commercial district at 89 Dearborn Street with the connivance of Dave Oakes, a well-known faro dealer. "The two proprietors took turns steering suckers into their den and robbing them" the *Chicago Herald* reported. "The place was 'pulled' [raided] every day and was in very bad odor. McDonald and Oakes ran their [crooked] 'skin' game at 89 Dearborn for three of four years."[22] The "pull" never amounted to much. After posting a trifling bail, the gamblers were back at it, sometimes the very same day of the arrest.

To steer business his way, McDonald assembled a gang of renowned criminals, "bunkoists," and thimble-riggers (shell-game operators) ; men whose colorful nicknames, personal flamboyance, and superficial charm made them celebrities in their own right. They were tolerated just so long as they remained judicious and exercised caution in their choice of victims. The easiest "marks" were the gullible businessmen, farmers, tourists, and commission merchants from the rural countryside, exiting their trains at the Rock Island and Pacific Railroad depot on Van Buren Street. Armed with a passenger list easily secured through petty bribes paid to the stationmaster or published newspaper notices announcing a hotel convention, the "bunkoists" prowled the train platforms and waiting rooms, knowing beforehand the names of their intended victims, easily recognized by their clothing style and rural mannerisms. Among the bunko fraternity and the cops who were paid to look the other way, the innocent country dupe was known as a "Granger." The richly appareled con-artist would make a fast approach, extend his hand in warm familiarity to the bewildered visitor, offering to extend all due "courtesies of the city" to the guest.

"Good evenin' Mr. Smith, when did you leave Davenport?"

"Well good evenin' but you've got the start of me; don't believe I ever seed [sic] that face afore," replied the Granger.

"Why Mr. Smith, don't you know Messers. James Sullivan & Company of your town; the most extensive produce-dealers and commission merchants west of Chicago?"

"Certainly I do, have known them for years."

"Well, my name is Henry Sullivan, oldest son of the senior partner and I have been cashier of the firm and right-hand man for several years."

"Don't tell me!" exclaimed the countryman. "Why you know if you know me, and have lived in Davenport as you say you have, that my farm is less than two miles from the city and that I most always trade with Sullivan & Co. But I be hanged if I remember that I ever saw your face afore."

"Very probable," said the bunkoist. "But you are undoubtedly well aware that the cashier of so extensive a firm as Sullivan & Co. is always wrapped up in his own duties, seldom or never knowing what is going on around him in the matter of buying or selling and consequently the faces that have shown themselves there hundreds of times, would not be noticed or recognized."

"Mebbe but . . ."

"Mr. Smith, where are you going to stop in the city? As for myself, I have to return this evening. I came up on special business."

"I dunno where I'll stop. I want to stay a couple of days."

"Well then, let's walk up Clark Street and that leads past the business portion of the city and we'll talk of mutual acquaintances."

The pair chatted amicably about subjects of mutual interest as the bunkoist led his prey in the general direction of the faro banks and gambling resorts run by McDonald lining Clark Street.

"By the way, I have a lottery ticket which I wish to get cashed upstairs here, and if you will go up with me and see that there is fair play in the operation we'll then do the town at my expense. This is the business that brought me here from Davenport." The Granger trailed close behind.[23]

Post-Fire Chicago, where the liberal proponents of the "wide open city" jockeyed for political power against the rising power of Prohibitionists, was a haven for slick operators previously escorted to the state line by police officers in other municipalities less tolerant of their presence. Harry Martin; "Appetite Bill" Langdon; "Snapper" Johnny Malloy; "Kid" Miller; Snitzer the Kid; "Dutchy" Lehman; Tom Wallace and his brother John; the murderous Jere Dunn; "Hungry" Joe Lewis, who clipped the famed English author and playwright Oscar Wilde for a couple thousand in 1882; "Dutch" Hendricks; Tom O'Brien, the "King of the Bunko Men"; Matt Duffy; Jim Parrish; "Red" Jimmy Fitzgerald; and the notorious gold-brick swindler George "White Pine" Martin—all were either in McDonald's direct employ or frequent overnight "guests" in Mary's hotel rooms on the upper floors while hiding out from the law.[24]

These men were recruited from the streets and remained close to McDonald throughout the 1870s, the decade when he amassed the bulk of his fortune through gambling, his liquor business, and lucrative criminal rackets. The "split" from their thieving enterprise was divided three ways: 40 percent to the "house;" 20 percent to the police; and 40 percent for their personal take. As his stature and financial resources grew, McDonald supplemented the payroll with twenty full-time "witnesses," whose only task was to supply carefully rehearsed statements on behalf of any member of the gang taken in by the police and arraigned on criminal charges. A reserve fund was maintained to pay "straw bail" (a worthless bond signed by someone with no licensing authority) for their immediate release, with other monies earmarked for the bribery of jurists. The revenues earned by "Cap" Hyman and George Trussell from the modest success of their Randolph Street keno operations during the Civil War paled in comparison to the whirlwind that the McDonald syndicate reaped in the decade following the surrender at Appomattox.

From time to time, there were setbacks and reprisals. It was commonly understood that it was bad policy for the army of bunko steerers to rope in an established Chicago business leader or State Street merchant only to have that individual seek redress in the criminal courts. The itinerant salesman, conventioneer, or out-of-town visitor was less likely to report the fraud, fearing the wrath of a spouse back home or professional embarrassment within the ranks of his company or local community. It was a simple matter of human nature.

Clean-shaven young men, callow and inexperienced in the ways of the world, were preferred marks, although in October 1868, one such lad, a humble assistant cashier with the Chicago Dock Company named Charles Goodman, nearly drove McDonald to the edge of bankruptcy and forced more than one member of his gang to temporarily scatter to the four winds. Goodman, a boy not yet out of his teens, was an easy mark for Harry Martin, one of McDonald's most skillful ropers, who received information that this young cashier was given access to his company's safe and was responsible for protecting the contents when the head cashier was out of the office. Inside were stacks of signed checks with the dollar amounts left blank.

Lured to the faro table at 89 Dearborn Street late one night, Goodman was plied with liquor, cigars, food, and the warmhearted encouragement of McDonald, who urged him to "play on," with the inducement of an occasional winning in order to keep him anchored to his chair. Hoping to change his luck, Goodman engaged Martin to sit in for him as his "deputy," figuring that the older, more experienced man was a friend looking after his best interests. After losing $15 the first night, Goodman, who lived with his parents on the West Side, was induced to go back to the office safe to fetch $100, then another hundred, and so on, until he was in the hole for $19,000.

The plan was to compel Goodman to empty the entire safe. With the stolen checks in hand, McDonald intended to open a "traveling" faro bank crisscrossing the country. Goodman was signing over company checks totaling $100 to $200 every evening, until Mr. Atwater, the secretary of the company detected fraud and began asking around. Alarmed, McDonald and Oakes suggested to the boy that he should steal one last lump sum—$28,600 in bank checks—before skipping town. Meeting with their "pigeon" in the back of Otis Fields's saloon, McDonald solemnly vowed to "force a compromise" with the Chicago Dock Company on his behalf, and while these negotiations proceeded, the boy should not trouble himself any further. Goodman, whose trusting nature must seriously be questioned, obliged. Meanwhile, Martin fled to Cleveland to stake out the city with a fistful of greenbacks in hand. With no other recourse but to run for his life, the hapless teenage victim boarded a train for California with Pinkerton detectives hot on his trail.

The story of the swindle might have ended there if only Goodman had not suffered pangs of guilty conscience and returned to Chicago to report the defalcation to his former employer. Making a clean breast of things, he said he had "entrusted" McDonald and his associates with the money. McDonald denied the charge but was promptly arrested and would stew inside a jail for the next two months while Alderman Thomas Foley, a champion billiard player with important connections in the First Ward, raised the money to post a $60,000 bail and was indemnified against loss.[25] After long delays, the case finally went to trial in the April 1870 sessions of the Superior Court. McDonald and his team paraded a line of witnesses to swear in open court that Goodman was a "fast young man" who squandered the money on prostitutes and gambling through his own volition. It was not McDonald's affair that this boy should be so reckless with his employer's money, they all agreed.

The trial was a farce but "was listened to with intense interest by a dense throng of spectators including very many members of the bar," the *Inter-Ocean* reported.[26] Judge Joseph Gary's courtroom was packed with Mike's supporters, and the gambler was acquitted. But the cost of defending himself was nearly ruinous. To help pay off the legal fees and settle the $60,000 civil suit brought by the Chicago Dock Company, he set himself up in business as a hack driver for Young's Omnibus Line, picking up passengers at the train depots and conveying them to and from their hotels, offering subtle encouragement to drop by one of the Randolph Street clip joints where he had an interest. It was a humbling, but temporary, loss of prestige.[27]

The ink was barely dry on the first round of subpoenas in the Goodman affair, when McDonald was dragged into court a second time on the complaint of one Baker Forsyth who, in a drunken state, accompanied McDonald, Paige, gambler William T. Swift, and John McDevitt, the reigning national billiard champion, to a faro bank at 72 Randolph Street one night. With $400 burning a hole in his pocket, Forsyth signaled his willingness to play, despite pleas to the contrary from a friend who warned him of the likely consequences of associating with the likes of these men.[28]

Enraged, McDonald struck the Good Samaritan in the face and warned him to be quiet, as he ushered Forsyth into the robber's den to play the "brace game" of faro. The ominous phrase was well known to police and frequenters of gambling houses. "Brace boxes" were quite simply dealer boxes rigged up with secret springs to control the issuance of cards dealt to the player so that the house would rarely, if ever lose. Important distinctions were already being made between the more upscale and honest "gentleman's game" and the treacherous "brace house."

McDonald was known to manage both varieties, acquiring competitor operations through a generous buyout offer or as a result of direct coercion. If the initial offer was refused, he knew he could achieve better results by forking over a portion of his purchase money to the police as an inducement for them to close down the rival parlors. Before very long, he had a controlling interest in nearly every gambling game in town—be it the objectionable brace house or the "square" game.

The legitimacy of this particular McDonald holding was the crux of the matter before Justice Winship of the Police Court as he listened to the complainant, Forsyth, who said he was gainfully employed in a reputable business on South Water Street and the $400 was taken from him by dishonorable means. In this instance, and most other reported cases, the justices were inclined to assess a small fine and dispose of the matter in the pragmatic belief that the victim should not have been so gullible as to not have known what he was getting himself into in the first place. McDonald, McDevitt, and Paige were held over for a bench trial that resulted in an acquittal. The predictable outcome of these proceedings naturally enraged the sensibilities of the business class and the meddlesome reformers. The gambling fraternity and the saloon keepers were excoriated by the Republican press as the real culprits for the surge in lawlessness witnessed during the postwar period.

Attacks upon persons and property escalated to an alarming degree in all three geographic divisions of the city. With boldness and impunity, travelers were waylaid on the remote suburban roads leading into Chicago. Gangs of footpads and garroters assaulted citizens in all neighborhoods, only to be discharged in the police courts through the intervention of "runners" employed by the justices of the peace. The runners were marginal figures on the fringe of the underworld loitering at the foot of the courthouse stairs to solicit bribes from defendants in return for a guaranty of leniency.

The laissez-faire attitude of the former actor, Mayor Rice, and the growing alarm that an organized "gang" of criminals supported by saloon Democrats was usurping the powers of the Republican mayor, seizing the mechanisms of city government, the police board, and the "justice mills," took root among the blue-blood alarmists.

"It may be well to cast a glance at the real or supposed causes that have led to the inauguration of the carnival of crime and the introduction of the horde of criminals with which Chicago is presently infested," the *Chicago Tribune* editorialized. "Why is Chicago today the general rendezvous of Western, to say nothing of Eastern criminals? The natural answer to this must be because they find the Garden City best adapted to their vocation."[29]

The reformer's hue and cry became a strident appeal to common decency, echoing across every social stratum of the young city.

~ 3 ~

A Department Store of Gambling

UNDER THE GASLIGHT LAMPS OF CLARK STREET, THE BETTING action was tightly packed from the Chicago River south to 12th Street—the "Black Hole of Chicago," as one morally proselytizing journal of the day described it. With the deaths of Trussell and Hyman, the location of the gaming houses gradually shifted southward into an integrated district running along Clark Street from Randolph to the Near South Side. Beginning in the 1850s, local merchants noted with growing alarm the presence of "young sports," attired in gaudy waistcoats and yellow gloves, making mischief with the female passersby—such men were called "mashers" in the parlance of the day.

The city was "free and easy," and by some contemporary accounts, a latter-day Sodom and Gomorrah for its tolerance of gambling and the great "social evils" of prostitution and vice. Those who decried the moral turpitude of Chicago after the Civil War attached symbolic meaning to the devastation wrought by the Great Fire of October 8, 1871, a calamity that left three hundred Chicagoans dead, ninety thousand homeless, and property losses pegged at $200 million in its wake. The central business district, the shabby residential tenements of the West Division and Near South Side, and the notorious Cheyenne District ringing the commercial houses and municipal buildings of downtown were swept away in the all-consuming conflagration. In the minds of the devout, the Fire, as tragic an event as there ever could be in the life of a great city, symbolized God's moral authority and the will of the faithful to "cleanse" a wicked and vile place.

Social utopians and the righteously indignant—a "Committee of Seventy" and a splinter "Committee of Fifteen" organized to close saloons on Sunday—added up the pluses and minuses and were encouraged. They looked toward a bright new day and the opportunity to live and work in a city scrubbed clean of moral decay. Presumably, such unholy places as Cheyenne, Conley's Patch, and the so-called Hair-trigger Block would vanish into history, leaving the shabby, immigrant poor to their own devices and the white picket fences and steeples of antebellum downtown fully restored. "With the saloons closed, the temptation would be removed and the Lord's Day observed as it should be," exclaimed Judge S. B. Gookins at a committee gathering inside the Thirty-first Street Presbyterian Church a year and three days after the Great Fire. "Crime would be diminished and the devil's stamp removed from Chicago."[1]

So, while the Committee of Seventy sermonized, the intrepid city merchants whose buildings were ruined in the fire erected temporary wooden shanties measuring up to eighteen feet high along the lakefront in which to transact business and sell their wares, while building contractors busily, and noisily, commenced work on a coming utopia—a fanciful illusion, as it turned out.

Chicago, a city "built as if to invite its own destruction," in the opinion of author-historian Donald L. Miller, "got back on the ground quickly. Even while the ground was still hot they were rebuilding. And then they rebuilt the entire city, literally, in a matter of a year and a half. But it was built exactly as it had been built before; it was again susceptible to fire"--and susceptible to an ambitious and reinvigorated criminal underworld.[2]

Before the full extent of the devastation and the final human toll could be added up, and less than two months after the last of the blazing ruins was finally extinguished, the city gambling hells and houses of ill fame were up and running and advertising their attractions. Mike McDonald's wine and liquor depot and other holdings on Dearborn Street between Randolph and Washington had been destroyed in the conflagration, leaving him with an uninsured $30,000 loss. However debilitating the financial setback, he too was quickly back in business and up to his old tricks within weeks of the disaster, this time with a new watering hole at the corner of State and Harrison Streets, a few blocks east of the Cheyenne District.[3]

"All night saloons and riotous establishments of every description have come to the surface," the *Chicago Times* complained on January 21, 1872. Variety shows that were thinly veiled fronts for prostitution were advertised in the *Town Talker*, a newspaper of the street describing in visceral detail the charms of a "dozen nymphs in a dozen degrees of nudity preparing for the stage and several blasé youths who seem to be waiting for their divinities."[4] The racy "Chicago Varieties" operated in a dozen dilapidated buildings near the southeast corner of Randolph and Canal Streets. "These places are the direct outgrowth of the Fire," commented the *Times*. "Before that event there was but one in the city, and even that [the old Winter Garden] was thought to be the climax of all nastiness."[5]

Displaced faro banks and illegal card games sprouted quickly on West Madison Street in small, nondescript buildings that had managed to escape the path of the onrushing flames, and they prospered like never before. John Dowling, one of Chicago's most famous gamblers and a longtime McDonald confederate, opened a new establishment at 73 West Madison that featured heavy blinds to prevent the glare of the chandeliers from attracting the attention of the police and all "good citizens" of a moralistic bent. All around, on the periphery of the "burnt district" (as the ruins of downtown were called by Chicagoans of that generation), there was gambling and vice. No utopia could Chicago ever hope to become despite attempts on the part of the Committee of Seventy to inject the temperance cause into the city electoral process.

Mayor Joseph Medill defeated the Democrat Charles C. P. Holden in the citywide election held November 7, 1871, on a "fireproof" ticket that pledged to rebuild shattered Chicago, close the saloons on Sunday, and remedy the criminal scourge that had only grown worse under the watch of his immediate prede- cessors—Medill's personal mandate.. First, he attacked the gamblers through legislation—State Representative Robert H. Foss of Cook County introduced a bill in the General Assembly appending the Illinois Revised Statutes of 1845, calling for more stringent criminal penalties against the keepers of gambling dens.[6] The measure passed overwhelmingly, was upheld by the state supreme court, and suddenly many of the "small-fry" sports in Chicago were scurry- ing for the train stations. Meanwhile, Mike McDonald and the syndicate of gamblers under his protection (routinely supplied with recognizance bonds) dug in for a long fight.

The threat posed by reformer Medill, ridiculed as "Joseph I, Dictator" by publisher Anton Casper Hesing, the powerful, left-of-center, German-born publisher of the *Staats-Zeitung* newspaper, was an early catalyst for Mike's segue into the realm of electoral politics. He led a defiant opposition of saloon operators backed by liquor trade associations and gamblers. In February 1872, McDonald lashed out at the Foss bill and its backer in city hall. "Every new broom sweeps clean, but it wears out in time," he confidently predicted. "It's the same way with the gambling laws. If a man wants to risk his money at a square game, I'd like to see the law that can stop him."[7]

McDonald said that the police and the new regime of bluenosed disciples of Medill were unfairly targeting him. Mike denied long-standing accusations that he was "roping in" the greenhorns and penny-ante gamblers. "Oh well, that's all damned nonsense," he snapped. "We don't want any ten-cent players around a first class place, but what can you do with them? We have less trouble with the squealers in this town than any other place I know of, and that shows the class of people who play. They seldom pull us on complaint. The profitable players are fellows who can lose a hundred or two without winking. The ten- cent people are a nuisance."[8]

The "pulls" (police raids) commenced in early December 1872, five months after Medill discharged William W. Kennedy, the incumbent police superintendent, for "general incompetence." Kennedy hesitated to enforce the Sunday saloon-closing measure and was reticent about closing down the illegal games. Elmer Washburn, the former warden of the Joliet Penitentiary, a political outsider and Protestant Yankee who unequivocally supported Medill, replaced Kennedy, the Irish Catholic who cowered in the presence of McDonald.[9]

Under the weak-kneed Kennedy, it was McDonald's habit to drop by police headquarters following token gambling raids and taunt the superintendent; asking him pointed questions about just how much he and his staff had "stolen" from the fraternity the night before. He would piteously rebuke Kennedy and remind him that he, Mike McDonald, "ran the city," and the gamblers under his protection had already recovered double the amount the following evening. Shamefaced, Kennedy stood idly by, suffering the mocking jest in silence because he knew the full power of the police commission supported the captains, and the captains were of course beholden to McDonald. But Washburn's defiant refusal to turn the other cheek was entirely unexpected, and his noncompliance caught McDonald off guard. Angrily, Mike vowed to "drive him out in 90 days."[10]

Elmer Washburn ignored the threats and zealously dispatched his bluecoats into the Clark Street rialto. The raiding parties carried out furniture, faro-dealing boxes, checks, bushels of cards, and accounting ledgers from the houses, as the seething proprietors and their outside "ropers" were driven off to the Harrison Street lockup in the "Black Maria" paddy wagon. The raids were a costly nuisance, despite McDonald's braggadocio. The keepers of the "first-class" dens had outfitted their rooms with the best tapestries, most expensive wines, and finest furniture. While raids of this nature represented a minor inconvenience, with charges routinely dismissed in court or a nominal fine assessed by the justices, the loss of the impounded goods and the destruction of the gambling paraphernalia by police was no joking matter. The high rollers were not likely to patronize the lower-class "dinner pail" resorts—they counted on the best accommodations worthy of gentlemen in an agreeable, parlor-house setting, but it took time and money to rebuild once such an establishment was ransacked by police. A system had to be put in place.

Pressure was brought to bear on McDonald to nullify the police threat, but he quickly discovered that not even his own place at 427 South State Street was immune from the Washburn raiding parties. He did his best to provide bonds for all of the detainees from Clark Street in the lockup, but at the same time strongly urged his colleagues to unite with him and contribute to a "special fund" that might be turned over to the superintendent as proper inducement to "lay-off."[11] In that way, he reasoned, this nemesis could be neutralized. But Washburn was undeterred, and the raids continued. Next, McDonald sent out another emissary, this time with instructions to double the bribe money and offer Washburn the sum of $25,000. The superintendent again refused, compelling the syndicate to divvy up the money and divert it to the rank-and-file bluecoats who were actually assigned to carry out the gambling raids. The patrolmen were said to have happily accepted the cash inducements, even if their superintendent would not. Meanwhile, a private bank account earmarked to "drive Washburn out" was opened.[12]

Before the year ended, McDonald would emerge the surprise victor in this test of will against the mayor, Washburn, and the Committee of Seventy. Internal political disputes pitting the police commission against Medill undermined Washburn, who received his comeuppance from all sides. Rank-and-file police deeply resented the superintendent because he was an outsider; the authors of the first published history of the department reaffirmed prevailing attitudes: "He would listen to no suggestions, simply waving his subordinates off. . . . He lacked every requisite supposed to be necessary to the successful management of a police force."[13]

Matters came to a boil on January 28, 1873, when the three-member police commission fired Washburn for making "unauthorized raids." By design, the state legislature had vested power in the commission to conduct gambling raids by working through the captains of the three police districts—not the superintendent. Medill protested the action, and it went to court, but the mayor had no power to wield. The commission's decision was upheld, and they appointed the board secretary—an interim chair-warmer—to run the department while a more suitable man could be found. With Washburn's dismissal, the sluice gates of graft, chicanery, and unchecked vice and gambling in Chicago reopened.

Then in July 1873, the mayor unexpectedly resigned his post and sailed off to Europe with his wife Katharine and their three daughters for an extended tour of the continent. Coincidental with Medill's sudden abdication was the news that City Treasurer David A. Gage defaulted on his bonds and had diverted $507,703.58 of city funds into a private account.[14] Gage, a second-term Democrat, provided McDonald and his cohorts with grist to use against the regime, even though the mayor had "inherited" Gage and later said that his office "could not be held personally responsible." Public opinion was understandably aroused, because all the while the mayor was preaching municipal integrity and castigating the Tweed Ring of New York and other corrupt sachems of the political world, he was oblivious to similar offenses occurring within his own administration.

Confidence in Joseph Medill and his designated successor, interim mayor Lester LeGrand Bond, was fractured by allegations that Medill had acted in a cowardly fashion. Gossip spread that the only reason for the incumbent mayor's decision to run off to Europe was to protect his family from contracting the next deadly outbreak of cholera many believed was at hand. The rumor, likely started by political foes Carter Harrison and Anton Hesing, was hotly denied by Medill, but it circulated around Chicago and gained credence over the next ten years.[15]

Despite many good intentions, it was a supreme irony of Medill's public life that his capitulation should usher in a fifty-year period of unbridled municipal corruption, open gambling, and segregated vice in the city of Chicago. Ex-mayor and newspaper publisher Joseph Medill's surrender made it possible for the ascension of Mike McDonald to the status of an unelected "czar" of city politics, an influential "kingmaker" prowling the corridors of power, who remained true to his word that he "ran the city." Firmly anointed as the "boss" of the underworld, McDonald would have much preferred to be thought of as a civic-minded provider of "hospitality" services with weighty responsibilities in the public sector.

In September 1873, with the reform movement in full retreat, an economic panic unleashed in national financial markets, and the Foss bill mostly ignored, Mike opened his "Store"—the grandest, gaudiest, and most brazen twenty-four-hour gambling palace in the Midwest, in the same league with Richard Canfield's Club House in Saratoga.[16]

Located at the northwest corner of Clark Street and Monroe (45.5 feet of frontage on Clark Street and 90 feet on the Monroe side), McDonald started slowly by subleasing space in a small saloon on the ground level. As his business prospered, he spent $15,000 outfitting the five-story building into a deluxe gambling parlor on the second floor, with keno in the rear room and the faro tables, roulette wheels, *rouge et noir,* and games of hazard running full blast in a room accommodating up to fifty players that faced the street.

The saloon and his wholesale liquor and cigar depot—the "legitimate" business enterprise—occupied the first floor. Overnight accommodations advertised in the city directory as the "Palace European Hotel" were available to overnight guests on the third floor, with a "clubhouse" for political friends and allies, and apartment living quarters for his family on the top floor. McDonald maintained a private residence on Wabash Avenue through the 1870s, but very often the children slept upstairs.

There were two entrances, one by the common staircase on Monroe and the other through the bar on the ground floor on Clark. The building was honeycombed with trapdoors concealed under expensive carpeting. Curious little peepholes were drilled through partitions, and several hidden closets allowed for concealment of patrons during raids.

The "Store," at 176 South Clark Street, was originally leased by one Festus B. Cole, the original tenant, but in April of 1873 he assigned the lease to Edwin Walker, owner of the Chicago and Lemont Stone Company, who sold limestone from his South Suburban quarries to the City of Chicago at inflated prices through the crooked machinations of the Cook County board.[17]

Ed Walker's business dealings with McDonald and members of the county board were extensive, beginning in the 1870s after Walker established his business along Waterfall Green, one of six major stone cutting firms located in Lemont, lying adjacent to the Illinois-Michigan Canal. The abundant "Athens Marble," another name for the rich limestone deposits in the region, was used to construct many public buildings in Chicago and across Illinois, despite common complaints about the yellowed appearance of the stone after exposure to the elements.

However, Mike's building was constructed of Ohio sandstone and Milwaukee brick—trimmed with ornate stone cornices to McDonald's precise specifications. It stood adjacent to the Kent Building and Constitution Block; both were post-Fire office and commercial incarnations constructed carelessly and in great haste inside the burnt district. Real estate speculation was rampant in the months following the Fire, as downtown land values and rental rates soared. McDonald invested heavily in the Store and other downtown properties as a hedge against the unpredictability of the green cloth trade. His various enterprises, stratagems, and associations with men in the "upper world" ingeniously insulated his core business from attack. As much as the Republican press and the clergy assailed the Store as a "gambling hell," the written record suggests that the mass of Chicagoans were indifferent, or benignly amused by the enterprising McDonald and his many games.

Legitimate business entrepreneurs entered into alliances with Mike with their eyes wide open. Godfrey Snydecker, a German banker and member of the board of directors of the Chicago Life Insurance Company, was granted the assignment of lease from Walker. Then on December 8, 1874, the assignment of lease reverted back to Edwin Walker, who collected the monthly rent as "business agent"; but before the ink was dry on this latest deal, Walker assigned the lease to Lazarus B. Silverman, proprietor of a reputable private banking house who had been doing business for a number of years as a note-broker.[18] Walker, Silverman, Hy Hartt, and a myriad of other individuals whose backgrounds are lost to history all ascribed their names to the leasing agreement for building space, thus confusing the police and the courts as to who could be legitimately arrested and prosecuted as true proprietors of the "Store," and who could not.[19]

Then, as the monies from the enterprise accumulated, Walker made Mike a full business partner in his Lemont limestone quarries. By branching out in this way, McDonald sharpened his business acumen and built a secondary fortune and a valuable set of contacts separate and apart from the average tinhorns trolling through "Gambler's Alley."

Day-to-day operation of the gaming parlor was left to trusted associates from the underworld. It was a twenty-four-hour operation demanding constant supervision. The game was "worked" in two shifts. One set of dealers reported for duty at 9:00 in the morning and stayed on until 7:00 P.M. The overnight crew relieved the day shift and worked the tables until the following morning.[20]

Skilled bunko artists Harry Lawrence and Morris Martin shared the profits in McDonald's saloon and ground floor cigar and liquor distribution business until 1877, when they branched out and opened their own place on Madison Street. James Winston supervised the dealers running the roulette table and a wheel of fortune that was always in play upstairs. Charley Winship, a quiet and well-mannered gent, dealt faro. Brother Ed was brought into the business as the poolroom cashier after failing to make the grade in a sixteen-month engagement as a furnace and heating salesman. And old Pat Casey, Chicago's most famous pre-Fire barkeep, whose "Silver Fountain" at Madison and Market Streets advertised "Old Number Six," a potent whiskey concoction designed to get the imbiber "drunker than he had ever been in his life," signed on with McDonald, and for many years thereafter served as head bartender at the Store.[21]

The bunko artists working the street corners and hotel bars checked in each morning to glean the latest intelligence from McDonald before testing the gullibility of strangers and the corruption of the police. Mike usually opened the meetings with a critique of their performance for the past week, based on the size of their envelopes, and excoriated and embarrassed the nonperformers. "You're no good Snoozer. Why can't you tumble to a paying racket? Here you have every advantage in training, but I'm hanged if we can make anything of you. You're a dead loss to the house. You haven't brought in a nickel in a week. We can't have it. You're no good for genteel work. You'll have to try the sneak-thief line; you might do enough there to keep from starving."[22]

California Jack, Jere Dunn, and Sir James Arlington (a.k.a. James Gannon, stabbed and killed in a one-sided quarrel outside the Store in 1875 by "White Pine" Martin)—the bunkoist with the fake English accent to charm the visitors from across the pond—stood in rapt attention as McDonald dispensed his orders for the day. "There are a pretty good-looking lot of strangers at the Pacific [Hotel] this morning. It will do to look after them. I understand there are a lot of 'John Bulls' stopping there. Maybe you can catch 'em for a drawing. There are three or four country stockholders of an Iowa railroad there; they ought to be pretty good game. The bank is running light. Try and do the best you can. Jack, you take a look around Kuhns's and the Brevoort. Jim, you might look into the Palmer, and Johnny you take the street corners. Follow 'em close boys. Don't get scared at [Judge John] Summerfield's flurry; that will be alright. Snoozer? Do try to make a man of yourself."[23]

The Store offered its financially well-equipped patrons all the first-class amenities, and the genial host was ever ready to stake thousands on the turn of a card to high rollers. The cigars were imported. The wines were of an exceptional vintage, the food sumptuous, the furnishings the most elaborate that could be procured, and from the balcony, a string band serenaded the gamesters with all the popular tunes of the day, among them "Champagne Charlie," "Captain Jinks of the Horse Marines," and "Shoo Fly."[24]

Important men from the world of commerce, city, state, and national politics, and the arts, as well as scores of visiting dignitaries, frequented the establishment.

Sir Charles Russell, an Irishman who obtained great prominence in Parliament and before the English bar, insisted upon visiting the Store during a Stateside tour in 1883. He had heard from no less than the distinguished gentleman Charles Stewart Parnell, that "this man McDonald" was prominent in the affairs of the great American city of the Midwest. After proper introductions, Sir Charles agreed to accompany McDonald to theater and later, a "private, but friendly game" of poker at the Store. The diplomat lost $500 and accepted it in good humor. A lark, that's all. The next day Sir Charles remarked that Mike was a "jolly good fellow, and rather generous too." "Oh yes, he's generous," came the reply. "Don't you know he gave back the $500 for the cause of home rule in Ireland?"[25]

Senator James G. Fair of Nevada was a frequent guest on his way to and from Washington, D.C., during the one term of office he served. A McDonald dealer said the esteemed Western politician and silver speculator was no piker. "One morning just after I had begun to deal, Mr. Fair came in and went to backing kings at $500 a king. In half an hour he lost $6,500. 'Well,' he said then. 'I guess I'll get some breakfast.' He went out and I never saw him again."[26]

Chicagoan Fred Ebersold remembered the largesse of the boss gambler as he greeted the public with a firm handshake from inside the sample room.

> I was passing "176." Boy-like, without thought of propriety or ethics, I entered, walked up to an important looking man and asked for Mr. McDonald. "I'm Mr. McDonald. What can I do for you?" he asked.
>
> "I'm collecting money for missions," I replied, handing him my book. He took it, scanned the list of quarters and dimes and without a question as to my identity or creed, entered the word "Cash," at the same time handing me a good sized bill. I thanked him and hurried out, elated.[27]

Such goodwill gestures drew praise, and the stories were inevitably repeated from one person to another down through the years, until Mike acquired the patina of a latter-day Robin Hood. The legend took root and grew.

"I was there one afternoon when a woman with a baby in her arms came in to complain that her husband gambled away his salary every pay day," reminisced one old-timer in a published 1921 interview.

> She had not a cent in the house to buy food for the children and herself. Mike asked her name and learned her husband was a clerk in a department store. He went upstairs and asked if such a man came there and left word to be called when the man appeared again. Then he opened the safe and gave the woman $50 remarking: "Madam, your husband won't come here much more. I am not looking for such small fish."
>
> When the man appeared that evening and was pointed out to McDonald, Mike caught him by the shoulder and told him if he ever came back he would be thrown through the window and to emphasize his

remark gave him a kick as he started down the stairs. I never saw the man there again.[28]

Not every penniless, foolhardy clerk was so fortunate. In an 1878 incident, a carter named Fitzgerald from the firm of Hibbard, Bartlett, Spencer stole money from his employer and gambled it away at a faro table inside the premises. A business agent for the hardware company, upon discovering the larceny, went straight to Mike McDonald and demanded return of the money.

Without uttering a word, McDonald went to his safe and withdrew six Smith and Wesson revolvers that Fitzgerald had put up as collateral against the house and handed them over to the businessman. Mike pressed his claim against Fitzgerald and obtained a favorable judgment from the court in a civil suit, but the man was unable to pay back his debt. Confronting him on the street in front of Jeff Hankins's gambling house not long after, McDonald again demanded satisfaction, but after being told "where to go," the gambler plunged a penknife into the debtor's arm and walked away while the police stood by, saying and doing nothing. This, too, added to his personal "mystique."

Among the legends and twice-told tales circulating around Chicago about the comings and goings inside the elegantly festooned parlors of the Store, none were more compelling than the indiscretions of the "lady of the house"—the fetching and vivacious Mary Ann Noonan—joined in the bonds of matrimony to Mike McDonald at St. Mary's Catholic Church on December 5, 1871.[29]

Born not far from McDonald in Lockport, New York, in November 1847 to John T. and Mary Ann (Armstrong) Noonan, natives of Ireland (he a descendant of merchantmen in County Clare and she of the Armstrongs of Sligo), Mary Ann relocated with her parents to West Perry Street in Tiffin, Ohio, when she was only two. The bustling river town hugging the bank of the Sandusky was an important glass and porcelain manufacturing center in the mid-nineteenth century and the seat of Seneca County. After John Noonan passed away in 1866, Mary's mother, in desperation to do right by the five kids married William Graham, a local Tiffin man. . Graham provided the means for his new wife to raise the three sons and three daughters from the first marriage in a proper household. But there were problems. "She [Mary Ann] was a passionate child with a fiery temper and she gave us some trouble," recalled Mary Noonan Graham of her spirited daughter in an extended interview with a *Times* reporter.[30]

Mary was a queer sort of girl, defiant to her mother, rejecting convention, yet easily swayed by powerful religious figures entering into her life at key turning points. "When not quite 17 years-old she was on a visit to Cleveland where she met a Catholic priest, the Rev. Father Noonan who claimed to be a distant relative, who induced her to go to Chicago where he secured her a situation. She also met M. C. McDonald in Cleveland and the acquaintance was renewed in Chicago."

Married at age fifteen and giving birth to a son, Harley Cassius Goudy, in Wayne County, Ohio, on January 18, 1866, and a little girl named Mary Cecilia ("Birdie") Goudy in 1868, Mary's budding romance with Mike McDonald kindled not long after her union with the hometown boy, John Goudy, fell apart. As a condition of her promise to marry Mike, he had to first agree to take in the two children. McDonald gave them his last name and raised Birdie and Harley as his own children, although the name change was never formalized in court.

It was reported by envious men who glimpsed her beauty that Mary Noonan was "the handsomest girl in Chicago," albeit a willful, hotheaded, emotionally unstable young woman possessing a streak of wild jealousy that knew no limits. One night she became insanely angry toward a young woman who had accompanied Mike and his sister-in-law to the theater. The next day, Mary tracked the woman down and beat her until she was bloody. She then aimed two pistols at her heart, before finally composing herself, lowering the weapons, and sending the injured woman on her way. Mary's willingness to brandish a loaded gun or a dagger at a stranger when her hot temper overtook the last semblance of reason and logic earned her a reputation as dangerous.

Mary nearly killed a Chicago police officer during a gambling raid against the Store on November 23, 1878, after three bluecoats, Michael LeBounty, Al Hoffman, and Florence Donohue, pushed their way up the stairs to search the family living quarters where the children were sleeping. Armed with a jimmy to force open the door if necessary, LeBounty declared that he held a warrant for Mike's arrest in his hand, but Mary kept the raiding party at bay, warning them not to take a step closer or she would shoot them straight up. Ed McDonald positioned himself behind her and blocked the door. "I will protect my family and my guests from annoyance. Defend yourselves!" screamed Mrs. McDonald.[31]

The order to raid the McDonald abode had come directly from Captain Michael C. Hickey, a notoriously corrupt demagogue and political enemy of Mike who was nominally aligned with the city Republicans. Because of long-standing political differences traceable to McDonald's growing influence in city hall in the post-Medill period and his ability to siphon power away from the police captains, Hickey "had it in" for the gambler-boss. But in his haste to humiliate Mike and disrupt his operation, the captain was careless, and the raid ended up a complete fiasco.

The reckless Donohue ignored Mary's directive to stand fast and advanced toward her with the intention of wrestling the gun away and knocking down the door. Mary discharged the pistol twice, but her aim was poor. The bullets tore through the officer's coat sleeve and settled into the wall. Taken into custody and arraigned on a charge of attempted murder with her brother, John Noonan, and the hapless Ed, it seemed almost a certainty that Mary McDonald was to be bound over for the penitentiary and the children removed from her custody.

Backed into a corner and having to answer to yet another nuisance charge of keeping a gambling house, Mike turned to Alfred S. Trude and Emery A. Storrs to save Mary, keep his family intact, and secure a favorable verdict from the court after the mayor dared to revoke his liquor license. Just twenty-six, Trude was an ambitious, but dirt poor, young trial lawyer from Lockport, New York, who had drawn the favorable attention of Mayor Medill during his war with the gamblers at the outset of his administration. Medill named him city prosecutor and told him, "I want you to go over to the West Side and prosecute Harry Lawrence and Morris Martin, the bunco men. This city must be rid of bunco." The lawyer did the work, and he did it to the satisfaction of the mayor, although there was no future in it and little chance of financial reward.[32]

Not long after, Trude and McDonald struck up a friendly acquaintance while sharing a bench on a Wabash Avenue express wagon. All of the horses of the city were down with the epizootic that particular week, and a serendipitous meeting between a gambler and a city prosecutor blossomed into a lucrative, lifelong association that would serve both men well. As a result of Trude's fine work for Medill, two important bunco men in the McDonald syndicate were driven out of the city and had jumped their bonds. Mike asked Trude if he would consider defending the bonds, and after a moment's hesitation, Trude said he would. It was a matter of economics. McDonald paid Trude $500 to handle the matter—whereas the City of Chicago's standard compensation rate was $5.00 for similar work.

Trude's amiable dealings with McDonald and sudden windfall abruptly ended his prosecutorial career. Seeing the unlimited potential in criminal defense work, Trude took up with Wilbur Storey, publisher of the *Chicago Times,* and defended him in five hundred criminal libel lawsuits spanning a ten-year period. At the same time he was defending and befriending his neighbor Mike McDonald (in later years these transplanted New Yorkers lived in nearby mansions on Drexel Boulevard), he was counsel for the Chicago City Railway.

During the 1890s, while McDonald was easing out of public life, Trude was a member of the Chicago Board of Education, eventually rising in rank to president of a municipal agency the *Tribune* derided as a "street corner clique" of insiders on October 28, 1894. Active in Democratic politics through the duration of his professional career, and one of McDonald's most able lieutenants during periods of internecine warfare among the splinter factions of the party, Trude was a delegate to the 1896 and 1900 national nominating conventions. Through his influence and connections, he advanced the appointment of his first son, Daniel P. Trude, to a judgeship in the municipal court and pushed his brother George for city attorney in 1895.

In a colorful, forty-year career before the bar, A. S. ("Asa") Trude defended the dregs of the Chicago streets: murderers, bunko steerers, vagrants, and all the other McDonald henchman who fell into the grasp of the long arm of the law. The champions of law and order vilified him. "His whole life and ability," growled the *Chicago Herald,* "was shown to be devoted to an unprincipled series of plots against justice in the defense of gamblers, thieves and murderers. He was represented as bribing bailiffs, packing grand juries, suborning witnesses, tampering with petit juries, and accomplishing his end by crooked means."[33]

In the first serious test of his abilities, Trude secured for Mary a change of venue before a judge less inclined to convict. The McDonald case was heard by Cook County Circuit Court Judge William King McAllister, a strict constitutionalist and partisan Democrat whom the *Chicago Times* praised as a "man of tender-heart and the most generous sympathies."[34] McAllister was no friend of Captain Hickey or the rough tactics employed by the men under his command.

After a searching examination of the facts of the case, McAllister found for the defendant: the actions of the police constituted an unlawful "invasion" of Mary's private living quarters because the raiding party lacked sufficient warrant to authorize such an entry. The McAllister decision was immediately assailed by law and order advocates, but it set an important precedent for years to come; one that would provide a modicum of protection to the gambling trust. The police had to be more circumspect in the proper execution of gambling raids. "Copies of the law should be in the hands of every policeman," opined former mayor "Long John" Wentworth. "A policeman is like a soldier—he is always anxious to distinguish himself."[35]

That same week, a "sweet scented" (compromised) grand jury ended its labors and found among other things that Mike McDonald did *not* keep a gambling house, which is akin to saying Lake Michigan is a dry gulch. It was asserted that three of the grand jurors—Alderman James Hildreth, J. W. Hersey, and J. C. Harrington—visited the Store to confer with McDonald during the hearings. When they left his establishment, the three decisive votes were firmly in Mike's column.[36] The liquor license was restored, and Mary returned home to 176 South Clark humbled, but satisfied.

From the outset of their marriage, relations between McDonald and his wife were strained. Liquor consumption, the constant threats of police harassment, so many shady characters lurking about the place, and the anxieties of child rearing in a fractious home environment took a heavy toll on the couple. Violent quarrels ensued; Mike had a short fuse and an overbearing temperament. Easily provoked, he beat his wife in fits of unbridled rage. "The trouble between my husband and me grew out of his brutality," she once said. "He was a big, red-blooded man but when under the influence of liquor he was rough and disorderly. He often struck me at such times and mistreated me in cruel ways."[37]

Mary and her children divided time between the mansion on Wabash and the upper floors of the Store. Too often the young ones bore witness to the nightly row, the appearance of uniformed police officers turning up at unexpected hours, the gunplay and the fisticuffs between inebriates that were becoming increasingly common occurrences.

During a deadly outbreak of yellow fever that overtook Memphis and other cities below the Mason-Dixon line in 1878, the children watched in silent horror as a Southern physician named Dr. Reilly (who contracted the disease in New Orleans) suddenly collapsed inside their father's saloon. The man was nursed by Mary, but her ministrations were futile, and he died in her arms. With such frightful scenes and such unhappiness and domestic chaos playing out before them at so tender an age, it was almost inevitable that the McDonald scions would have an enormous struggle to reach adulthood in firm possession of wisdom, sound judgment, responsibility, and respect for other human beings. There was also the constant unpredictability of their father's occupation to contend with.

In the opening days of the Washburn raids, when a handful of honest police officers, undeterred from carrying out their duty by offers of bribe money, were closing down Mike's faro games, "brace" houses, and bunko scams (thus scaring off patrons and forcing McDonald to temporarily relocate operations to secret hideaways on the North Side), Mary begged her husband to practice fiscal restraint, if only for the sake of the children. But Mike craved the excitement, even if it meant gambling with large sums of his own money.

Fearing that a pauper's grave was to be her husband's final destiny if he were to continue down this ruinous path, she prevailed upon their mutual friend, Police Captain William Buckley, to remove her husband from Watt Robbins's faro bank on Clark Street one night where, she was told, he had squandered upwards of $6,000. The captain was, of course, discreet. He sent a "friend" in plain clothes to the resort to whisper sage words of advice in McDonald's ear. "Come home!" was the message given, but the message sent back spewed four-letter epithets and physical threats.[38]

Believing that happier times lie ahead if only her husband would consent to withdraw from Chicago for an extended period of time, Mary badgered Mike to escort her abroad and roam about Europe in a carefree manner, as was the custom of the rich and wellborn of the Gilded Age. Such an excursion, she reasoned, might draw them closer together. But as Mike's profits from the Store multiplied and control of the political mechanisms of the city seemed within his grasp, McDonald brushed aside his wife's incessant demands to undertake a European junket. He would not under any circumstances allow her cravings for a travel adventure to disrupt his self-contained world, nor did he pay much attention to how she was spending her leisure time.

Alienated from her husband and disenchanted with the dreadful routines of maintaining a lodging house inside a gambling casino, Mary soon became a regular attendee at Hooley's Theater matinees every Wednesday and Saturday—and fell hard for the star attraction, Billy Arlington, America's foremost banjo player and minstrel show impresario, starring in the traveling company of *California Minstrels!* with Rickey Barney, Ben Cotton, and the Reynolds Brothers. Jack Haverly, kingpin of Chicago stage productions, who "arranged with the prominent managers for the services of all the meritorious artists in the minstrel world," booked the popular entertainers into Hooley's for this latest engagement.[39]

Billy Arlington was a stage name; the persona of a skillful seducer of needy, socially prominent women isolated from their husbands and trapped in desperate marital situations.[40] His dalliance with the wife of Michael C. McDonald was the latest in a long string of conquests that scandalized Chicago. Born Valentine Bunell, the stage lothario established roots on the South Side of Chicago with his wife, Julia, a frail woman in delicate health who gave birth to a daughter named Amelia. The girl was placed in a San Francisco convent when she was only sixteen.

An African American entertainer and public speaker of high visibility and national renown, Arlington bridged the prejudices of the era through amusing, lighthearted audience repartee and depictions of life in the antebellum South. He delighted several generations of white theatergoers in Northern and Western cities and built the Myers Opera House on Monroe Street after the Fire, and he renamed his troop Arlington, Cotton, and Kemble's Minstrels. He was an enormously popular lecturer on the Chautauqua circuit of the 1870s, delivering topical addresses injected with humor and pathos. Returning to Chicago in October 1877, he filled the seats at McCormick Hall and had them rolling in the aisles with his talk on "Life's Problems." With industriousness befitting the times in which he lived, Arlington had the means and the determination to elevate his status from an itinerant circuit performer to financier by shrewdly investing in two independent theater ventures. Arlington, Leon, Kelley, and Doniker's Minstrels built and operated the Academy of Music on Washington Street, until it was destroyed in the Great Fire.

It was Mary who initiated contact with the performer through a written correspondence inviting him to a clandestine meeting and late-night supper arranged at Buckminster's downtown restaurant. By early March of 1876, Arlington's backstage, lonely hearts flirtation with Mary had escalated into a full-blown sexual affair. Mary occupied center aisle, front row, at his twice-weekly matinee performances, and her loving inscription accompanied a horseshoe of flowers delivered to Arlington's residence on South Park Avenue, where it was received by Billy's heartbroken wife.

Arlington was known to be a serial romancer. His reputation as a roué chasing after wealthy white women was common gossip. On April 21, 1873, the *Chicago Journal* reported that Billy had "borrowed" a certain society lady's jewels, ostensibly to loan to another woman for a party, but in truth he put them up as collateral to finance the printing of posters and advertising materials for his theater. The matter ended up in court. In the only published account of the McDonald-Arlington affair on May 3, 1876, the *Chicago Times* reported that "there are said to be women in houses of prostitution here, whom he beguiled from happy homes, and their sorrow-stricken parents yet live in the city to mourn the disgrace that cannot be forgotten."

He did seem to fear detection, the barrel of one of Mike's custom-made pistols, or an angry husband's retribution likely to be carried out by the murderous Garrity brothers. Billy and Mary were in love . . . for the moment at least. His poetic nature appealed to Mary's desperate cravings for tenderness and flattery in order to salve her lack of self-esteem. More late-night tête-à-têtes followed; he called her "Mamie" because that was the pet name she preferred, and one that Mike often used in their tender moments. In turn, she addressed her cache of secret love notes to "Val."

Emboldened by her husband's inattentiveness, it was not long before the love-starved matron was swept up in Billy Arlington's arms. While dining with Mike at Tivoli's Restaurant one night, she spied her paramour seated across the room and asked her husband if he would fetch the waiter and invite "Mr. Arlington" over to their table, so everyone might be "properly introduced." Oblivious to the intrigue afoot, McDonald of course complied, if only for Mary's amusement. And thus he shook the hand of the man who was bedding his wife. Later, McDonald was forced to admit that Arlington had been "playing him for a rank sucker," a bitter, but ironic twist to his now-famous "there's a sucker born every minute" mock of public gullibility.[41] The supreme irony was that despite the nature of his business, where a gambler's ability to gauge human nature and understand a person's underlying motivations was a business prerequisite, Mike could be so thoroughly blindsided. But when it came to his wife, his children, and those who depended on him, he had a trusting nature.

In December 1875, Arlington was invited to Cincinnati to play a limited engagement at one of Haverly's opera houses. Mary left home under the pretense of visiting her mother in Ohio, but spent the week in Billy's hotel room. She returned with the minstrel troupe undetected, but was so closely veiled as not to be recognized by acquaintances in Chicago. In early March, Arlington was booked into McGuire's Opera House in San Francisco with Billy Rice, another headlining minstrel performer.

Sick at heart and longing for her secret lover, Mary contrived a scheme to pry loose $350 of her husband's money to travel to San Francisco to be with Arlington. She complained of persistent ailments; a bout of catarrh (an inflammation of the mucous membranes) had laid her low, and the bitter cold Chicago winter was too much to bear in her present condition. McDonald was sympathetic to her every complaint and forked over the money to cover her travel expenses. She suggested to Mike that her daughter Birdie accompany her on the excursion; a disarming gesture no doubt intended to alleviate suspicions.

Arriving in Denver two days after her Chicago farewells, Mary penned a jarring letter to Mike from her hotel room. She accused her husband of infidelity and called up a long-forgotten moment of marital tension. What prodded Mary to fire off an unprovoked emotional tirade after departing the city on pleasant and agreeable terms was unfathomable to Mike—but he exercised the greatest patience and determination in this latest domestic ruckus. He telegraphed the Denver hotel, where he was informed by management that Mary and Birdie had checked out and were en route to San Francisco but had left no forwarding address.

On the seventh of April, Mike arrived in the Bay Area intending to get to the bottom of the mystery and bring her back by force, if necessary. With the aid of private detectives, he was able to trace her movements to the newly opened Palace Hotel, a majestic public house located on Montgomery Street. Examining the hotel registry, he was thunderstruck by the incriminating signature written in a bold hand: "V. B. Arlington, wife, and two daughters." The detective pointed out a certain livery stable nearby where Arlington was in the habit of renting a rig each morning for a canter through the city with Mary by his side. "That would be the best place to meet up with them, Mr. McDonald," he was advised.

Positioning himself inside the stable, he awaited their return, with two fully loaded pistols. The unsuspecting couple returned from their morning drive chatting and laughing. But the laughter ended abruptly when they gazed down at the vengeful husband who was aiming at Arlington's head. "Get down from there, you damned darkie!" barked McDonald, using a crude racial epithet that was common for the times. In an effort to shield Billy from Mike's wrath, Mary uttered a shriek and bolted down from the carriage. "Mike, shoot me! I don't deserve to live!" she wailed. The star of the minstrel circuit wheeled the horses about, applying the whip, and managed to escape a potentially lethal showdown.

Mary was repentant but denied the accusation that she had "run off" with Billy. "I went alone," she said. "I went to San Francisco and visited with friends, and while there I met with Arlington. He was only a casual acquaintance."[42] She threw her arms around her husband and muttered words of contrition through her veil of tears. Mike instantly forgave her, wanting to believe that her feeling for Arlington was little more than platonic affection. After a few days had passed, Arlington presented himself at the hotel to offer a humble apology, affirm Mary's claim, and issue a promise not to trouble them again during the marital rapprochement.

Favoring reconciliation over divorce, Mike promised to cut down on his drinking and to escort her to the grand Centennial Exposition to be held in Philadelphia later that summer as a token of goodwill. Together they boarded an east-bound train. But in Salt Lake City she was restive and uncommunicative. One morning, she gazed intently at her husband as he tried to read the morning paper. "Why Mamie, you look as though you want to kill somebody."

Turning her back on him, Mary retreated to the sitting room. When she returned, she aimed a loaded revolver directly at his chest. He spoke to her in gentle, soothing tones, and at length, she lowered the weapon. Further proof of her disturbed mental state was unnecessary, but McDonald refused to consult an alienist or consider an extended recuperation period in a hospital. He was convinced that with the healing hand of the church and parental obligations she would regain her senses.

In Omaha, Mary reunited with one of her brothers, while Mike continued on to Chicago to mitigate a public relations disaster and potential humiliation with the gentlemen of the press. After conferring with the city reporters, Mike was able to get them to agree that the sordid details would receive no mention in the newspapers. Not even the combative *Tribune* deemed it appropriate to publish this explosive story. Only Wilbur Storey defied the gentlemen's agreement. The curmudgeonly editor ran a two-part article in the *Chicago Times* in mid-May, informing his readers that because nearly everyone on the street was gossiping about the McDonalds' discord, he would print the true facts of the case, including the publication of several love letters purportedly written by Billy Arlington and turned over to the *Times* by one of Mary's brothers in Indianapolis.

Calling Mary his "Precious Angel Wife," Arlington said he "cried until tears ceased to flow." He spoke of Mary's planned trip to the Centennial Exposition and the chance to reunite in Philadelphia and New York, but was realistic about their hopes being slim for becoming legal husband and wife. "Oh My God Mamie, we can never be together as long as we live. He would kill us both and follow you to the ends of the earth, and I feel confident he has no idea you love me or that we have been intimate with each other. Why did he take you from me? Oh darling, when you shook my hand at parting, I thought I would die. My God! I can't go back to her again, so no, God forbid! And yet what am I to do?"[43]

At the same time Arlington was pledging eternal love and devotion for Mary Noonan McDonald, he was writing pitiful letters of contrition to his wife Julia, pleading for forgiveness and reconciliation. "You have always been a true and faithful wife to me therefore I cannot forget you. We will let bygones be bygones and live for the future," he wrote.[44]

McDonald's decision not to file for divorce, despite the damning content of the letters published in Storey's paper, was as much a sound business decision as it was an affair of the heart. Mike had consigned a number of his real estate holdings to her name, and there were the children to think of. The near-tragic consequences of the Arlington business and Mary's commotion with the three Chicago bluecoats convinced Mike to remove his family from his place of business and into a private residence a safe distance from the betting action downtown.

With his personal wealth pegged at three-quarters of a million dollars and a keen desire to obtain social prominence driving him, he sold the Wabash

Avenue home and purchased a three-story, eighteen-room mansion with horse barn on a 100- by 148-foot lot at the northeast corner of Ashland Boulevard and Harrison Street (308 South Ashland). The home was one of the stately, dignified French Renaissance marble-stone dwellings covered with ivy and bordered by trees and decorative urns. Many of Chicago's most prominent and wealthiest citizens had migrated to the West Side after the Great Fire, forming a veritable social register of old-line Protestant families living side by side in luxurious Ashland Boulevard mansions. Directly north, the magnificent Episcopal Church of the Epiphany at Adams Street and the Fourth Baptist Church served the devotional needs of a tightly woven social hierarchy where old family fortunes and the time-honored customs and rituals of Chicago's society dictated good taste, proper decorum, and social standing.

Nearby lived William J. Chalmers, president of Allis-Chalmers Steel Company, and millionaire William P. Rend, owner of a string of Pennsylvania coal mines supplying product to city of Chicago furnaces, who collected works of art and counted their money. Dr. Florenz Ziegfeld, founder of the Chicago Musical College and the father of "Flo" Ziegfeld, the genius of New York's "Gay White Way" where his *Follies* were a staple of Broadway culture for decades, lived at 1448 Adams Street. The famed poet Lydia Jane Cadwell and William A. Pinkerton, heir to his father's nationwide detective agency, were among the cordial neighbors, although they did not necessarily care to socialize with the Irish Catholic McDonalds or deem it proper to welcome them to garden receptions after Mike and his family settled comfortably into their Ashland Boulevard residence early in March 1882.

Mayor Carter Henry Harrison, a political ally and Bourbon Democrat who owed his 1879 mayoral election victory to McDonald's political patronage, purchased his family abode at Ashland and Jackson in 1876 from Henry Honoré, father of Bertha Honoré Palmer, the queen of Chicago society.[45] Harrison lived two blocks north of Mike, but he too had to make compromises in order to gain an entrée and overcome the snobbish attitudes of the privileged aristocrats toward the "unwashed" class of politicians, gamblers, and *nouveaux riches*.[46] In one outrageous stunt that violated society protocols and raised eyebrows, Harrison staged an afternoon tea for *the husbands* of Chicago's society mavens. "To find a man presiding at the tea table was certainly an innovation but it was an innovation that was attractive," reminisced his daughter-in-law Edith Odgen Harrison.[47]

They were a proud, enviable, albeit arrogant lot, these old-line money people. One longtime resident had this to say about the social milieu of Ashland Avenue in the 1890s. "I am certain that the people of the West Side could give the residents of the other side pointers as to how to enjoy life and not merely exist. Perhaps, however, it is all due to the many advantages the people of the West

Side have over the residents of the other side. Why do I live on the West Side? It is perfection."[48]

Mary was delighted with her new surroundings, despite the rigid social caste system she faced. She called Ashland Boulevard her husband's "love token" and happily cut off further communication with Billy Arlington. Nor would she dare to speak of him again. For the next seven years, she remained a loyal and dutiful wife, supervising the domestic help, barely tolerating the presence of the irksome and judgmental Grandpa McDonald, and giving birth to two sons: Guy Cassius, who was baptized with the surname of Mike's sainted mother; and Cassius Michael, born five years later, in 1885. She embraced her Roman Catholicism with renewed conviction and with a manic, religious fervor, as the storm clouds that seemed to be hovering over her and Mike McDonald and their troubled union dissipated—but only for the time being.

~ 4 ~

Tammany by the Lake

In THE PRE-FIRE DAYS OF CHICAGO'S HISTORY, THERE STOOD A rather plain-looking, three-story, basement-frame hotel at Wells and Kinzie Streets, brushing up against the Galena and Chicago Union Railroad depot. The political people and all classes of Chicagoans currying favors with the "men who had it in right" knew this dilapidated building as the "Hatch House," named after the long-forgotten builder.

John T. Corcoran and his brother Michael, both zealous, two-fisted, Twentieth Ward Democratic organizers, bought the place in 1859 and spruced it up to the tune of $25,000. They rented rooms in this "handsome and commodious" hotel, 134 of them, many with running water, for $2.00 a day, while at the same time, they carried out acts of voter intimidation that became legendary.[1]

In its heyday, the Hatch House was a notorious robber's roost and the closest parallel one could find to New York's Tammany Hall. When the first hostelry burned down in the Great Chicago Fire, a gaudier public house sprung up from the smoking embers of the conflagration in January 1872 at Clark and Kinzie. The two Hatch Houses are principally remembered for their gin-soaked sample rooms doubling as a "clubhouses," where the old-time politicos banded together for the purposes of welding an effective organization through the recruitment of worthy youngbloods like McDonald with a knack for organizing. John Corcoran drew around him swaggering bullies whose political methods and physical comportment were patterned after the New York Tammanyites with respect to protecting the rights of all citizens to drink, whore, and gamble as they pleased. "Clabby" Burns, Eddie Hall, "Bad Jimmy" Connorton, "Kid" Murphy, "Scully the Robber," and "Coonie the Fox," men who are forgotten in the mists of time, were some of the most noted criminals of "Little Hell" who made life exciting in the back alleys of the Twentieth Ward. They were said to be the guardians of the Hatch House. "Many an inebriated man was robbed in that den, and there is no record of the mysterious disappearances which might have been traced to the Hatch House if the police had not been completely under the control of the gang," the *Chicago Tribune* reported.[2]

Not unlike the rough and tumble antics of the Tammanyites of 14th Street in New York, Corcoran and his strapping *boyos* tossed paving stones into the club-houses of rival ward organizations, poked, prodded, and submerged captured political rivals in horse troughs, nearly drowning them in pools of fetid water polluted by horse spit and offal until they screamed for mercy. Every election day, gangs of "repeaters" (men paid to circulate the precincts casting multiple votes under the names of the long deceased, culled from stone grave markers in the cemetery) were hired to influence the final vote tally.

The Hatch House Gang made life miserable for the few remaining Swedish residents, large numbers of Irish, and the arriving Italians laboring on the docks of the Chicago River and the smoky factories of the neighborhood. Too much liquor and too little order earned Market Street (today, Orleans Street) from Grand Avenue north to North Avenue and the district encompassing Larrabee Street to Goose Island a sinister reputation as the "Plague spot of the North Division" and the lasting moniker "Little Hell," borrowed from one of the poorer neighborhoods on the east end of London.

"Squalor and filth reign here supreme," noted a *Tribune* editorialist. "The faces that stare and glare from these hovels are bloated and bleary-eyed, telling the monotonous story of wasted lives—lives over-powered, stupefied and brutalized by the insidious monster Intemperance. There is room for missionary effort in 'Little Hell.'"[3] In time, the missionaries and settlement house workers would arrive, but the results were marginal. The poor and downtrodden were not much interested in hearing the "Hallelujah chorus" when their children were starving in the streets and gangs were terrorizing the neighborhood. It remained "Little Hell" and an immigrant slum through the 1920s and well into the 1930s.[4]

A contemporary journalist commissioned by the Hatch House toughs to polish their image in the face of such damning editorial censure authored this contemporary assessment of Alderman John and his so-called popularity in the slums of the Twentieth Ward: "On account of his facility of gathering political strength and his facility in organizing, Mr. Corcoran has often been compared to the late John Kelly of New York, and by his many friends he has been dubbed the 'Sachem.' He is genial in disposition, weighs 240 pounds and is five-feet eight inches in height."[5] His brother Mike's criminal record, however, belies the better judgment of sycophants.

Convicted of armed robbery in 1868 and sentenced to fourteen years at the Joliet Penitentiary, Mike traded on Brother John's aldermanic powers and was granted a formal pardon by Governor John Palmer, sympathetic ally of his Hatch House supporters in Chicago, after serving only eighteen months.

Important connections and expedient alliances between city, county, and state politicians were forged in the streets once Mike Corcoran was back in town and operating at full throttle. At election time, the Corcorans "assisted" the Democratic ticket in every Chicago ward and congressional district where the party was being challenged, and when necessary, across state lines. It was reported in October 1880 that the gang "sent to Indiana reprobates, Italian peanut vendors, tramps, and every portable voter they could lay hold upon in Chicago, who would go for a consideration to run the risk of being sent to the Penitentiary for illegal voting."[6]

The Corcoran brothers befriended McDonald early in his career, inculcated the techniques of grassroots political organizing at the ward level into his business plan, and established a "satellite" office in one of his downtown gambling dives, opposite the twenty-four-hour magazine depot maintained by the Western News Company, a nationwide distributor of periodicals directed by John R. Walsh, the former "train butcher" known to Mike McDonald from his Michigan Central days. It was a most curious and ironic pairing of two willful men who reached the same fork in the road at an identical moment, but had chosen completely opposite paths.

Born two years apart to poor, working-class Irish immigrant families, Walsh and McDonald were friendly, but never close. They shared some common adventures, as well as a few business dealings, and had much to learn from one another. Both were ambitious and yearned for wealth, privilege, and the joys of a stable home life. But as Walsh achieved his many successes through discipline and innovation and by serving a Horatio Alger–like apprenticeship that in time earned him all the personal rewards denied Mike McDonald, the blithe gambler took unfortunate short-cuts in life because he never completely understood himself nor was he able to come to terms with the world he had made.

That McDonald was a persuasive man with the ability to organize and manage groups of people with the skill and aplomb of one of his early political mentors, John Corcoran, no one ever questioned. That he was a forceful presence and energetic in his pursuits, he proved time and time again. That he attained his wealth by setting high moral standards in the company of principled people while maintaining domestic bliss at home, he never claimed, nor would anyone else claim it for him.

In his three-volume Gilded Age opus touting the accomplishments of Chicago's most noteworthy businessmen and public figures, Alfred T. Andreas excluded McDonald but praised Walsh and declared that he was "justly entitled to the credit of having materially contributed to the welfare and convenience of the great reading public of the West."[7]

Operating on the other side of the street from Walsh and standing shoulder to shoulder with the bruising Hatch House Gang and their hired poll sluggers, McDonald was seen as a creature of the back alleys, political clubs, and saloons of 1870s Chicago, inspiring greater levels of public loathing than respect, based on newspaper dispatches reporting his warm relations with the political "bummers," conmen, and thugs armed with jimmies and brass knuckles who surrounded him.

In the early years, before the attainment of a polished veneer, a house full of servants, a footman, and the patronage of well-heeled politicians who were to become his consuming obsession, McDonald was less than circumspect in his choice of companions. In the same fashion as the twentieth-century crime bosses, he relied on street "muscle" to enforce his will and the lessons taught to him by the Corcorans when it came to dealing with deadbeat gamblers, police officers, and others pressing their complaint. The four Garrity brothers, "big, uncouth dirty sneaks," from the saloons and low dives of Illinois Street near the Chicago River, were "the nearest approach which this city has ever shown to metropolitan tendencies in the way of crime," complained the *Tribune*.[8]

Hugh, John, Mike, and Tommy Garrity were Hatch House ringers who performed certain criminal "services" for Corcoran and Mike McDonald, but their postwar stock and trade was to cheat honest men out of their money through clever swindles and bunko scams orchestrated by McDonald and initiated inside train stations and hotels.

"At an early hour last evening, Hugh Garrity, one of the most unscrupulous confidence operators and thieves in the city, succeeded in victimizing a stranger to a considerable amount by the practice of the old threadbare game," the *Tribune* reported on June 30, 1868. "The transfer of the funds was made at or near the Michigan Southern depot, and immediately after when he imagined himself unobserved Garrity jumped into a hack and drove off." The victim of the con game followed in pursuit, and with a well-aimed toss of a brickbat that hit its mark, brought Garrity tumbling into the street. When he tried to escape on foot, a police officer's bullet pierced his left hip. Wounded, but not severely, Garrity was seized with five confederates, arraigned on a charge of vagrancy, and placed on trial two months later. Each was fined the modest sum of $100 before being discharged.

Inside the all-night saloons of State Street, the Garrity brothers terrorized and pistol whipped any individual who gave offense. Their crimes were lengthy and their reputation was alarming to honest and true men, and those operating on the right side of the law, or just trying to get along. J. H. Romaine, a Board of Trade member, was smashed over the head with glass and crockery by John Garrity inside Batchelder's resort on March 2, 1877. The same day, Garrity was arrested for tearing apart Mollie Fitch's house of ill fame on Fourth Avenue.[9] When both cases came up at the Armory Police Court, neither the victims nor the witnesses bothered to show up, and the matters were quietly dropped.

Later that same year, Mike Garrity, with brothers John and Hugh, was arrested and charged with mayhem for kicking, gouging, and disfiguring Johnny

Dowling as he relaxed in the comfort of "the Store." McDonald and three other men rescued Dowling from certain death, after Hugh smashed a champagne bottle over his head and nearly severed the injured man's nose with a fierce bite of his teeth. "And you can bet your last penny if you can find takers, that I will prosecute to the bitter end," Dowling gasped from his hospital bed.

McDonald retained a legal team to represent Dowling in his complaint, but after many continuances, a change of venue to Kane County was ordered. In the end, following two hours of closed-door deliberation, Hugh and John were let off with light, two-year sentences. Someone had "influenced" the jury.. "It was believed that had all been honest and square, as there was only a one-sided case, they would have returned in a few minutes."[10] While McDonald had made a grand show of "helping" out his friend Dowling, he was not going to lift a finger to send the Garritys away for a protracted period of time. McDonald and his associates who witnessed the unprovoked attack ignored the subpoenas to appear in court to testify on behalf of the victim.[11]

By employing the Garritys and protecting them in court, the Hatch House Gang and McDonald relied on tried and proven methods of street intimidation, knowing they could get away with committing egregious acts. A review of the criminal court calendar for April 1870 shows that John and Hugh Garrity were arrested for vagrancy—the common charge filed against bunko schemers and gamblers—and fined $101.50. The charges were suspended in order to save the county the expense of another useless trial.[12] The Garrity brothers tested McDonald's patience, even as he stood behind them in court, allowed them to turn his saloon into a bare-knuckle free-for-all, and furnished bail for their various offenses. In an 1884 case involving a robbery charge against Mike Garrity, the gambler posted a $1,000 bond, but the offender jumped bail, leaving McDonald to pay back the forfeiture.

The emboldened Garritys attached an exclamation point to every criminal act committed, while crooked judges and the police looked the other way. In separate incidents a year and a day apart, Mike McDonald and the Garrity family of "shoulder-hitters" were responsible for two assaults against well-known citizens that underscored the gambler's violent side as he built a political underworld network in the blood and beer of the Clark Street rialto.

The evening before the gala opening of the city's 1873 Inter-State Industrial Exposition, a stellar triumph of commerce and industry hosted by Chicago's mercantile leaders just two years after the Great Fire, McDonald, Morris Martin, Dowling, and the rest of the thuggish troop loitered outside Jake Wolford's saloon at 128 Clark Street, taunting passersby with their swagger and bravado. In a sudden and shocking show of sadistic fury, Hugh Garrity seized a stranger, threw him to the ground for no apparent reason, and kicked him in the face and stomach while Mike and John stood back, observing the savagery with benign amusement. The bloodied victim crawled to a nearby lamppost and staggered to his feet. McDonald, his boots shined and his silk shirt and waistcoat cleaned and pressed, flicked the man's hat from his head and struck his arm. "Leave go, damn you! You're not hurt!" he screamed into the victim's ear. A small crowd gathered. Hearing the murmurs and observing the frowns of the witnesses, Mike stepped back and told the crowd, "He's not hurt. It was just a misunderstanding, that's all!"[13]

Two women negotiating a horse-drawn phaeton tried to pass by the street brawl without drawing attention, only to find John Garrity blocking their path. Garrity tried to commandeer the coach, but one of the ladies stood up and horsewhipped him. A police officer, hearing the melee, spied McDonald and his bodyguards and said, "this will never do," but then inexplicably walked away from the scene without intervening. Minutes later, the Garritys besieged Wells Sherman, a retired Chicago police deputy superintendent and pounded him to a bloody pulp with a set of brass knuckles. Sherman was pulled from the gutter and spirited off to the home of John Corcoran, where a three-inch cut over his eye was treated, apologies accepted, and a promise not to prosecute was received from Corcoran. "Sometimes the boys get a little out of hand," he apologized, or with words to that effect.

The brutish Garritys were still not finished. Next they pounced upon Samuel J. Medill, city editor of the *Tribune* and the former mayor's brother as he strolled down Clark Street toward his room at the Grand Pacific Hotel, pausing briefly to inquire about the Sherman affray. It was past 11:30 P.M., when from behind, Hugh Garrity struck the newsman in the back of the head with the brass knuckles, driving the dignified old gent to the ground. Only then did the McDonald party finally retreat. They walked back to Watt Robbins's gambling house near Monroe, but were refused admission. Enraged, Dowling and Garrity discharged their revolvers into the door. With shots fired, the police had no other recourse but to quell the disturbance. Watt Robbins and his doorman were arrested and charged with vagrancy—the saloon was closed for the night. "Meanwhile no steps were taken to secure any of the gang of roughs who only escaped being murderers by accident and that fortune which protects bullies and roughs in Chicago."[14]

A well-publicized example of Mike McDonald's retaliation methods against opponents occurred inside James McGarry's saloon at 115 Madison Street, days ahead of the city election of 1874. Described as a "quiet and respectable place," McGarry's establishment was in fact a rollicking political clubhouse; and the proprietor was the most famous barkeep of nineteenth-century Chicago, having been immortalized by journalist-author Finley Peter Dunne as the real-life inspiration for the fictional "Martin Dooley," the wise and philosophical Bridgeport tavern owner whose epigrams and sentimental musings about Irish American immigrant life amused and delighted the reading public in both newspapers and books.[15] As a result, McGarry was one of the best-known Chicago characters of the late Gilded Age. His original saloon at 121 South Clark was destroyed in the Chicago Fire. He reopened in a basement hovel at Dearborn and Madison not long after, enforcing firmly established rules of the house.

Mixed drinks were barred while McGarry was on duty and serving. Straight whiskey, various ales, and beer were the only beverages of choice. Thirsty patrons knew better than to order a blended drink or a cordial. "We sell only liquor here," McGarry barked. "There's a sody fountain around the corner and I think Tommy Newman across the street knows how to make 'em, but we don't spoil liquor and digestion for any price!"[16]

McGarry neither operated in Bridgeport, nor was he particularly philosophical, gracious, or as amusing in person as the good-hearted character portrayed by Dunne. He was a well-seasoned politico, outspoken on matters of public interest, and his barroom an important rendezvous for judges, bankers, politicians, and county board members who spent money prodigally. It was known to all as a tough "Democratic saloon" with beer barrels propping up wooden planks doubling as a countertop.

On the night of infamy, McDonald was informed by one of his henchmen that McGarry had insulted his honor and reputation by calling him a public thief in a Chicago newspaper and had promised he would see to it that the prison bars slam shut on Mike if he could help it. Around 8:00 P.M., McDonald, armed with a pistol and accompanied by Nick Geary and John Garrity, elbowed his way past an assembled throng of judges, theater people, and the Cook County treasurer, who were enjoying a taste of election-eve lager. In a loud voice, Mike demanded to "settle up" with McGarry.

"How are you, 'Red Jim'?" McDonald sneered, as he brandished a walking stick at a man he once called his dear friend. He knew that "Red Jim" was not a moniker to McGarry's particular liking. "Jim, I hear that you said I was a thief, and you would have me put in the penitentiary. If you said that you are a lying, thieving bastard!" McDonald drew a pistol and aimed at the barkeep's forehead. To prevent the county treasurer from intervening on McGarry's behalf, Garrity struck the man with a vicious blow. The affair was of brief duration. The gun was hastily snatched from McDonald's fist by Clem Periolat, a political spoilsman and supplies contractor to the Cook County Board of Commissioners, before a shot was fired.

The combatants were separated and McDonald was "escorted" to the Armory Police Station in the comfort of a fancy carriage and was let out on straw bail through the connivance of Captain William Buckley, said to be on the gambler's payroll. McGarry demanded redress from Buckley, but was curtly informed that McDonald was "alright" and had been released into the custody of his attorney, Alfred Trude.

The McGarry matter went before a judge and was quietly settled the following December. One witness after another was paraded before the jury to testify to the fact that McDonald's gun was empty at the time and the affray was just a "falling out" between two old and devoted friends. The jury acquitted McDonald amid loud and raucous cheers coming from the spectator gallery. Afterward, every important politician, judge, county board member, fire and police commissioner, and even the mayor himself accepted invitations to feast at a lavish banquet and champagne celebration at the Store. All of the heads of the major city departments and a Catholic priest showed up to toast—and roast—McDonald in a jesting, good-natured kind of way. "It was a grand burlesque," sniffed the *Tribune*. "The fact that Mike's friends knew he would be acquitted accounts for the completeness of the preparations; the actors it will be seen were well up in their parts."[17]

Inside the Store, glasses were hoisted long after the midnight hour tolled. The liquor flowed easily, and lusty rhymes and humorous parodies were recited until dawn. The "actors" and orators, including the city clerk of Chicago, who good-naturedly lampooned McDonald and his association with their friendly ally, Mayor Colvin, arose from their chairs.

> Here on this bosom–
> My Michael, come rest;
> Your arms 'round my neck,
> Your face on my vest.
>
> Too long have we lived–
> Asunder, apart;
> Divided in body,
> United in heart!
>
> The proof of our union
> The city shall see;
> McDonald and Colvin,
> The firm name shall be!
>
> You pluck the Granger;
> No odds 'tis done–
> Chuck-a-luck, roulette,
> Faro, vingt'un;
>
> I shield you from danger,
> Befriending your game;
> As my share of the swag,
> A third I shall claim!

A stand-in for Police Superintendent Jacob Rehm (already in trouble with the government for complicity in the nationwide "whiskey ring" scandals and because his deputy, Michael Hickey, owned a stake in a Chicago house of ill fame) offered toasts and the compliments from the "boys" back at headquarters. Mike McDonald, enjoying his victuals and fine wines, gazed contentedly at his flock this chilly Chicago evening, knowing his "gang" was looked after and well-protected by police and city officials as long as the normal perquisites were paid.

The thugs surrounding Mike in the formative post-Fire years profited under the centralized command of their boss following Mayor Medill's providential decision to resign from office. These men with long criminal records were essential to the operation, although privately, McDonald held most of them in deep contempt, viewing them as a temporary means to an end, nothing more. Jere Dunn, a "sporting man" from Oswego, New York, was the worst of the lot, but one of lawyer Trude's most regular and dependable clients. He, too, was a McDonald man down to the bone, and the amount of business he brought to the syndicate compensated for legal expenses that were charged back to the gambler's enterprise.

Dunn, who served terms in a Pennsylvania prison and at Sing Sing penitentiary in New York State on two separate murder counts, was brought to Chicago by McDonald in the early 1870s to organize illegal horse races on the lakefront and perpetrate clever bunko swindles on the witless "Grangers" passing through town. Dunn was a persuasive and ambitious sociopath—a real moneymaker who rose quickly in the ranks of the McDonald syndicate. With funds drawn from his bulging purse, Dunn (although he had been previously convicted of animal abuse in 1880) purchased "Lady Alice," a prized trotter who fell dead upon the track from exhaustion after running a race in Michigan. With the insurance money received from the untimely death of the steed, Dunn opened a Chicago saloon to further his connections in the athletic and political realm. While passing through Chicago, John L. Sullivan, the famed bare-knuckles prizefighter, frequented Dunn's tavern and agreed to allow the ex-con, erstwhile killer, bunkoist, and Chicago barkeep to represent him as a booking agent.

Jere Dunn handled the affairs of other champion prizefighters of the era, including William "the Solid Man" Muldoon in coast-to-coast engagements. He provided insider "tips" to Mike McDonald in order to affect the betting odds on these well-publicized bouts back home in Chicago. In return, McDonald showed his gratitude by placing at his disposal the services of expert legal counsel in the person of Alfred Trude, Leonard Swett, Emory A. Storrs, and Colonel Dan Munn, the former federal revenue collector in Chicago. All four were respected in legal circles and accorded high praise for their brilliance of mind, their clever tactics, and refined courtroom demeanor. And yet, all of these accomplished barristers, who were warmly welcomed into the sanctum of the Union League Club, the Hamilton Club, and the Chicago Bar Association, rarely turned down the chance to represent McDonald or other scoundrels within his domain.

By dabbling in the world of sports, whether it was owning a racing stable or promoting prize fights and crooked horse races, Jere Dunn and his ilk became minor celebrities and their names familiar to a national audience who kept up with all the news of the ring and the turf. Wherever John L. Sullivan, the "Boston Strong Boy," traveled, Jere Dunn was sure to be lurking in the background making useful connections and peeling off greenbacks from the champ's purse. In December 1883, Dunn arranged an illegal match for Sullivan in Chicago through Charles E. "Parson" Davies, a gambling proprietor, nationally known fight promoter, and owner of the "House of David," a rival faro bank that had been a minor irritation to McDonald for many years.[18]

The "Parson" was well regarded and one of the leading "sports" of the city after booking John Ennis in a one-hundred-mile walking race against Dan O'Leary in the Glass Palace along the lakefront. Ennis was beaten, and Davies took O'Leary on a European tour and made him a star. Cornelius Vanderbilt tagged Davies with his famous nickname while watching O'Leary perform at Madison Square Garden. Seeing Davies, the commodore asked, "who is the clerical gentleman?" When told that Davies was O'Leary's manager, Vanderbilt said he looked more like a parson than a sportsman, and after that the nickname stuck.

Davies had under contract James Elliott, a hot-tempered fighter twice arrested, for robbery and for assault and battery. Eager to make a name for Elliott, Davies counted on an early knockout of the champ that would confer national celebrity on his charge. A match with hard gloves was set to go off at McCormick's Hall, but the police had other ideas and abruptly cancelled the fight. The enraged Dunn accused Elliott of being a coward and afraid to meet Sullivan man-to-man in the ring. These were hard words for Elliott to swallow, the code of honor among thieves being what it is. The two men exchanged taunts and vowed to settle matters with gun, knife, brass knuckles, or whatever other suitable weapon could be found. Mike McDonald later testified that Elliott was an "un-caged ruffian," who uttered repeated threats to the effect that "If Dunn doesn't shoot me in the back I'll crawl to him and chop his head off!"[19]

The inevitable brawl between the two men occurred inside William "Appetite Bill" Langdon's Tivoli Saloon at Dearborn and Calhoun Place in "Gambler's Alley" on March 2, 1883. Langdon, a reformed cardplayer and bunkoist whose place was a favored after-hours haunt and the "resort of fast women, gamblers and pimps," according to the *Chicago Herald,* misspoke when he accused Dunn of carrying out "cold-blooded murder" after shots were fired between the two, with Elliott laid cold by Dunn.[20]

Other witnesses swore to it: Elliott didn't stand a chance, and Dunn had shot him down like a dog in the street. But this isn't what Dunn's influential friends wanted to hear from the witnesses. At the coroner's inquest the next day, Mike's erstwhile political ally and fixer in the Twentieth Ward, Joseph

Chesterfield Mackin, Alfred Trude, and a score of Clark Street gamblers were present to plead Dunn's case before the coroner's jury. "I'll bet that if you got to the bottom of it, Trude has already a strong tie to every man on the jury," said one spectator. "I mean he's got some way of influencing them or rather he thinks he does."[21]

Not even the great Trude could stave off a coroner's ruling of homicide or forestall Dunn's indictment. He bowed out of the case, but secured a new presiding judge for McDonald after Egbert Jamieson was dismissed for showing prejudice against the defendant. Opening their wallets, Mike McDonald and Chicago gambler Pat Sheedy paid $100,000 and engaged Emory Alexander Storrs, politically a Republican and twice a finalist for the office of U.S. attorney general during the presidential administrations of Rutherford B. Hayes and Chester Arthur, to represent Dunn. The retention of Storrs and McDonald's dealings with individuals of high social rank philosophically opposed to the class of men reputed to be under the gambler's wing illustrate that party labels and reformist ideology easily blurred with the proper cash inducements.[22]

As a courtroom orator, Storrs had few peers, and in the Dunn matter he easily outshone the Cook County state's attorney. He created confusion among jurors by summoning William Pinkerton, head of America's foremost detective agency, to testify that Dunn was no murderer, despite a long and impressive rap sheet submitted from law enforcement officials in three different states. When McDonald's turn on the witness stand came up, State's Attorney Luther Laflin Mills assailed him and all the other "saloons, Dago dens and dives [that] had given up their inmates" to appear in court.[23]

The jury came back with the only possible verdict they could render: Not Guilty, agreeing with Storrs that it was a simple case of "self-defense" against a crazed and unpredictable ruffian. Allegations of McDonald's attempt to pack the jury circulated in the streets but were never acted upon. Nobody expected them to be, and "the expenses of the defense of Dunn were borne by the class with whom he is associated," sniffed the *Herald*. "And they alone of all the people in this great city have the right to reckon their comrade's restoration to liberty as a personal triumph."[24]

Jere Dunn said that he had counted on nothing less than a full acquittal and was off to preview the Kentucky Derby. He vowed that he was through with Chicago forever. A year later, Dunn turned up in New York, where he resumed management of the great "John L.'s" career. He hunted down a friend of Elliott's known as "Logan No. 2." This individual had vowed to avenge the slain fighter and shoot Jere Dunn on sight. But Dunn got the best of him inside a Park Row saloon. The coroner's jury ruled it "justifiable homicide," and Jere Dunn carved a fourth notch into his gun handle, adding yet another drinking story to his breezy barroom braggadocio.[25]

~ 5 ~

The People's Party and the Overturn of Puritan Rule

JOSEPH MEDILL AND HIS POLICE SUPERINTENDENT, ELMER WASHburn, made a desperate but honest attempt to break up organized gambling, but not for a day did it stop. By means of informants, alarm bells, and other contrivances, the gamblers usually knew in advance when the bluecoats were going to strike. They secreted their dealer boxes and paraphernalia in hiding places, leaving only the furnishings of the house to the special police details to smash and destroy.

In the aftermath of the police wrangles and Medill's failure to suppress gambling, Mike McDonald and his flock consecrated Clark Street's once-respected commercial district, anchored by the Bank of Chicago at Randolph and Clark, into a gaudy, nonstop, twenty-four-hour Monte Carlo–style casino "strip," with dens ranging from deluxe emporiums for "high rollers" down to the common nickel-and-dime places known as "dinner pail" resorts catering to the working man, who presumably carried his lunch with him to the playing table. There, the common laborers could wager their meager earnings on the most popular parlor house game of the day—faro.

Up and down the street, gambling houses catering to every pocketbook hung out their shingle in the wide-open 1870s. For indigents or those suffering "gambler's ruin," the dinner pail resorts operated by the Hankins brothers—Jeff, Al, and George—were often the last refuge for a hot meal and a schooner of beer. Unless the patron made a nuisance of himself, the boss gamblers plied their customers with free food and beverage, often served by an African American wait staff delivering home-cooked meals directly to the men seated around the gaming table.

For nearly thirty years, the Hankins brothers were enormously influential in parlor house gambling and thoroughbred racing circles—second only to McDonald as "persons to see" about getting up a big game in Chicago. But they lacked Mike's political savvy and did not care to hobnob in socially prominent circles outside of the sporting world, where they won and lost fortunes as easily as breathing the morning air.[1]

George, Al, and Jeff were true to their calling and operated gambling dens in the heart of the commercial district and outlying areas for many years. Their principal establishments were at 134 and 121 South Clark Street where, it was reported, the "artistically frescoed walls" were covered with "a magnificent $1,000 mirror; its floors are clad in a rich Brussels carpet; its furniture is a mass of elegantly carved woods and its walls adorned by richly-tinted drapery, while on a marble-topped sideboard the most delicate viands, wherewith to satisfy the waning appetite and the choicest stimulants to drown the waxing cares, are gratuitously laid out."[2] It is clear by this account that the brothers recognized that while the dinner pail trade brought in a steady stream of foot traffic and regular cash flow, it was also incumbent upon them to provide luxurious accommodations for the more discerning gambler of more affluent means.

The brothers were born to farming people in McHenry, Illinois, well north of the Chicago city limits in McHenry County. Inspired by a reading of the popular novels of the day and the lure of adventure, Jeff abandoned the drudgery of farmwork, and Al, an apprenticeship with a harness maker, and they took off for Alder Gulch, a crude mining camp in Virginia City, Montana. Barely out of their teens, the Hankins boys opened their "California Exchange," featuring two billiard tables, card games, and a stock of cigars and liquor they sold from the back of a prairie schooner to the rough-and-tumble miners panning for gold in their red flannel shirts and slouch hats. Drinks were sold for 75 cents a shot, and "placer" gold nuggets or a pinch of the precious "dust" were put up as collateral for a drink or a turn at the roulette wheel.[3]

In the midst of the Civil War, Jeff moved on to Blackfoot City, where he opened a one-room gambling hall and saloon for the local miners in Ophir Gulch. "Such a rich field did he find for industry and enterprise of his sort that he persuaded his illustrious brothers George and Al to unite their fortunes with his." They opened a much more pretentious resort dubbed the "Headquarters," where Al Hankins, the quiet, lean, solemn-visaged brother who looked more like a poor dirt farmer than a tinhorn, took command. "Al, before many months residence at Blackfoot City . . . was stamped as one of the worst of the unsavory society of the camp. By even the vicious, depraved wretches that frequented the "Headquarters," he was regarded with an awe excited by his deeper villainy. He became recognized as an outlaw, a swindler and a thief."[4]

Law enforcement was nonexistent—the camp was beyond the reach of civilization—and there were very few women living in the area. But with the arrival of Eastern people and their imported refinements, a citizens' "Vigilance Committee" was soon organized to drive out the town's undesirables. The Hankins trio fiercely resisted the vigilantes through the countertactics and gunplay of a gang of toughs they formed called the "Regulators," but the Western foray ended unhappily for Jeff, Al, and George when they were driven out of the camp on a rail. The only alternative was a hearing before "Judge Lynch" and a certain appointment at the "hanging tree."

Although officially out of business, Jeff held title to vast acres of mineral-rich land in Montana and the Dakotas. He grew wealthy by it, but at great personal cost. Fleeing from an armed posse while in the midst of his gambling and land speculation, Hankins tumbled from a fast-moving wagon and mangled his leg, rendering him crippled for life. Short and rotund and hobbling along with the aid of a cane, Jeff crept back into Chicago with a $10,000 insurance settlement and reunited with his brothers three years after the close of the Civil War.

The laissez-faire attitude of the city government in the years leading up to the Great Fire encouraged the brothers to open a string of gambling dens, each operation independent of the others and run as a single proprietorship, although the three often pooled their resources when necessity dictated. George Hankins referred to his cumulative holdings as the "clubhouse business," a cachet that borrowed heavily from McDonald's upwardly mobile pretensions. "One-eyed" Wally Winchester, said to be the "first gambler to reach Chicago" during the Fort Dearborn days, was their principal croupier and house manager. In addition to their Clark Street properties, the Hankins brothers hung out their shingle on Washington Street in plain sight of Marshall Field's ornate department store; at Clinton and Jefferson, west of downtown, where "Iron Face" Barker and Billy Knight looked after the family interests; and at various satellite dens operating on the South Side.

All the while, they vigorously sought out the "piker" bets—wagers of 10 cents or so that McDonald refused—as a throng of anxious bettors were served daily by an army of sixty-eight dealers in their employ. It was reported that in one month alone, eighteen suicides were reported to police, all of them due to financial losses sustained at the Hankins's establishments—all of which suffered a poor reputation as dishonest "brace houses." The curious thing is that despite all of the hostile publicity surrounding their crooked dealings, the businesses ran full-throttle through the duration of the parlor house era extending from 1870 to 1895, long after the brothers had a falling out and agreed to split their holdings and go their separate ways.

Along the rialto, Alderman John Corcoran, erstwhile friend and elder mentor of McDonald, ran a faro game almost uninterruptedly in the House of David until Billy Fagin bought him out. George Holt, a former Board of Trade man and a "well fixed" anomaly among the cardsharps, operated at 71 West Monroe and also held a stake in the House of David. Holt was reported to be a regular churchgoer until he fell in with a bad crowd and renounced his religious beliefs. But his gambling house appealed to the professional men and grain speculators. The police rarely interrupted the game in progress.

John Belknap's place at 119 Clark Street was another "gentleman's game," rarely disturbed by the bluecoats. "The proprietors are suave, gentlemanly fellows, always courteous to those whose acquaintance they desire and whose pocketbooks are sufficiently plethoric to tempt their stupidity," the *Inter-Ocean* observed.[5] At 98 West Randolph, Curt Gunn and Sy Jaynes welcomed the professional gamblers to the table to "buck the tiger" (play faro) into the wee hours of morning, if that was their choice. The partners grew wealthy and opened gambling resorts in Hot Springs, Arkansas, and Saratoga Springs, New York, until Jaynes's eyesight badly deteriorated along with his bank account, leaving him penniless.

After leaving McDonald's employ, thereby provoking the Garrity brothers to commit murderous assault against him, John Dowling opened a small house at 148 Clark catering exclusively to the gambling bosses who were often the victims of their vices—and not the Grangers, high rollers, or dinner pail crowd in shabby clothes. Lucky at cards, but unlucky in the art of self-defense, Dowling once played a lone hand that was worth a cool $60,000 to $70,000. Liberal with his money, he never allowed an unlucky gambler to leave the table dead broke.

Among the fraternity of gamblers, none were more curious, nor as vilified as, "the pirate of the basin," Julius "Black Jack" Yattaw, "commodore" of the *Chicago Harbor Yacht Club Boat House* and the *El Tempo*—two large, flat, dimly lit scows moored in Lake Michigan. The major attraction aboard the city's most famous "bumboats," run by Yattaw and his principal competitor, Bartholomew McDermott, were gambling and cheek-to-cheek dancing that appealed to prurient tastes. Government Revenue Service cutters and succeeding mayoral administrations tried in vain to scuttle Yattaw's vessels.

Driven out of Buffalo in 1872, Yattaw and his mistress, Maggie, a "degraded woman from one of the low dives of the city," dropped anchor and set up housekeeping in the physical squalor of the Cheyenne brothel district of Chicago, earning their sustenance from the offshore pleasure-boat business.[6] A man not easily discouraged, the "commodore" was harassed with raids and assessed petty fines for failing to maintain proper nautical lighting, operating a saloon without a license, running a floating brothel, and other offenses, but he always managed to scrape by, despite daily censure.

"Yattaw ought to have been sunk in the lake three years ago when he was weak," growled the *Tribune*.[7] Surprisingly, the U.S. government came to the gambler's rescue by permitting the bumboat fleet to moor in the breakwater, two miles off of Van Buren Street, at the federal pier during the summer resort season. With gleeful impertinence, Yattaw advertised his nightly "soiree" entertainments and made a fortune serving refreshments during the day.

In 1882, the Chicago authorities all but gave up the notion of trying to inveigle Black Jack to leave town. In the belief that his underworld associations might be useful to the detective bureau, they appointed him a policeman. But Yattaw was discharged from his duties in a moment of personal cowardice for allowing a desperado named Bill Allen to escape a police dragnet after killing an officer one night. It was back to the bumboats for Jack and the missus. They conducted their floating dance halls until the early 1890s, when Sid McHie and a contingent of West Side bookmakers modernized and updated the bumboat concept by outfitting an aquatic poolroom to clock bets on the horse races safely offshore.[8]

Billy "the Clock" Skakel was another scalawag of the saloons, but unlike Black Jack Yattaw, Skakel thrived in politics and stock swindles and made a fortune. Billy was only twenty years old when he opened a faro bank near Clark Street and the Chicago River in the early 1870s.[9] Keno was his racket, and a decade later he moved five blocks south down Clark Street with partner John Walpole. At times, he worked for McDonald and Morris Martin; the men of the Store provided him with introductions to important First Ward Democratic politicos.

Skakel's large clock and stock ticker "fixed" the readings of shares listed on Wall Street, but the actual price of shares had no bearing whatsoever on his quotations. The mechanical contrivance was a variation of the old faro dealing box—slips of paper with so-called stock quotations were substituted for playing cards. Billy would fix the ticker in advance the night before the "boys" stopped by his bucket shop in Gambler's Alley, where "short selling" went on in the shadow of the nearby exchange. Each morning the suckers, the greenhorns, and the compulsive gamblers who simply couldn't help themselves ducked into the alley to place wagers on the price of stocks. No one other than Skakel knew what the clock would read. Morris Martin and Harry Lawrence invented the stock swindle scheme in the early 1870s, and it flourished for nearly twenty years until the early 1890s, when laws against short selling curtailed the activity.

In the months following Mayor Medill's European retreat, the *Chicago Times* reported that there were "seven-hundred bunko men and bucket shop short sellers in the city and skin games of every description in nearly every block."[10] The city was as wide open as it would ever be for these gamblers and the more dangerous elements of the criminal underworld; the only modern parallel to the complete takeover of Chicago by a cabal of underworld figures in league with the city administration would occur during Prohibition in the1920s. Despite the setback, "Medillism," as a popular movement among the native-born, was not vanquished. The Committee of Seventy stitched together a party platform under the aegis of interim mayor Bond.

The task before McDonald as the November 1873 city election loomed was formidable: to unite this ragged fraternity of professional gamblers, liquor dealers, bunkoists, foreign-born Germans and Irish, and all good men of a "liberal bent" in common purpose to thwart the ambitions of the Medill coalition, now reorganized under the banner of the "Citizens' Union Party," and to emerge from the bitter affray unscathed and as the acknowledged "kingmaker" of a new political movement. It was to McDonald's great advantage that Mayor Bond became the unwitting mouthpiece of the Committee of Seventy, still championing a Sunday-closing law, the imposition of a $3,000 saloon licensing fee, and the right to deny any applicant deemed morally unsuitable. He sermonized about the need for cautious spending and sober retrenchment in the midst of the Panic of 1873, but these opinions were quickly drowned out by the tumult and the shout of the opposing forces of the temperance issue.

Tarred and feathered as a "Know-Nothing" anti-Catholic, antiforeign zealot, Bond stood little chance of articulating his views and moving the Citizens' Union Party past this one divisive issue and toward the political center, because McDonald and the influential German publisher Anton C. Hesing had succeeded in unifying the Irish and Germans behind their "People's Party" incarnation, dedicated to the overthrow of Puritan rule. It was a remarkable and historic accomplishment for the pair who found common ground because, as the *Tribune* observed, "this coalition could never have been brought about except by an attempt to interfere with social customs and traditions; and to make the Fourth Commandment a measure of city government. The antagonisms between the two nationalities were too deep-seated and of too long-standing to have been reconciled in any other way."[11]

The Germans and Irish found they had much in common through shared involvement in the liquor trade and the Liberty League, a protective association and political lobby dedicated to repealing dry laws. McDonald was an early and active member, and though he was never interested in assuming the mantle of leadership, he worked quietly behind the scenes to draft the candidates and get them to agree on principles and a winning slate.

Within easy access of Hesing's office at the *Staats-Zeitung* and Wilbur Storey's rival *Chicago Times*—the Democratic sheet bestowing upon the People's Party only a lukewarm endorsement—the nominating convention was appropriately staged in the upstairs hall of the Evans and Hickey saloon and liquor wholesaler on Randolph Street. Party leaders stepped forward, including Bernard Caulfield, the former rebel plotter; Twentieth Ward alderman John Corcoran, "given to wine and association with women," according to the *Times*, and his Hatch House thugs; brewer Peter Hand; Jake Rehm, the ex-police superintendent who owned a brewery on 12th Street; Henry B. "Buffalo" Miller of the National Distillers and Wholesale Liquor Dealers Association cognoscenti; former alderman John H. McEvoy, another wealthy brewer looking to advance his own business interests; and the billiard player and city alderman Tom Foley. McDonald and Hesing drove the nomination of Charley

Kern, for years a political "nine-pin"—a loser in several earlier attempts to become sheriff—and for mayor, they advanced Harvey Doolittle Colvin, an executive with the United States Express Company, as the standard-bearer of the People's Party.[12]

With great emphasis, Colvin promised skeptical Germans voters, who had counted on Hesing to be their candidate, to drive the nomination of one of their own for police chief. And with Kern added to the ticket, the New People's Party presumably represented a fusion of the best elements of the two older parties. Their principal aim, he said, was to stamp out the corruption of the past and protect all good working people against intrusive, unwanted temperance legislation.

Colvin, born on a Pennsylvania farm in 1813, yearned for high office and was easily flattered. He wanted to be mayor; but he was a political cipher who garnered little respect among the insiders within the Hesing-Corcoran-McDonald ruling triumvirate looking to deliver the city into the hands of the People's Party. Hesing, a former Cook County deputy sheriff, made his compact with the gamblers: promising Corcoran a nomination for circuit court judge in return for a plurality in the Twentieth Ward; and to McDonald, a fistful of appointments in the First and Second Wards and necessary influence within the Cook County Board of Commissioners.[13]

At stake for Mike was gaining control of law enforcement, the sheriff's office, the bail bonding racket, and the mechanisms for running city elections. Before 1886, it was legal for polling places to set up inside taverns, where the barkeep might exchange free whiskey shots or a cold stein of lager for a vote. Theoretically, the sale of liquor was prohibited on election day, but if the proprietor was also the alderman of the ward, what bluecoat in his right mind would dare instigate a raid? The bar was open for business, usually in the basement, upstairs anteroom, or kitchen of the premises.

Massive fraud preceded the city election. Dan O'Hara, clerk of the Criminal Court of Cook County, instigated a voter registration scheme by deputizing barkeepers from the city's eight thousand saloons to run a "naturalization mill," providing foreigners with citizenship papers and careful instructions to vote the People's Party ticket. Inside the Store, McDonald registered his fair share of hungry immigrants and provided every supplicant with a hot meal and gambling chips in consideration.[14]

There was nothing retiring or diffident in Mike's nature. He did not retreat from his pledge to work the city wards on behalf of Colvin or shirk his duties in any way. Voters were plied with free beer in saloons kept open in defiance of the election-day closing laws, and gangs of "repeaters" (men paid to vote twice) were driven from precinct to precinct to vote the "Sour Mash" ticket, as the *Tribune* often referred to the party. The apolitical Hankins brothers were recruited for the same useful purposes, and Corcoran's Hatch House thugs tossed voters sympathetic to the Citizens' Union Party in the Seventeenth Ward into the ditch. Black eyes and cracked craniums were reported across the city, forcing the *Tribune* to concede that the People's Party; this mottled assemblage of "O'Hesings," were better prepared and much more organized than the loyal "American" voters. "We warned the Committee of Seventy repeatedly that a rigid, cast-iron rule applying to every beverage that a man puts in his mouth, and attacking national customs harmless in themselves, would not command a majority vote in this city, composed so largely of persons of foreign birth."[15]

With public sentiment in his corner, Colvin was elected with more than 60 percent of the vote. On his fourth try, Kern was elected sheriff. O'Hara was swept in as city treasurer on the strength of the Irish vote. He replaced the disgraced David Gage, and his election was another feather in McDonald's cap.

From inside the warm and comforting glow of Kingsbury Music Hall on election night, a grand celebration hosted by the principal architects of this stunning victory over Puritanism carried on through the night. Earlier in the day, the jubilant but arrogant Hesing cabled Medill, "that sojourner in Paris," and sent him a taunting message. "Your policy has been defeated by 10,000 majority!" Hesing promised that the Prussian flag would be hoisted high above the *Staats-Zeitung* editorial offices before dawn the following morning.[16]

The ex-mayor seethed, but prudently resisted the impulse to fire back a terse reply. Instead, he checked his temper and wired his editors back in Chicago and advised them that for the sake of Republicanism he would try to mend his fences with Hesing and the German community upon his return, but he also made it perfectly clear that he would not be a candidate for office again.

The People's Party had good cause for celebration. And with his trusted inner circle of Alfred Trude, Tom Foley, and Al Hankins by his side, Mike paid tribute to liberty and lager. In the second precinct of the First Ward, Mike personally registered 130 more voters than were counted in the city census.[17] "The irrepressible Mike McDonald was as busy as a bee," the *Chicago Times* noted. "And if the Hesing-O'Hara party is grateful, they will give him some good fat office. His name has been mentioned in conjunction with that of superintendent of police, but this would be insulting Mr. McDonald. It is well-known that he runs Captain Hickey. If Hickey is appointed to the vacancy it would all be the same as if Mike were superintendent."[18]

The *Times* was wrong about Hickey—there was great enmity between Mike and the captain—but in the subtle jest, Wilbur Storey had shrewdly recognized a defining, but unmistakable, turn in Chicago politics: the christening of the city's first real political boss; a boss up from the gutters, whose ability to dictate policy and make appointments established the foundation of a system of municipal government that would endure for more than a century.

In his first official act upon taking the oath of office, Colvin bypassed Mike Hickey and elevated Mike's friend Jacob Rehm to police superintendent, due in part to a pragmatic desire to distance the People's Party from embarrassing allegations of Hickey's part-ownership in a downtown brothel and earlier scandals dredged up by the *Tribune*. Jake Rehm was acceptable not only to McDonald, but to the German voters and Hesing, who was counted as a close personal friend despite Rehm's token affiliation with the Republican Party and his ambition to use his position as a springboard to an appointment as city collector of the North Division.

Rehm, a former police commissioner who had resigned his post after a falling out with Medill, began his third stint as the head of the police department. Within the year, he would block proposals to clean out the detective department and would demonstrate great laxity in dispatching raiding parties into Gambler's Row. It was understood and agreed at the time of the appointment that Colvin would dissolve the police board so that no more "Washburns" could infiltrate the police cadre and intrude upon the gamblers with "unauthorized" raids. Real arresting power would henceforth rest with Superintendent Rehm and his successors.[19]

Outside of Mike McDonald's Store, throngs of hungry and shivering people, laid idle by the crash of the local construction industry (precipitated by the September collapse of Jay Cooke and Company of Philadelphia), huddled in the shadows. They were thankful for the "People's" victory and freely joined in the New Year's Eve–style celebrations inside the festive and brilliantly lit palace saloons and bowling alleys stretching from Clark and Lake Streets to the Pacific Hotel. But in the coming weeks, when the idled men looked to Colvin and his People's Party for hard answers—and a swift reckoning—the mayor's reply was muted.

Thus began the nation's worst depression since 1837, a crisis that would drag on through the next four years. In Chicago, one out of three workers lost their jobs; many were construction workers who had migrated to the city after the fire to rebuild the burnt district. The incoming city hall coalition promised a rebirth of democracy, suffrage, and humanitarian aid for the poor and downtrodden. But Chicago in December 1873 was dark and grim for beleaguered city residents. Armies of homeless tramps roamed the streets. Families were going hungry. City workers were paid in scrip, and desperation mounted as five thousand unemployed people beset city hall demanding that Colvin provide public works jobs or force the charitable organizations to disburse the remainder of the Chicago Fire relief funds. The mayor met the crowd at the door of city hall and promised to use whatever resources he could to alleviate hunger and homelessness during the long winter months.

"I never saw a time in Chicago when so many people were out of employment," sighed Cook County State's Attorney Charles Reed. "I never knew a time when I had so many applications for employment as now. The banks I understand have lots of money, but there is not the business doing to remove it from the bank's coffers to the pockets of the poor."[20]

Enmeshed in the interests of the gamblers, saloon politicians, and Liberty League distillers who formed the nexus of his administration, there was little the incoming mayor could do to heed the people's call for bread and sustenance.

Bummers, Gutter-Rats, Whiskey Soakers, and Saloon Loafers

ONE HUNDRED WOMEN OF SOCIAL PROMINENCE AND HIGH MORAL notions, all of them earnest and inspired workers in the cause of temperance, crowded into the city council gallery the afternoon of March 19, 1874, to pray for the soul of Harvey Doolittle Colvin, the former city treasurer who had campaigned for mayor on a platform of reform and economy.

But now the mayor, despite the stern admonition coming from the Presbyterians, the Congregationalists, the Methodists, and Miss Frances Willard, president of the Women's Temperance Union, was preparing to sign into law a compromise measure to reopen the saloons on Sunday, provided that patrons enter from the rear of the establishment.

A petition signed by fifteen thousand citizens was presented for his consideration, but it would be hard for the reformers and Prohibitionists to make inroads. "We the women of Chicago, earnestly entreat you to refuse to give the sacred sanction of the law, or your approval to the house which is the way to hell going down to the chambers of death!"[1] Particularly objectionable to the church ladies was the deliberate omission of a clause to enforce gambling prohibition inside the saloons. "Here is a door thrown open for an additional and dangerous inducement for young men to spend the Sabbath in saloons, which, we submit, was not contemplated by many who supported the People's Party."[2]

If the good people who voted in the self-anointed "party of the people" with high expectations of improving the lot of all Chicagoans, they were badly deceived, or worse—terribly naïve and Pollyannaish in their thinking. Colvin of course, refused to bend. He reminded the ladies of the deputation that he was already "pledged."

"I adopted the platform of the People's Party when I was nominated," he said. "Now this is part of the platform. In honor there is no way in which I could refrain from signing that ordinance. 'Long John' Wentworth tried to suppress the gambling houses which only caused gambling dens to be established in the top rooms of buildings all over the city. A similar mistake would be made if an attempt was made to suppress the saloons." One alderman observing the proceeding was more to the point. "He would sooner resign his seat than veto the ordinance. If he went back on his party he would be called a cur."[3]

As Colvin's star dimmed, a secret government within the city government had emerged; a government ruled by liquor men and the affiliated brewery trade associations, the gamblers, the Corcorans, and Mike McDonald took charge in the midst of an economic depression that showed no sign of loosening its grip across the city. A letter to the editor of the *Tribune* noted, "It is a common boast that he runs the City of Chicago and that he cannot be convicted or punished for anything. They say he owns the mayor and the chief of police, as well as many other city officials. If high officials are owned by Mike McDonald, the public would like to know how he acquired title, and what was the consideration paid?"[4] The author of the letter cited as one example of McDonald's influence the intervention of State's Attorney Charles Reed, who blocked a second grand jury from launching a more thorough investigation into McDonald's armed assault against "Red Jim" McGarry.

That Colvin was only the "caretaker" of the People's Party by his own admission was soon evident. With the repeal of the Sunday law, he found himself unable to guide this one-issue coalition toward other practical matters. By late 1873 or early 1874, a dramatic power shift from the Mayor's Office to the gamblers and their allied aldermen had the press up in arms.

"This man McDonald. . . . is a man of ability and energy, and for that reason all the more dangerous," noted the *Tribune*. "This man today is the boldest and most conspicuous of all the champions of the Hesing ticket. He has a grievance to redress and an interest to serve."[5] Addressing the larger question of whether or not McDonald exercised citywide control as a "supreme boss," the suddenly hostile *Times* concluded that because "it was not openly arranged that the depository of the city funds should be The Store, the blacklegs came in for their share of the 'swag' through the election of [George] Von Hollen [as city collector] and one or two other judiciary officers."[6]

As precarious as the financial condition of the city was in 1873, the fiscal picture worsened over the next three years. The city treasury was dragged down by wasteful appropriations and an enormous floating debt of $5 million, all bearing high rates of interest. By the spring of 1876, not a dollar could be borrowed, nor was there the legal authority to borrow money. Bills were paid in worthless municipal scrip, and the City of Chicago's "paper" was accepted under protest in nearly every banking office in the nation.

The leaders of the People's Party, responsible for escalating the crisis through graft and plunder, were political hacks of the worst stripe, ill-prepared to administer the affairs of a great city during the financial panic. Patronage appointments were doled out as payoff to Mike McDonald and Anton Hesing, with disastrous results. McDonald's choice for sheriff, Charles Kern, conspired with the Cook County board to cut the per diem cost of food per prisoner at the jail from thirty-five to twenty-five cents a day. It was strictly an "off-the-books" agreement, and Kern was said to have pocketed ten cents in meal money for every inmate in his custody. Officially, the cost to the county remained at thirty-five cents a head.[7]

Corrupt arrangements like this one were all too common. And while Kern escaped indictment, others did not. Between 1874 and 1876, the gates of the penitentiary swung open to admit a cadre of embezzling Colvin appointees. The lucky ones escaped to remote regions of Canada, where extradition was not a possibility. City Collector Von Hollen looted the city treasury of $100,000 in order to pay back massive gambling debts accumulated at the Clark Street faro banks belonging to McDonald, Watt Robbins, and George Hankins and his brothers. "He soon fell into constant and intimate association with gamblers and the habitués of low saloons, and at last he has run through his riotous career at a cost of $100,000 to the people of Chicago," commented the *Tribune*, which campaigned hard, but failed, to abolish the collector's office after this disgrace.[8]

The common council demanded an accounting and subpoenaed Robbins, Harry Lawrence, and Jeff Hankins to testify to their dealings with the politician. By then the city coffers had been bled dry. Von Hollen plotted his escape and left secret instructions to his friend and legal counsel Alfred Trude to sell his brewery holdings to his business partner and forward the money to a postal box in Canada, where he fled to avoid prosecution. The Von Hollen defalcation was just a modest foreshadowing of even more egregious acts in the city of Chicago.

The Whiskey Ring, one of the most damaging public scandals of the 1870s, was a part of a wider conspiracy hatched by Colvin men (and others) engaged in the liquor trade to falsify the quantities of liquor manufactured and sold for public consumption. General John A. McDonald, the corrupt district revenue collector in St. Louis, and affiliated distillers and public officials in Milwaukee, St. Louis, New Orleans, San Francisco, Cincinnati, and Chicago defrauded the federal government of taxes—a practice that had gone on for a considerable time. Federal revenue collectors were being routinely bribed to allow the large distillers to retain tax proceeds that had steadily risen since the end of the Civil War.[9] Massive fraud within the Internal Revenue Service involving the failure to collect taxes on politically connected distillers in five cities had long been suspected. Allegations of fraud and bribery dated back to the administration of President Andrew Johnson. The scandal reached into the White House, further tarnishing the troubled presidency of Ulysses S. Grant, whose appointment of General McDonald in 1870 was made in good faith on the advice of his personal secretary, Orville Babcock, also deeply implicated in the conspiracy.

In Chicago, Jake Rehm, Mike McDonald's handpicked police chief, was called the principal organizer and extortionist for the local faction of the Whiskey Ring. Large portions of uncollected tax revenue earmarked for the Internal Revenue Service were siphoned from the distillers and saloon owners into Rehm's private account. Anton Hesing, it was charged, received $40,000 from one company, the Lake Shore Distillery Company, and Superintendent Rehm, in excess of $70,000.

"He [Rehm] accepted hush money from gamblers and from prostitutes and from thieves, mock interlopers, from bunko men and confidence operators," thundered attorney Robert Ingersoll, one of the most mesmerizing political and courtroom orators of the age, when the Chicago trials opened in May 1876. Lashing out against government witness Rehm, who agreed to "tell all" in order to avoid penitentiary time, Ingersoll said that the superintendent "grew rich from bribery and corruption. It means he was in partnership with the rascality and all the crime in the City of Chicago."[10]

It was established that Rehm and Hesing shared the profits of a distillery that distributed gin spirits to local saloon keepers in Chicago without paying the government excise tax. The tavern owners were rewarded with $500 a month for keeping separate inventory records and advised in advance when revenue collectors were expected in the city.

Referencing the accused's earlier business dealings with gamblers and prostitutes, Ingersoll nailed Rehm to the cross for accepting $30,000 from Mike McDonald—a charge Jake hotly denied under cross-examination. But there was no denying that in Superintendent Rehm McDonald had found a sympathetic ally in law enforcement to protect his interests. Not since the days of William W. Kennedy had McDonald been so warmly received inside police headquarters. Rehm's door was always open to his old friend, and for two years Mike reaped enormous political payoff for fronting money to the People's Party candidates. Enjoying his patronage perks, McDonald gained unlimited access to the police judges, the right to examine the arrest blotter, share sensitive intelligence exchanged between Chicago and other cities, and schedule daily debriefings with his bail bondsmen and their detained clients inside the interview rooms.

From September 1873 until October 1, 1875, when things got too hot for Rehm in Chicago, the superintendent presided over a thoroughly corrupt and demoralized police department. Then, on New Year's Eve, just two months after submitting his "voluntary" resignation papers, Rehm, Hesing, and Henry B. "Buffalo" Miller were arrested at their homes and taken into custody for the whiskey frauds.

Jake plea-bargained his way into the same county jail lockup he once oversaw—stoic, unaffected, and ready to serve his six months and admit that he had "made arrangements with government collectors, and received and distributed money." But he never kept a dime of it for personal profit. It "was all for political purposes," he alibied to the grand jury. The *Tribune,* previously sympathetic to Rehm because he was loyal to the Republican Party, called the government deal "a defeat of justice."[11]

Jake was the first of many McDonald allies who, over the next decade, glimpsed the inside of a jail cell. He was assessed a $10,000 fine and retired from public life with his riches intact following discharge from prison. Rehm expressed deep sorrow for his friend Anton C. Hesing, the publisher the *Tribune* branded "a dishonest tyrant' leading a band of "Cut-throats and thieves," who was sentenced to two years and ordered to pay a $5,000 fine. The opposition press decried the verdict as a travesty of justice in light of Rehm's minor inconvenience. Hesing's sympathizers echoed the sentiment and signed petitions. Their favorite served less than six months of his sentence and once freed, he used his paper to upbraid the "scoundrel Rehm" as the real mastermind of the frauds.[12]

"Buffalo" Miller of Hyde Park, the former printer's apprentice to Wilbur Storey who served in the legislature and as Colvin's second city treasurer, was another shabby example of the type of politician endemic to the big cities in the 1870s. Miller registered neither surprise nor disappointment after his six-month sentence was handed down.[13] Seventh Ward alderman James H. Hildreth, a former streetcar conductor and one of Colvin's floor leaders in the city council, fled to Canada until his lawyers could negotiate safe passage and a jail-free return.

As desperate ringleaders and lesser lights scurried for passage on Canadian trunk lines under assumed names or surrendered information to the grand jury in an effort to extricate themselves from an appointment in the lockup, McDonald was mostly ignored and left unscathed. During the long hours of tedious grand jury testimony, his name surfaced repeatedly in connection with alleged payoffs to Rehm and for harboring a criminal fence from Detroit named Louis Cohn— wanted for questioning in the Milwaukee phase of the whiskey deliberations.

McDonald, standing comfortably behind the curtain throughout, grew stronger politically and seemed to be forever immune from prosecution, even as the tattered Colvin regime crumbled in scandal, amid the woeful state of the city's finances (the policy of paying bills in city scrip drove the city to the edge of bankruptcy) and a barrage of adverse publicity. But Mayor Colvin would not give up. The charter election of 1875 established that the incumbent mayor would occupy that office until 1877, because the date of the city election was shifted from November to April.

The constitutionality of the election was challenged in court, but Colvin believed that it justified his right to hold over until the spring. Public outrage soared. At a mass meeting of thirty thousand disgruntled citizens shoehorned into the Exposition Building in April 1876, moderate Democrat Thomas Hoyne was nominated for mayor.[14] Fed up with the antics of the People's Party, Hoyne was carried into office with 33,064 votes against only 819 ballots cast for Colvin. The will of the people was clear, but Colvin refused to surrender his office and would not yield the gavel or his chair in city hall, based on the dubious 1875 charter election. For twenty-eight days, Chicago had two mayors, until the matter was resolved by the incoming city council. Hoyne's election was voided by the circuit court, and another election was called in July 1876. This time the Republican reformer Monroe Heath, formerly of New Hampshire, prevailed, ending one of the most bitterly contentious and peculiar episodes in all Chicago political history.

Hildreth was deposed. Hesing and Rehm were behind bars, and the defeated Colvin set his sights on more achievable political goals—retiring to a safe position with the United States Express Company—while plotting a return in the next election. Meanwhile, a "reform" city council, elected by the people, backed Heath, who promised Chicagoans economy, retrenchment, and a new day of political openness.

Surveying the debris of the failed Colvin movement, McDonald correctly sensed a new and dangerous threat to his operation. He vigorously pushed Perry H. Smith, a wealthy North Side socialite and Bourbon Democrat sympathetic to "liberal causes" who eyed the Chicago mayoralty with only a modicum of interest. Smith was chairman of the Cook County Democratic Central Committee and a committed Illinois delegate for Governor Samuel Tilden of New York as the party's standard-bearer in the November 1876 presidential election, but Smith lacked the ambition to *become* an officeholder himself, despite the urgings of McDonald and the "bummer" factions.

Mike McDonald and Alfred Trude adroitly assembled the leftovers of the People's Party and steered them back into the Democratic camp where they could renew their battle against the temperance reformers. McDonald's interest in the national political scene up until the moment he first cashed in on the whiskey tax swindle was only cursory. In 1868, he supported the candidacy of the Democrat Horatio Seymour against *General* Grant in passing, but he broke ranks with the party four years later and "did a great deal of local work" for *President* Grant in his reelection bid against Horace Greeley.[15]

The federal patronage well, although desirable in itself (for many politicians of the age, *the only reason* to seek high public office), did not reach far enough down into the depths of the Cook County government to make any real difference to Mike or his confederates, until his dealings with the crooked federal liquor gaugers (excise men) of the Grant administration changed the dynamic.

Perry Smith opened a campaign office at 77 South Clark Street, just around the corner from the Store, as preparations for the national convention in St. Louis heated up. McDonald was Smith's confidential adviser in the choice of

Illinois delegates, although Mike supported Tilden guardedly, with reservations, despite the New Yorker's reputation as a "hard-currency," gold-standard
reformer and "Eastern man, with Eastern sympathies."

McDonald was building important alliances beyond Chicago and looking
to the future. He accompanied Smith and the delegation to St. Louis in late
June, less than two months after confronting his wife and her lover outside of
San Francisco's Palace Hotel. Believing that indelicate matter was satisfactorily
resolved, McDonald, though not a delegate, arrived in the Mound City to march
in the grand procession to the Exchange Hall where the nomination was to
take place and to make important connections in the private smoking rooms
of the convention hotels. This was the first national nominating convention
to be held west of the Mississippi River, and it drew an immense concourse of
visitors from all parts of the United States, including the powerful New York
gambler John Morrissey and his entourage, there to support the ambitions of
Governor Tilden.

The presence of Morrissey, a former Five Points street-thug and gambling
boss who shaped Saratoga Springs into the Las Vegas of its day, "is perhaps
the first instance in the history of Christian civilization when a prize-fighter
came up to a political convention to exhibit his broken nose as a trophy or war,"
scolded Henry Clay Dean, Methodist clergyman and former wartime Copperhead, "and perhaps the only instance in which the proprietor of a fashionable
gambling hall has ever ventured among the shadows of the spires of Christian
churches to engage in a general revival, and hurry up the millennium of political reform. It is a shameless neglect on the part of the railroads that a special
car was [not] provided to bring him here."[16]

The active role the gambling fraternity played at the state and national level
in the 1870s was the inner dynamic of the Democratic Party's growing urban
"machine" base, but their support of Tilden was puzzling. Given Tilden's history
of prosecuting the Tweed Ring earlier in the decade, McDonald's allegiance
might have been a shadow pretense in order to gain exposure to the national
party, vis-à-vis private introductions to Tammany Hall "sachem" John Kelly
and other Eastern Democrats staying in the hotels.

Whatever suit of clothes a man chose to wear—Republican, Democrat, or
Independent—the key thing was the color of the lapel. In other words, whoever
could provide the most expeditious means to an end received support. And in
this case, McDonald staked Perry Smith for mayor in the all-important 1877
city election. His money and connections played well, but the German and
Irish party leaders were suspicious and resentful of this "silk-stocking" Anglo-
Saxon in their bailiwick. But Smith's money bought a lot of Tilden votes in the
Fifth, Sixth, Seventh, and Eighth Wards in November. Samuel Tilden pulled a
seven-thousand-vote plurality from these city wards, and that helped him carry
Illinois, albeit in a losing effort.

McDonald returned to Chicago after a relaxing summer interlude at the Philadelphia Centennial Exposition to confront a growing problem with the unctuous new mayor. Heath, a former dry-goods salesman before entering public life, signaled his intention to crack down on the gamblers in the same fashion as Medill and Washburn had done five years earlier.[17] A new police chief, but an old enemy—Michael Hickey—had taken over for Jake Rehm.[18] As political payback for supporting the Democratic national ticket in a hotly contested election and embarrassing Mayor Heath because he could not deliver Cook County for the Republican Party, Hickey vowed to crush the gamblers. He reserved his most purposeful enmity for McDonald and set out to destroy him, as much as such a thing was possible. The new chief removed or transferred half-a-dozen detectives who had become friendly with the Clark Street sports, or proved to be complacent in their duties with respect to suppressing gambling.

In a direct blow against the fraternity, Mike's designate at the Armory Police Station, Captain William Buckley, was dismissed for failing to close the Clark Street faro dens. His replacement, Captain Simon O'Donnell, was a fearlessly honest police official who had no reservations about putting the big-shot gamblers in their place and upholding the superintendent's General Order No. 43, issued November 9, 1875, to rigidly enforce all gambling and vagrancy laws.

By Christmastime of 1876, Heath glowingly announced that all of the clip joints and gambling houses were forced to close. By necessity, McDonald temporarily retired the dealing boxes, roulette wheels, and poker chips and converted the Store into a "bucket shop," a fraudulent operation where a naïve investor could buy and sell stock on the street, although the transaction was not with a legitimate brokerage firm.

In these lean times, Mike had to make do matching up buys and sells to increase his own profit until the political winds of Chicago blew more favorably, or at least until he could cook up a revenge scheme of his own to take down the devious Hickey, a moral hypocrite the habitués of Clark Street knew all too well.

The disgruntled ex-police detectives, having lost their sinecure, gathered inside the Store, hoping that McDonald might be able to contrive a way for them to get their jobs back. Over drinks and cigars, former detective Martin Flannigan was the talkative one. He revealed everything he knew about Hickey's treachery: his secret partnership with the brothel madam, Lizzie Moore, and his ownership of a run-down "mansion" at Biler Avenue and Harrison in the Cheyenne district that was leased to Daniel Webster, a large black man working as a bail bondsman who kept the place as a house of ill fame and doubled as a criminal fence. It was charged that Webster paid Hickey $3,500 so his operation would not be molested.

The rumor was first published in an evening newspaper belonging to Alfred Trude at McDonald's insistence. Anonymous letters revealing Hickey's shady dealings were sent to Heath, but the mayor dismissed them as a vicious smear campaign and called the accusations scurrilous fiction invented by the McDonald clique. "They are not worth repeating," he told a *Tribune* reporter sent to investigate. "I cast them all in the waste basket."[19]

Probing further, the reporter discovered that Hickey was not as clean as the mayor presumed, and he sought out Dan Webster for comment. "Whom do you rent this house from?" he asked.

"I don't rent the house at all. I bought it."

"Whom did you make the payment to?"

"A lady," came Webster's reply.

"What's her name?"

"I don't know exactly. She's Mr. Hickey's wife's mother."[20]

Convicted on a federal charge of counterfeiting, Webster was incarcerated and then let go after Hickey signed a petition for release. Thereafter, the emboldened Dan Webster threatened to have any police officer "put off the force" if they raided his parlors. At least one of the disgruntled detectives discharged by Hickey failed to heed the warning.

McDonald's intrigue started a firestorm inside city hall. Despite the mayor's vote of confidence for his embattled superintendent, the Police Committee of the city council launched an investigation into his private dealings with criminals and vice mongers. Alfred Trude, appointed to the prosecution team, flailed away at Hickey as lead counsel, but emotions ran high and tempers frayed. Hickey had his supporters—many of them patronizing the same saloons as McDonald and Trude.

When Mike showed up with Trude in Kirchoff's beer hall on Clark Street following a light supper at Tivoli's and an evening of theater, his exchange of hot words with W. T. Gough, a city express man, provoked another vicious assault. Gough was speaking in loud, unruly tones, expressing sympathy for "poor Hickey," knowing that his incendiary words were easily overheard by McDonald, who was drinking heavily and in bad humor following newspaper criticism of Trude's methods that afternoon. McDonald slammed his glass on the table and pounced on Gough before he could defend himself. A smashing blow from McDonald's fist broke the man's nose and sent him sprawling to the floor. Lawyer Trude rushed into the fray and began kicking the prostrate Gough in the stomach and head as he curled up into the fetal position, bleeding profusely.

Pistols were drawn by Gough's friends—then a McDonald henchman produced a six-shooter and aimed it at the heckler. After a minute of stone-cold silence as the combatants assessed the situation and thought the better of it, the guns were lowered and the standoff ended. The badly injured Gough was led away. He filed a useless criminal complaint at the Central Station, but was told to take it over to the Armory near the Cheyenne district.[21]

Meanwhile, the *Tribune* and the mayor stood gamely behind their man Mike Hickey, making hay out of McDonald's latest barroom brawl escapade and accusing the city hall Democrats of initiating a baseless, slanderous attack against a "good and decent" line officer. Webster, they countered, was a "valuable informant" against McDonald's operation, and because of it, open gambling was on the decrease in Chicago. "Under these circumstances, what was the duty of the Mayor?" the *Tribune* irritably complained. "To allow a faithful officer to be disgraced and ruined in order to satisfy the hatred and revenge of disreputable characters who assailed him? We say no—a thousand times no!"[22]

It was a vicious battle that broke down along strict party lines. The same acts of malfeasance and bribery condemned by the *Tribune* against scores of Democratic politicos and all their allies who had gone before were now being committed by a powerful Republican responsible for upholding the laws of the entire city. While Hickey set out to punish the gamblers and Jake Rehm the police-appointees friendly with McDonald who had crossed him, Hickey left the vice merchants alone. Conversely, Rehm went after the whorehouses with zeal but ignored the gamblers and the saloons, because, as was demonstrated in his whiskey trial, he had an interest in their business and it was important not to disrupt that business.

Hearing the testimony of the fired police officers, various gamblers, and assorted ne'er-do-wells, the Police Committee filed a majority report recommending that Michael Hickey be discharged from the force. The question was left to the mayor to decide what was to be done. Heath wasted no time. On November 14, he ordered Hickey back to duty with his salary and title restored after the suspended police chief appealed to the mayor's sentiment, *ad hominem,* in a closed-door meeting with Heath.

"Well sir, what to you propose to do about it?" Hickey wanted to know. "You see we have made this fight and as I warned you, the gamblers have responded. Now are you going to stand by me or shall I resign? I know I am innocent, but those fellows have convinced a good many people that I am not, and you cannot sustain me without a misconstruction of your motives and injuring yourself. I am willing to yield if you wish it."

"It would have simply been the act of a coward to have gone back on Mr. Hickey," explained Heath.[23]

By now, even the city bluebloods and civic elites had a bellyful. A strongly worded communiqué signed by Levi Z. Leiter, Robert Todd Lincoln, William Blair, and other conservative-minded Republicans demanded Hickey's ouster and the immediate reappointment of Elmer Washburn. The appeal was ignored. Certain members of the City Council tried to push the matter further, by lobbying for Heath's impeachment, but there were not enough votes to sustain such a drastic action.

Neither would the issue go away. Hickey had exposed Heath's vulnerabilities, and it became the singular campaign issue in the April 1877 election. The gamblers and their party hacks took their cue from McDonald and anointed Perry

H. Smith, Mike's reluctant protégé, as their choice for mayor at the Democratic city convention held at the North Side Turner Hall. Smith easily surpassed Harvey Colvin, unelectable and out of favor among "the boys" but still pushing his credentials, by a vote of 76–54.

Smith mounted the dais and acknowledged his nomination to the throng. "It is with grateful heart that I tender you now my most sincere thanks for this generous, unanimous [sic] marked expression of your confidence and so far as it may lay within my power I will carry out your just and honorable intention with reference to the conduct and management of the affairs of the city."[24] In the back of the room, Mike McDonald and his boon companions, Harry Lawrence, Johnny Dowling, and Alfred Trude, puffed their cigars and smiled contentedly.

It wasn't so much that they looked up to Smith's high-minded idealism—he ran a one-man platform espousing the need for educational reform and the immediate construction of new schools to accommodate the city's growing population—but rather the gamblers counted on his family fortune and the deep pockets of well-heeled business associates willing to generously feed the coffers of the Democratic Central Committee.

Called a "professional tax eater" by Heath and the Republicans, and excoriated by the *Tribune* as a tool of the "Bummers, gutter-rats, whiskey soakers, saloon loafers, and the underground population of the slums," the hapless Smith ran an earnest, straightforward, but short-lived campaign. Late in the electoral season, the realization set in that he had been badly duped by McDonald.

The scheme to elect an "idealist" and control him through directives emanating from the Store fizzled hours before the polls were scheduled to open. A dispatch arrived at the *Tribune* editorial office from Smith announcing his intention to withdraw from the race and throw his support to Mayor Heath in the belief that he was "betrayed . . . by injudicious friends whose affection was not pure, but rather a greed for our wealth. I was admonished that Chicago needed reform, and on that basis I consented to run. I learned what becomes necessary for the election of a Democrat, even if he is not elected, and when I contemplate the society into which a Democratic candidate is thrust, and the wear and tear on the lining of the stomach . . ."[25]

Among the North Side society swells who could not fathom the motivations of a young man of Smith's advantages and social position being so reckless in his choice of associates, a sarcastic little rhyme began making the rounds:

> Go bury young Perry far out in the woods—
> Where politics are never heard—
> Where his neat little legs can be folded to rest;
> To the song of the wild mountain bird.[26]

Heath was swept into office by eleven thousand votes, and Perry Smith faded back into the billiards room of his private club. With a fresh mandate, Superintendent Hickey renewed the attacks against McDonald's gambling dens, until he was halted in his tracks as a result of the near-fatal shooting encounter inside the Store between Mary and Officers LeBounty and Hoffman. Thereafter, Judge McAllister's ruling against the department effectively put a stop to the police harassment of Mike's business and made him virtually immune to prosecution as the 1870s drew to a close. The *Tribune* reported that "Judge McAllister had held that Mrs. McDonald would have been justified if she killed all of the officers who made the raid on Mike's place. . . . [The police] would not order another door broken open until they were assured of protection."[27]

The city was broke. The recession was slow to heal, and a climate of bitter recrimination, fueled by growing militancy within the labor movement, hung in the air. Meanwhile, the "bummer" Democrat and the Republican "reformer" seemed blithely untroubled by high unemployment, the nonstop graft, and the mixed messages they were sending to the electorate. One party promised tolerance and personal liberty, the other stood behind honesty in government and economy. These ideals were trumped by the mutual animosities of self-serving factions within each party.

Dangerous times were at hand. In late July, tensions among Chicago's working classes boiled over. A national railroad strike begun in Baltimore ignited urban rioting in the nation's major urban centers and eventually spread to Chicago.[28] Lawless street mobs roamed through the city, creating mayhem in their wake. The Deering Street Police Station was swarmed and taken over by an angry mob. According to John Flinn and John Wilkie, "Strikes were in progress from the lake to Western Avenue; from the North Side rolling mills to the Town of Lake. The disposition of propensity to strike became a mania. Workingmen who had no earthly cause to complain, who could not call to mind a grievance, threw down their tools, tore off their coveralls, snatched up their coats and hats, shook their clenched fists at their employers—and joined the nearest mob."[29]

With truncheons liberally employed, the police counterattacked. Across the city that summer, rioters were put down by whatever means necessary. A gathering of German tradesmen agitating for the eight-hour workday inside the West Side Turner Hall on 12th Street resulted in eighteen dead, with hundreds more injured. At issue throughout the ordeal were the rough tactics of Michael Hickey's bluecoats, complemented by five thousand untrained, but brutal, volunteers called up by the mayor and reorganized as a military unit with army ranks assigned to the ruling cadre. Hickey, who had organized a regiment at the outbreak of the Civil War and sent them off to fight while he remained safely behind in Chicago, informed his men they should address him as "Colonel."

The superintendent/colonel's ham-fisted suppression of the workers' right to assemble was evaluated and criticized, but in the end, Hickey's downfall came about only because Mike McDonald had finally mustered enough resources within the City Council to reject Hickey's reappointment by a vote of 22–11 when the matter came up for debate on July 8, 1878. Two powerful aldermen, Arthur Dixon of the First Ward, and Edward F. Cullerton of the Seventh, aligned the Democrats behind Mike for the roll call. The outcome was split straight down party lines.[30]

When asked why Superintendent Hickey was not retained after his brilliant work fighting organized gambling and cracking the craniums of dangerous anarchists, the Democratic aldermen euphemistically shrugged their shoulders and said "no particular reason, it was time for a change, that's all."[31]

Nonsense, whispered one grizzled city hall veteran. "If you want to find out the real reason why Hickey was let go," said one, "go ask Mrs. McDonald."[32]

∾ 7 ∾

The City Hall Swindle

AN EMBITTERED MICHAEL HICKEY WAS VANQUISHED BUT FULL OF wrath against a police department he believed had turned its back on a brother officer so that it could heel before the dictates of a vicious criminal. A series of anonymous letters directed to the members of the city council's Police Committee accused the worthy gentlemen of shirking their duties and pointed out that the Clark Street gambling dens were back in business and left mostly unmolested by the new superintendent, Valorous Seavey, who held the world-weary belief that gambling suppression was futile. When the identity of the letter writer was exposed by a simple comparison of his handwriting specimen to Hickey's signature on police communiqués, Hickey was pilloried in the court of public opinion. His criticisms of police indifference to the gambling kingpins made him look petty and vengeful. His remonstrations fell on deaf ears.

The McAllister decision effectively neutralized the police and shielded the gamblers from warrantless searches. Seavey was not of a mind to subject his men to the threat of harassing lawsuits and costly litigation when there were more serious crimes to contend with and rising fears of anarchists running loose in the city. Meanwhile, with his approval rate sagging, Mayor Heath inauspiciously finished out the last two years of his term. He no longer posed a threat to Mike McDonald, who had expanded his operations well beyond the sponsorship of rigged hotel confidence games and "brace" faro. Now, the whole of Cook County and beyond was up for grabs.

The "King of the Gamblers" sold fine wines and imported cigars in his downtown liquor depot. He dabbled in commercial real estate, construction, and the buying and selling of land parcels to developers pushing beyond the pre-Fire city limits. However, the essence of McDonald's personal fortune stemmed from gambling and the sale to the city of Chicago of Lemont limestone carved out of south suburban quarries he jointly owned with Edwin Walker, who had constructed the Store in 1872–73.

Driven from the city offices they occupied during the repudiation of "Colvinism," the McDonald "corruptionists" had regrouped and infiltrated the offices of Cook County government and the various agencies with control of appointments, private-sector contracting, and oversight of millions of dollars of tax apportionments.[1] "It is also a notorious fact," reported the *Tribune*, "that Mike McDonald, under various names, has been a contractor for the city in supplying stone sidewalks, vault-roofing, and other work and that he always had the inside track. The County Board has increased taxation to the uttermost limit of the law and has a floating debt of uncollected taxes, another floating debt representing expenditures beyond appropriations, and a third debt representing arrearages to contractors on the Court House Building."[2]

The contract award to Mike McDonald and his business partner to supply building stone to city construction crews replacing the old courthouse and city hall annex, both destroyed in the Chicago Fire, was larceny on a stupendous scale. A full year before the bidder's contracts were awarded, the *Tribune* cautioned taxpayers of the certainty of cost overruns and the inevitability of county board chicanery.

"The building of the courthouse, which will have to be undertaken some time in the near future, will open up a rich mine of thieving contracts. It was ascertained that one man, [Clemmens] Periolat virtually has a monopoly of furnishing the most profitable supplies to the County. His contracts were taken out in the names of various clerks and drummers [salesmen] in his employ."[3]

Clem Periolat, the county bigwig who snatched McDonald's pistol before Mike could discharge a fatal shot into the skull of "Red Jim" McGarry in the saloon row a year earlier, controlled expenditures and the bid-rigging process. The county board was an engine of corruption; and Periolat, as a private contractor wielding enormous influence, drove that engine.[4] After losing $180,000 worth of assets in the Chicago Fire, Clem found a way to recoup his business losses by gaining a toehold among the county politicians. A commercial furrier and wholesale grocer by trade, Periolat and his partner, James Forsyth, sold food products inferior in weight and quality from his company warehouse to the county poorhouse, the insane asylum, and the Cook County Hospital at above-market prices. He furnished the county hospital with Irish potatoes worth fifteen cents per barrel, but Cook County paid ninety cents, per the contract specified by Periolat. For the year 1875–76, Periolat sold goods worth $13,701 for $25,669, an overcharge of nearly 100 percent. His contracts embraced practically all the items purchased by Cook County, amounting to $280,000 annually. He had such enormous influence that it was understood no one could hold office or do business in the county without Periolat's consent.

While the political situation in the city wards was carefully assessed from behind the closed doors of McDonald's Store, the county Democrats who controlled the board continuously from 1873 to 1877 gathered inside the McCormick Building at Randolph and Dearborn, where thirteen rooms were rented to the men of the Union Club to socialize, gamble, fund-raise, screen job seekers, and plot election strategy. Periolat, a man of endless resources and a newfound obsession, was the club's first elected president. He rigged grand juries and brokered the contracts with stakeholders of companies favored by the commissioners or their allies.

The *Tribune* lampooned the Union Club, derisively calling it the "Bean Club" and the home of "the Ring"—the former designation a mocking reference to the purchase of one hundred barrels of Boston baked beans at $1.50 each, and the subsequent loss of the goods to a heavy rainstorm. Flood water had seeped into the barrels, causing the beans to expand and explode before they could be distributed to the city almshouse, or so it was explained by Periolat years later.[5]

By any name, the Union Club—or "Bean Club"—was a political clearinghouse for jobbers and job seekers. Ed McDonald, laboring as a cashier at the Store at the time Periolat marshaled control of the board, was one who greatly benefited from being sent over by his brother with a note of introduction. Ed was no gambler, and his arrest during the ill-fated Hickey raid had badly rattled him; he didn't have the stomach for it. But Mike contrived with Periolat to secure Ed an appointment as assistant engineer at the House of Corrections—a well-paying political plum of a job with many perquisites.

Less than a year later, Ed was promoted to head engineer at the Cook County Hospital, and with it came the opportunity to reap a rich harvest by "skimming" money off the top of padded contracts agreed to by the merchants who supplied the institution with goods and services. Plumbing contracts were his specialty, because one of Ed's lucrative side businesses was a plumbing supply firm doing business as Boyle and Company. It was a silent, secret partnership—Ed McDonald and D. T. Boyle owned the company and sold supplies to the hospital over the signature of the warden, who lacked the oversight power to veto questionable appropriations.

Ed and his family settled into a comfortable, well-furnished hospital apartment with his every need and want attended to and paid for by the county, down to his laundry, fuel, lighting, and the upkeep of a saloon he purchased at 600 West Van Buren Street. Mike's aimless and melancholy younger brother found his calling in life and over the next decade grew rich through the ancient evils of institutionalized patronage, nepotism, and graft.

Conditions inside the hopelessly overcrowded hospital wards were deplorable. Bed linens were not changed until they had become black and fetid; the rooms were cold and drafty in winter and sweltering hellholes in the summer months. Meanwhile, the hospital staff lived above their means, and the "Ring" celebrated their good fortune by spending taxpayer monies on the finest meats, champagnes, and cigars. Commissioner William Wood, the lone dissenter among the den of thieves, later remarked that "the credit of the County, both financially and morally—[was] destroyed. Its orders forced upon its employees and contractors, being sold at discounts of 15 percent; its hospitals filthy, dilapidated and disorganized, and a system of contracting for supplies to the various institutions, so loose that all *reputable* merchants and dealers refused to send in propositions to fill our requirements. The difference between the lowest bid and that which was accepted was divided between the contractor and the Commissioner, by whose votes the contract was awarded."[6]

Ed McDonald's growing fortune was incidental compared to the monies pouring into Mike's account from the county courthouse swindle. The genius of the thing was the clever "bait and switch" scheme involving the stone contractors: William McNeil and Sons theoretically "won" the bid process after chartering a private train stocked with venison and wines to ferry the commissioners out to the Lemont stone quarries. In truth, McNeil turned out to be the front man for Edwin Walker, who paid the county board a $5,000 "incentive" in order to win the contract. The $5,000 bribe was put up by McDonald through an operative, one "Henry Cockayne," who delivered the ultimatum to Walker and his wife Mary that they must sign over the trust deed to the Store as collateral. The deed was signed and executed on July 27, 1876. An investigation later revealed that "Henry Cockayne" was the birth name of the notorious gambler and bunko man Harry Lawrence, Mike's floor manager who supervised the betting action at the Store.[7]

After handing over the payoff, Walker was called upon to supply McNeil's bond. Following the formal ratification of the bid, McNeil yielded to the demands of the "Ring" and the unseen hand of McDonald by surrendering power of attorney to Walker and with it, all fees, emoluments, and gratuities from the county. Walker's bid to supply limestone from his Lemont quarries was $200,000 higher than that of Patrick Fanning, who could have furnished the same kind of stone from his Excelsior Stone quarry in Lemont. But Fanning offended the board by refusing to pay the commissioners for the right to do business with the county. Then he turned down a buyout offer of $24,000 from McDonald and Walker in return for a promise to withdraw his name from consideration and keep quiet.

"I saw Walker, McNeil, and [former Cook County Sheriff] Frank Agnew around McDonald's place. They were holding conferences and I knew I was throwed out [*sic*]," Fanning revealed. "They got hold of some of my copies of my agreement and destroyed all they could lay their hands on."[8]

Underfinanced and ill-prepared to meet his contractual obligations Walker operated on the margins. More than anything, he needed time to straighten out his affairs, such as they were. But time was in short supply for McDonald, who contrived with the board to bleed Walker dry. He secured arrangements with the clerk of the county board for Walker to borrow liberally (at a high rate of interest) on the faith of forthcoming estimates—money the Lemont Stone Company had *yet* to earn.

McNeil, described as a "capable man" by the *Chicago Tribune*, was just a straw man, and the board had no confidence in his abilities. "Why, I wouldn't trust him to build a woodshed!" sneered Commissioner John McCaffrey. Realizing rather belatedly that he was being set up, McNeil broke ranks from Walker and pulled his men off the jobsite, demanding revocation of the bond and power of attorney. Walker was in a tight spot. A competitor firm obtained a judgment barring the Chicago and Lemont Stone Company from quarrying stone when it was found that Walker's men had been mining on land that did not belong to Walker.

Walker threw up his hands in frustration and said that without the line of credit and the removal of the injunction, he could not possibly supply the necessary materials or pay the 425 workmen. The credit line was not extended and matters worsened. Not long after, the master stone mason who built the Store for McDonald was bankrupted and left out to dry. In a swindle of this magnitude Mike McDonald was not inclined to grant cash dispensations to defaulters. He ruthlessly pounced on his partner's misfortune, ruined him financially, and then appointed Harry L. Holland, his trusted bookkeeper and private secretary, to reorganize the Lemont quarries after Walker's company was thrown into receivership on May 1, 1883.

With McDonald and his contractors calling the shots, project oversight was nonexistent; there simply was no accountability. Project superintendent L. D. Cleveland was blind; the principal architect, James J. Egan, was young, inexperienced, employed by the county, and thus subordinate to the whims of the Ring, although he was the first to report back that the Lemont limestone was of inferior quality. The county not only overpaid for it, but the product was not thick enough to meet the original contract specifications. It was easily soiled and unsightly to behold after prolonged exposure to the wind, rain, and snow. Worse, Walker had padded his bills with unwanted "extras" in a desperate attempt to stave off financial ruin.

The opposition press drew attention to the sad state of affairs in the months following the July 4, 1877, groundbreaking. The Ring fended off criticism from the Citizen's Association and switched tactics. They ordered Egan to make frequent changes to the original design in order to cover up the steal. Finally, they met and agreed that there were additional monies to be made in buying Hallowell granite from a certain quarry that a certain commissioner did business with in the state of Maine. Accordingly, large quantities of the granite were ordered for the three entrance ways and the interior wainscoting of the building. And just as the back taxes of earlier years were used to pay off Walker and

McDonald for their porous, inadequate limestone, the Ring employed similar tactics in pushing through a new bond issue for the granite appropriation.

"There is really some truth that those using [granite over limestone] care no more about soiled and unsightly walls than they do about the ruins of Jerusalem," noted the *Tribune* with disgust. "Such an opportunity for plunder comes but once in a lifetime."[9]

When the increasing county taxation reached the utmost limit, the voters finally had enough and voted the Ring out in November 1877. Five new commissioners, four Republicans and a Democrat, took office. The whole extent of the wastefulness and extravagance of the previous four years was soon laid bare, and the Citizen's Association demanded that the grand jury investigate. Edwin Walker's financial miseries were compounded by an indictment for perjury.

Clem Periolat, branded a "skillful manipulator" and the "treasurer" for the Ring, was betrayed by his friend, James Forsyth, a supplier of wearing apparel to the County Alms House, who traded testimony for leniency. It was revealed in testimony that the thieves were stealing from one another: Forsyth was removing funds from Periolat's business and depositing funds in a secret "K" account—named for fellow conspirator George Kimberly, meat wholesaler, warden of the insane asylum, and secretary of the Cook County Democratic Committee. The private books of the Ring were opened up for all to see, confirming the truth. But even with the evidence damning, few Chicagoans believed that any of these well-heeled grafters would occupy cells in the Joliet Penitentiary alongside the hardened criminals of the working class. And certainly not McDonald, who once again stood innocently off to the side as Walker, his broken former partner, answered to the charge.

Emory Storrs and Luther Laflin Mills led for the state, but the applicable statutes were vague, contradictory, and against the common right—the *accepted* privileges of office—that were common at that time. Who would want to occupy an office at an annual salary of $500 per year if the usual perquisites were to be denied? That was the real issue to ponder. The law and the incriminating facts of the case were therefore impotent because a long line of office holders who had gone before and who had profited from the ills of the spoils system were not prosecuted. It was a precedent that the jurors and the court were all too aware of.

Clem Periolat, Kimberly, and the "Colvinite Commissioners" were all *acquitted* just two weeks before the November election. And with that acquittal, the hope that future county boards might serve the public in a more responsible manner faded. Within a decade, an even more rapacious and venal group of commissioners than the Periolat Ring assumed office. The members of the 1883–87 Cook County board—the insatiably greedy "County Boodlers," as history records— were the handiwork of Michael C. McDonald.

Meanwhile, work on the new Cook County Courthouse and City Hall complex on LaSalle Street between Washington and Randolph Streets progressed at a glacial pace, hampered by labor strikes and revisions to the blueprints. The delays would continue for the next seven years. New contractors and suppliers hired by the "reform board" were fired on a whim. The job was completed in 1884, but in fact the building was not ready for occupancy until February 1885 because the board decided at the last minute that a fireproof roof should be installed—a bitter irony as it turned out.

When the invoices were collected and tallied, the final cost of the imposing French Renaissance–style structure with massive, thirty-five-foot Corinthian columns and garish statuary and accoutrements covering the exterior came in at \$2,424,668, though some pegged the actual cost at \$4 million.[10] Praise for the architectural design of the six-story building was muted; in fact, it was nonexistent. After such a great expenditure of public money, citizens who were left to foot the bill for the pork-barrel extravagance and greed of the old county board were disappointed and angry with the politicians—with justification.

In the next five years, complaints were voiced about the building's poor ventilation system. The office space proved to be unsuited and inadequate to meet the demands of the expanding county agencies; the visible cracks in the foundation and the dingy appearance of the yellowing limestone were the subject of an investigation. The Courthouse was less than five years old, when the stone began crumbling, forcing the Cook County board to issue a bid solicitation for exterior renovation.

In a rush of revelation, Mike McDonald privately communicated to the commissioners a "solution" to their problem. "Boys," he said in his customary show of familiarity. "I have a proposition for you; one that will restore the luster and grand appearance of this magnificent building. Let me introduce you to the wonders of the *Lundberg Process.*"

Among the grifters, bunko men, three-card monte cheats, and brace gamblers of the big cities, there is what is known in the trade as the *short con*. And then there is the *long con*. The short con is a quick one-off swindle; "skinning a sucker," then beating a fast retreat into the shadows before the dupe knows he has been had. The long con—the carefully planned, elaborate scheme to bleed a victim dry over a period of months, in this case, years—is the craft of the swindling artisan. The Lundberg Process was the climax to the long con—the thirteen-year courthouse project. In 1886, Michael McDonald brought his long con to a spectacular conclusion by pulling off the "putty and paint" job—more grand larceny against the good taxpayers of Cook County.

Five years earlier, an inconspicuous notice had appeared in the newspaper, placed by "Professor" Charles O. Lundberg, forty years a newspaper man, and thirteen years a flimflam inventor, that guaranteed "Stone and brick can be cleaned, preserved, and made water- and fire-proof by the 'C. O. Lundberg Stone Preserving Process.' Samples and certificates will be furnished by calling on C. O. Lundberg at 20 Bryan Block, 166 LaSalle Street."

Lundberg was a doddering, slightly addled laboratory tinkerer who earnestly believed in the remarkable restorative powers of his liquid "compound" for brick and stone. Harry L. Holland, who worked in Mike's new downtown office in the Montauk Block and who made it his business to find out about such things, kept tabs on Lundberg, until finally Holland was invited to present the Lundberg Process to members of the Committee on Buildings. By no coincidence, it fell on a holiday: Decoration Day, 1886, when the reporters were not likely to be roaming through the building.[11] The invitation was proffered by architect Hansen, who was promised a 5 percent commission if he could help push this thing along.

The "Professor," who had earlier applied his formula to a small section of the County Hospital at the invitation of Warden William McGarigle, was unaware of Holland's impending meeting. He did not need to understand the particulars of the contract, only to produce the chemical and keep his mouth shut, McDonald reasoned. Thereafter, Lundberg signed on as a supplier-subcontractor working under the direction of Holland, McDonald, the Cook County Commissioners, and three ward heelers in their employ: Joseph Chesterfield "Oyster Joe" Mackin, L. P. Crane, and Arthur Gleason, who was appointed company "secretary."

The courthouse, much of it constructed with shabby Lemont limestone, was crumbling on the upper floors, and a select committee on public works had been appointed to recommend a remedy. E. R. Brainerd, a political hack who came up with a construction estimate, was awarded $183,000 to remove porticoes and granite stone from the Washington Street side of the building and replace the copings with a cheaper grade of Bedford stone. Commissioner John Evelyn "Little" Van Pelt, a close friend and political stooge of Joe Mackin and Mike McDonald who boasted that he descended from the "Knickerbocker" aristocracy of New York, was elected to the county board in 1883. He was to be the point man.

The short-lived "reform board" finished its term and was replaced by what Chicago history records as the "Boodle Board." Over the next four years, their intrigues and grafting schemes eclipsed even the shockingly low standards set by the Periolat Ring. The failure to convict these men of wholesale thievery in 1877 had set a dangerous precedent: the implied promise of official immunity for dishonest commissioners. Emboldened by the impotence of the Citizens' Association and other like-minded reform groups a decade earlier, McDonald and his flock rebuilt the county board in the image of the bunko steerers of old, applying the same corruptive tactics of the mid-1870s with panache. "Little" Van Pelt, the glib, diminutive grain trader from Jerseyville, Illinois, was appointed chairman of the Cook County Democratic Central Committee in 1882 and chairman of all the important county committees a year later.

According to the *Tribune,* Van Pelt had suddenly "blossomed as a geologist" in his strong advocacy for the cheaper grade of Bedford Stone provided by E. R.

Brainerd.[12] The three dissenters—the reform minority—were shouted down in heated debate, and the bid was awarded to Brainerd. Next, Harry Holland stepped forward with a piece of stone that had allegedly been taken down from the court-house and treated with the Lundberg Process eighteen months earlier. Holland pointed to the lustrous appearance of the stone. "See gentlemen!" exclaimed Holland, a nimble and resourceful promoter whose father was an Episcopal clergyman back East. "This scientific wonder formula will rescue our public buildings in the years to come!" Holland's asking price was 30 cents a foot. The board estimated that the process would need to be applied to 127,000 square feet.

Pulling McDonald aside, the commissioners agreed to cut the deal with Holland—they knew the Lundberg Process was a scam, the old "brick trick" warmed over—but the money was real enough. The board demanded a $14,000 bribe from McDonald as their price for approving the contract. The money was to be passed to "Little" Van Pelt and distributed among the "boys" on the Building Committee: Dan Wren; Christian Casselman; Christian Geils; the foppish Clark Street gambler Harry Varnell; Mike Leyden; Mike Wasserman; "farmer" Richard McLaughery of Palos, Illinois; the rough and tumble James "Buck" McCarthy from the Stockyards District; and Richard Oliver—to do what they pleased with it.

Warden McGarigle, the former Chicago police chief who owed his foray into elective politics (and his $5,500 a year salary plus the usual perquisites of plunder) to McDonald, was appointed "bag man." He carried the bundle of cash to the eternally optimistic Van Pelt who shook hands and said he truly believed that the Lundberg Process was "a good thing for the building."

McDonald was sullen, resentful, and taken aback by the subversive intent of his handpicked appointees. "Those stiffs want too much money!" he grumbled. But he also understood it was the price of doing business, and the axle had to be greased.[13] The contract to coat the upper three floors of the courthouse and city hall was awarded on June 7, 1886, and the job was completed the following October. The public was assured that the total value of the contract was only $30,000. But when Holland presented the final bill for payment, the original sum had mysteriously swelled to $181,250. The invoice charged the county for 440,000 square feet of treatment—though the original measurement was only 240,000 square feet. The usual complaints emanated from the Citizens' Association. An investigation was ordered and payment to Holland was withheld.

Separate paint samples from the Lundberg Process were sent to Professor Walter S. Haines, a scientist of the Rush Medical College for chemical analysis. The first sample turned out to be a cheap grade of linseed oil. Sample two was nothing more than paint, consisting of linseed oil, white lead, turpentine, carbonite of lime, silica, oxide of iron, and alumina.[14] The formula was no better and no worse than the common varieties of lead paint sold over the counter in Chicago hardware emporiums.

Another "reform board" elevated to office in 1886 reconsidered the payment of Holland's original invoice. He submitted his warrants on October 31, but the treasurer was instructed not to pay them. Incensed, McDonald's bookkeeper filed a civil lawsuit seeking a $131,250 settlement of his unpaid claim on August 4, 1890. A spate of appeals and denials followed. Holland would turn it into his personal crusade. If anything, Harry was a patient, if not obsessive man. The matter would require eighteen more years of laborious and bitter litigation to resolve, depriving McDonald of his "putty and paint" windfall and Charles O. Lundberg of his fees.

Mike was already in the grave when a civil jury ended the matter by awarding Holland a generous $33,500 cash settlement on December 5, 1908. By the time Harry finally cashed out, gone too was the county courthouse and city hall that had inspired the contretemps. The shabbily constructed public building that had cost the citizens of Cook County so dearly was declared unsafe by structural engineers. The three to ten tons of coping on the top three floors that E. R. Brainerd and Harry Holland promised to "secure and protect" in their original proposals came loose from their underpinnings. County officials were warned that a terrible disaster was imminent.

The 1904–5 board pondered possible remedies, but could not reach consensus. It was predicted with certainty that the slightest tremor in the ground would unhinge massive blocks and send them hurtling to the ground. There would be substantial loss of life if the calamity were to occur during normal business hours. The five-million-dollar bond issue required to build a new and better city hall hinged on receiving voter approval. The pain in all of this was the knowledge that the next city hall would have to replace a building that was barely twenty-three years old.

The timetables to build public support and appropriate money for the next city hall and courthouse accelerated following a fire on January 17, 1905, that caused considerable damage to the upper floors. City and county offices had to be transferred to other buildings. A painter, trapped in the flames, perished, sparking a press outcry to demolish the old building. The original "fireproofing" compounds had proven useless. "It is architecturally monstrous—it is abominable as a workhouse," the *Tribune* bitterly complained. However, by 1905, a new generation of reporters and city rewrite men failed to evoke the name of Mike McDonald in connection with the deficiencies of the county building. By then, Mike was a name from the past, and the neophyte newspaper scribes had no living memory of those earlier times and the role he played—certainly not the same vivid impression of the man evoked by a reporter who compared Mike's methods with the late, lamented William Marcy Tweed, who had built the City of New York a city hall by doling out no-bid contracts to political friends and employing much the same "business practices." "Mike McDonald wants to be the 'Boss' Tweed of Chicago and in that role he would be as much more dangerous in public interests as he is more vicious and corrupt than Tweed was. Tweed was content with political power and the means it gave him to reward his friends and accumulate a fortune. McDonald goes still further that in addition to personal profit, he shall be enabled to protect certain criminal classes with whom he has more or less associated for many years."[15]

Less than a week after the 1905 fire that rendered the old government building useless, the resolution was adopted to build a new city hall and county building. Architect Daniel Burnham envisioned a classic structure arising from the pile of Lemont limestone rubble that formed the masonry of the old temple of graft; one so impressive and awe-inspiring that it would humble the county schemers and discourage the saloon grafters passing through its doors. Who among future generations of Chicago lawmakers would dare trammel the spirit of Progressivism by pilfering the public coffers in this new temple of democracy?

The cornerstone was laid in solemn ceremonies on September 21, 1906. The finishing touches were applied less than two years later. In 2008, the functional, rock-solid building celebrated its one hundred years of service to the citizens of Cook County, although Burnham's noble vision of a new age of honesty, dignity, and openness in state and municipal government evaporated . . . about thirty seconds after the opening gavel signaled the start of the first meeting of the city council.

~ 8 ~

Our Carter

IT WAS MCDONALD'S DESTINY TO BE DAMNED AS A STREET THUG and called a loathsome criminal—while at the same time he was warmly regarded by influential city attorneys, judges, and politicians as a master organizer who resurrected the moribund Cook County Democratic Party in the decades following the end of the Civil War.

Standing before the First Ward electorate inside crowded public meeting halls to whip up sentiment for aspiring Democratic candidates who appealed to him for political muscle, Mike's sense that he was an important "boss," with the power to help unify splinter factions of the party and shape public policy by anointing the favored few, was reaffirmed. However, as much as he saw himself as kingmaker, he could never escape his past or strip away an unwanted reputation as the flashy, conniving "King of the Gamblers." The bad behavior of the saloon habitués; the nightly shootings, and the criminal acts of the class of men lurking in the grog shops, hotel lobbies, and card rooms of Clark Street made it impossible to separate his name from the intrigues, the violence, and the chaos of the streets. After all, many of these men were his *clients*.

When a dissolute, drunken bunko steerer and pimp named John Turner (a.k.a. Hank Davis) gunned down Charles D. Whyland, owner of St. Elmo's Restaurant, inside Kuhn's hotel, accusations were leveled at McDonald as the instigator of the unprovoked assault. Davis was connected with a pawn shop operating across the street from the Store, and by extension, was assumed to be one of Mike's agents. Davis said he was liquored up but could not remember the reason why he produced a gun. While admitting he was probably guilty of the crime of murder, he denied being one of McDonald's bunko men.

The unprovoked, Thanksgiving Day shooting of a popular restaurant owner by a debased man at the bottom of the social order stirred deep public outrage.

"I was in California in vigilante times, and San Francisco was never as bad as Chicago today!" complained one man. "There are more lampposts than there are bunko ropers," offered another. "Wouldn't it be a good thing to join the two things somehow?" A man who described himself as a "merchant" added that "The murderer was one of Mike McDonald's men and there are a hundred others who, like him, are liable to kill any one who chances to come in their path. The first thing that ought to be done is to clean out the Store. When that is done, there can be some hope for the future—but not before." And this: "Is the life of any citizen safe while such a scoundrel as Mike McDonald is recognized as a power by the City Government, tolerated by its officials and treated as an equal by the very men who should place him inside a prison? In order to restore some resemblance of law and decency in Chicago it will be necessary to drive this McDonald and his pack of cutthroats away from the city."[1]

With the blood of a well-known citizen on his hands, and the matter not so easily disposed of as, say, a common charge of keeping a gambling house, McDonald issued a rare public statement—and he published it in the Chicago newspapers.

"I have, Mr. Editor, for sometime past, sought obscurity rather than noto-riety. That my place of business is as quiet as any in the City of Chicago, and is as free from any dangerous element as any in the city, for the truthfulness of which utterance I refer you to the Captain and Chief of Police or the merchants in my neighborhood. I would be silent as I have been in the past, were it not for the fact that my continued silence would be misconstrued. Every murder committed or burglary done is charged to the McDonald gang, whereas in fact I never knew the man charged therewith or interested myself in their [business]. A gambler I may be, more than that I am not."[2]

In words intended to evoke a sense of victimization, McDonald attempted to firm up his reputation by demonstrating that he was a man of principle and honor. But neither was he entirely willing to disassociate from the gambling hoi polloi who depended on his name, his bail bonding racket when they got into trouble, and his influence in dangerous times.

Hank Davis was convicted of murder and dispatched to the Joliet Peniten-tiary for twenty-one years. McDonald was censured—but no direct link to Davis or the murder could be established. This was not the end of it however. Five years passed. Davis's widowed mother solicited Mike's help in getting up a petition to free her son from prison. She said she was penniless and in the streets; and her late husband, a Presbyterian minister, had left her without funds. Her boy was prone to epileptic fits, in grave danger, and likely to die in the stir unless Mike could intervene. McDonald, guileless in the presence of a tearful woman, made a reckless decision. He enlisted the support of the sentencing judge, several aldermanic chums—even Mayor Carter Henry Harrison—and hand-delivered a signed petition to the Illinois State House and the warden of the Joliet Penitentiary, where Davis was a model prisoner. Then "Mrs. Robinson," the widow woman, was exposed as a fraud; a pathetic character of the streets who earned her keep by feigning illness to collect charity from strangers.

Davis would remain locked inside his jail cell for the time being, but McDonald's poor judgment compromised the credibility of Chicago's new mayor early on in his administration. Harrison was subjected to public ridicule by McDonald's serious faux pas, the first in a long series of unfortunate incidents that would strain the delicate bonds of friendship between Harrison and McDonald; a friendship that catapulted the Kentucky-born ex-congressman into Mayor Heath's vacated chair on April 1, 1879.

Before Harrison, Chicago mayors were caretakers, and city politics was, in the opinion of essayist Edward Kantowicz, "a bipartisan jungle of rival bosses and factions."[3] There had been no "strong mayors," but there were many strong ward leaders, and there was of course Mike McDonald to nudge the party brokers to favor his handpicked candidates. However, when the party caucuses convened in the early winter of 1879, there was no clear Democratic preference. The wealthy State Street merchant Levi Z. Leiter, a Democrat, applied, but the "dirty shirt" faction—McDonald's "bummers"—nipped it in the bud.

To effect a compromise, the "dirty shirts" and the party "silk stockings" agreed in principle to nominate a man who would stand well with both factions. Carter Harrison (1825–93), an old and familiar name in Chicago, was their choice. Born in a log hut in a canebrake in Fayette County, Kentucky, Harrison was a cousin of Thomas Jefferson and a distant relative of President William Henry Harrison. The family line could be traced all the way back to the time of the "Protector," Oliver Cromwell. According to various historical accounts, an ancestor of the Chicago mayor, also named Harrison, led King Charles I of England, condemned as a tyrant, to the chopping block at Whitehall on January 30, 1649.

Harrison completed his Yale Law School studies before gravitating to the city in 1855. With his wife, Sophie Preston, a genteel Southern woman who bore him ten children (six died at an early age), Harrison launched a career in real estate. His first piece of property was the Adams House Hotel at the corner of Harrison and Clark Streets, which he converted into a private residence. He entered politics after the Chicago Fire and was elected to the first Cook County Board of Commissioners. In 1874 he won a seat in Congress as a Democrat from the Second District.

Harrison was in the dumps politically when McDonald solicited his intentions for city office. His bid for reelection to the Congress had failed the year before, and his politics was suspicious to both bummer and silk stocking. The odor of scandal hung over his term of service in the Forty-fifth Congress. Harrison, as chairman of the Committee on Reform of the Civil Service, had pushed through the payment of benefits to four alleged Union Army veterans who asserted that they were permanently disabled by their wartime wounds. The claims were previously disallowed because none of the five had actually *served* in the Civil War, let alone suffered egregious injuries.[4] One of the claimants was a newspaper editor who had never ventured south.

The Greenback Party and the Socialists actively courted Harrison to head their ticket, and as a "Border State" native married to a woman from the Deep South, he had at times expressed open sympathy for the Confederate cause during the Civil War. Could a suspected "Copperhead," conflicted in his loyalties, claim city hall? These issues clouded the city election. For their part, the Republicans, as was their custom, failed to put up a worthy candidate palatable to the working men and women of Chicago. After Mayor Heath declined to stand for reelection, the conservatives chose the porcelain Abner M. Wright, a Board of Trade member described as "too cold, too bloodless and calculating."[5]

McDonald and his faithful apprentice "Oyster Joe" Mackin, with Alderman Ed Cullerton, Frank Agnew, Alfred Trude, Mike Corcoran, his Hatch House "shoulder hitters" (nineteenth-century term meaning "thug, bully, brute"), the millionaire Perry Smith, and Dave Thornton, owner of the "House of David" gambling hall were all solid for "Our Carter" (his most famous appellation).[6] Harrison was a man of enduring charisma, wry humor, and personal flamboyance. An oversized slouch hat and black cape were his famous trademarks. More important, he stirred the passions of the common man. It was an unbeatable combination.

The *Tribune* expressed its usual apprehension and warned voters that Harrison's election would constitute a "bummer restoration." These concerns were swept aside, however, because Harrison's experience on the national level placated the conservative Potter Palmer and Levi Leiter Democrats, and his liberal views toward liquor consumption and the right of men to gamble as long as they could afford to do so convinced McDonald to throw the full weight of his ward organizations behind the campaign.

As the emblem of his cause, Harrison adopted a pet eagle perched upon a rickety pedestal and driven around town in a dray pulled by six horses. The campaign banner affixed to the wagon read: "Carter's Eagle and Victory." Dismissed as a cheap trick by the Republicans, the frightened and squawking bird injected an element of good humor and frivolity to the campaign. Starchy and unappealing, Wright was unable to stir a similar passion, even among his friends on the Board of Trade. Twenty-six of them bolted the party to vote for Harrison, who by now was affectionately dubbed "the Eagle" by the man on the street.

There was no heroic grandeur to Carter Harrison. He was a methodical politician unimpressed by high-minded ideals uttered by officious psalm-sayers. He lacked a great liberal vision of the future and profound moral principles, but he understood human nature better than most. A self-made millionaire, he gauged voter opinion much better than any of the five mercantile Republicans who would mount challenges to his rule over the next two decades. The "Harrison Dynasty" (between father and son, they would serve ten terms of office as mayor between 1879 and 1915) was hatched on April 1, 1879, when "the Eagle" coasted to a five-thousand-vote victory margin over Wright, despite the Socialist candidate's siphoning away eleven thousand likely Democratic voters. The Republicans were stunned by the defeat—candidate Wright immediately cried fraud and accused the police of complicity. "The thing is a fraud from alpha to omega," complained Wright. "Fraud, top, middle and bottom." At his urging, the *Tribune* launched an independent investigation.

The gamblers had performed their duties admirably—and the *Tribune* attested to it. Wagonloads of "repeaters" were ferried around by Dave Thornton to various precincts to vote for Harrison as many times as they could get away with, for small cash inducements. Mike McDonald had personally appointed State Street saloon owner and gambler Joe Suits to the First Ward Democratic Committee, and he worked the hotels and saloons. McDonald "registered" and certified seventy-five Harrison voters, some of them underage, but all of them claiming permanent residence at the Store.

"Votes were received from persons who were non-residents in the precinct and even from some who were not citizens of the United States," reported the *Inter-Ocean.*[7] At Brown's Hotel, a shot of whiskey was served to any man who presented himself to an election worker. William McNeil, the courthouse contractor about to be cut out of the "swag" by Ed Walker and the county board, led sixty workmen to the polls, introducing them as residents of a nearby First Ward lodging house.

Democratic wheelhorse "Oyster Joe" Mackin made the rounds of the saloons and back alleys to personally escort unregistered winos and assorted ne'er-do-wells to the polls. Born in Philadelphia, Mackin stepped off the train just two months after the Chicago Fire. His first meaningful employment was at the Sherman House Hotel, bartending for Frank Clyne. He opened a basement saloon and political club on Dearborn Street in 1875. There, it was said, he invented the "free lunch," supplying a purchaser of a fifteen-cent shot with a fried oyster and a fork. Mackin was a quintessential nineteenth-century Chicago "saloon politician," full of good cheer and flaunting his connections. McDonald hired him as a private secretary in 1880 at a salary of $3,000 per year after taking note of his "extraordinary" service to the Democratic Party in 1878–79 as ward heeler and functionary. Mackin's duties were entirely political—he stayed away from the gambling action. Touted by the bummers for his organizational skills and his willingness to engage in election fraud to aid and abet their schemes, Joe was elevated by McDonald to secretary of the Cook County Democratic Central Committee.

It may be said that of all the gamblers, politicians, and hangers-on, Joe Mackin, Harry Holland, and Alfred Trude were the closest to McDonald, his true inner circle, and their loyalty was unwavering. As a result of McDonald's sponsorship, Mackin's political power grew exponentially until he was recognized as one of the most influential Democratic politicians in the state of Illinois.[8] The city election of 1879 was his springboard to power.

Two police officers were detailed to every polling place. Outgoing mayor Heath called them "efficient, non-partisan men" and denied any instances of fraud, but minus the presence of poll watchers and competent election judges, the opportunity for fraud existed—and was acted upon by McDonald's gang. "The man who goes around like a roaring calf shouting fraud, fraud makes a fool of himself," editorialized the *Daily News*. "How much better is it to submit cheerfully, and acknowledge that you are done for. It relieves you wonderfully, and it relieves your friends too."[9] Wright withdrew his accusations—and the new regime took over.

Carter Harrison and Mike McDonald built an immediate and strong rapport. Harrison frequented the Store, respected McDonald as a persuasive man of ability, and was known to lay down a bet or two at the roulette wheel. He scoffed at the reformers seeking to deprive working men of a good time during the after-hours, as long as the games were "square." Philosophically, the two men were in accord—at least during the early years of the Harrison Dynasty.

This Bourbon Democrat from the Kentucky canebrake accepted McDonald's campaign "subscriptions" and his organizational genius, and he looked the other way when accusations of voter fraud in the city's so-called bummer wards were flying fast and furious, but he demonstrated a troublesome streak of independence that could not be compromised. Unlike the pliable Harvey Colvin, Harrison the First was a contrarian who battled Mike over appointments and slate-making and occasionally struck hard at his gambling interests in retaliation for untoward actions that would embarrass or discredit his administration.

Despite the frequent airing of dirty laundry in the press—their squabbles were a matter of public record—McDonald reached the apex of his political power under the elder Harrison. In the fall of 1879, Mike took over as chairman of assessments for the Democratic Central Committee—responsible for fee collection and revenues levied against the myriad of ward clubs scattered across the city. In August, the First Ward organization, with the blessing of the mayor, formally sanctioned Mike's behind-the-scenes contributions to the party by anointing him precinct committeeman. A splinter faction of "Young Democrats" from the Twelfth Ward denounced McDonald as a "notorious gambler and the representative of a disgraceful element of the city." In a moment of rare nonpartisanship, the *Tribune*, giving the devil his due, said that the action of the Twelfth Ward men "is very rough on McDonald, without whose active aid the Democracy has never been able to achieve much in this County."[10]

McDonald deserved credit for the restoration of the Democratic Party and the success of his political cohorts in the recent election. Dr. Swayne Wickersham, one of the key Camp Douglas plotters, won an aldermanic seat. Harrison was elected, and campaign gossip among Republicans accusing him of being a wartime traitor subsided. In any other Northern city, the chances of such a thing occurring were slim. The 1870s and early 1880s are remembered as the height of North-South divisiveness, when Republicans waved the "Bloody Shirt" and dredged up old and painful memories of secession as a means to win elections. Barney Caulfield went to Congress, and the local party organization in Chicago was mostly cleansed of a traitorous image that plagued the Democrats on the national level in every election up through the end of the nineteenth century.

On an August evening in 1880, the clubroom of the Palmer House was filled with two hundred party regulars assembled to pay tribute to Mike and ridicule the Twelfth Ward "long-hairs" (as reformers and idealists were commonly satirized). "Individual members of the crowd arose and with tears in their eyes declared the keeper of the Store to be all that is good, true, and beautiful in a political and social sense." Deeply moved by the affection of the "boys," McDonald acknowledged Magistrate John J. Prindiville of the county justice court occupying a seat of honor and made a few gratuitous remarks before settling comfortably back into his chair alongside Oyster Joe, recognized by the organization as Mike's second-in-command—a true-to-the-cause Irish *consigliore*.[11]

Now would have been the opportune moment to shed old and dangerous associations with the shoulder hitters and bunko steerers and to extricate his family name from the gambling racket, the bail bonding racket, the protection racket, and the "greenhorn swindles." Mike could rightfully claim a share of the credit for rebuilding the party of Andrew Jackson to a position of strength from the ashes and disgrace of Civil War "Copperheadism."

Already a wealthy man of property who indulged his children and his wife in sumptuous upper-class surroundings, McDonald was no longer entirely dependent upon the revenue streams derived from illegal enterprises for his sustenance. He was a dynamic force in Chicago politics. Yet, he seemed unwilling to break with his past. McDonald continued to leverage his political clout for the benefit of his underworld allies and other vagrants and criminals seeking his sponsorship in Chicago. The scams grew bolder, and the schemes more audacious. With the benefit of political sponsorship, police protection, and Justice Prindiville obliging Mike by imposing minor fines with no accompanying jail time for the accused, the emboldened criminals organized under their patron.

Michael Cassius McDonald would not relinquish the sporting world until it ceased to be of personal benefit—anymore than he would voluntarily surrender his wayfaring wife to a sweet-talking minstrel performer. It was the "action" he craved. The game was afoot, and the temptation to build a Democratic platform from a position of strength and still remain the "czar" of the underworld rackets in Chicago was a powerful inducement. Celebrity criminals were always made to feel welcome at McDonald's Store, provided they remained "square" with the proprietor by keeping pistols holstered and their bankroll visible.

Jimmy "Nosy Jones" Carroll, one of America's cleverest bank robbers, was wanted for the Farmer's and Mechanic's Bank heist in Galesburg, Illinois, and a dozen other "scores" committed with his gang—Billy Burke, Tom Bigelow, Mart Davis, "Paddy" Guerin (the famous Devil's Island escapee), and John Larney, also known as the sneak thief "Molly Matches"—when he paid a social call to 79 West Monroe to catch up on old times with McDonald and Joe Mackin.[12]

Mayor Harrison had been in office less than three months but was certainly aware that Carroll was hiding out in plain sight within the city. On the night in question, Assistant State's Attorney Edward P. Weber and some newsmen were enjoying McDonald's company when Carroll joined them at the craps table. After a round of drinks and a friendly toss of the dice, Mike and his guests repaired to the Pacific Garden Theater, where the curiosity of a circus elephant provided the evening's amusement. Everyone was liquored up and in good spirits—Weber apparently did not catch on to the fact that he was trading jokes with a feared bank robber whose image adorned every police station in the state. But a resourceful detective in plain clothes did—and without benefit of due process, Carroll was handcuffed and escorted to the Central Station in a carriage.

Assistant State's Attorney Weber protested the affront, calling it a "kidnapping" and in violation of the Constitution, adding that he cared "not a wit" for McDonald and his gang, he was merely questioning the legality of the arrest.[13] McDonald furnished the necessary bonds for the Carroll gang and a forger named Charles Brockway. Carroll returned to Galesburg on his own recognizance, declaring that he was prepared to stand trial. McDonald assigned Alfred Trude to travel downstate to represent him, but was surprised when Carroll jumped bail and ran off to Canada, a safe haven for corrupt politicians and criminals on the lam. Safely over the border, Carroll compulsively continued to rob banks, until his luck ran out and old friends from Chicago were no longer there to save him from the stir. Carroll was arrested in Toronto and sentenced to five years in the St. Vincent De Paul Prison.

Hearing of his plight, Carroll's friend and confidant "Oyster Joe" Mackin got up a petition imploring the Canadian authorities to grant a formal pardon. The names of the prominent men of Chicago and downstate Illinois who affixed their signatures to the document ended in public scandal. State Street merchant E. J. Lehmann, former mayor Colvin, six Chicago aldermen, an equal number of Cook County commissioners, a bank president, four Illinois state senators, a respected physician—and Mayor Carter Harrison—admitted under questioning from the media that they had all signed the document. To a man, they said they were hoodwinked and had done so only because the bearer of the petition, a ward character named Charley Johnson, who listed the Store as his home address, had tricked them into believing the document was to assist the impoverished family of some poor unfortunate unjustly convicted "up North." Being busy men, they said, they had not bothered to take the time to actually read the petition, that they signed many such official documents in the course of a business day, and that on the word of the wily political hand Joe Mackin, whose name Johnson invoked, they had freely attached their signatures.

"The only thing I object to is that they printed my name at the bottom of the list," quipped McDonald, who professed ignorance of any "scheme" to spring Carroll. But it was no laughing matter to the mayor, who vented his wrath against William Pinkerton, son of the famous Civil War era detective, whose agency was headquartered in Chicago. Pinkerton, who was on cordial terms with McDonald, explained that the photographic images of Carroll were old and it would have been impossible for him to have recognized the bank robber in Chicago. It was a moot point—Carroll had been bonded out and was long gone. Canadian officials considered the petition, before rejecting it in the belief that some or all of the signatures had been forged.

Harrison was not easily placated. He ordered the Store and Mike's other satellite dens "pulled" and made no bones about it. This was pure political retaliation—and when the dust settled, there followed the usual reconciliation. "The police department and myself in consultation, came to the conclusion that it was time to strike at McDonald and show him that he must not interfere for these thieves," said Harrison, but it was only a temporary inconvenience for Mike.[14]

Bail bonding was an important cash racket, and McDonald sought ways to protect it. Despite taking the party boss and gambler to the woodshed for the Jimmy Carroll embarrassment, less than a year later the mayor obliged his uneasy ally by removing crusty old Simon O'Donnell, who had been indefatigable in his attempts to suppress the gamblers, from the superintendency of the Chicago Police Department. O'Donnell had an important role to play in the arrest of Jimmy Carroll—it was one of his detectives who had been sent out that night to bring Carroll in after gaining reliable street intelligence about his whereabouts. This was done without the knowledge of the police, who were routinely funneling information to McDonald.

O'Donnell had struck hard at McDonald by "cleaning out" the Armory Station of a gang of professional bail bondsmen after one of them, George Eager, offered him a $5,000 bribe.[15] During Hickey's reign as police chief, Eager furnished "straw bail" to the demimonde of the Cheyenne District and to African Americans trapped in the justice system. In these intolerant times, George Eager and Dan Webster held a virtual "monopoly" on black prisoners taken in to the Armory Station for arraignment; the shady lot of bail bondsmen who hovered around the police courts like hungry vultures drew the line if the applicant was a harlot from Cheyenne or a person of color. George Eager, once a respectable livery stable owner who sunk to the lower depths through unfortunate business reversals, handled the red-light bonding trade for McDonald. It was not widely publicized at the time, and sexual vice was counter to the grain of McDonald's Catholic upbringing. But there was profit in it, and profit always trumped piety.

After years of handing out business cards in the Biler Avenue whorehouses, George Eager was arrested by O'Donnell and charged with running a burglary and fencing gang. Mike did not bother sending Trude to the rescue; not this time, although in a half-hearted gesture, he wined and dined the grand jurors empanelled to pass judgment on Eager at a dinner party in the Store. It didn't count for much, because Eager was sentenced to two years. Before the scheduled day of imprisonment, the convicted man died in Crittenden's Road House in South Chicago of a sudden heart attack. McDonald did not attend the funeral or send flowers but filed a $200 claim against the widow, claiming the money was due him because he had been "stiffed" by George on a business loan.[16]

Losing George Eager was not a fatal setback—there were many more like him; but Simon O'Donnell was emerging as a major annoyance, in the Elmer Washburn tradition. Not long after, McDonald whispered in the mayor's ear, and O'Donnell was replaced with the snap of a finger and an official order. It was reported on November 30, 1880, that the superintendent, a senior officer in his fifties, "voluntarily resigned" his position in order to return to his previous assignment as captain of the dangerous West Side "Terror District."

"Simon as you know is a man of quiet tastes with a fondness for outdoor exercise," Harrison explained, but he wasn't fooling anyone. "He hated bother and disliked wire-pullers. He has often expressed to me his desire to get out of his present position in order to be away from the worry naturally attendant on it. It is his own free will that he should again become a captain. He will tell you so himself."[17]

Others related an entirely different story. Simon O'Donnell's letter of resignation was never made public, fueling speculation that he was driven out by McDonald. The night of O'Donnell's testimonial dinner at Burke's Hotel, Harrison tucked the letter into his lapel pocket where it would remain hidden away, because the mayor did not want it to get out that enjoying some "refreshing exercise" out in the woods was the furthest thing from the superintendent's mind. O'Donnell allegedly wrote a terse note revealing how he had been overridden and countermanded by the same unnamed wire-pullers Harrison had spoken of, and resignation was the only means of maintaining self-respect.[18]

The appointment of O'Donnell's successor was a paean to McDonald's knack for political one-upmanship. He submitted to Harrison the name of Captain William J. McGarigle of the Third Precinct—a Republican no less—as a man of impeccable credentials who was certain to please the doughty Citizens' Association and earn the mayor high praise from the silk stockings for his show of nonpartisanship. Harrison was not so sure; he favored John Bonfield, a head-cracking, law-and-order man who wielded his truncheon against suspected anarchists and trade union organizers with deadly efficiency. But McDonald was persuasive; McGarigle was a college-educated man, and he had some high and mighty notions about improving police service in Chicago, including a proposal to organize the first traffic division. "Do I need to remind you Mr. Mayor that Mac served as Elmer Washburn's private secretary, and you remember Elmer of course?" The genius of the thing rested in the irony of the situation.

Washburn's man became McDonald's man, and to no one's surprise McGarigle voiced his strong support for liberalizing the public statutes against gambling. Explaining his official position, McGarigle said, "I have all along been in favor of licensing the gamblers as the only way to regulate the evil successfully. It cannot be suppressed entirely, for men with a passion to gamble will always find means and a way to indulge it."[19]

It was a pragmatic view shared by Harrison, whose attitudes on the subject were a matter of public record. "The Eagle" was not opposed to allowing the more opulent dens to remain in business. It was the brace houses and robbers' dens, whose mission was to pick the pockets of the dinner-pail gamblers, that he so strongly opposed. In the spring of 1881, the mayor ordered all of the remaining keno dens cleaned out; the game was always considered the most dishonest of them all. Billy Skakel, the resourceful bucket shop swindler, defied the edict and stirred the mayor to action by introducing two new games, "Pique" and "Rocky Mountain Jack," a variation of keno substituting a deck of cards for the numbered balls. McDonald and the "main line" gamblers, not wishing to see their operations compromised or their patron in city hall agitated, said they did not welcome new games being introduced in Chicago and expressed support for Harrison.

The Hankins brothers, who had to defend themselves in scores of civil suits filed by "gambling widows" and out-of-town "Grangers" accusing them of cheating, did not fare well under Harrison's rule. Their choice boiled down to heeling before the mayor or relying on McDonald's pull to save them from the raiding parties. As the decade wore on, George, Jeff, and Al recognized that the time had come to divest their downtown casino holdings and turn full attention to thoroughbred racing as their primary business. The Sport of Kings was taking hold in the public conscience, and the brothers invested heavily in a stable of prizewinning thoroughbreds that would compete on the national level.

The new police chief winnowed down the list of gambling dens approved for raids to a mere handful. William McGarigle was only twenty-nine years old when he took over the reins of the scandal-ridden department. He introduced numerous procedural and administrative reforms in the next two years, but owing to his youth and political inexperience, he was a pliable tool in the hands of McDonald, who was already looking ahead to the next election and the chance to run McGarigle for sheriff. At stake was the continuing control of the bail bonding rackets and the chance to firm up his political rule countywide through a young and eager apprentice with a burning ambition to advance in public life—and by extension, advocate his viewpoints at important administrative levels within the law enforcement community.

At a meeting of the nation's police chiefs who gathered in Chicago in December 1881, McGarigle implored his colleagues to consider measures to do away with the grand jury system in the belief that "the time has come when instead of being assistance in the administration of justice it has become an obstacle of the gravest dimensions."[20] This was one of the important planks in the McDonald platform, perfectly articulated to law enforcement professionals by Mike McDonald through the Chicago superintendent.

It was already clear to the reform Democrats that McGarigle was the gambler's "Trojan Horse"—McDonald slated him to run for Cook County sheriff in the November 1882 election—a calumny against the Democratic Party, according to General Israel Newton Stiles, who assaulted his record as superintendent: "he had proved so entirely satisfactory to the criminal classes that they rallied as one man to his support."[21]

The *Inter-Ocean,* the *Journal,* and the *Tribune* likened the nomination of McGarigle to a blueprint of the coming apocalypse—the fear and paranoia that consumed the Republican press was nearly overwhelming, and their daily tirades against the bummers spread throughout the city electorate. "The sheriff's office is of special interest to every class of crime from murder to petty larceny. The bail-bond business as systematized and pursued by Mike McDonald includes the entire catalog of offenses against society, or as it might specifically be called, of one individual against another. With a sheriff of their selection, whatever his personal character, the criminals could prey upon honest folks with a degree of impunity, the remote prospect of which, even, must gladden the heart of every thief and thug in Chicago."[22]

Harrison shrewdly sensed a growing public backlash against "McDonald rule" and urged his friend and ally to withdraw McGarigle's name from the ticket—but the superintendent had already switched parties and declared himself a Democrat. "There is McGarigle," Harrison mused. "He never entertained a suspicion that he was a scoundrel until he ran for office and the newspapers informed him."[23]

Harrison believed McDonald was causing irreparable damage to the party with his advocacy for McGarigle. Ignoring the warnings, Mike took to the campaign hustings to whip up public sentiment for his man. At a Democratic ward meeting on the North Side, a brass band struck up a rousing rendition of "See the Conquering Hero Come," as McDonald entered the packed hall where he was greeted by thunderous applause. McGarigle, whom no one seemed to notice, followed close behind. Mike had grown a full beard, radiated his usual confidence, and extended his hand in friendship to all. "Gentlemen, I didn't get up to make a speech, but to treat you to beer!"[24] Within a few moments "the boys" had emptied a keg of beer and stuffed free campaign cigars into their coat pockets. While McDonald expertly worked the room speaking in calm, measured tones, his obedient candidate stood off to the side dispensing the frothy lager like an errand boy, or worse, a common Clark Street barkeep. The Republican press was taken aback by McGarigle's betrayal of the party and his subservience to Mike. They stepped up their attacks against "gang rule."

McDonald ordered each of the leading gamblers of the city to kick in a $500 campaign "donation," but there was open revolt within the ranks. Johnny Dowling, whose facial features were rearranged by the Garrity gang, said he could not in good conscience cast a vote for one such as McGarigle. There were many other bolters, particularly in the South Side immigrant Irish wards. Still, at the eleventh hour, the odds-makers favored Mike's candidate by a 2–1 margin. Seth F. Hanchett, the Republican opponent, was a Prohibitionist. It seemed inconceivable that the Germans and Irish would buck the Democracy and Mike's dictates to vote for a man opposed to their self-interests. But in a dramatic and stunning turnaround, Hanchett polled forty-nine hundred more votes than McGarigle.

The *Daily News* dismissed the boastful claims of Joseph Medill of the *Tribune* and William Penn Nixon, publisher of the *Inter-Ocean*. Each took immense personal satisfaction and 100 percent of the credit for alerting the populace to the perils of McDonald-McGarigle rule. The real story, however, unfolded in the Irish wards where the election was lost. In this hard-fought city contest, gambling and liquor took a back seat to the cause of Irish nationalism. Victor Lawson, publisher of the *Daily News*, observed that McDonald "put on the ticket a man who was tinged with the colors of the Orange men."[25] McGarigle was an Irish Protestant, hostile to the aims of the Clan-na-Gael and other secret Irish Catholic societies funneling money and arms back to the *auld sod* to fight the British.

The failed campaign was costly and unnecessary. McDonald's control over the County Board of Commissioners remained absolute, and the bail bonding rackets were never seriously threatened. His dealings with Harrison were as cordial as they would ever be—the mayor called Mike a "devilish good Democrat and a clever fellow," despite their differences of opinion.[26] But McDonald would not allow McGarigle, a political tenderfoot, to retreat to private life without pushing him back to the well one more time. It was his ornery determination that his amiable young friend from the North Side should achieve national stature in Democratic politics through his machinations. The cost of "moving up" would be prohibitively high, and like so many others who fell under Mike's spell, McGarigle would pay dearly for the privilege.

$$\sim 9 \sim$$

Oyster on the Half Shell

In NOVEMBER 1884, THE SKIN GAMES AND BUCKET SHOP INVEST-
ment swindles practiced by the Clark Street bunko men answering to Mike
McDonald reached the Oval Office in the White House. The exposure of a
gigantic confidence game was so infamous in its design and execution by a
gang of remorseless Chicago "sharpers" that it made midnight burglary look
respectable by comparison.

The investment scam was alternately known as "Fund W" or "Fund K,"
depending on the plan selected by the duped victims from across the United
States and around the world who sent in their nickels, dimes, and dollars to
"the firm of Fleming and Merriam" at the "Public Grain and Stock Exchange,"
a commission business at LaSalle Street and Washington Boulevard promising
to earn a generous 15 to 30 percent monthly interest. From the spring of 1881
until the winter of 1882–83, this "mutual cooperative fund" for speculation in
the buying and selling of grain, provisions, and stocks on the Chicago Board
of Trade and the New York Stock Exchange raked in an estimated $1 million
to $8 million, depending on the source, through enticing advertising circulars
published in newspapers and distributed to the gullible "Granger" element
across rural America and overseas. More than eight thousand hopeful investors
responded to the Chicago post office box address.

Fund W was the stratagem of William W. Miller, a Chicagoan peripherally
connected to the London banking and brokerage firm of Field and Company.
Convicted of chattel mortgage loan fraud in 1872, Miller served his time and
then took in one John Fleming as a junior partner with Frank L. Loring, whose
brother Dan was a wheelhorse in New York State Republican politics and an
intimate of President Chester Alan Arthur. At first, enough dividends were
paid to investors to allay public suspicions and encourage further investment.

But postal inspectors in Chicago, overwhelmed by the volume of the incoming mail, shut down the operation until the legitimacy of the enterprise could be properly established.

Before the ink on the first indictment was dry, William Miller fled to Canada. The London firm he was connected to had already failed, and with it, $100,000 of Miller's cut that was on deposit from Fund W disappeared. Miller's wife finagled a promise of immunity for her husband if he would come back and give state's evidence against Loring and Fleming. An agreement was reached, and the two conspirators were arraigned. Back in Chicago, Mike McDonald was named in the proceeding as someone who was central to the scheme and who had lent support to the defendants, but he somehow managed to wriggle free from an indictment. Unfazed, Mike provided surety for Frank Loring and retained top legal counsel to act on his behalf. Loring was, after all, a fellow New Yorker and someone to reckon with because of his brother's important political connections back East.

The case went before Judge Henry W. Blodgett of the U.S. District Court for Northern Illinois in November 1883. Emery Storrs led for the defense, and his pleas were eloquent and impassioned. It was the Post Office, he charged, that was the guilty party. No one would have lost a dime if the government had not suspended the business. Judge Blodgett, whose integrity was called into question for other rulings in his capacity as a member of the federal bench, raised eyebrows with his show of sympathy for the defendants. His attitude was peculiar, and it stirred talk in judicial circles. Back in 1877, Blodgett was a "law and order" man who did not hesitate to sentence Anton Hesing and "Buffalo" Miller to prison for their roles in the Whiskey Ring frauds.

But in the Fund W diversions involving the theft of far greater sums of money, he let Loring and Fleming off with a meager $500 fine and a term of imprisonment in the Cook County jail of twelve months—or until the defendant's fines were paid in full. There was understandable outrage in the reform camp—and complaints from Loring's friends and family who had expected that there would be *no* jail time.

A clique of prominent New York "machine" Republicans who drank and socialized and brokered political appointments with President Arthur when he controlled patronage as collector of the Port of New York City monitored the proceedings and attempted to intervene on behalf of Loring. They wanted nothing less than a full pardon for their bosom pal, and to these ends they dispatched Mike Cregan, the short, stocky, sunburnt political boss from New York City's Sixteenth Assembly District to Chicago to enlist McDonald in the scheme. Cregan checked into the Grand Pacific Hotel but spent much of his time wining and dining at the Store and at McDonald's abode on Ashland Boulevard. Although they represented separate political parties that were, in theory, philosophically opposed, Cregan and McDonald were of the same mind politically. Both were kingmakers and kindred spirits, and they struck up an immediate friendship.

In October, Mike traveled to Niagara Falls ostensibly to visit his boyhood home and rekindle some favorite boyhood memories. It was the first time in two years McDonald had ventured outside of Chicago, but the matter was of the greatest urgency and demanded his involvement. Dick Crowley, a Lockport, New York, political boss, debriefed him on the situation and explained that the key to the whole thing was to circulate a petition in Chicago for Loring's pardon and to inveigle Judge Blodgett to sign it. That would tip the scales with the president, Mike was assured.

McDonald, who had some experience working the "pardon mill" on behalf of bank robber Jimmy Carroll, said the matter would be quickly and quietly disposed of. Defense attorney William C. Goudy visited Blodgett, who unhesitatingly affixed his signature to the document. The envelope was sealed and turned over to Mike, who proceeded on to New York City, where he checked into the Fifth Avenue Hotel to plot strategy and take in the attractions of the town. There he met up with Barney Biglin, a political chair-warmer from the Eighteenth Assembly District who held a fat contract worth a $100,000 a year with the commissioners of immigration, and Dan Loring, who boasted of his "influence" with Arthur, recalling in visceral detail the roistering good times enjoyed at the president's Lexington Avenue residence when "Chet" was still just "one of the boys" and could eat and drink any man under the table.[1] The three political fixers, no strangers to the wages of sin and the attending dangers in the "rialto" districts of their respective cities, ventured into the Bowery to tour the saloons and consort with the dance hall slatterns of this vice-ridden "Strand." Tipsy and bleary-eyed from too much drink, McDonald fell prey to a thug of the New York underworld inside one of the Bowery hellholes and was relieved of a small pouch of diamonds he carried with him for safekeeping.[2]

Escaping with his life intact, but his dignity badly bruised, McDonald returned to Chicago to get the petition drive going. He called in his chips and secured the signature of Potter Palmer, Chicago's famous hotel man and the reigning "king" of Chicago society who was known to host Democratic caucuses and high-stakes poker games for the "boys" in his guest rooms. Palmer was owed substantial money on a property leased to Loring, and he reasoned that the only way he could recover what was due him was through Loring's release. Former mayor John Rice and a host of other luminaries, including Judge Blodgett—the key to the whole thing—all followed suit, although Mayor Harrison would take no part. Relations were becoming increasingly strained between the two powerful Democrats. Harrison laid it on the line to McDonald and ordered him to make the hard choice: to pursue a career in politics or to continue on with parlor house gambling, but not both. The Eagle was showing signs of open revolt against gambler rule.

Harrison said he would not tolerate the gamblers' antics much longer—although he never refused a campaign donation from them either. "Why, a gambler votes with his money," Harrison told a reporter. "If I refuse their money they withhold their votes. I accept their money, get their votes, and after the election return their money. I want their votes, not their money."[3]

In an interview with McDonald, the Chicago correspondent of the *Kansas City Times* reported that Mike was considering bowing out of the game. In a discouraged tone, he said he was contemplating a move into a Michigan Avenue mansion (although he chose the West Side). "I am getting pretty well along and my children are growing up about me," Mike said in a moment of self-reflection. "I have noted that nine-tenths of the gamblers who stick to the game die in their houses. I don't intend that any man should point me out in the street in rags and say, 'There goes Mike McDonald the gambler.'"[4] More likely, the statement was an example of his habit of baiting the press at opportune moments; the time was not yet right to fold up the Store, the satellite gambling dens, or the bonding business. There was still good money in them, but his desire to move up in the world and associate with a better class of people was an underlying ambition.

Very much enticed by the prospect of a private audience with the president, Mike raced back to New York in November to present the petition to his new friends and anxiously await the inevitable summons from the White House. The "boys" did not have long to wait. Continuing on to Washington, Loring, McDonald, and Cregan were escorted from the Willard Hotel to the White House and presented to President Arthur and Attorney General Benjamin Brewster. The meeting lasted nearly a half-hour. Pleasantries were exchanged and reminiscences of old political battles were recalled as Arthur studied the petition and found it to be in good order. He signed his name, and the two swindlers whose elaborate "Ponzi scheme" was among the most audacious frauds of the late nineteenth century were set free. Back home, the *Tribune* was outraged. Not sure whether he should censure the Republican president, Joseph Medill prudently checked the impulse to excoriate the party's standard-bearer, choosing to lambaste McDonald's cant instead. "It must have been a novel experience for the Chicago gambler, bondsman, jury fixer, and bunko steerers' companion. Thus to find himself transferred from his den of rascality to the private audience room of the Chief Executive of the nation." The next day, Medill vented his anger in another editorial:

Mike McDonald is a great power in Chicago. He has become very rich. Like the octopus, his tentacles reach out in unexpected directions, and seize unsuspecting victims. Mike McDonald works through others and rarely shows his own hand. The others constitute "the gang." They make up the [political nominating] conventions, furnish the votes, stuff the ballot boxes, do the "fine work," endure the curses of the community and stand the occasional trials which come up in the courts. Mike McDonald himself is never reached. His hand never appears. He holds no office and wants none. He prefers to be the "Warwick" of the corrupt Aldermen, County Commissioners, and Judges. He seeks his reward in money, not in honors. His love of power is more gratified by conscious exercise thereof than by ostentatious display. He desires that his agents shall have full credit for all the mischief that is done while he enjoys the profits. He is loyal to them as long as it pays him to be so. When there is any revolt against his dominion he knows a way to bring the refractory spirits to their senses.[5]

How much of a fee (or other considerations) Mike received for his services by the New Yorkers cannot be ascertained, but the pardons racket opened up fresh new opportunities. Before he could turn it into a new revenue stream and a decided advantage on the national level, however, an open revolt broke out within the ward organizations of the Cook County Democratic Party. It was during Harrison's second term, in 1883, when the first serious breach in the Democratic alliance occurred between the mayor, a faction of independents, and the McDonald "machine." Joseph Mackin, the debonair ballot-box stuffer asserting his political muscle, expected to be appointed the mayor's private secretary in return for helping to "defray" the expenses of the 1883 reelection campaign through gambler money. The "Oyster" was sorely disappointed when the position went to someone else, but McDonald was more annoyed by the corresponding loss of patronage. Mackin, who personally had little to fear from Harrison's administration because he was secretary of all of the powerful party committees, began operating the "machine" to the mayor's detriment.

Apprehensive of McDonald—Mike was gaining prestige on the national level, and the ward leaders looked up to him and not city hall for their marching orders—Harrison, probably sensing his own vulnerabilities, looked with favor upon William P. Whelan, a former altar boy and popular Madison Street barkeep everyone knew as the "Mockingbird" because of his set of "golden pipes." Harrison quietly encouraged Whelan to battle Joe Mackin for a First Ward aldermanic seat with the intention of giving the "McDonald-Mackin-Trude Machine," as it was now called, its comeuppance. The Mockingbird was no reformer and did not pretend to be, but he agreed to run as an "Independent Democrat," enlisting the support of the good-government people against Mackin, a man the mayor so thoroughly despised.

Mackin and McDonald called the young upstart the "Fat Boy of the First." "I want to show the political tramp Mackin that the 'Fat Boy' has got something of a pull here!" Whelan fired back.[6]

At first, Harrison used diplomacy to inveigle Joe Mackin to withdraw his candidacy, but when that tack failed, McDonald was summoned to the private chambers. In forcible language intended to bring McDonald to terms, the mayor ordered him to oust Mackin at once or face reprisals. McDonald's active support of Mackin offended and infuriated Harrison, and when Mike took no immediate action, the mayor made good on his threats and ordered the new police chief, Austin J. Doyle, to raid the gambling dives "up and down the line." Police wagons were quickly filled with roulette wheels and various paraphernalia from the "tiger's lair" and thrown into a hot furnace at the Des Plaines Street station. The value of the destroyed materials was pegged at $8,000. Summoned from his West Side home to provide bond for the arrested gamblers, McDonald's buggy pulled up in front of headquarters where the reporters were waiting for him. "What do you think of it?" asked a *Times* man.

"I don't know anything about it!" Mike shot back. "I was at home attending to my little boy who is sick with diphtheria when word came over that I was wanted downtown, as there might be some young fellow I would have to bail out. I suppose that it is First Ward politics. It is a way that the Mayor has got to get even with Joe Mackin for his opposition. He raided everything in which he thought I had a moneyed interest. I don't own a gambling house and don't know anybody who does.

"The raiding of a few insignificant gambling houses—what does it amount to?" he wondered, trying to downplay the seriousness of the situation. "It is an exemplification of Chicago politics, and it is not connected with either party. It don't hurt me so I have nothing to say."[7]

But it *was* an expensive problem for the gamblers, a *very* expensive one. Whenever Mackin showed aggression and turned the resources of the machine against Harrison, a raid was ordered and then another. Torn between personal loyalty to Joe and practical considerations—the protection of the Store and the other establishments of the mainline "sports" from further harassment, for example—McDonald had no choice but to pressure the "Oyster" to give it up.

The day before the spring 1884 aldermanic election, Mackin sullenly withdrew from the race rather than see Mike continue to suffer financial setbacks because of Harrison's vindictive actions.[8] The field was left wide-open to "Mockingbird" Whelan, who entered the council pledged to fight McDonald's machine by embracing the agenda of a handful of men who had the courage to stand up to him. One of them was John Gelder, a Second Ward reformer or "kicker," as his breed of Democrat was termed, who had spoken out against McDonald rule in the council halls of the party one too many times.

The fight between the machine and the "kickers" escalated to an ugly street brawl when McDonald spied Gelder and his young son walking slowly past the Store one bright June afternoon in the 1884 election season. According to Gelder, McDonald, who stood on the sidewalk, called him over. "I understand you have been abusing me," he said in a threatening tone.

"I don't know that I have said anything that I did not have a right to say," Gelder retorted. "If you set yourself up as a political leader, you must expect somebody to take the opposite and talk about you. If I have said anything I had no right to say I am a man of property—you have your recourse."

"I don't care anything about your property!" snapped McDonald. "If you say anything more about me I'll cut your ears off!"

Gelder shook his head, muttered a few words and walked away. Enraged, McDonald pounced upon the Second Ward man, knocked him to the ground, and repeatedly kicked him in the midsection. The scrap, although a brief one, attracted a large crowd. The throng cheered lustily—Mike was known to them; Gelder was an outsider. Mike's official version, told to the police, varied significantly from Gelder's account. [9]

"I had just driven up to my place with my wife and boy when Gelder, the little rat, who was standing on the corner, was pointed out to me as the man who had been roasting me in the Second Ward meetings. I went up to him and asked him what he meant by it, telling him that I lived on the West Side and wanted the Second Ward to let me alone. Gelder got his back up at once and reached into his pistol pocket and declared that he would use my name wherever and whenever he pleased," McDonald explained. "With that I slapped his face and as he turned to run away I helped him along with a kick in the fleshy portion of his pantaloons." [10]

McDonald, by virtue of his money and his associations, neither feared arrest, a criminal indictment, or lawsuits from injured parties. He was an intemperate man; violent and easily provoked. He cared not a wit about the consequences of flashing his famous temper or the usual press censure certain to follow, because the cops were compliant and as a rule the victims of these vicious, unprovoked street brawls elected not to sue for damages. They had no leverage with the corrupt bluecoats and even less in the police courts.

In a fierce intraparty political scrap, such as the one that unfolded in 1884, McDonald counted on the loyal support of his machine men. Gelder and the other "kickers" were easily shouted down and outmaneuvered in boisterous party caucuses held at the Palmer House and the ward meeting halls. A witness to the proceedings summed it up thus: "After the smoke of battle has cleared away you'll find that Mike is at the old stand and as strong as ever. He may not be in the whiskey business, because he has his stone quarries and real estate to look after, but he will be the same politically; always sticking to his friends and favoring the best candidate." [11]

Sensing Mayor Harrison's growing disaffection with the machine and his friendly overtures to the "kickers," Mike considered Mackin's sage advice to aid him in "putting the old man in his place." McDonald's rumblings to the press indicated that he was of a mind to punish Carter Harrison for his treachery. Boasting of his abilities as a kingmaker, McDonald told a *Herald* reporter, "Lots of fellows come along here going to City Hall, and slapping me on the shoulder, they say, 'Mike, you made him, and you can down him.' If the Mayor thinks he can make me call Mackin off he is mistaken, because I am willing to spend both time and money for my friends."[12] Privately, Mike much preferred peaceful relations to a political war with the mayor. The challenge he faced was reigning in Harrison's ambition to build a legacy at the expense of those cherished friends from the saloon trade and faro banks of Gambler's Alley.

To the extent that Michael Cassius McDonald and Joseph Chesterfield Mackin emerged as the de facto rulers of Chicago politics in 1884, the record suggests that Mike's braggadocio was not far from the truth. Mackin's mission to Washington, D.C., in February to secure the national nominating convention for Chicago offered further proof.

With the Cook County Democratic Club and the grafting members of the county "boodle board"—"Little" Van Pelt, Mike Leyden, and Mike Wasserman— in tow, Mackin and the "boys" pledged to the party committees the full support of the McDonald machine to Samuel Tilden over New York governor Grover Cleveland. Tammany boss John Kelly hated Cleveland, and the Chicago political underworld was sympathetic to the aims of the New Yorkers and pledged support. But due to the various infirmities of advancing age, Tilden wrote a letter to the delegation advising of his intention not to be a candidate. In a weakened field, Kelly cast his lot with Senator Thomas F. Bayard of Delaware, a noted Bourbon politician.

On the eve of the convention in Chicago's Interstate Industrial Building (the "Glass Palace"), the divided factions of the Illinois State Democratic Party huddled in Peoria to select their delegates and the delegates at large. The enemies of the McDonald-Mackin coalition did everything in their power to defeat the machine, but they were outflanked. Carter Harrison coveted the role of delegate-at-large, but he was opposed by both machine politician and "silk stocking." McDonald, representing the Third District, shrewdly dangled a ticket to the convention before Harrison as a bargaining chip. He saw it as his best chance to mend fences.

Alfred Trude; William McGarigle; Judge Prindiville; "Little" Van Pelt; Johnny "de Pow" Powers, a newcomer from the immigrant wards of the teeming Near West Side, loyal to the machine; Jim Hildreth, back from Canada and returned to his city council seat—all of the important McDonald factotums were on hand to support Mike and draft the party's official position on tariffs and foreign affairs—dry, but weighty matters they knew little about. But the preservation of federal patronage was a key issue on everyone's mind, and familiar ground to these wizened Chicago ward bosses.

Mayor Harrison, unhappily positioned in the minority, was touted for governor or possibly senator by a splinter faction of "kickers" who recognized his popularity and strength among the electorate. A crack in the door opened for

"The Eagle," and he said he would be receptive to a change of address to Spring-field or Washington "if the boys were willing" to back him. Mackin, stood in the way. He was less conciliatory to the old man than McDonald, and with a few whisperings made to the downstate Democrats, Joe Mackin checked Carter Harrison's budding candidacy for the Senate at the door.

The gubernatorial slot was still open, but Harrison was an economic protec-tionist, and the party platform, as it was drawn up by Mackin and McDonald, was linked to free trade and strong opposition to tariffs placed on foreign goods. Harrison's ambition to win a Senate seat was thwarted, but the Peoria legislative caucus went ahead and slated him for governor anyway—likely knowing the election was unwinable. Illinois had not elected a Democratic governor since Joel Aldrich Matteson in 1853, but Mackin reasoned that either way he would come out ahead in the bargain. If the old man won it, it would remove him from Chicago and allow Joe to "spread his wings" in city hall. If Harrison lost, he would be diminished politically, or so Mackin envisioned.[13]

Mike was soaring to the apex of his influence and political power. He played a winning hand and appeased Joe, his friends, and his foes masterfully. He gave his place as delegate-at-large to Harrison and took for himself the honor of being an alternate-at-large. Much pleased with his sabotage against Harrison, Mackin was appointed a district delegate to the convention and a state com-miteeman-at-large. All the important district battles were won by the machine. "That Mackin, Mike and the machine had everything their own way the result of the convention shows," commented the *Tribune,* cautioning anyone "who would underrate the organizing capacity, the corralling ability, and the execu-tive talent of Joseph Chesterfield when backed by Michael Cassius."[14]

The ride back home aboard the nine-car Chicago and Alton Railway "Chi-cago Special" was a star-spangled Fourth of July hoopla. "The boys had little sleep during the night; a number of them red-eyed—soiled plug hats, and here and there a bottle of Peoria sour mash," one reporter observed with a hint of sarcasm. "At Joliet they marched through the town. The penitentiary was pointed out to them, but none of the boys recalled having seen it before. The kickers of the [Cook County Democratic] Club, including the 'Mockingbird' who were on the train, had apparently forgotten that they had been kicked out of the convention, for the crowd was good-natured throughout and no rows were reported."[15] Gilded Age politics in Chicago was four-fifths bluster and one part burlesque.

Mike McDonald, treasurer of the Cook County Democratic Party.
Chicago History Museum.

Mike McDonald's "Store" and the Palace European Hotel, northwest corner of Clark and Monroe Streets, 1880s. Chicago History Museum, ICHi-21715.

Tree-lined Ashland Boulevard, looking south from Adams Street, c. 1900. McDonald's mansion stood at the northeast corner of Congress and Ashland. Chicago History Museum, ICHi9852.

THE TIGER'S PREY.

Shall MIKE McDONALD Rule the COUNTY as well as the CITY?

CHICAGO. PHOTO   W.Y.BARNET. DES.

McDonald depicted as a predatory "Tammany Tiger," crushing Mayor Harrison and the chief of police under the weight of his political power, which extends from City Hall to the Cook County building. The tiger also symbolizes the game of faro. Lithograph, c. 1883. Courtesy of James Conway, Aah! Rare Chicago.

Anton Casper Hesing, who spearheaded the People's Party's opposition to Sunday closings and the temperance movement in 1873, was the influential publisher of the *Staats-Zeitung* newspaper. Chicago History Museum, ICHi59199.

Alfred S. Trude, McDonald's attorney and confidant for over thirty years. Chicago History Museum, DN-0068252. Photographer: *Chicago Daily News.*

Mayor Monroe Heath, who succeeded Harvey Colvin in 1877, fought a losing battle against Mike McDonald and the gambling fraternity. Chicago History Museum, ICHi24444.

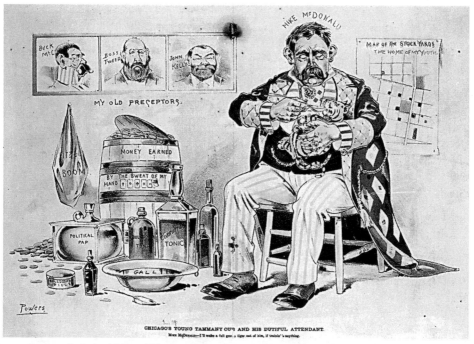

Cartoon depicting McDonald feeding Chicago's young "Tammany Cub," representing the Chicago syndicate that was modeled after New York City's Tammany Hall organization. Chicago History Museum, ICHi11659.

Seventh Ward Alderman "Foxy" Ed Cullerton, powerful chairman of the City Council Finance Committee, who kept getting elected by large pluralities despite accusations of fraud and graft. Author's Collection.

Studio portrait of Mayor Carter Henry Harrison, 1893. Chicago History Museum, ICHi20086.

MICKY MACKIN

Incidents in His Public and Private
Career Portrayed with Pen
and Pencil.

His Progress from the Barroom to the
Position of Champion "Smooth-
Worker."

The Transition from Serving an Oyster
with a Drink to Wholesale Bal-
lot-Boxing.

Cartoons lampooning the career of "Oyster Joe" Mackin, professional barkeep, master politician, McDonald's secretary, and ballot-box stuffer. From *Chicago Tribune,* December 28, 1884. © 2009 *Chicago Tribune.* All rights reserved. Used by permission.

Chicago City Hall and Cook County Building, c. 1886, which was plagued by cost overruns and shabby construction—but produced more boodle for the gang. Author's Collection.

John "Little" Van Pelt (*left*) and Cook County Hospital Warden William McGarigle, convicted ringleaders of the 1883–87 Cook County "Boodle Board" of Commissioners. Author's Collection.

High-living Harry "Prince Hal" Varnell,
gambler, proprietor of the "Turf Exchange"
saloon on Clark Street, and warden of
the Cook County Asylum at Dunning.
Author's Collection.

Billy "the Clock" Skakel
(1843–1925), Chicago gambler,
politician, stock speculator,
and "bucket shop" proprietor.
Courtesy of Dorman Nelson.

Alderman John Powers, boodle
politician of the Nineteenth Ward and
McDonald's city council ally. Chicago
History Museum, DN-0072434.

DeWitt Clinton Cregier,
twenty-sixth mayor of
Chicago, 1889–91.
Author's Collection.

McDonald's Lake Street elevated line looking west. Chicago History Museum, DN-0004591.

Hempstead Washburne, twenty-seventh mayor of Chicago, 1891–92, closed the Garfield Park Racetrack and fought McDonald in court. Chicago History Museum, ICHi23786.

15th Ward

Altgeld

Democracy

meets

Every Night

at 8 o'clock
at

1509

Milwaukee Avenue.

Every Citizen favoring
the building up of a
progressiveDemocracy
invited to join.

John P. Altgeld

Mass Meeting

on Friday, March 17th, at 8 P. M.

Wendel's Large Hall, 1504 Milwaukee Ave.

The Intellectual and Fearless

CLARENCE S. DARROW

will speak. Also **WALTER F. COOLING,**

Editor of the "Municipal Ownership Bulletin"

Jacob Engenthran   A. T. Johnson   I. W. Hicks

Geo. Hankel, Union Printer, 418-420 Dearborn St.

John Peter Altgeld's gubernatorial campaign poster, 1892. Clarence Darrow, an assistant corporation counsel under Mayor Cregier, helped McDonald direct Altgeld's run for governor. Chicago History Museum, ICHi27038.

The mansion on Drexel Boulevard acquired by Mike McDonald in 1898.
United Press International Photo.

Webster Guerin, the young artist McDonald's second wife, Dora, was accused of murdering. Chicago History Museum, DN-0004681.

The pearl-handled revolver Webster Guerin gave to Dora McDonald, with which he was killed. Chicago History Museum, DN-0004683.

Mike McDonald (*right*) and his son Guy during the 1907 murder inquest.
Chicago History Museum, DN-0005145.

McDonald (*right*) arrives at the jail to see his wife, Dora, arrested on suspicion of murder.
Chicago History Museum, ICHi21714.

Dora Feldman
McDonald
in court, 1907.
Chicago History
Museum, DN-0052222.

Webster Guerin's relatives leaving court: Ben (*left*) and Archie Guerin, Webster's brothers; and Avis Dargan, Archie's fiancée. The boys' aunt, Nellie Fitzgibbons, stands behind Ben's right shoulder. Chicago History Museum, DN-0052227.

Attorney (and future U.S. senator) James Hamilton Lewis, who defended Dora in her trial for murder. Chicago History Museum, DN-0052240.

Archie Guerin, who was browbeaten by defense attorney Lewis during cross-examination, went to work for Lewis not long after the trial. Chicago History Museum, DN-0052253.

Mary Noonan Grasshoff, the first Mrs. McDonald, returned to Chicago in 1907 to lay claim to her late husband's fortune. *Chicago History Museum, DN-0005338.*

$\sim$ 10 $\sim$

Boodle for the Gang

THE HOT AND SULTRY WEATHER FAILED TO DAMPEN THE ENTHU-
siasm of the visiting Democratic delegations that descended upon Chicago in
early July 1884 to nominate their party's candidate for president. A. T. Andreas
reported that the festivities "far outrivaled the Republican gathering in point of
excitement, enthusiasm, fireworks; the noise of the brass bands and the speeches
of agitators who endeavored to control local feeling."[1]

The drama, the pageantry, the intensity, and the utter unpredictability of
nineteenth-century political conventions greatly overshadow what the modern-
day American electorate has come to expect from the political process. Today
a national nominating convention is essentially a coronation; an anticlimax
to months of state caucuses and primaries where the outcomes are fought and
determined long before the final roll-call of the state delegations.

In the days of Mike McDonald, the routines of daily living in the big cities
were temporarily suspended by the spectacle of democracy at work. The great
national issues of the day, for example, tariff protectionism versus free trade, or
the debate over a national civil service, were dry and mostly incidental to the
man or woman on the street, compared to the excitement of marching bands and
the appearance of elegantly tailored delegates in silken headwear, waistcoats,
and flashing campaign badges and battle ribbons proudly signifying their membership in a club of partisans whose allegiance was with this or that candidate.
The electoral season was the Fourth of July and the arrival of the traveling circus,
all rolled into one. It was the colorful bunting from the cornices of the Palmer
House, the Tremont, and the Grand Pacific Hotels; catchy slogans, bombastic
oratory, villainous satire, fireworks lighting up the evening sky—and with the
Democrats in session—free-flowing beer and whiskey for all.

The arrival of 750 delegates, friends, and members of Tammany Hall at the Lake Shore depot on July 6, festooned in their white hats and red sashes, brought out a crowd of several thousand fired-up partisans who lined the streets to catch a glimpse of these well-known political celebrities. At the front of the column, Mike McDonald and Carter Harrison proudly marched arm-in-arm with Tammany Grand Sachem John Kelly and Senator Thomas F. Grady.[2]

Amid the lusty cheers of men and women chanting "Kelly! Kelly!" there was McDonald, this rogue gambler, reveling in his high attainment as an alternate delegate to the national convention. Oh, to be recognized in such a way as this! Arguably, it was his finest hour in politics. Seated among the credentialed delegates on the convention floor, Mike drew considerable attention to himself. Upsetting established protocols, he had entered the hall with his four-year-old son Guy Cassius, fully recovered from his recent bout of diphtheria and dressed up in a muslin waist suit with a big Cook County badge pinned to the lapel. Mike deposited the boy on the stenographer's table near the Illinois delegation. The young prince was doted upon by the wives of the prominent Democrats and praised for his all-around "good behavior" by the *Tribune,* adding that the lad was the objective point of "25,000 pairs of eyes. The pretty child is all unconscious of the situation he is producing or the blushes and mortification that later years must certainly bring."[3]

The *Inter-Ocean* located the gambler-politician "lean[ing] up against the Arkansas banner looking at the revered gentlemen. He was arrayed in a natty suit of fine blue broadcloth and his small, delicately shaped hands looked as though the manicure had but shortly finished them. Mike looked more like the rector of a swell Episcopalian church than the proprietor of a gambling den."[4]

Indeed, it would have taken all the inducements of an Episcopalian minister to arbitrate the raging party disputes among the Illinois delegates. But such a man was not available. Carter Harrison, recalcitrant and disagreeable as ever, arose from his chair to attack the free-trade plank and moved to strike. But he was heckled and shouted down by his fellow Illinoisans, and his support of Grover Cleveland was bitterly assailed. However, Harrison was a wily old political hand with a few tricks to play on Tammany and McDonald's faction who were philosophically opposed to Cleveland's candidacy. The mayor told no one that he had secretly agreed to second the nomination of the New York governor. Hours before the nominating speeches commenced, Harrison allegedly ordered the Chicago police to pack the galleries with every sympathetic Cleveland man that could be pulled off the streets. The mayor did not want to risk hearing the catcalls and jeers of the Tammany holdouts and others when the moment came to ratify Cleveland's nomination. Holes large enough for men to slip through into the hall were bored into sections of the building. The Tammanyites, no strangers to this kind of political trickery, accused the Chicagoans of hustling hundreds of paid "ringers" into the Exposition Building.

"I heard that Chicago enterprise *did* cut a hole," Harrison concèded, "and probably a dozen got in but our police checked it. I promised fair dealing. I meant it, and our people are carrying it out." Few were convinced of the Eagle's sincerity, but the effect of his intrigue was remarkable. Cleveland's nomination was greeted by thunderous applause. Support for the other candidates, especially among the Western delegations, melted away. "They love Cleveland for his character but they love him also for the enemies he has made!" exclaimed Edward Bragg of Wisconsin, shooting a glance toward the Tammany men.[5]

McDonald sensed that Cleveland, hated by Kelly's supporters who viewed him as an enemy Orangeman, was likely to withhold his patronage appointments as punishment to all who continued to oppose him. Further resistance was futile after the New York delegation bolted from the Kelly camp. McDonald realized that in order to salvage patronage he would have to move his Illinois men into the Cleveland column. There was simply too much riding on the outcome to do otherwise.

The national election, pitting the dour but pragmatic New York governor against the former Republican secretary of state, James G. Blaine, dubbed the "continental liar from the State of Maine" by his many foes, was memorable for its mud-slinging and the intense passions both candidates stirred among voters. The smart money was on Cleveland, and the pool sellers along Clark Street and Gambler's Alley were finding it hard to clock bets on election night. "The facts are the boys who drink also bet," said one bookmaker, "and they have all got their money upon the election. The boys have put up about all they have and are now standing around with their hands in empty pockets."[6]

A procession of Democratic supporters tramped past McDonald's Store and the nearby Iroquois Club—a Tammany-style political headquarters—hoisting an effigy of Blaine in the air. The gamblers lit firecrackers and "shooting rockets" and stationed a corner player atop a building portico playing "We'll Hang Jim Blaine on a Sour Apple Tree," and "Marching through Georgia," to the delight of the festive masses. It would require another two full days of waiting before Grover Cleveland could be reliably certified as the victor. Locally, Harrison was spurned by Illinois voters in favor of the Republican, Richard Oglesby. "I have never cared about being the governor," Harrison said. "Whatever interest I feel is therefore in Cleveland's success."[7]

Nettled and highly displeased by the party's preference, McDonald called his fellow Democrats a bunch of "dough heads" and "fossilized specimens." Cleveland, he said, was a "cold, close, tight-fisted man. It is a shame," he added, "that with the talent in the Democratic Party it could not get anything better than a 'hangman' to carry the standard. If there is anything an Irishman detests next to an Englishman it is a hangman. There is an old word in the original Irish—or Celtic, or Gaelic or whatever you may choose to call it—that means hangman. It is the most opprobrious epithet that one Irishman can apply to the other, and, of course it is invested with a peculiar significance in connection with this campaign. Blaine gathered in the Irish at a great rate. The selection of Cleveland was very unfortunate."[8]

It was equally opprobrious—and politically damaging to McDonald—to vent his disgust to the one Chicago newspaper closely monitored by the party men in Washington. His unfortunate remarks tested the patience of the incoming president, who read the *Tribune* dispatches from Chicago. Cleveland's first few months in office would be consumed by an endless stream of office seekers and political spoilsmen descending upon the capital pursuing payback in the form of job appointments. Each delegation had its own short list of loyal party men to present to the chief executive for consideration. Experience and competency counted for very little, because in nineteenth-century politics, to the victor belonged the spoils. Would Cleveland finally break with tradition and choose qualified men?

The Iroquois Club and the machine men traveled to the capital to attend the inaugural and celebrate the victory of the first Democrat to claim the White House since James Buchanan. Although he had called the president a "dough head" and a "hangman," McDonald counted on receiving his just due with the elevation of William McGarigle to U.S. marshal of the Northern District of Illinois, Alderman John Colvin to collector of the Internal Revenue, and whatever leftovers there were going to Joe Mackin to dispense as he pleased. McGarigle's candidacy, Mike asserted, was supported by six out of ten Illinois congressmen, and Mac was a member of the Iroquois Club in good standing and a marshal in the Cook County Democratic Club.

"I think Mr. Cleveland is a machine man from the crown of his head to the soles of his feet," Mike confidently boasted to a reporter inside the Willard Hotel, where only a few months earlier he had registered as a guest prior to his meeting with President Arthur. "He believes that a party without a machine is simply a mob. This is going to be a machine administration for the president is surrounded by machine men—[Daniel] Manning and all the rest of them."[9] When asked if a grateful administration would likely remember him, Mike modestly replied, "I don't want anything sir, of any description. Moreover I am out of politics and am going to tend strictly to my own business. I had a friend once who got quite well-to-do in just that way."[10]

The "McDonald machine," represented in Washington by "Little" Van Pelt, Congressman Frank Lawler, Johnny Corcoran, and Aldermen Hildreth and Cullerton, lobbied hard for McGarigle's appointment and carried on the fight for the next two months. It was a remarkable expenditure of time, energy, and money on behalf of just one man, and it raises a question about how far Mike reasonably expected to advance the Cook County Hospital warden in public life, or more importantly, *why?* A friendly U.S. marshal would benefit McDonald's bail bonding business and discourage forfeitures, always a costly business risk.

The Chicago "dough heads"—the antimachine men of a reformist bent—feared that McGarigle's appointment was a prelude to a more sinister possibility: McGarigle for U.S. attorney general.

Mindful of the stakes, Seventh Ward alderman "Honest" John Comiskey, father of the future founder and president of the Chicago White Sox baseball team, rushed to the White House to warn the president. "When I heard Lawler tell the President that the Democrats of the Northern District would be disappointed and broken-hearted if McGarigle was not appointed Sheriff, I bought my ticket and came to Washington to tell the President that there were some good Democratic hearts in Illinois that would not break if he turned his back upon the gang. I am convinced the President will make no mistake," Comiskey predicted.[11]

On the theory that one could not draw clean water from a dirty well, Cleveland heeded the advice of the dough heads and named a political unknown, Frederick Marsh, sheriff of Ogle County, as U.S. marshal. Howls of protest emanated from the political saloons and city hall over the appointment of a "hayseed" and an Englishman no less![12] "From a narrow, partisan point of view, the Republicans would have reason to rejoice over the appointment of McGarigle or some such member of the gang," commented the *Tribune*. "It would have been a notice that the Administration is in sympathy with the tough element of the Democratic Party in Chicago—the crowd led by Harrison, Van Pelt, Lawler, Hildreth, Ward, Colvin, Cullerton, Mike McDonald, Mackin, and so on. But this party advantage would have been gained at a serious cost in placing the United States Marshal's office under the control of a corrupt political cabal."[13] President Cleveland spurned political machines in Ohio and Indiana in his selection of office holders. According to historian Geoffrey Blodgett, when a German American leader called for fewer appointments of Irish Americans, Cleveland appointed more Germans.[14]

As the names of Mackin and McGarigle circulated among lobbyists and spoilsmen making the rounds of the capital trolling for high-level appointments, back home these two loyal McDonald henchmen were already under fire for fraud and corruption. The first to fall was "Oyster" Joe Mackin for illegally influencing the outcome of the 1884 Sixth District state senatorial contest pitting the Democrat Rudolf Brand, president of the Brand Beer Brewing Company and a powerhouse within the liquor trade associations, against the Republican opponent, attorney Henry W. Leman, no friend of the saloon owner or the liquor lobby. A Brand victory would have assured Democratic control of the thirty-fourth General Assembly and a golden opportunity to select the Democratic successor to General John A. Logan, the outgoing U.S. senator.

An examination of the tally sheet in the second precinct of the Eighteenth Ward showed that after the locked ballot boxes had been delivered to the county clerk for validation, the original ballots were replaced with facsimile copies marked in favor of Brand over Leman. Mackin, a master schemer and accused ballot-box stuffer, was charged with forging the spurious tally sheet and the names of eleven election judges and clerks.

The *Daily News,* instrumental in exposing Mackin's role as the ringleader of the fraud, revealed that the bogus Eighteenth Ward ballots were printed at P. L. Hanscom's commercial printing house on Madison Street and hand-delivered to Joe at his private suite in the Palmer House. Mackin was a personal friend of Potter Palmer, who provided Joe with free bed and board. *Daily News* publisher Melville Stone, the only truly nonpartisan journalist in a highly partisan news-gathering age, swore out a warrant for Mackin's arrest and the apprehension of his three confederates, William "Black Bill" Gallagher, Henry Biehl, and Arthur Gleason—the latter serving as chief clerk of the Cook County Clerk's office. Despite forceful evidence of election fraud, the indictment against Mackin was dropped while Gleason and Gallagher were prosecuted to the fullest extent of the law before Judge Blodgett.

Although Joe squirmed out of the more serous charge of election tampering, he was indicted for perjury by a special grand jury after telling a lie about the procurement of the ballot tickets from Hanscom and Company. Mike McDonald raised a $10,000 war chest to pay the legal fees of defense counsel Emory Storrs and was a daily visitor to the Cook County Jail during the entire duration of Joe's trial. It was widely rumored McDonald would make a direct appeal to President Cleveland should the jury vote to convict.[15]

Brand was elected, but Mackin was found guilty and sentenced to five years in the Joliet Penitentiary. Gleason and Gallagher each received two years. An exhaustive appeals process followed. Mackin's case made it all the way to the U.S. Supreme Court, but the appeal failed and the prison doors slammed shut behind him. Soon after, the bill for legal services came due. "Chesterfield" Joe (he preferred to be addressed as Chesterfield) had assumed the $10,000 Mike raised in his name was enough to cover Storrs's bill. It wasn't. Just $150 was expended for that purpose. Where did the rest of the money go? McDonald used it for other matters, of course, leaving Joe's wife Clara with a terrible financial burden to bear alone.

Clara Mackin, a marvel of energy and perseverance, worked tirelessly the entire four years her husband was away petitioning public officials at every level of government. There was a surprising show of sympathy for the Mackins in their hour of need. Joe was a scoundrel but an otherwise likeable chap, and Judge Blodgett, as was quickly becoming a habit, softened his attitude toward the man he had put away. Blodgett directed a personal letter to Governor Oglesby pleading for Mackin's release, but it would require another change in the State House in order to spring Joe from his cage.

Swayed by the pleadings of Clara Mackin, Governor Joseph Fifer, a Bloomington Republican, issued a formal pardon on July 2, 1889, not long after he took office. "His perjury was purely a defense and was not destined to affect the life, liberty or property of anybody," Fifer explained.[16] The *Chicago Globe*—the Democratic news journal Mike McDonald and a consortium of partisans launched in 1888, praised the work of "Private Joe" Fifer and bestowed their usual platitudes on Mackin. "He has borne that heavy judgment manfully, and in his days of misfortune earned the respect and sympathy of all who knew him."[17]

In a more earthen tone, Joe paused to reflect on his time away. "I did my bit," he snapped. "And I don't owe the State of Illinois anything. The case cost me and my friends $1,000,000 but Joe Mackin didn't squeal. He still maintains his self-respect and can look every man in the eye."[18] The *Daily News* believed Mackin's chicanery contributed to a general improvement in polling methods and that parole was a just outcome. "Mackin will now become a good citizen. He will probably have the good sense to go quietly about his business and keep fool friends from making a show of him. Any attempt on their part to treat him as a martyr will be viewed with disgust by the public which wishes Mackin well in spite of the past."[19]

Joe returned to Chicago to catch up with old acquaintances, open a real estate business, and work for the good of the party—but with far greater discretion. Stripped of his position as secretary, Mackin was diminished politically and would never again be the same force in local politics. It was a blow to McDonald's machine and the first of a series of unfortunate and ill-timed public and private setbacks in the second half of the decade that jarred his perfect sense of order and the belief in his own political infallibility.

Mackin put on his best game face and greeted the old Clark Street gang pleasantly. He raised his stein of lager like "a good old scout"—because that is how he saw himself—but revealed nothing about the hardships put upon his wife by McDonald's underhanded withdrawal of the $10,000 defense fund. Two weeks after his release from prison, a deadbeat gambler named Peter Gabel—a heavy loser at Sy Jaynes's faro table—paid a friendly call on Joe at his office in the Temple Block. He had a proposition in mind and suggested a way for Joe to get back at McDonald for his dirty double-cross.

He said he had heard of some "corrupt treating" going on inside the city council chambers. Didn't Mackin *know* that Mike and his business associates at the Chicago City Railway Company had paid nearly $50,000 in bribes to six Chicago aldermen and another $15,000 to Mayor Harrison's corporation counsel, John P. Green, for their votes and the "right kind of opinion" to pass an ordinance granting them exclusive rights to build an elevated line along West Lake Street? "Well didn't you, Joe?"

The bribe estimate seemed suspiciously high, but Peter Gabel held to it and threatened to expose the whole rotten scheme if Mackin were only willing to provide him with the affidavits of the men who were known to have accepted the money. He said he knew where the affidavits were and might be able to supply the key to the locked office where they were stored. Party loyalty was one thing, but ten grand was after all, still ten grand. Mackin was no "squealer," but his patience was already tested. He told Gabel he would have to sleep on it.

Meanwhile, William McGarigle, the "loyal Mac," an important stakeholder in county government because of McDonald's sponsorship, vowed to run the Cook County Hospital in a "fashion of true economy" and said he would "provide for a proper improvement of the grounds and buildings." Those were his words upon taking office as warden on September 3, 1883.[20]

The City of Chicago and the State of Illinois have had their share of ambitious up-and-comers like McGarigle who enter the political arena saying one thing and doing something else; passionate and committed young liberals who pledge reform, economy, and openness in government, only to betray conviction and find a prison door awaiting them. In the twentieth century, three Illinois governors, Lennington Small, Otto Kerner, and Dan Walker, the latter two considered idealists with a liberal agenda and a good plan, were among the scores of elected and appointed officials beating a path to the gates of the penitentiary for what boiled down to a personal belief that their station in life made them impervious to the rules.[21] This mindset was dramatically underscored on December 8, 2008, when the most shocking corruption scandal in state history unfolded after Governor Rod Blagojevich, a product of the Chicago Democratic Machine and the eternally ambitious son-in-law of Dick Mell (a powerful, entrenched Northwest Side alderman and ward boss whose influence helped propel Blagojevich into the governor's chair), was arrested by federal law enforcement and charged with conspiracy to commit wire fraud and soliciting bribes. In addition to his shady dealings with convicted fund raiser and political operative Tony Rezko, the bullying Blagojevich attempted to "sell" the vacated Senate seat of President-elect Barack Obama to the highest bidder in a "pay for play" modern-day scheme that seems designed from the blueprints of McDonald's County Board swindles of the 1880s. As a gubernatorial candidate in 2002, Blagojevich touted ethics reform, increased state aide to public education, and instituted an ambitious capital development program. On the surface of things, candidate Blagojevich seemed to present ideal credentials as a dedicated Illinois "liberal reformer." Commented FBI chief Robert Grant: "I can tell you one thing, if [Illinois] isn't the most corrupt state in the United States, it is one hell of a competitor" (*Chicago Sun-Times*, Dec. 10, 2008).

The treachery of the 1876 Cook County Board of Commissioners went unpunished, and the same derelict system of private firms anteing up hefty "commissions" for the privilege of doing business with the fifteen elected commissioners (ten from Chicago, five from the suburbs), then charging back whatever they pleased for the delivery and services (or no services at all), was firmly entrenched in the political culture. It was a pox upon local government in the decade following Clem Periolat's disgrace.

By 1885, the "boodle" commissioners controlled by McDonald comprised a majority of the Cook County board. Mike had retooled the board with new machine men even more rapacious than Clem and his gang. McGarigle and his cohorts allowed the courthouse steal to go through without a second thought; the Lundberg process and all the other notorious swindles received requested appropriations.

Harry A. "Prince Hal" Varnell, the dapper Clark Street gambler, race track railbird, and saloon owner no more qualified to run the affairs of a public health care institution than the lowliest pickpocket sleeping in the bridewell, was appointed warden of the Cook County Insane Asylum at Dunning, a distant outpost lying northwest of the city and far from the prying eyes of the Citizens' Association, reform-minded citizens who would later reorganize as the Civic Federation of Chicago.[22] "Prince Hal" was one of the younger set of city "sports" and an aspiring politician angling for prestige and influence—achievable through the sponsorship of his two pals, Mike McDonald and Alderman Hildreth. With $100,000, he fitted up a sumptuous gambling parlor and saloon at 110 Clark Street, wrapping himself in luxury and elegance. As county warden, nothing less would do.

The *Tribune* reported that Varnell had outfitted his private offices and his home on hospital grounds with costly Persian rugs, Brussels carpets, and lace curtains. He ordered strawberries for $3.00 a dozen in April and grapes in March. Using taxpayer money, he paid for the living arrangements and personal effects of his nephews, cousins, and friends downtown. An unlisted drug store infirmary on the hospital grounds at Dunning served as the official "clubhouse" and headquarters for the members of the "ring" who spent more time attending dances, social soirees, and private feasts hosted by Harry—that all around "good fellow" described by a contemporary as a man of "warm nature and sympathetic impulse"—than attending to their duties. Meanwhile, "the poor, the lunatics, and the sick have fared none too well, but those who have been hired to take care of them live in luxury."[23]

The only limit to a warden's authority was the right to dole out high-level patronage appointments. All staff assignments had to first be cleared with McDonald. Office seekers were escorted to the Store for their job interview with Mike. In a personal memoir published by New York author Victor Robinson in 1919, Dunning staff pathologist Dr. Shobal Val Clevenger recounted the strange circumstances of his posting in the early 1880s.

> The Superintendent of the asylum, Dr. J. C. Spray [Varnell's predecessor], was favorably disposed toward him and one day proposed: "Come along with me and see if you can pass muster." To Clevenger's astonishment he brought him into a drinking saloon on Clark Street. The proprietor, an ordinary looking fellow, was leaning on the customer's side of the

long counter. Spray went over to him and Clevenger heard him whisper to him, "This is the doctor I was telling you about." At these words the saloonkeeper raised himself, looked at Clevenger for a moment, nodded quietly and put out one finger for him to shake. "I congratulate you," smiled Spray to Clevenger. It seemed like a joke, yet they were in a serious place; on the first floor were the wines and liquors; on the second were the roulette wheels and faro layouts—yet that den was the true city hall of Chicago and Clevenger had touched the hand of royalty. It was "King" Mike whose nod made him special pathologist to the Cook County insane asylum. It smote the conscience of Clevenger to accept a position from Mike McDonald—yet it was his heart's desire.[24]

Mike's handpicked commissioners reported directly to him and no lesser authority. James J. "Buck" McCarthy, a former prizefighter who had worked as a meat packer in the Stockyards District, joined the board in 1884. Boastful, arrogant, and a political windbag, McCarthy sneered at the threat of prosecution. "There are only two powers over the board, one is the Almighty, the other the grand jury, and we have to draw the grand jury." McCarthy added that he was no "squealer."[25]

Charles F. Lynn, a stoop-shouldered man with prominent features and a long, flowing beard was the weak link—the "squealer." Lynn was McCarthy's protégé, a deputy sheriff and county commissioner from Hyde Park, who admitted he was in it solely for the money he could extort. Expressing withering scorn for Philip Armour and other powerful Chicago industrialists who refused to contribute to the corruption fund, Lynn exposed McGarigle as the "collector of boodle" for the ring and the unanimously elected "bag man" for Boss McDonald by the eleven corrupt commissioners under his sway.

As Warden McGarigle grew wealthy and sated from the perquisites of the job, conditions at his hospital were unimaginable; worse than Hogarth's descriptions of eighteenth-century London squalor. In the contagious diseases ward, a cramped, fetid, 18- by 40-foot room, men and women were forced to lie on the floor side by side waiting to die. There were only six beds in the room. The nurses were frequently intoxicated; partially understandable, given the awful stench of corpses awaiting transport to the morgue and the sickening quality of food they were forced to serve to the patients; at times the meat was putrid.

Only a minuscule percentage of the tax monies was actually budgeted for the critical supplies and services most needed to ease the sufferings of the poor and downtrodden languishing inside Warden McGarigle's infamous cesspool. Rather, the public money was spent in more "practical" ways. McGarigle commissioned a private horse stable for his personal use. Imported damask draperies and expensive china cuspidors were placed inside his office and outside in the hallway. A *Daily News* reporter counted twenty-four lightning rods, purchased from a supplier friendly with the board, mounted onto a toolshed. The writer noted that there was a "lightning rod on every chimney, every alcove, every corner, and every crevice" of the wooden shed.[26] Hal Varnell, former business agent for P. J. West, a lightning rod manufacturer, put them there.

The wastefulness and unsanitary conditions were the same in the county hospital, the poorhouse, and the Dunning asylum, when the Executive Committee of the Citizens' Association pooled their resources and allied with publishers Melville Stone, Joseph Medill, and J. Frank Aldrich and with Charles B. Farwell of the Union League Club of Chicago to break the power of puppet master McDonald and his commissioners to control the selection of the grand juries that had protected them from criminal indictments for well over a decade.

In November 1886, after the Republicans succeeded in establishing a beachhead with the election of Aldrich and fellow Union Leaguer Murry Nelson to the board as a way of fighting the boodle faction, a one-million-dollar deficit was reported in the county budget—easily traceable to the extravagance of the ring. The Mooney and Boland Detective Agency, engaged to investigate financial improprieties, found that the eleven corrupt commissioners had also used an extensive number of tax warrants, whose legality was doubtful.[27]

The Union League men, the newspaper publishers, and the civic elite were outraged and said they would stand for it no longer. Cook County State's Attorney Julius S. Grinnell, who had made his mark prosecuting nine trade unionists accused of exploding the bomb in Haymarket Square that killed seven police officers during a labor demonstration on May 4, 1886, pounced on the Dunning drug store and clubhouse on March 11, 1887, seizing the records of the board and placing them in the hands of a special grand jury. Warrants were served on McGarigle, Varnell, and Warden Charles L. Frey of the county almshouse, but Mac was defiant and unapologetic. It was the fault of the prevailing system, he explained, and he just went along with it—as everyone else did. "I don't even care if the same system prevailed in heaven, there would be boodlers. The temptation is too great and the restraint absolutely nothing. Men are but human, and as long as the County Board is a big committee just so long will dishonesty prevail."[28]

Harry Holland, a pivotal figure in the county building larceny, stood by McDonald and uttered not a word as Charles Lundberg accused him of fraud and failing to pay his men for their work. "We have done about $50,000 worth of work, but stopped because Holland did not pay us as per the contract."[29]

An attempt to pack the grand jury was thwarted, and the honest and true men who refused to be bribed or intimidated returned 306 indictments against Holland and eleven county commissioners, including McDonald's brother Ed, plus five private contractors who were a party to their schemes. Not surprisingly, no evidence of personal wrong-doing could be traced back to Mike, who laughed off a reporter's suggestion that if he wasn't careful, he too would be measured for prison stripes. "Well, according to the newspapers I'm into everything nowadays," he joked. "But I notice after it's all over I show 'em a pretty clean pair of heels and I'll do it this time or I'm very much mistaken. Most everybody's a boodler nowadays, you know."[30]

"The grand jury did not vote upon the question of indicting Mike McDonald," explained Assistant State's Attorney John R. Bensley. "In Mike McDonald's case, an indictment could not be framed to hold. When a man lays all his plans coolly and deliberately beforehand with the express purpose, apparently, of preventing any tracing of crookedness to his door it is an extremely difficult thing to get at him with legal evidence."[31]

Oddly, Grinnell congratulated the jury for not indicting McDonald, agreeing there was a lack of evidence. Freed up from the annoyance of having to defend his name in court, Mike placed his fortune at Ed's disposal. Alexander Sullivan, William S. Forrest, and Luther Laflin Mills, among the finest legal minds in the city at that time, were deployed on behalf of the indicted men. Two prolonged and tedious trials were to follow. In June 1887, McGarigle and Ed McDonald were brought before the bar of justice; the next month the "omnibus" phase against the remaining commissioners commenced. Judges Henry Shephard and Egbert Jamieson of the Superior Court heard the two cases respectively.[32] Shephard was the city attorney for Chicago in 1873, and as a judge, presided over a number of famous cases including the celebrated society divorce trial of Mrs. Leslie Carter in the 1880s. Shephard was a Democrat and an early champion of the eight-hour workday. There were fears on the part of the prosecution team that Shephard would extend leniency to McGarigle and Ed McDonald.

The prosecution's efforts to coax Warden McGarigle to turn state's evidence and expose McDonald's complicity in the steal in return for a promise of leniency were hastily rebuffed. McGarigle, like McCarthy and Varnell, was no "squealer." Mike, sporting a long, flowing beard in the fashion of presidents and statesmen, used all of his skills and persuasive powers to aid his brother and those defendants who remained loyal and true. He was seen everywhere—the county building, the federal offices, and as a daily spectator seated in the front row of Shephard's court. Twice he had to be reprimanded for making hand gestures and signaling to Ed as his brother patiently answered the prosecution's questions in the box with a surprising air of unconcern.

Tiring of the deliberations one afternoon, McDonald strolled down the hall and into the office of John Peter Altgeld, a protégé of gambler Joseph Martin, a city sport who paid Mike McDonald a third of the house proceeds each night for the right to operate a faro and stud poker parlor at Madison Street and Dearborn. Martin, with Mike's contrivance, secured a judgeship for Altgeld in the Superior Court during the fall 1886 city election.[33] Altgeld greeted McDonald warmly. Since the judge settled into Chicago's North Side German enclave in 1875 to begin his law practice, McDonald had kept his eye on the young liberal opportunist, knowing that he was never too proud to keep company with the machine Democrats. Judge Altgeld looked to them for political support and counted Mike as a friend.

"How'de do Judge," greeted McDonald. "I have just been listening to that little brother of mine. I had a little experience with a jury once over there in the courtroom. They had me charged with gambling. I let my lawyer pick out eleven of the jurymen until he came to Miner T. Ames the coal man. My counsel objected to him. I said no. Well, he stayed on the jury and was the only man who stood out for conviction. The other eleven wanted to acquit. If I ever have any experience with juries I'm going to leave it to the lawyers." McDonald turned and walked back to the courtroom. Out of earshot, Altgeld turned to a reporter and remarked with due sincerity: "Smart man, smart man; one of the smartest men in the country."[34]

On June 18, 1887, the jury McDonald unsuccessfully tried to pack returned a verdict of guilty against McGarigle and Brother Ed, fixing their punishment at three years in the penitentiary. Bond was denied for both men. The testimony of Fred Bipper and Nic Schneider, two private contractors paying bribes to the county board, was convincing despite accusations of perjury from the defense team. "Little Van Pelt was the real schemer," Bipper told the court. "He's bright and full of charm." When asked about his personal feelings toward the boodling commissioners, he added, "They are a lively set. They like fun. Some of them gave their women places in the County institutions."[35]

Bipper helped seal the fate of the principal architects of the swindle and helped bring dramatic closure to Chicago's most sensational corruption scandal of the late nineteenth century. Later that summer, other dominoes fell during the "Omnibus" phase of the trial. "Little" Van Pelt was convicted. He raced off to Canada, thought the better of it, and returned to accept his punishment. "Farmer" McLaughery, "Big" Dan Wrenn, a sweating three-hundred-pound bear of a man, Hal Varnell, Michael Leyden, and Michael Wasserman all served time in the Joliet Penitentiary. "Buck" McCarthy, a belligerent old cynic, had a friendly juror in the box and was let go with only a minor fine to pay; he was later elected to the Chicago City Council. Harry Holland was another who had evaded prosecution. Others, like Commissioner George Klehm, saved themselves from prison by making reparations or agreeing to aid the prosecution.

Ed McDonald and William McGarigle occupied adjacent cells in the gloomy Cook County Jail on Hubbard Street. Both men were well fed by the cooks at the nearby Revere House Hotel and received a procession of visitors and were accorded special privileges befitting their status. They understood quite clearly the deeper implications of their crimes—they were washed up politically. As the hours dragged by, Ed and Mac had ample time to contemplate the bleak circumstances that landed them in this mess. If not for his brother, Ed might have remained an itinerant merchant seaman, and McGarigle (it is not unreasonable to believe) might have been rewarded with an appointment to a federal post, had he trusted in his own abilities instead of allowing Mike and his snake-oil salesmanship to dictate his future course.

Tragedy followed. Nine-year-old Eddie McDonald, the only son of Mike's jailed brother, fell to his death from a fire escape at the Cook County Hospital while playing a game of chase with his schoolyard friends. A frail, sickly lad with spinal trouble, Eddie slipped on some loose boards that formed part of the roof of the landing on the top floor and crashed to the lower level of the building, twenty feet below. The freakish accident might not have occurred if hospital workmen had properly sealed off the area or tightly secured the hole in the floor the boy had fallen through.

The stricken father was granted a furlough to attend the wake held at the county hospital and the funeral at St. Jarlath's Church. Sprays of white roses and lavish floral arrangements bearing the inscription "Gates Ajar" (after the Elizabeth Stuart Phelps Ward novella of the same name) filled the room—paid for by Van Pelt, Varnell, Alderman Hildreth, and other county bigwigs who followed Mike, Mamie, the McGarigles, their children, and the rest of the procession out to Mt. Olivet Cemetery on the South Side, where the casket was interred at the McDonald family mausoleum.

Left to his sorrows, in his county jail cell, Ed McDonald lapsed into deep depression. Studying his friend's despair and sense of hopelessness, McGarigle confronted the specter of his own grim future and decided to act fast. The recent tragedy, the stifling June humidity making his cell intolerable, his impending transport to the Joliet Penitentiary, and the sickening thought of sharing space with hardened criminals he had once arrested, all motivated McGarigle to make independent arrangements for his removal from Chicago after refusing Grinnell's final demand that he give Mike up.

Cook County sheriff Canute Matson held the keys to Mac's freedom, and Mac played upon his sympathies well. The sheriff felt bad for McGarigle and was easily coaxed into granting his request to visit his wife Anna and the children in their Lakeview home on July 22, 1887. Earlier that same afternoon, Varnell, McCarthy, Mike McDonald's private physician, Dr. Leonard St. John, and the attorneys conferred with McGarigle inside the cell in a meeting that lasted for nearly two hours. The lengthy conference failed to arouse the suspicion of the sheriff, who might have suspected something was up, given the number of indicted felons and politicians who had crossed the Canadian border ahead of the jailer in recent years. Dr. St. John was not inquiring after McGarigle's health. He owed his hospital staff appointment to his mentor, and he owned a fast Canadian schooner named the *Edward Blake,* presently moored alongside a grain elevator at Ashland and Archer Avenues. St. John put his medical career and professional reputation on the line to aid his friend and boss.[36]

True to his word, Matson, having no deputies available that day, personally delivered McGarigle to his residence on Grace Street that evening and waited patiently in the front parlor while his prisoner went upstairs to take a bath and "freshen up." Half an hour passed, and the house had suddenly grown very quiet. Anna McGarigle was asleep in the next bedroom. Alarmed, Matson raced upstairs, only to find that the bathroom window had been flung open. The water in the tub had been drawn, and the suit of clothes McGarigle came home with were strewn across the floor. It was plain as day: the prisoner had jumped out the window and was whisked away by a confederate.

The tracks of a buggy and the imprint of horse hooves on the ground confirmed the obvious fact. Matson suddenly recalled McGarigle's prophetic comments from only a few weeks earlier: "If I had a ten-minute start, I could get away from the Chicago Police and every detective in the County. It would be much easier to hide here in Chicago than endeavor to get to Canada by the ordinary routes."[37]

The real plan was to reach Canada through the Straits of Mackinaw. With the aid of Dr. St. John's fast schooner, McGarigle slipped past patrol cutters and a ship hired by the *Tribune* to assist in the pursuit and was let off at Green Island Shoals, a desolate beach near Point Edward. From there he made his way to Banff in the distant British Northwest Territory, where he settled easily into the rhythms of country life. Mac bought into a livery business and invested in a local hotel. He joined the church choir and was nominated for chief of the village fire department during his time of exile. Without an extradition treaty in force, the U.S. government was powerless to intervene. Weeks after McGarigle's flight from justice, a bottle washed up on the shore of Grand Haven, Michigan. The message was delivered back to reporter Charles Chapin in Chicago, who promptly published it as an exclusive in the *Tribune* the next day.

> To my friends in Chicago: A few more hours and I will be safe through the straits and in Canada. Sheriff Matson, please accept my thanks for the bath, but I have concluded it in British waters. Oh Ed, I wish you were here with me! Goodbye till we meet!—W. J. McGarigle

Is He Not a Typical Democrat?

AND, FOR A TIME, THE PEOPLE OF COOK COUNTY BENEFITED FROM a scandal-free board. The McDonald machine was driven into temporary retreat and forced to conduct its affairs with prudence, sagacity, and moderation—but only for a brief time.

The Citizens' Association said it "hoped that future generations will learn wisdom from the experience, especially as kindred frauds in other parts of the country are being unearthed and punished at the same time that our community has brought to light and castigated offenders against our welfare and integrity. An epidemic of fraud has been followed by the corrective antidote of punishment."[1]

The reformers had at last scored a significant victory, albeit a momentary one. They failed to take into account that corruption in municipal and county government and corruption in big-city police departments are cyclical events. Typically, a highly publicized political scandal involving individuals or groups of office holders engaged in a conspiracy to commit fraud hastens the hue and cry from the media "to do something," and a clamor for reform is echoed throughout the city. Cursory actions are taken; indictments returned; the malefactors dealt with; and in the aftermath, a period of time elapses during which no further news items about the scandal or its consequences are reported in the daily press. The matter is quietly forgotten. Then we learn painful lessons that the "system," the culture of corruption as an accelerant of public malfeasance, is highly resilient and resistant to change.

The optimistic hope for lasting reform faded not long after the close of the "Omnibus Boodler Trial." Less than two years later, following another election and a partial restoration of machine-friendly commissioners, it was widely reported that the new "reform board" had illegally appropriated a vast sum for road repairs in the town of Cicero and Hyde Park (then a suburb before annexation in 1889) when it had no authorization to do so. "The worst steals of the McCarthy–Van Pelt gang were connected with the gravel road jobs. It is an insidious scheme in the direction of boodlerism!" shrieked the *Tribune*, and it called the new county hospital administration "loose, inefficient, and scandalous." James G. Strain, McGarigle's replacement as warden, was no improvement and was soon forced to resign.[2]

By the end of the 1890s, the so-called Gray Wolves of the Chicago City Council were firmly implanted and driving the vehicle of corruption. They had learned valuable lessons in the intervening years, and their doings were not nearly as flagrant or indiscreet as the profligacy of "Little" Van Pelt, "Mac" McGarigle, or Ed McDonald. The *Tribune* unhappily noted that "the fate of the County Commissioners did not deter them, for they knew they were not doing business after the clumsy fashion of their brethren on the county side of the square. They are boodling now without fear because in all human probability their deals cannot be exposed." Resigned to it, Murry Nelson said that "the trouble with reform is that the reformers won't stay mad more than six months."[3]

What happened to the county boodlers in the aftermath is a parable of Chicago's checkered political history. Ed McDonald spent the next seventeen months behind the grated doors of the North Side jail, living easier than his fellow prisoners, but nevertheless confined. Mike had spent $50,000 trying to save his brother. The best he could do was spare Ed the hardships and indignity of incarceration at Joliet and keep the heat on the appeals court. The persistence of the high-priced defense team finally paid off on November 17, 1888, when the Illinois Supreme Court freed Ed on technical errors and the theory that Nicholas Schneider had perjured himself as a prosecution witness. General Israel Newton Stiles, the lead prosecutor, indignantly accused Mike McDonald of "wicked influence on the administration of justice."

Brushing off the accusation, Mike raced about town spreading the glad tidings to his friends and associates. "When I heard the news I almost thought it was too good to be true," he said. "Then I went into the parlor where Ed's father was reading. The old man's face fairly beamed with joy and rising from his chair, he exclaimed: 'Thank God! Hereafter my sleep will be undisturbed.'" Mike was philosophical. "Great reform periods strike this city from time to time. Everybody is then suspected of wrong-doing. You can't prove your innocence," he said. "The papers, the judges, the people, everybody is against you. You can't get fair play to save your life. Then the thing blows over. I tell you, a better man than Ed McDonald never lived! He was nothing but a great, big-hearted engineer who never took his hands off the throttle."[4]

Trading on his brother's connections once more, Ed McDonald had no trouble assimilating back into society with a new job at a substantial income. Mike formed a partnership with Michael J. Tierney, the former city boiler inspector and owner of the Western Tube Company. He sunk a sizeable amount of his money into the enterprise in return for an agreement to place Ed in a respectable position that would not subject him to ridicule or embarrass him professionally. It worked out well for Ed, and within a year, he organized the Globe Steam Heating Company with Tierney.

Few people, including the McDonald brothers, believed William McGarigle would take the risk of returning to Chicago, but early freedom for Ed raised hopes for Mac, as his powerful friends in Chicago diligently greased the wheels. Wealthy State Street merchant Edward J. Lehmann, owner of the Fair, a discount dry-goods department store, was a McGarigle patron and a close friend of Mike McDonald. Not only had he funded the purchase of McGarigle's Lakeview home and funneled money to support Anna and the four children while Mac was away in Canada, he offered to pay whatever court fines would be assessed if an amicable settlement could be reached. Lehmann presented a petition to the new state's attorney, Joel Longnecker.

The time was right for McGarigle. On May 30, 1889, a tall man wearing a broad-brimmed slouch hat and a gray traveling suit confidently strode into Judge Shephard's courtroom, trailed by Longnecker and Lehmann. Audible gasps were heard in the courtroom as several bailiffs and spectators rushed to greet William McGarigle with a handshake and a slap on the back. The fugitive had accepted a plea agreement with the state's attorney that allowed Lehmann to pay his $1,800 fine in exchange for a guilty plea. No one seemed to be terribly perturbed by the court's willingness to let Mac off so easily. Nor was McGarigle vilified as a rank coward by the McDonald machine for leaving Ed to shoulder the burden of punishment alone, as some people predicted.[5]

He settled easily into private life; opening the famous "Round Bar" with Ike Lansing on Clark and Washington Streets where bets were taken and many a drunken gambler was hauled off to jail. "Bad" Jimmy Connorton, one of the city's worst street thugs and the publisher of a scandal sheet called the *Siftings*, engaged in a furious shootout with West Side gambler Mike "Bull" Haggerty inside the dining area of McGarigle's groggery in September 1890. Haggerty died, and Connorton was acquitted of murder, but the reputation of the place suffered.

Perhaps the worst indignity befalling McGarigle occurred a year after his discharge from justice, when, in a chance meeting at a saloon on Clark Street, the disgraced ex-sheriff Matson called Mac a "miserable thief" and punched him in the nose. "He violated his word of honor to me and placed me in a most unpleasant light before the public," Matson said indignantly. "I struck him in the face and neck and he bellowed like a baby as he ran behind the bar."[6]

After exhausting their appeals, the five convicted boodlers were shipped to Joliet in May 1887. They served less than two years, were praised as model prisoners, and returned to Chicago in February 1890. George C. Klehm, who avoided prison, resumed his duties as a justice of the peace in the north suburbs. "Buck" McCarthy was elected alderman of the Stockyards District on the Democratic ticket and was a delegate to the 1896 nominating convention. "Little" Van Pelt, the only one to suffer a serious financial reversal as a result of his time away, resettled in New York as an electrical contractor.

Despite the county board debacle, a glare of unwanted publicity brought down upon him by Ed's imprisonment, and the loss of Joe Mackin and other key allies, Mike McDonald did not retreat from political life. If anything, his rapid rise in party circles during the early 1890s encouraged him to heed Carter Harrison's advice and dispose of his gambling holdings, including the Store—the crown jewel of Clark Street and the best-known rendezvous of gamblers west of Saratoga Springs. The history of the house with its big play, dazzling scenes, and fortunes won and lost in an hour was the hallmark of a passing era. The transfer of title of 176 Clark Street to gambler Harry Perry on September 1, 1888, signaled the coming decline of the "parlor house" trade as it had existed since the Chicago Fire.

Perry and his associate, Charles E. "Parson" Davies, the fight promoter, financed the purchase of the Store through a chattel loan (personal property) secured from McDonald.[7] The gaming tables were hidden away in a second-floor room accommodating fifty patrons playing stud poker, faro, roulette, and hazard. Behind the wooden door bearing the name "The Club," an African American porter admitted all who were known to the house. Perry and Davies kept him on staff, along with two members of Mike's old gang, Charley Winship and George Norris.

McDonald continued to utilize the upper floors of his old place for political gatherings and to settle street disputes. An effective arbitrator who could resolve the quarrels between warring factions of gamblers before they resulted in bloodshed or loss of life, McDonald coaxed his friend Davies and Pat Sheedy to settle a long-simmering feud over fight dates between the respective pugilists each managed. McDonald sequestered them in the Store and persuaded both parties to schedule their boxers for a match in San Francisco—neutral ground. What Mike could no longer do was guarantee Davies absolute immunity from police raids when the political winds blew unfavorably.

Billy and Matt Pinkerton were on friendly terms with Pat Sheedy, whose "Turf Exchange" saloon competed with the Store for the gambling trade. Despite the peace agreement brokered by McDonald, raids against the Store were nonstop during the mayoral regime of the Republican John Roche (1887–89), a "law and order" reformer who interrupted Carter Harrison's string of election victories. In the early 1890s, the Pinkertons were behind many of the costly raids instigated by the Civic Federation of Chicago in their mission to drive the gamblers out of downtown. Davies held out as long as he could before sailing for Europe with his stable of fighters in 1893. Harry Perry went to work at Hal Varnell's place and sold the Store to "Bad Eyed" Cliff Dougherty, who was always unlucky, as a four-year prison term in Joliet would attest.[8]

Mike McDonald could not extricate himself entirely from his former associates. He was still their protector and unofficial ruler, but he had moved up in the world. No longer referred to as "Sure Thing Mike," "he is Colonel McDonald, and Michael Cassius McDonald, Esq.," smirked the *Tribune*. "He is addressed thus in the perfumed notes of the Iroquois Club, by the figurehead chairmen of the Campaign Committees, and by all the committeemen and secretaries. And why not? Do not the candidates depend on him to pull the boys in line? Is he not a typical Democrat?"[9]

In the long aftermath of the War of the Rebellion, it seemed that nearly every nineteenth-century man of high station in the United States adopted such military affectations, whether justly deserved or not. There were more so-called captains and colonels about in the land in 1890 than when Grant took Richmond. It was of no consequence to Mike that his wartime dealings were shady. He was to be forever addressed as "Colonel" McDonald by the sachems of the Illinois Democracy, the young Turks, and the old "aristocracy."

Parading down State Street wearing a high silk hat and sitting erect atop his steed during the presidential visit of Grover Cleveland in 1887, Mike was at the head of a column of the city Democratic clubs. The gala parade came not long after an ugly incident at Uhlich's Hall, when McDonald's raucous supporters shouted down a party resolution to endorse Cleveland's policies at a meeting of Democratic partisans.[10] By now, Joe Mackin's star was in eclipse. McGarigle kept his money but had lost his self-respect and could not be slated for county dog catcher, if that had been his true aim, and Van Pelt had gone back East. There were some lean days ahead for the Chicago Democrats, and the once invincible Carter Harrison was the victim of voter backlash.

With the greatest reluctance, Harrison angrily and bitterly withdrew his name from the 1887 mayoral ballot, knowing that the seed of public resentment over his handling of the Haymarket Riot and, to a lesser extent, the county board scandals, had taken root. For the moment, the Harrison dynasty was in tatters, and efforts to elect the Eagle to the U.S. Senate were doomed to failure. McDonald was busy grooming new leaders for 1889 and beyond—leaving behind a political vacuum in 1887, a "throw-away" year for the Democrats. In disarray, the party did not bother to slate a candidate, leaving the field wide open to the Socialist/Labor Union Party and its candidate, Robert S. Nelson, to challenge the fiscally cautious Republican, John A. Roche.

Machine Democrats and gamblers, anticipating the looming battle between the supporters of communism and the forces of anarchy versus blue laws, Prohibition, and Protestants, threw their support behind Roche—in their mind, the lesser of two grave dangers. Expressing the sentiments of many, Alderman Ed

Cullerton declared, "I regard it as a sacred duty to aid in preventing the triumph of the party of anarchy and socialism."[11] Only Harrison, actively courted by the socialists to run on their ticket for city controller, withheld his support from Roche. Branded a "Red serpent" and an anarchist, Harrison said that a Nelson election would not necessarily be a bad thing for Chicago and cautioned his former supporters along Clark Street that their zeal to see Roche elected would hurt them in the long run and would hasten the passage of more unpopular blue laws. The gamblers, under orders from Mike to support Roche, believed that they had helped stave off a city revolution, only to be rewarded with nonstop raids after the Republican was swept into office by 27,000 votes—the largest victory margin in city history up to that point in time.

Inside the city council chambers on Mayor Harrison's last day in office, an immense floral display in the shape of an eagle was laid before the old man's desk in tribute. More than one hundred specially favored well-wishers were invited to attend the farewell party, utter words of congratulations, shed a few tears, and share their fond remembrances. Neither Mike McDonald nor the habitués of Gambler's Row, so instrumental in sealing his first election victory in 1879 and every one thereafter, were asked to attend. The snub was intentional and an obvious betrayal of the support the outgoing mayor willingly accepted all those years from the bummers and cardsharps of the "machine" he now looked down upon with such scorn and contempt. All along, Harrison's hypocritical policy had been to accept their money and organizational skill in the city wards while holding out his palms and looking the other way in mute silence. In his published 1944 memoir titled *Growing Up with Chicago*, Carter Harrison II forcefully rebuts the notion of an enduring strategic political alliance and warm personal friendship between his father and Mike McDonald.

> The truth is that from 1880, when father had been mayor for a single year, the two men were hostile, and it was only in politics that there had ever been intercourse between them. They class Mike as [a] collector of graft from the underworld. He was all that. Presumably the collection was for the coffers of the local Democratic machine, which made up as it was of boodle aldermen, political contractors and ward heelers, was every whit as corrupt as Mike himself. From it Mike undoubtedly considered himself entitled to a liberal squeeze. For him no money was so tainted he did not like to hear its jingle in his pockets. Mike was at no time more than a low type gambler and a cheap politician. There were two Chicago gambling houses which the police kept under vigilant scrutiny, Mike's "The Store" and the George Hankins resort in Gambler's Alley; the latter known as a dinner-pail dump. Politically Mike never stacked higher than the underworld's representative in the 1st Ward, where tough saloons, gambling dens and houses of ill-fame had their habitat. Even Chicago's

tolerant world of politics of the 1880s took such scum and human offal with reservations.[12]

The dutiful and loyal younger Harrison served his political apprenticeship as the editor of the *Chicago Times*, his father's newspaper acquired from the estate of the late Wilbur Storey. Into the early 1890s, the Democratic sheet was the mouthpiece of anti-Republicanism and anti-McDonaldism. The son's deep and abiding enmity for Mike McDonald that stayed with him into old age stemmed not from the gambler's objectionable choice of associates or the nature of his business, but Mike's sabotage of the elder Harrison's efforts to win a Senate seat and to reclaim the mayoralty in 1889.

To bolster the machine, Mike needed to cultivate a new generation of leadership, fast on their feet, coupled with a skillful job of political reorganization. The remnants of the "dirty shirt" aristocracy and the young turks of the streets coalesced under McDonald, their old master, as the "Elegant Eighties" rolled into the "Gay Nineties." Mike's new money man and city council point man during this time was William "Black Bill" Fitzgerald, former county commissioner, alderman of the Third Ward, and political monarch of the South Side Stockyards District. "If I don't represent the party in Cook County, I don't know who does!" Fitzgerald boasted to Billy Whelan in 1889. Fitzgerald was full of swagger, and he much preferred his constituents to address him as "Colonel," and not as "Black Bill," a moniker earned in the streets because he was in the habit of wearing a black hat pulled well down on his head. With lawyer Alfred Trude, "Black Bill" Fitzgerald comprised Mike's old-guard aristocracy—transplanted upstate New Yorkers and kindred spirits. Fitzgerald kept control of the Democratic state committees and looked after the commissions inside the gang.[13]

The new generation of ward characters; creatures of the back alleys eager to share in the boodle leftovers, lined up behind McDonald and carried out orders on Election Day. Preeminent among them was the nimble downtown barkeep Michael "Hinky Dink" Kenna, admired for his brains, wit, and guile. He promptly got himself arrested for intimidating voters and preventing them from registering to vote for gambler Billy Skakel, aldermanic candidate running against Kenna's First Ward ally, "Bathhouse" John Coughlin in 1890. An unsavory collection of saloon toughs and First Ward lodging house bums received their marching orders at Columbia Hall from Kenna, Coughlin, Sol Van Praag, "Fatty" Lawless, and "Big" Sandy Walters. Over on the West Side, the immigrant and hod-carrier vote was "guaranteed" by Johnny Powers.

Powers opened his uncle's corner grocery store at Harrison and Jefferson as a Democratic campaign headquarters in 1888 and was rewarded by party slate-makers with an aldermanic seat in the impoverished West Side Nineteenth Ward. He exchanged the grocery store for a saloon, ran a card game in the back room, and with the exception of one term served in the Illinois state senate, Johnny "de Pow" Powers served as alderman continuously until 1926.[14]

Jane Addams of Hull House, scores of indignant settlement-house reformers, Democratic challengers, and the press assailed John Powers as the rapacious "Prince of Boodlers" year after year in blistering speeches and in the written word. The *Chicago Herald* lashed out, "Powers is as fit to be an alderman as an elephant [is] to take part in a roller skating match! It is generally acknowledged that the average Chicago alderman is a great deal worse than he ought to be, and yet it would be difficult among all the sixty-eight members to find a worse representative than Powers."[15]

After 1889, the old McDonald-Mackin machine was henceforth known as the McDonald-Powers-Fitzgerald faction. Alderman Powers had risen quickly in the inner circle. He was elevated to the chairmanship of the Committee on Streets and Alleys West, which meant that he controlled a big chunk of appropriations for "civic improvements" on the West Side—including Mike's boldest scheme yet: to build an elevated railway above Lake Street with his partner Fitzgerald. At stake was several million dollars. Powers's support and a cooperative mayor were the key to the whole thing.

∽ 12 ∽

A Flighty and Excitable Woman

DESPITE THE BEST INTENTIONS OF MIKE MCDONALD TO PROVIDE a tranquil setting for his wife "Mamie," his wheezing, cantankerous father, "Grandpa" McDonald, and the two excitable little boys, Guy and Cassius, in the magnificent mansion at 308 Ashland Boulevard, with its Turkish carpets, hardwood floors, and inlaid grand piano, his efforts brought only more domestic heartache to the family. Carved marble busts of Mike and Mary, sculpted at great cost, adorned the mantle; fine raiment, costly jewels, blooded horses for riding and driving, exquisite furniture purchased from the Tobey Company of Chicago, and a full complement of cooks, butlers, and footmen attended to Mary's every want, but they all failed to satisfy this flighty, emotionally un-stable woman or provide much comfort and peace as she marked her fortieth birthday in 1887.

It was a house, a shelter, a local curiosity, but never really a home.

In a day and age when politicians were popular culture celebrities, an endless parade of favor-seekers, gamblers, and fugitives, as well as sightseers who were simply out to take in a famous local attraction and everyday people of Chicago passing by would march up the walkway, seeking out Mike McDonald. Public figures were more accessible and unencumbered by the presence of security guards and barriers then than today. Often a simple knock on the door brought the common person face-to-face with a mayor, a senator, or perhaps even the president himself.

In the rear of the McDonald home, the horse barn doubled as a polling place on Election Day. The younger Carter Harrison remembered his father casting a vote:

> A dozen plug uglies gave us the dirtiest looks along with unflattering remarks in whiskey-husky tones they neglected to modulate. The evident

144

desire to create an excuse for a brawl made us hold our peace. Through a panel in one door six feet above the ground a slot had been cut; it was just large enough to permit the passage of a man's hand. This was the procedure: a voter gave name and address to a wooden door to be met with a gruff "Hand in yer ballot!" Who took it or what became of it was a secret, for no watcher unapproved by Mike had access within either during the voting or the count. On the little finger of his left hand, Father wore a gold band with a small diamond. When his demand that the door be opened met the suggestion: "Hand in yer ballot or get the hell out of here!" with his left hand he neared the slot, holding the right in reserve for possible attack. Mike grabbed his arm: "Don't do that! The boys'll get that rock if they have to cut your finger off!"[1]

The James Thurberesque parade of mysterious and threatening characters arriving at the house at odd hours to confer with her husband destroyed Mary's hope of privacy. She never knew what jarring event to upset the equilibrium would happen expect. One night in April 1884, hours after Mike had retired for the evening, burglars broke into the home. It was four in the morning, and for a second or two the shadowy outline of an intruder could be seen outside the bedroom door. McDonald roused his wife from a deep sleep and told her to go touch the burglar alarm, but it was disconnected. "By this time I had reached into the closet and got 'Pete,'—that's my twenty-inch revolver—and started downstairs. My wife ran to the front window and looked out. There were two of them on the front steps and she began to holler for the police. I ran to the window and fired down at them four times before they got away. The neighbors said we made as much noise as if a powder magazine had exploded. I believe I must have wounded one of them. They didn't take anything away except a few trinkets belonging to my father."[2]

Mary McDonald's deepening hostility toward her father-in-law made her regret that the burglars failed to carry off "Grandpa" along with his little trinkets. The presence of the old man and his habit of interfering with nearly every aspect of her married life and her relationship with the two little boys heightened growing tensions. Mary's frequent mood swings oscillated between religious fervor and her waking dreams of escape from an untenable marriage. Year after year, she pleaded with Mike to take her to Europe for the grand tour and for the chance to reunite with her blood relations in Ireland, but McDonald kept putting her off. There was always something to attend to; another project to finish. Mike had no interest in running off to Europe on a lark and risk being undercut by his party rivals.

Mary was restless and dissatisfied, but she never abandoned hope, even if it meant leaving her two youngest children behind in the States. The son from her first marriage, Harley C. (Goudy) McDonald, was a grown man running a fur business from an office in the Masonic Temple that lost more money than it managed to take in. Harley understood his mother's plight, but he had his wife Theresa and a newborn son to think of and mounting financial problems. He was little help. One day Mary confided in her mother her intention to go to Europe before the year was out, with or without her family. She was defiant and would not listen to reasonable advice to the contrary. She left the house in a huff and returned to Chicago. A friend and neighbor of the McDonalds later remembered Mary as a " flighty and excitable woman. Her uncertain moods and hot temper [were] notorious and I had heard that she was examined some time ago on account of some mental trouble."[3]

Mike McDonald, for all of his faults, was a generous benefactor of the Catholic Church. Perhaps out of guilt or obligation to his father's wishes, Mike donated large sums to the Archdiocese of Chicago. He frequently opened his home to the hungry priests of his West Side Parish, serving them rich meals they were otherwise unaccustomed to. In 1888, Father Price, a visiting priest from Asheville, North Carolina, took a guest room in the mansion while he raised money for construction on Notre Dame de Chicago, a parish for the French Catholics at Loomis and Sibley (now Flournoy) Streets. The McDonalds aided the effort by sponsoring a fund-raising musical recital in their home that netted $500.[4]

Father Price was granted a dispensation from the church to say mass inside the home a few times a week before a temporary saint's altar set upon a bureau in the day room. By Mary's personal account, the altar was taken down when Father Price departed the residence—after all, the Catholic Church did not sanction the giving of communion or receiving confessions in private homes—but a story that gained currency and set the tongues of gossips to wagging held that it wasn't just a "temporary altar" that had been set up for the convenience of a priest, but an elaborate private sanctuary behind locked doors where Mary surrendered her passions to Father Joseph Moysant, a twenty-seven-year-old French American priest born and reared in Aurora, Illinois.

Father Price made the introductions. He had invited Moysant to join him at the McDonald dinner table one night, not imagining the strange and fateful outcome. Mary exhibited great sympathy for Moysant, a man in reduced circumstances—physically withered, tired, and sickly. At Mary's helpful suggestion, Joseph was given free bed and board and regular medical appointments with Dr. Leonard St. John until such time as he was restored to robust health.

Moysant, a good-looking man, described as "rather foppish" in his dress, inspired pity as he told of his circumstances. He said he was ordained in 1887 at St. Viateur's College in Kankakee and assigned to the Church of the Immaculate Conception. That summer, he was transferred to St. Patrick's Church in Dixon, Illinois, to relieve Father Tracy; but what he neglected to say was that within a few weeks he had seduced a married woman from Chicago, Mrs. J. C. Gandy, who was observed lurking about the Waverly House Hotel with her religious "companion."

The Waverly House was Moysant's trysting nest. He took Mary and other women there, but one too many indiscretions were noted by Katie Loftus, a domestic in the parochial house in Dixon, and by the manager of the Waverly House. News of the incident reached Archbishop Patrick A. Feehan in Chicago. Clergymen familiar with the situation were summoned. They described Moysant as too much of a "woman's priest," that is, he was at the very least a compulsive romancer—and a sexual predator. Stories of priests who play the seduction game right up to the point of breaking their vows of celibacy abound. Such men revel in the power and the control they exercise over their female parishioners desperate for romance and affection denied them by indifferent husbands.

Once the game of manipulation is up, however, and the lecherous tactic exposed, the archdiocese quietly transfers the offender across the city or to another town to avoid further embarrassment. In due course, Father Moysant was suspended—"silenced" by the archbishop for his tryst in the Waverly House of Dixon and the Grand Pacific in Chicago, but the cunning seduction of Mamie McDonald continued.

"Father Moysant was a greasy, ill-mannered reprobate—little better than a tramp when he came to my house," Mike McDonald told the *Chicago Daily News*. "He came there for food and shelter, out at the toes and the elbows. He ate with his knife till I gave him a quiet tip that that was not quite the correct fashion, and wiped his nose on his cuff till I furnished him with a handkerchief. I put up with him for charity's sake and never had words with him but twice—once because he smoked opium cigarettes in the house and again because he presumed to reprove my little boy at the table."[5]

Mary purchased a nun's habit and fancied herself one of the "Sisters of Charity," a voluntary membership association of Catholic women.[6] The devotional altar to practice her faith was installed at Moysant's suggestion and with Mike's consent. It was situated in an adjoining room where the priest had spent many nights. "She, poor woman, doubtless thought it was for devotional purposes," McDonald revealed. "I am now satisfied that it was a bit of his cunning—a blind for me. She was weak mentally and he was strong mentally, and under his powerful leverage, the church, he made her an easy mark."[7]

McDonald was convinced (and with justification) that the priest plied Mary with doses of cocaine and hashish. Moysant ingested opium in Mike's presence—then secretly hooked Mary on narcotics as a means of keeping her under his spell. After a drug-high sexual tryst, she would give him her confession and receive absolution for the sin—thereby squaring accounts with God and Mike. It was further alleged that Mary and her priest exchanged gold rings on the altar of Notre Dame de Chicago.

"He was living at my expense and practicing a sneaking treachery upon me at the same time," McDonald stated, "and for the amusement of myself and anybody else, making my little baby boy kneel down and fold his hands together while he blessed him. It is enough to make a man wild just to think of the infamy of it."[8] Moysant and Mary carried on this way under the McDonalds' roof for nearly two years. By the time Mike was in command of all the facts, Mary had abandoned the family home and her children. She informed Mike of her intention to visit her mother in Tiffin to purchase a plot in the local cemetery where she planned to relocate the remains of her late father. McDonald gave her $100 in traveling expenses—she said she needed no more than that. Less than three days later, on July 27, Mary was back in Chicago and garbed in the attire of a Sister of Charity. Mike questioned her about her odd raiment and why she had returned so quickly from Ohio. Mary's feeble explanation satisfied her husband's curiosity—Mike desperately wanted to believe the truth of her words, and in matters of the heart he was as naïve as a callow schoolboy. Later, after he had set off for his downtown office, Mary slipped out of the house and was driven to the train station with Moysant at her side. The priest had grown a beard to disguise his appearance.

Realizing that he had been cast in the role of cuckold a second time by this woman, the furious McDonald interrogated the domestic help to determine their level of complicity. One of the cooks confessed that Mary had pushed her against the wall, seized her by the throat, and threatened violence if the girl revealed anything to the master of the house. Hugh Mullaney, the family coachman, said he took Mary to the train station but deliberately withheld the information from the master of the house. He had promised Mrs. McDonald that he would not say anything for a week. Enraged, Mike fired him on the spot after learning the truth.

Tickets for the Atlantic voyage were secured by Mary through a French sailing line at Jersey City. The fugitive wife demanded a berth on the next steamship set to depart New York Harbor—the *La Normandie* sailing for Paris on July 29. Mary, dressed as a Sister of Charity with spectacles and a gray wig, entered the ship's deck blindfolded by Moysant. And so this bizarre *tableau vivant* was reported in visceral detail by eyewitnesses. They arrived at La Havre on August 5, but their final destination was something of a mystery. Many believed them to be on their way to the Père Hyacinth colony outside Paris, where the marriage of priests was sanctioned.[9] However, when questioned later, Mary offered reporters a sanitized version of the story. She described Moysant's hasty departure from Chicago the same day as her flight from the city as "purely coincidental." He had gone on to Montreal, Quebec, Mary explained, while she purchased a one-way ticket in New York for the transatlantic voyage to reunite with her sister, Mrs. Catherine Philvot, see the sites, and escape the miseries of life on Ashland Boulevard with "Grandpa" McDonald and an objectionable maid Mike refused to discharge, in spite of her pleadings. Or so she said.

Mike appealed to the Archdiocese of Chicago for redress, but neither the archbishop nor Father Achille L. Bergeron of Notre Dame de Chicago (facing a public relations disaster of some magnitude as he solicited donations from both rich and poor to pay for the new church) were inclined to admit that an impropriety had occurred in their bailiwick under their watch. Bergeron stood accused of "encouraging" Moysant to sidle up to the wealthy gambler and his wife in order for the archdiocese to pry loose $25,000 in charitable donations for the church building fund. Bergeron professed innocence of the charge and said that Moysant "has not had any connection with our church for more than a year before this scandal occurred. I was greatly relieved when Father Moysant went away."[10]

The *Chicago Times,* now owned by the resentful Harrisons, reveled in McDonald's discomfort. They kept the story prominent and reported every salacious rumor. The *Tribune* and the *Inter-Ocean* provided far fewer details of the scandal and sympathized with the husband's misfortune. The *Inter-Ocean,* a sworn enemy of McDonald in former years, lamented "the futility of human hopes and surmises. Just when this man had got to a point in his life when it seemed nothing could upset him, when he had amassed money, drawn away from the old entanglements that had kept him before the public and was reaching for a better hold on the public's opinion, there came upon him the cruelest blow that could befall a human being."[11]

Divorce papers were immediately drawn up by his old friend and legal confidant, Alfred S. Trude. There was no going back now. Mike had all the proof he needed. "Were not the servants in my house helping them to be together and to deceive me? Oh I have such proof of their guilt that it is enough to madden a man to think of it!" Then, in a rare, unguarded moment, McDonald broke down and shed tears of bitter remorse in the presence of reporters. He said he believed that Moysant intended to poison him while living under his roof. "I can't understand how a man can be so confoundedly low and mean. A priest?! Well, say, I'll bet you couldn't find a rounder on Clark Street that would turn a trick like that on a man that had been white to him. No sir, not one."[12]

Mary arrived safely in Paris, but she did not join the Père Hyacinth colony, as many people back home had expected. Nor does the evidence suggest that she remained in the company of Moysant very long, lending credence to Mary's assertion that her flight from Chicago had nothing to do with a desire to wed the priest. In fact, the affair seems to have dissolved rather quickly and with finality. After less than two months touring the City of Lights, with a trip to England where Mary complained of being shadowed by Mike's detectives, the sojourn ended, and she sailed back to the States aboard the steamship *City of Chicago*—accompanied by a clergyman and his wife. She used two assumed names to book passage and fool the detectives and the press dogging her every move: "Josie Raymond," and "Mrs. C. Armstrong," the latter being her mother's maiden name. Word of her impending arrival reached McDonald in Chicago and immediately he sent cables to New York seeking an audience with his estranged wife. Then he dispatched Pinkerton detectives to the Fifth Avenue Hotel to report on her every move.

Her attempt to slip into her hotel suite incognito failed. Accosted by an agent bearing a handwritten letter from Mike requesting her immediate return to Chicago, Mary reacted violently. Near the marble staircase of the hotel lobby, she screamed at the red-faced man, who explained that he was a friend of Mike's, nothing more. She could not be assuaged. Mr. Phillips, the hotel detective, not wishing to alarm the other guests, escorted the hysterical woman and the object of her white-hot anger into a private office. "You tell me who you are and don't think to blind me!" she screamed at the Pinkerton man. "What are you watching for? I want to tell you that I am a match for you and a dozen detectives." Mrs. McDonald produced a dagger from her bag and threatened the detective with bodily harm unless he agreed to leave her alone.[13] The man kept his composure and exited the hotel without further incident.

On October 12, Alfred Trude and Mike McDonald arrived in New York for a showdown with Mary. Lending his personal assistance, Archbishop Feehan requested that a priest from New York City act as intermediary between the combative McDonalds when they agreed to meet inside the blue parlor of the Fifth Avenue Hotel. Mary demanded that Grandpa McDonald find another place to live as the most important condition of her return. Mike replied that he would not oblige her on that score. Mary drew a breath and asked for more time to rest up and ponder her next move—she had contracted a bronchial infection before disembarking from the steamship and said she needed a few more days to convalesce.

Reluctantly, Mike returned to his suite of rooms in the Brunswick Hotel to await her final decision. When he did not hear from her the next day, or the day after that, the desk clerk at the Fifth Avenue Hotel was contacted. He said that she had checked out—but left behind a farewell letter for him. The message blinded McDonald with rage. Mary said she had decided not to come back—and to add insult, she said she was betrothed to Moysant in Tiffin, Ohio, months earlier—a lie of course, but salt for the wound. "I am contemplating taking a role on the stage in a stage dramatization of El Cid," was her parting shot. She said she would return all of her jewels and worldly possessions to be rid of him.

A furious search of New York hotels was ordered by Trude, but the Pinkertons said that she had vanished into the city and could not be found. Several days passed before word filtered back to McDonald that Mary had sailed back to Europe on the City of New York. With a heavy heart, the gambler-politician turned the page on this sad episode of his life and returned to Chicago to devote his time and energies to more practical matters: the building of an elevated streetcar line, irrespective of whether the people wanted one or not.

"Parson" Davies, the celebrated fight promoter and the new proprietor of the Store, asked McDonald—this man of the world who had tricked the devil—how he could have been so gullible in affairs of the heart. "I can't understand it Mike, a man of your experience . . ."

McDonald thought for a while and slowly replied: "My God man, when you cannot trust your wife and your priest, whom can you trust?"[14]

～ 13 ～

Bribing the Gray Wolves for
an "Upstairs" Railway

ALFRED TRUDE PRESENTED MIKE'S SUIT FOR DIVORCE TO JUDGE
Jamieson of the Superior Court—certainly no stranger to the McDonald kin.
The gambler-politician laid bare his soul, calling Mary "wholly unfit" to be a
mother and revealing secret information from the Pinkertons that Mrs. Mc-
Donald was "unduly intimate" with Moysant inside the two hotels. It was a time
of anguish and introspection for Mike—animated by his anger after being so
cruelly humiliated by the perfidy of his wife. Lawyer Trude asked the court to
grant Mike custody of the two children and ownership of the house and all
of its contents. But forty more days would have to elapse before the decree as
specified by Trude could be granted. That would allow Mary the necessary time
to respond to the charges.

The forty days passed quietly. Mary did not challenge the divorce. She sent
word to Mike that she had no defense to make and would not be returning
to Chicago. On November 22, McDonald entered the courtroom dressed in a
well-fitting suit of sober black with a high silk hat wrapped with a wide brim
of black crape. In the wake of the divorce action, more tragedy followed. His
married stepdaughter, Alice "Birdie" McDonald Pyott, adopted by Mike during his ill-fated union with Mary, passed away at age twenty-two and had just
been laid to rest. As Trude reviewed the essential facts of the case, McDonald
sat at the table, head bowed, with eyes shaded by his hand, before Ellsworth
Walton of the Waverly House gave testimony that he had delivered pitchers of
twenty-five-cent beer to Mary and her lover. After they had slipped out of the
hotel at 2:30 in the morning to catch a train back to Chicago, Walton removed
a slip of paper that had been stuffed into the keyhole of their room to prevent
nosy snoops from peering inside their room.

An audible gasp was heard from inside the courtroom as these details were recounted. The judge ordered the testimony written into the record, and a decree of divorce was granted. Mary's beautiful home—a "love token" given to her by her husband as a symbol of his eternal affection—reverted to Mike. It was not the outcome he had intended but one that was inevitable. McDonald exited the courtroom brushing off reporters' questions and wiping away a tear. It had been an anguishing time for him these past two years. Death had taken a much-beloved nephew and a daughter. Prison had removed his brother and closest political allies from his side, and now, at the age of fifty, with his personal life in shambles, he stood alone to bear the responsibility of single parenthood.

McDonald did not sequester himself behind drawn curtains inside his Ashland Boulevard mansion or drown his sorrows inside a bottle of rye. He went about his business as before and was soon back in city hall, championing a pet project to establish the Lake Street elevated railway franchise with a new partner in tow, "Colonel" Morris H. Alberger of Philadelphia. The plan was Alberger's great inspiration, but he lived in a rented room at the Richelieu Hotel and was suspiciously viewed as an opportunistic Eastern dude pushing a scheme to line the pockets of Boston businessmen with hefty franchise fees—"pork" for their own political plate. In one particularly stormy session, Alberger, the Western business agent for the Meigs system, an experimental steam-powered monorail manufactured in Boston, went before the Committee on Streets and Alleys to advance a proposal to bring the system to Chicago, but he was taken to the woodshed by the boodle aldermen who asked the logical question, "what's in it for me?"[1] Alberger cried "blackmail" and "fraud," realizing that minus Mike's divine guidance and political acumen, competitor companies would be awarded the Lake Street franchise. The Adams Law, an 1883 measure sponsored by Congressman George E. Adams, requiring Chicago's transit companies to secure approval signatures from a majority of property owners before building each mile of the proposed route, was another impediment to overcome.

The new Democratic mayor, DeWitt Clinton Cregier, represented McDonald's next-to-last great triumph as the Democratic kingmaker of Cook County. Slight in figure, Cregier had served as chief engineer of the Chicago water system and later as commissioner of public works under Harrison, but he made an enemy of the mayor when his ambition to succeed the Eagle was made known. A widening schism developed in the party between the resentful Harrison faction and McDonald's machine, now dubbed the "Wine-and-Whiskies" (or "Wino-whiskies"). The Eagle had let everyone in the "gang" down. Harrison had proven unreliable—he was no longer a friend to the McDonald interests. Cregier was the new man of the hour. He had pledged his support for the Lake Street "L" and the Wine-and-Whiskies went all out for him.

The Democratic candidate owed his election to McDonald's eleventh-hour intervention. With the aid of Mike Corcoran, "Captain" Jim Farrell, and George

Hankins, Mike raised a hefty $30,000 war chest for the Cregier ticket and bought up the support of the labor leaders after the Republican Roche spurned an offer of a brokered agreement that would have allowed the games to run wide open in return for political support. Mike was named chairman of the Cregier campaign committee, and Hankins the deputy chairman. McDonald went east to raise money from New York gamblers, while back home his operatives ran in two thousand bogus votes in the First and Eighteenth Wards to ensure a Cregier victory.

Cregier campaigned as the public face of the reform movement—it earned him a share of the "good-government" vote—but once elected, he allowed the gamblers free run of Clark Street. The public face of reform disappeared. All-night saloons were back in business, and the midnight closing law was universally ignored. The gamblers got what they wanted—Hankins reopened "Old 134," and within a week the Clark Street rialto was a blaze of light and the nocturnal playground for blacklegs pouring in from every corner of the nation.

A disgusted Marshall Field, who provided Cregier his required bond after taking office, threatened to withdraw it unless something was done about the intolerable conditions. "Never before in the history of Chicago has gambling been as open as it is now," complained the *Chicago Times,* the Democratic sheet now in the control of the Harrisons. "Carter Harrison allowed public gambling but he also controlled it as far as he could. Harrison made no false pretenses in the matter and simply said: 'Yes I prefer to have open gambling so I can control it.'"[2]

Meanwhile, McDonald pushed his upstairs railway, and the new mayor seemed amenable to circumnavigating the Adams Law to support a franchise that would enrich *everyone's* coffer. In the three years leading up to his mayoral run, Cregier was superintendent of the West Side Railway Company. He was counted on to support the Lake Street elevated plan and help lift the cloud of uncertainty that had impaired Mike's proposed line during the regimes of Harrison and Roche.

Before leaving office in 1887, Mayor Harrison, with city council approval, had parceled out lucrative streetcar-line franchises to his former business partner and financial backer Harvey T. Weeks, president of the Chicago Passenger Railway, and to Charles Tyson Yerkes, the ruthless and predatory Philadelphia financier who had come to Chicago in 1881 with a new wife and $40,000 in working capital to open a bank, build streetcar lines, and cash in on the greed of arguably the most corrupt city council in the nation.

Yerkes played an important role in developing mass-transit systems in Chicago and London, and in his time he was a living symbol of the excesses of unrestrained capitalism. While serving as a financial agent for the City of Philadelphia's treasurer, Joseph Marcer, Yerkes risked public money in a colossal stock speculation. The venture ended in disaster when the Chicago Fire sparked a financial panic in Eastern markets. Left insolvent and unable to make payment to the city, Yerkes was convicted of larceny and sentenced to thirty-three months in the Eastern State Penitentiary. He served only a fraction of that time, before moving west to strike a new fortune in Chicago, where he was warmly received by a coterie of aldermen including Edward F. Cullerton, who expressed a willingness to exploit his connections and dole out fifty-year street railway franchises to Yerkes's companies for cash.

Within a decade of settling in Chicago, Yerkes's original $40,000 investment was worth fifty times that amount. Yerkes was chasing a monopoly. In 1886, Charles Yerkes and his business partners, Peter A. B. Widener and William C. El-kins, acquired a bare majority control of the Chicago City Railway, which owned patents for a cable system to replace the antiquated horsecar lines from the time of William B. Ogden, Chicago's first mayor. Yerkes paid the bargain basement price of $1,503,000, formed a holding company called the North Chicago Street Railway Company, and then issued $1,500,000 in bonds to pay for the original stock purchase. "The secret of success in my business," he reportedly told an aide, "is to buy old junk, fix it up a little, and unload it upon other fellows."[3]

His takeover of the North Side line precipitated a string of further buyouts, until he controlled a majority of the city's street railway systems on the North and West Sides. Like McDonald, Yerkes employed the necessary means to acquire street franchises and to build and extend these lines by suborning politicians for their favorable votes. Yerkes cajoled, bribed, intimidated, and sometimes reverted to blackmail schemes to compel members of the various city council subcommittees on railroads and on streets and alleys to obtain their necessary votes to pass enabling ordinances. He found willing allies eager for boodle in the "Big Four" aldermen, "Foxy" Ed Cullerton, James Hildreth, John Colvin, and John Powers, with considerable help coming from a Republican, Walter Scott Hull—all entrenched ward bosses franchising the streets, alleys, and public utilities to the high bidders.

On the night of a crucial council vote over whether or not to grant Yerkes the right to run his North Side cable cars through the LaSalle Street tunnel, McDonald settled into a comfortable wicker chair, urging his machine aldermen to "vote right"—vote for Yerkes. Mike was an important conduit to the city council in Yerkes's scheme to "buy up" the franchise rights. He also had a hidden financial interest in the Yerkes firm. The *Tribune* reported that Mc-Donald "predicted every move that was made, and when one of the boodlers wavered, he would remark: 'Now they must get down to business. There'll be no fooling!'" For the moment, Mike's interests were aligned with those of the Philadelphia financier, so long as Yerkes signed over the checks and did not attempt to interfere with his long-term plans for Lake Street.[4]

The *Chicago Daily Mail* cornered McDonald the day after the council voted to sell the tunnel rights to Yerkes for $125,000—about $425,000 less than the assessed value of the franchise. In light of the development, would Mike consider forming a combination with Yerkes? "No, the road is not for sale nor has Yerkes bid on it!" he answered emphatically. "I would not like the Philadelphia clique to tempt us with an elegant offer. I never met Yerkes but once in my life." Still, he candidly admitted that the tunnel ordinance was a fix. "Do I think there was any crooked work in the renting of the LaSalle Street tunnel? Of course there was fraud—so the papers say. But you know the fine workers don't paste up their transactions on the outer walls." A Yerkes spokesmen at the Chicago Passenger Railway Company answered the charge. "Mike was playing the scriptural injunction, 'Answer a fool according to his folly,'" adding, "He [McDonald] has a considerable interest in our road. So has E. J. Lehmann, but Carter Harrison hasn't a dollar."[5]

With only a slim margin for error, McDonald and Colonel Alberger pooled resources in the early months of 1888 to push through the Lake Street plan. Mike would agree to deliver the politicians; Alberger would work the Eastern financial markets. They organized a construction company with nine directors named, to build the road for $666,000 a mile and take their payments in bonds. The two courthouse scoundrels, Harry Holland and Edwin Walker, were added to the board with Fitzgerald, while McDonald was voted treasurer.

From the beginning, McDonald and his "Upstairs L Road" faced stiff opposition from the community and reform aldermen Walter Pond and Joseph H. Ernst, who introduced an ordinance to halt construction so the Lake Street residents could regroup and articulate their views in a public forum. Facing a likely injunction, "Black Bill" Fitzgerald and McDonald complained to the Department of Public Works. "It is hard for an *honest man* to obtain justice in this city!" thundered Fitzgerald. McDonald lowered his gaze and nodded solemnly.[6] Then he marched into Cregier's office, where he vented his displeasure to Assistant Corporation Counsel Clarence Darrow.

Believing the Adams Law protected their livelihoods from the intrusion of the "L," a West Side political rump group calling itself the "Lake Street Protective Association" organized to fight the McDonald syndicate because McDonald never bothered to consult with the business owners and residents who would be forced to live and work under the shadow of the noisy, smoke-belching cars running up and down their thoroughfare. Cregier sympathized with the people but was reluctant to go back on his promises to McDonald, so he stalled for time.

Mike's alliance with Charles Yerkes was never so simple as a clear-cut battle pitting the interloper from Philadelphia against the gambler McDonald for supremacy of the elevated lines, with the residents and business owners shunted off to the side. There were strong suspicions of McDonald's ulterior motives. He was fighting for control of a West Side racetrack located in Garfield Park near the Lake Street "L." Political enemies said that McDonald really would not give a damn about the road if the racetrack were to founder.

The real purpose of the Lake Street "L" from Mike's standpoint was to deliver thousands of railbirds to the gates of Garfield, nothing more. If the Republicans were to recapture the mayoralty in 1891 there would be bluenosed opposition to the track. Lose Cregier to the reformers, and the priorities would shift, meaning the future of the elevated line would have to be reevaluated. Then the key to the thing would be to inflate the value of the stock—sell it to Yerkes to "fix up" before he passed it off to "the next fellow." But that was in the future.

The untested Meigs system was considered impractical, risky, and unsuitable to hold up under the wear and tear of Chicago. The plan was soon scrapped when the city council balked at the installation of a double-track system, but Alberger was adaptable and lingered in the city a while longer. He severed his connection with Meigs after the syndicate failed to raise bonds among the Boston investment community.[7] Conventional steam engines and railroad cars would travel down a single track.

As the first postholes were about to be sunk along Lake Street, McDonald, Powers, Cullerton, Alberger, and Fitzgerald produced their slush fund, and fourteen city aldermen (including the remaining dissenters from the Streets and Alleys Committee) each received cash considerations in exchange for their favorable vote on the ordinance. These aldermen, representing both parties, were among the first to be dubbed city council "Gray Wolves" by the Municipal Voters' League (MVL).

The boodle aldermen were in it strictly for the money. The city paid its aldermen only $3 per council meeting, but those who were patient and in it for the long haul grew rich. The schemes these men cooked up for lining their pockets were varied and often ingenious. The gas companies, public utilities, and city railways were prime targets for shakedown because their operators wanted to do business with the city and had the means to pay up. McDonald therefore paid out the "usual and customary" perquisites to ensure the success of his ordinance, as table 13.1 illustrates.

With Mike pulling the wires, the Chicago City Council voted to grant the Lake Street Elevated Railway Company a twenty-five-year franchise and passed the enabling ordinance to authorize construction of a road beginning at Canal Street running west from downtown to the city limits. Colonel Alberger received financial backing from the Farmer's Loan and Trust Company in New York, and a cash deposit of $100,000 required by the ordinance was posted by McDonald. "This at least will be a relief to the people of Lake Street who have been clamoring for an 'L' road, and who are friendly to any company that promises even a partial deliverance from the odious Yerkes monopoly," praised the Daily News.[8]

Others were not so sure and thought that editor Victor Lawson of the Daily News was very naïve in his opinions. He did not understand who he was dealing with in Michael C. McDonald, nor did he seem to recognize the shadow

Table 13.1 City Aldermen Bribed by Mike McDonald for Their Favorable Vote on the Lake Street Ordinance

Alderman & Party Affiliation	Ward Represented	Bribe Amount
William P. Whelan—D	First	$5,000
Michael F. Bowler—R	Fifteenth	$3,500
Daniel R. O'Brien—D	Twenty-third	$3,000
John J. McCormick—D	Seventeenth	$3,000
Edward P. Burke—D	Sixth	$3,000
Charles A. Monear—R	Eighth	$3,000
James T. Appleton—D	Second	$3,000
John H. Oehman—D	Fifth	$3,000
Simon Wallner—R	Tenth	$3,000
J. N. Mulvihill—D	Seventeenth	$3,000
Thomas D. Burke—R	Twenty-second	$2,500
William A. Love—R	Seventh	$2,500
August J. Kowalski—R	Sixteenth	$2,500

Source: "Was There Bribery?" Chicago Tribune, June 25, 1890; Chicago Inter-Ocean, June 26, July 3–4, 1890.

of Yerkes lurking in the background, watching and waiting for the right moment to play his hand. The role of altruist was an unfamiliar one for "Colonel" McDonald, but there were some, like Lawson, who believed Mike was "good for the city," compared to this ruthless Philadelphia interloper who didn't care much for elevated railroads anyway.

William M. Beadle, a stenographer in the employ of Joe Mackin, would later tell the Cook County state's attorney how Aldermen Monear and Wallner received only a fraction of the $3,000 they were promised, and in disgust, they sought Mackin's assistance in getting what was due them. Unafraid of leaving a paper trail, Monear and Wallner signed Mackin's notarized affidavits attesting to their acceptance of bribe money and McDonald's subsequent failure to pay them their full share. The episode speaks volumes about political arrogance and the elected officials' sense of entitlement that they should present themselves, and not the citizens of Chicago they allegedly represented, as the aggrieved parties in this affair.

Peter Gabel, the conniving horse dealer who was chummy with Alderman Cullerton, attempted to drive a wedge between Mackin and McDonald by pressuring Joe to turn over the affidavits that would "send Mike to Joliet." Mackin, who had stuck by his word that he was no "squealer," waffled, and then thought the better of "ratting out" Mike, no matter how serious his differences were with his old partner. Desperate to cash in, Gabel made his pitch to the aldermen. He played upon Monear's anger and rising frustration with McDonald for stiffing him on monies due and proposed an alliance. Monear balked (because he was already in arrears to McDonald on an old gambling debt), and Gabel circulated bogus affidavits in Alderman Monear's ward to cripple him at election time.

Gabel's threats cost Monear his reelection and spurred State's Attorney Joel Longnecker to convene a grand jury to look into the matter, although Long-necker had his doubts about whether any indictment would stick. Monear and Wallner admitted their signatures were genuine, but they said they never signed an affidavit and were puzzled as to how their names ended up there. They must have been transferred through an ingenious forgery.

Mackin ad-libbed to the grand jury, providing his listeners with moments of hilarity and wit, but no one was really surprised when his memory proved defective. "I don't see why they want to mix me up with this thing when I've been trying to steer clear of every kind of notoriety."[9] As to his signature on the affidavit, did he recognize it? "Well really I can't say," Mackin told the grand jurors. "It might be." But then he couldn't say for sure.

Despite his wall of silence in court, Joe had exposed his dealings with the aldermen to his young clerk, Beadle, who told the grand jurors what Mackin could not. "Mackin suggested that I should leave town at once—until the thing blows over," Beadle testified. "He gave me a five-dollar bill and told me to avoid grip-sacks and downtown depots and to get on an outgoing train at some outly-ing depot."[10] In light of the contradictory statements and plausible denials of the accused aldermen, the grand jurors weren't sure who to indict, or on what charge—boodling or perjury?

At first, the *Tribune* argued that the entire project was rotten from its concep-tion. "All the circumstances in connection with the passage of the Lake Street 'L' ordinance indicate that greenbacks were used to grease the slides. Several of the aldermen who voted for it were the bitterest opponents in committee. The whole history of the road and the general reputation of those identified with it bear out the idea that it has been carried out in the spirit of its boodle conception."[11]

Despite compelling evidence of bribery, the grand jurors voted 12–9 not to return an indictment against the aldermen on July 12, 1890. They concurred with Longnecker that not enough evidence had been obtained to warrant conviction. As was customary following an important verdict of the court that turned out all right despite long odds, Mike rewarded the "boys" with a grand celebra-tion—this time two hundred Cook County Democrats accompanied by the fully uniformed members of the marching band led by Captain James Henry Farrell set off on an all-expenses-paid junket to Niagara Falls.

"Yes sir, we are going!" gloated Colonel Thomas Jefferson Dolan, an affable, but utterly useless political hanger-on from the Eighteenth Ward who collected his weekly government paycheck for doing nothing—he was quick with a joke and always good for a couple of laughs during their many long convention junkets, side trips to construction sites, pork-barrel land grabs, and country picnics.[12]

"You know Mike, and you know his ways," Dolan continued. "Well, he is going to unbuckle. This has been a pet idea of his for years. Mike is going to get a whole train of Pullman cars he is! He pays everything, so he does! It goes, he says, if it costs him $10,000! What's it to him? He's got plenty. So Mike will let loose. Won't them kazoos of hack men [cab drivers] at the Falls get a game though? They will play our excursion for marks. So they will. They will say: 'Oh my look at them millionaires from Chicago!' There was never a hack man at the Falls who could compare with our bunch! We are going to do the Falls in royal style. Nothing seen like it there since the visit of the Prince of Wales."[13]

McDonald's excursion back to his boyhood home under a far different set of circumstances than when he had left it as a lad of fifteen was a chance to catch up with his past, unwind from the recent turmoil of the divorce, and flaunt his political associations and business success to those who might still remember him from leaner times. The watering hole of the Clifton House at Niagara Falls enjoyed a brisk trade all that week as Mike shored up his political base in a remote port-of-call from Chicago. The trip to New York was a necessary one. McDonald was building consensus and adding support for an amendatory ordinance to expand the Lake Street charter, allowing him to extend the road east from Canal Street, crossing over the Chicago River on a drawbridge and proceeding east to Wabash, where it would intersect with the South Side line. The Meigs plan was scrapped, and steam engines from an Eastern firm were ordered.

The aim was to complete a fully connected above-ground rail system in the central business district in time to ferry visitors to the Chicago world's fair of 1893—the "World's Columbian Exposition." The New York financiers demanded it, and they did not expect McDonald to fail them. Costly infrastructure work and the condemnation of buildings along the proposed route on each side of Wabash Avenue and Michigan and points further west were required, but the property owners raised serious objections.

After being greeted with initial skepticism, McDonald's proposal was praised by his old enemies at the *Tribune* as a good one, even though it stood little chance of being adopted in the council. "Mr. Yerkes should have taken lessons from McDonald when he was engaged in his long negotiations with the Council for a South Side Loop. None of his plans were half so comprehensive and daring as this. The 'L' route as laid out, crosses at a favorable point all the most favorable streets in the business district. It runs alongside or within a stone's throw of some of the biggest stores and hotels."[14]

Remarkably, McDonald's visionary design of an elevated system encircling Chicago's downtown business and retail district—thus becoming the permanent infrastructure of the rapid transit system that would eventually form the nexus of the modern "Chicago Loop"—was several years ahead of its time. However, the political infighting, the greed of Yerkes and the aldermen, coupled with the obstructionist tactics of the business owners on both the east and west ends of the line, forestalled immediate adoption of the plan.

Mayor Cregier initially vowed support for the elevated road, but in a stunning reversal, he vetoed the amendatory legislation on the floor of the council on October 31, 1890, arguing that the property owners along the route had not been properly consulted. Cregier said he acted in the people's best interest—a shocking admission from an incumbent Chicago mayor. Ignoring howls of protest from Cullerton, Powers, and other "boodle aldermen," Cregier deferred the ordinance back to the Joint Committee on Streets and Alleys for further modification.

Over the next twelve to eighteen months, the McDonald-Alberger-Fitzgerald syndicate, with Harry Holland communicating progress of construction to the press, labored to get the consent of citizens to acquire the right of way to enable construction to proceed west between Lake and Randolph and from Ashland to California Avenue on the opposite end. McDonald traveled to Albany to strategize with his cronies in the Tammany Hall delegation before continuing on to Washington, D.C., where he solicited Joe Mackin's assistance to lobby legislators for transit funding. Mackin was living in a downtown D.C. hotel, and despite their recent differences, the "Oyster" arranged meetings with the politicians that mattered.

Very little came of it, and most of the Lake Street building owners were paid off with stock. "The fellows who gave us their consent to pass their property got stock according to their frontage," McDonald explained. "That is, so many shares for so many feet. I got a sweetener in stock for the money I let the company have on its bonds. There are 812 of those out—that is, $812,000. I hold conservatively over 200 of them and I paid par for mine too."[15]

Work stoppages were frequent, and for a time it seemed as if the whole venture would blow up. "We'll use our own money to make extensions," Holland vowed. "The New Yorkers who did negotiate with us haven't put up any, and they won't."[16]

Amid countercharges that McDonald had watered down the stock payouts to the point that the railroad held only $4 million in assets, rumors began to circulate that the Lake Street "L" was about to be put up for sale. The collapse of a New York investment house meant that the company could no longer hold its bonds on the open market. Heavy shipments of gold in financial markets made investment bonds for traction companies far less desirable in 1891–93 than in 1888.

"We have already expended a million, or to be exact, $996,000 on the road," Colonel Alberger revealed. "All of that money was put in by six persons."[17] Alberger attached a condition that the buyer would assume the obligation of completing the line. McDonald and his partners initiated buyout discussions with Edward Lauterback, a New York lawyer heading a syndicate of new East Coast investors, but his offer of $1.5 million was ridiculously low and immediately rejected. A month later, in June 1892, McDonald entered into high-level discussions with Frank L. Underwood of Chicago and Willard R. Green of New York, who were interested in buying out his interests and completing the road. The question of whether Mike grew weary of the endless wrangles and merely wished to "cash out" and devote his energies to promoting a new racetrack venture on the West Side and John Altgeld for governor in the 1892 election, or whether this was a sinister boodle scheme to bring about an eventual Yerkes takeover remains unanswered.

McDonald's Lake Street Line and the rival Metropolitan West Elevated Line (powered by electricity—a marvel of the age) posed a serious threat to Yerkes's designs for a monopoly. Acquiring both the Chicago West Division Railway and the Lake Street Line made the most sense to Yerkes, because it would mitigate a rising threat and allow him to develop a system of streetcar feeders to connect various surface lines to the West Side.

However, on December 23, 1892, after six months of negotiation, ownership of the project transferred to Green and Underwood for the sum of $2 million, with McDonald acting as trustee for the old stockholders. The company was reorganized with $6.5 million in bonds and $10 million in stock. New directors and officers were elected, with McDonald retiring from the board but retaining his stock, valued at $300,000. Additionally, he held bonds worth $400,000. "Black Bill" Fitzgerald stubbornly refused to resign and was unceremoniously ousted from the board the following month after a bitter stock fight. Changes in management were immediate. Former mayor John L. Roche was installed as president, but Colonel Alberger, who had remained loyal and true to the McDonald project since its inception, continued on as general manager. For the moment, the future of the West Side transit venture seemed assured with "honest money" behind the project.

Reaching a top speed of twenty miles per hour, the first steam locomotive of the new Lake Street Elevated Line inaugurated service on August 3, 1893. Flush with pride, Colonel Alberger and the New York ownership were greeted by cheering throngs of spectators lining the route of the *Clarence A*—named for Clarence A. Knight, general counsel for the corporation. (Another new locomotive, Engine 24, was named for McDonald—the *Michael C*.)[18] The opening of the road was hailed as a marvelous civic achievement, wholly endorsed by the West Siders who blessed it once all of the property claims were settled to their satisfaction. The Lake Street Elevated Railroad Company, however, was soon beset with financial setbacks and a disappointing lack of ridership. After only eighteen months, the New Yorkers were soliciting buyers.

After years of acquiring valuable Chicago real estate (literally block by block), Charles Yerkes closed the sale of the Lake Street Elevated Railroad, July 3, 1894.

On that day, he purchased controlling interest from Underwood and Green after the stock price had plummeted from $28 per share in February 1893 to just $18 per share in July 1894. The road reported a $146,000 loss, and the New York investors decided they wanted out.

A financial panic descended upon the nation following the close of the 1893 world's fair, and only Yerkes possessed the wherewithal to capitalize on the economic misfortunes of the elevated railroad. He paid $1 million for the depressed stock, convincing the bondholders to renegotiate their notes.[19] Former mayor Roche was replaced by Delancey H. Louderback, a loyal Yerkes man and an efficient money manager who previously ran the Northwestern "L" Company. At the first stockholder meeting following the takeover, President Louderback tersely assailed the financial acumen of McDonald, Fitzgerald, Green, and Underwood for allowing staggering construction cost overruns to drive the project to the edge of bankruptcy. "At a liberal estimate the six-and-two-fifths miles [the length of the route] should not have cost over $2,017,000," he reported. However, the final bill came in well over $3 million. "It is apparent that the road has been used to issue securities to the investing public regardless of its probable earning capacity."[20]

Yerkes ultimately achieved what McDonald and Alberger could not: the linkup of the Lake Street "L" road with the rival Metropolitan West Side Elevated Railroad and the South Side "alley" line in the heart of downtown Chicago, the final phase completing the "Loop" and the extension of rapid transit into distant city neighborhoods. On October 1, 1894, the city council passed the necessary right-of-way ordinances to extend the line 4,500 feet east to Wabash Avenue, and then from Lake Street south to Harrison, paving the way for the first train of the "Union Loop" to pull out of the Lake Street station on September 6, 1897.[21] A majority of the original directors were on hand, although there is no record of Mike McDonald being invited to participate in the ribbon cutting.

Following a series of sensational newspaper exposés in the *Chicago Record* accusing Yerkes of bribing juries and other corruptive acts, the titan of traction was driven from Chicago in July 1899. His scheme to secure a one-hundred-year traction franchise was foiled by many of the same boodling aldermen who once supported him in the Chicago City Council because Mayor Carter Harrison II was opposed to Yerkes and was more the reform politician than his father.

The Lake Street road failed to live up to financial expectations. It passed through a receivership in 1897 and never earned or paid a dividend. In the end, the property owners, who took their buyout in stock instead of cash, were snookered. In March 1904, the line was renamed the Chicago and Oak Park Elevated Railroad. On average, it carried only 800,000 passengers a year—by comparison, ridership on the Metropolitan was 41 million in 1903–4. It was not until 1924 that the four separate companies that owned the elevated lines were joined together into one system. The modern, municipally owned Chicago

Transit Authority (CTA) was authorized in 1945. On October 1 of that year, the CTA took over all "L" and streetcar operations, ending decades of unprofitability and fifty years of raging debate over who should own the roads: the City of Chicago or private corporations.

The history of the Lake Street "L" and the other privately franchised streetcar lines and railways is pockmarked by corruption. Yet these same men—McDonald, Alberger, Yerkes, and the "boodle" aldermen who vested them with the power to shape history—gave to Chicago one of its most enduring and iconic landmarks—a screeching, clanking overhead railway system extending from Lake Street on the North to Van Buren, south and out into the residential neighborhoods. Its cars twist and turn on ribbons of steel, its rail resting upon ancient, oil-soaked wood planking thirty feet above the heads of shoppers, office workers, and visitors who, over the generations, simply refer to the city it encircles as "the Loop."

The Garfield Park Racetrack War

MIKE MCDONALD'S IDIOSYNCRATIC QUEST FOR RICHES, RESPECT, and recognition from representatives of the "upper world" was congenital—but his alliance with the Chicago netherworld was enduring. He was still the boss gambler, fixer, and all-around rogue, despite his remarkable ascent into the world of high finance and politics and his having built the city an elevated line, presumably for the common good.

On the third day of September 1886, the Chicago Fair and Trotting Breeders' Association was duly incorporated for "the holding of meetings for turf sports, agricultural, mechanical and other fairs and the encouragement of the breeding of trotting horses."[1] The farcical wording of the act of incorporation suggested a higher purpose than the construction of a thoroughbred track for the purpose of making book and selling "pools," but this was the *only* purpose Ed Corrigan and his partners, David Waldo and Joseph Ullman, had in mind when they opened an enclosed racing oval adjacent to Garfield Park, near Madison Street and Crawford Avenue (now Pulaski) on the West Side.

Corrigan was a big name in national racing circles both as a successful driver of trotters and the owner of pacers. His horse "Riley" won the 1890 Kentucky Derby. Corrigan-owned stables produced prizewinning steeds at every level of competition. He bought up tracks and laid the ground rules by which the turf sports were governed, but members of the "Gambler's Trust" in Chicago viewed him suspiciously. To McDonald, who had his own designs on the Garfield Park track, Corrigan was an interloper; impossible to reason with, and spoiling for a fight. The fight came during the July 1890 race meet when the downtown gambling fraternity refused a request from Corrigan that they extend the courtesy of closing their betting operations so it would not interfere with his own trackside bookmaking business.

McDonald's "trust gamblers" had respected the directives of city hall during the annual Washington Park races on the South Side, but only because Washington Park catered to a "better class" of bettors: millionaire socialites, State Street merchants, and politicians who partook in the genteel traditions of the annual "Derby Day" and possessed the means to impose their will upon city hall. Derby Day was the high point of Chicago's summer social season, and its exclusivity was respected by every class.

Believing he was entitled to the same consideration as the Washington Parkers, Corrigan demanded the trust keep faith with the edicts of the law department that declared wagering on the grounds of the track was legal, while clocking bets in poolrooms or out on the street with "handbook" men was not. It was a thorny legal issue, because some legal analysts who weighed in on the matter asserted that state law made no exceptions—wagering was illegal wherever it was practiced. The vagaries of the Illinois racing laws could be interpreted either way, but in a decade-long tussle between Corrigan and the trust, victory went to those who wielded the biggest political stick—and in Chicago during the early 1890s, the man holding the biggest political stick was Mike McDonald.

Corrigan threatened McDonald, the Hankins brothers, and the other trust gamblers with raids carried out by private detectives against their downtown poolroom operations based on an 1887 statute that explicitly prohibited bookmaking in the city but in fact imposed only a minor inconvenience. "Oyster Joe" Mackin was one of the first to be arrested by the Pinkertons on a charge of maintaining a gambling den .

In retaliation, raiding parties led by Lieutenant Martin Hayes and a platoon of police department bluecoats descended upon the Garfield Park to close the bookmaking concession and disperse the crowds. Corrigan filed a lawsuit against Mayor Cregier, Superintendent Frederick Marsh, and the police department, accusing them of accepting payoffs from the gambler's trust and conspiring to injure his business through an unlawful restraint of trade. In frustration, Marsh voiced a common complaint about the traveling handbook men, one that would echo down through the years: "We arrest them wherever we find them, but we can do little with them for they carry their books in their pockets."[2]

Competition to operate a book inside the gates of the racing oval in the 1890s was fierce. At the crux of the matter was Corrigan's deliberate snub of McDonald. The bookmaking privilege was awarded to Joseph Ullman's Universal Fair and Exposition—reputed to have earned over $600,000 in a six-month period. Ullman and his operatives offered bets not only on the Garfield races, but for out-of-town racing as well—an illegal enterprise known to the railbirds as the "foreign book." The telegraph made it possible for betting operations to receive results from distant tracks across the country, accept bets minutes before post time, and communicate the results instantaneously to the house.

The rising popularity of spectator sports, particularly thoroughbred racing, in the late 1880s and 1890s foreshadowed the eclipse of Clark Street gambling, and with it the era of the lavish, high-stakes "parlor" resorts with their opulent furnishings and fine liquors began to disappear. The Civic Federation claimed much of the credit, but it had more to do with fundamental changes in public tastes, leisure pursuits, and the evolution of this section of the central downtown "Loop" into a thriving commercial business center.

Eugene Field, an essayist, newspaper columnist, and informed social critic, observed in 1895 that

> The old "Store" at the corner of Clark and Monroe is already half-forgotten although the building in which it was once located still remains and shows an unchanged front. Gambling was discontinued here in 1891, and in 1892 the Democratic County campaign committee took charge of the second floor and had the large rooms partitioned into offices. The heavy doors, battered by the sledge blows administered during many police raids, remained to tell the past glories of the "Store." For there was a time when politicians were made or unmade by a single word from the man who had his headquarters in these gambling rooms.
>
> Men who wanted nominations or were seeking promotion in politics came to ask his influence. Those were the days of free and easy voting, when 150 repeaters, thoroughly organized, rode from polling place to polling place to cast votes as long as the polls were open. The schemes which controlled elections were planned and executed from this corner. But every year seems to put the "good old days" further away, and the veterans of the street see new signs of degeneracy every day.[3]

As gambling dispersed into the outlying areas of the city and county, Ed Corrigan abandoned Garfield Park, the attending controversies with Hankins and McDonald, strident community opposition, and interference from the Democratic-controlled police force to build the first-class Hawthorne Race Course on 119 acres of land in the town of Cicero, skirting the western boundary of Chicago.

Hawthorne Park opened on May 20, 1891, a month before McDonald and his partners, Jeff Hankins, "Prince Hal" Varnell, "Paddy" Ryan, Sid McHie, and "Blind" John Condon, a former parlor boss from Logansport, Indiana, boldly filed for a permit to build an expanded wooden grandstand that would comfortably seat up to twenty thousand patrons with an eight-hundred-shed horse stable in Garfield Park. Incorporated with a capital stock of $300,000, the new "Garfield Park Club" was an impetus for completing the Lake Street "L." Billed as the "closest track to downtown," the swift completion of the commuter elevated line would mean that the downtown sportsmen and patrons living well west of the central city could be delivered to the track within minutes. The stakes were high indeed.

Garfield Park, established in 1869 as "Central Park" by the state legislature, was one of three large wooded areas interspersed with boulevards and conceived and developed for public recreation.[4] The West Side neighborhood surrounding the park was quickly filling in with single-family brownstones. It was an orderly, quiet existence in a garden spot not unlike the pastoral setting older residents of pre-Fire Chicago remembered fondly, and the Garfield Park neighbors aimed to keep it that way. They knew all too well the dangers a racetrack posed. Calling it an "intolerable nuisance" during the 1889–90 racing season when Corrigan was in charge, outraged residents filed an injunction to prevent this new venture from opening and becoming a fertile breeding ground for crime.

"The stench from the stables polluted the air; shouts, jeers and the noise of brass bands were heard at the homes of the complainants," the suit charged. "The gambling drew to the neighborhood a crowd of thieves, confidence men, loafers, tramps, beggars and adventurers and at all hours of the day and night houses were visited by beggars who sometimes carried revolvers to extort alms or food. Women and children could not venture from their homes for fear of violence or insult at the hands of the mob. Dog fights and prize fights were other attractions offered."[5]

The city council issued the necessary building permits over the strident protests of the West Side clergy and Carter Harrison, who blistered McDonald for weeks on end in the pages of his *Chicago Times*. "A cheap politician, he had himself assumed an importance which he never had attained," railed Harrison in a blind fury. "A mere mercenary, he was without honor or character. Every impulse of the man was scoundrelly. Without respect for law or decency, he was a fit manager of the unblushing scoundrelism, which in season, and out of season prevailed at Garfield Park."[6]

Declaring war, the vocal Corrigan said he had half a million dollars in cold cash to pass around, if necessary, to crush McDonald and Hankins. Corrigan held an advantage—his stable of horses was uniformly superior to the Garfield stakeholders. "Outside of location, Corrigan by far has the best of it and deserves public support," a stable owner told the *Tribune*. "The Garfield Park club must prove its quality against odds before the public will flock to its track, though novelty will give it good crowds for some days."[7]

McDonald and his associates opened in late July, "and in point of attendance Garfield Park is ahead, a natural advantage on account of location," commented a *Tribune* sportswriter.[8] That the ownership offered free admission to the grounds was a grave concern to residents—it brought into the neighborhood a shabby class of reprobates most feared by the residents.

The issue was brought into sharper focus as the 1892 racing season approached. The political pendulum had swung back to the Republicans. Former city attorney Hempstead Washburne, considered to be an honest and capable man, narrowly defeated Cregier for the mayor's office and set out to reform the police department and chase out the remaining gambling strongholds on Clark Street. His position on the racetrack question was more evenhanded. He granted the Garfield Park gamblers a thirty-day application with the hopeful intention of seeing all racing associations put on the same basis and a cessation of hostilities through equanimity; dispelling track concessionaire Hal Varnell's accusation that Corrigan's Chicago Racing Association offered to pay the expenses of a "mass indignation meeting" of angry West Siders against the Garfield opening.

More raids were to follow. After a race meet was interrupted by Inspector Lyman Lewis on September 3, an emergency writ of injunction was obtained by Hankins and McDonald. Police Superintendent Robert Wilson McLaughry and Inspector Lewis were named as defendants for obstructing the "true purpose" of the meet, held "for the purpose of developing speed and endurance in thoroughbred horses."[9] McLaughry and Lewis, it was charged, were acting as the agents of Corrigan. They replied that they were only upholding the law, and the law made it clear that the "foreign book" was not allowed on the grounds.

The matter went before a judge, and when summoned to testify in the Gambling Trust's lawsuit against the city, Mayor Washburne stunned the court with an admission that James Burke, a Corrigan agent, proposed to donate $50,000 to the Republican campaign coffers if the Garfield Park track was closed. The offer was refused, but it revealed a deepening rift between the mayor, who waffled on the issue, and the superintendent, determined to close Garfield at all costs.

The war between the gamblers was brought to a tragic, albeit spectacular conclusion, the very same day the McDonald-Hankins-Condon lawsuit was being deliberated in chancery court. Minutes after the third race of the day concluded, a large contingency of club-wielding, overzealous police under the command of Inspector Lewis descended on Garfield Park to arrest every bookmaker, jobber, hostler, and "sport" in sight and shuttle them off to the Harrison Street lockup for processing. It was an unauthorized raid executed without the mayor's knowledge or consent, fueling speculation that Superintendent McLaughry coveted Corrigan's offer of a $50,000 bounty more than upholding orders.

A great crowd of hangers-on loitered outside the Crawford Avenue gate jeering the police as they poured out of their paddy wagons. The bluecoats raced around the grounds blowing their whistles and chasing frightened spectators in a willy-nilly fashion. It was a scene of confusion and utter pandemonium when suddenly the sharp crack of pistol shots emanating from the southwest gate, near Harrison Street and Crawford Avenue, sent the police scurrying to the location.

Outside the wall of the track, they caught up with their fellow officers chasing a man of slight build wearing a gray suit and a slouch hat. The identity of the fleeing man was easily ascertained: it was Captain James E. Brown, a former Texas sheriff who maintained a stable of horses running at Garfield Park. Brown had a fearsome reputation as a hair-trigger gunman responsible for killing a dozen men back in the Lone Star State. He bobbed and weaved through the residential side streets adjacent to the park, desperately trying to elude his pursuers. The cops discharged their pistols into the air but Brown kept going, tearing past carpenters and plasterers building a row of new residential houses on Jan Huss Avenue.

The police closed in. Captain Brown turned and fired two shots from his pearl-handled .44 caliber pistol at Officer John Powell, sending a bullet through his hand and into his abdomen. Powell fell to the ground clutching his stomach and writhing in pain as Brown rushed toward his victim to administer the *coup de grâce*; he pressed his weapon up against Powell's chin and delivered the fatal shot.

The bitterly outspoken fifty-three-year-old horseman, who had been railing against the police harassment of honest stablemen racing at Garfield for many days, darted off toward a nearby alley, attempting to escape, when he was confronted by Officer Henry L. McDowell from the Des Plaines Street Station. "Don't shoot anymore! Put up your gun! I will not shoot!" the policeman ordered. "But I will!" Brown hotly replied as he took aim. With weapons raised, the two men faced each other from a distance of less than thirty feet. It was a dangerous *tableaux vivant* conjuring up the familiar image of two Western gunfighters squaring off in the dusty streets of old Laredo. The outcome was as expected: simultaneous shots were fired, dropping both Brown and the police officer to the ground.

Mortally wounded, McDowell staggered to his feet, walked a few paces, and then collapsed into the street. He expired at the Cook County Hospital less than an hour later. Meanwhile, a hundred vengeful Chicago police officers itching to extend the same courtesies to Brown as Brown did to Powell, circled over the remains of the Texan, but it was too late. Brown had passed into eternity with a glare of defiance on his face. "He died with his boots on," quipped one onlooker. An Arkansas sheriff watched in horror as the police kicked the corpse repeatedly and flailed away at the head with their truncheons. "For God's sake men! The man's dead! Don't treat him like that!" he protested.

The sheriff was promptly escorted away by the enraged police who had already beaten and manhandled many other spectators daring to criticize their rough methods.[10] An estimated eight hundred men were hauled away to the Armory Station on Harrison Street and the Des Plaines Street lockup, including Hal Varnell, George Hankins, and a dozen of the club jockeys. Al Hofmann, a McDonald bondsman and local brewery kingpin, furnished the bonds and apologized to each detainee on behalf of the club.

At the inquest, the mayor and the superintendent offered conflicting testimony. McLaughry was made to sweat by Mike's friend Alexander Sullivan, the high-priced legal counsel for the Garfield Park consortium, who grilled him relentlessly about the alleged Corrigan bribe and the whisperings that Brown's death was an assassination carried out by Lyman Lewis, the hired instrument of Corrigan. Put on the defensive, the superintendent essentially told the court the police were damned if they do and damned if they don't. "If you close the Garfield track they will say the administration was paid by Hawthorne, and if it is allowed to run they will say that the Garfield people put up the money. You can get as much done for doing your duty as for not doing it."[11]

Public opinion was decidedly against the police in the wake of the Brown shooting, although the coroner's jury returned a verdict exonerating the officers of blame for it. The *Chicago Globe* said that "Jim Brown died like a man" and had been "shot down like a dog" by "the offal of a crime-cursed city; the dissipated habitues of the vilest dens, rum-soaked wretches attired in blue uniforms, clubs in their hands, while in their pockets were revolvers loaded [and] ready to obey the chief's order."[12]

Strong words about police brutality and suppression of the public's right to peaceably assemble at a racetrack to bet on horses if it so chose provided McDonald with what he believed to be the necessary leverage to petition the city council to refrain from revoking the Garfield Park license—an action by the mayor that seemed not only probable but inevitable.

Alderman John Powers, the McDonald mouthpiece in chambers, introduced a measure to permanently license Garfield for a $100 per month assessment in the belief that this was what Washburne had intended all along. But Powers was badly mistaken. The mayor understood that if such a law were to be enacted it would effectively deny police the power to interfere in the conduct and management of the track. It came as no surprise that the bill was easily approved by the city council with only token opposition. But in the interests of public safety, Washburne vetoed the ordinance.

Alderman John "Bathhouse" Coughlin, the First Ward buffoon just beginning his long and colorful reign as political orator and protector of the Levee District, arose from his chair to deliver what the *Tribune* called a "wild harangue" in defense of the Garfield Park ordinance. "They [the police] invaded a peaceful amusement and lawlessly dragged my own father off to jail! Why, Mr. Brown was a high-minded citizen and sheriff of his own county! It was therefore the duty of the police to protect burglars!"[13] The Bath's unintentional slip of the tongue set off a gale of laughter, but the mayor's veto held; and the protection McDonald once enjoyed under Cregier evaporated with Republican rule.

The stockholders of the Garfield club admitted defeat but were left holding the bag for several hundred thousand dollars worth of building improvements and an ironclad lease signed with former judge Lambert Tree, who owned the land the park was built upon. As a last, desperate measure, Mike McDonald made an ill-advised attempt to bribe Police Magistrate Charles W. Woodman of the West Town District, a Republican partisan spotted inside the Garfield Park grandstand earlier that summer enjoying the afternoon sun, a schooner of beer, and a day at the races.[14]

In a packed courtroom inside the Des Plaines Street Police Station following two days of proceedings, Woodman discharged several of the detained Garfield gamblers, fined club management $100, and assessed minor fines to the small-fry gamblers. Alexander Sullivan gave the usual notices of appeal, when suddenly the routine call was interrupted by the loud bang from Woodman's gavel. He ordered the throng of gamblers, attorneys, and bondsmen jamming the courtroom to remain silent while he read aloud a prepared statement accusing Mike McDonald of offering him a $300 bribe.

Veteran observers of the justice courts were stunned. No one could remember a sitting justice of the peace or any other jurist of the civil or criminal courts making such a bold and dramatic statement while presiding over a trial. Woodman waved a thick wad of bills for everyone to see and asked if Mike McDonald were present in the courtroom and if so, would he please come up and retrieve it? "Are you assured that Mr. McDonald did not give you that amount by mistake in making payments on bad bonds?" queried attorney Sullivan.[15]

Woodman revealed that McDonald had visited his West Side residence on Fifteenth Street two nights earlier. His daughter had answered the door, and the mysterious caller introduced himself as "Mr. Mason," asking if this was in fact the home of Justice Woodman. She showed him upstairs where her father received the visitor, recognizing at once that it was the famous local gambler and politician. However, McDonald persisted in calling himself "Mason."

"McDonald said that he thought he would come over and talk with me regarding the Garfield Park club cases," recounted Woodman. "He said that it was exceedingly important for the association that these cases be disposed of at once and said that they desired to resume racing as soon as possible. He also had something to say in regard to the shooting of Col. Jim Brown and expressed the regret that the affair had occurred, as it created a prejudice against the club. In so many words he asked that I dismiss the cases and as an argument stated that two judges had agreed to grant an injunction restraining the Superintendent of Police from raiding the track if I would dismiss the cases."[16]

The subject then turned to politics, and McDonald brought up the candidacy of his man, John Peter Altgeld, for governor. "He said there was no doubt in the world that Altgeld would be the next governor. He talked as if he had great influence with Mr. Altgeld and personally assured me that I would be reappointed Justice of the Peace. He also said the election of a Democratic governor would ensure the election of a Democratic mayor and that there would be no doubt about my being reappointed under such circumstances."[17]

McDonald arose from the chair and remarked that as a bondsman, he believed he owed Woodman some money for the personal recognizance the judge had granted the arrested Garfield gamblers from the day before. The judge accepted the bills without counting them out, estimating that the amount due him was no more than $17. McDonald tipped his hat and exited the residence.

Only then did Woodman examine the bills and realize that he had been handed $300. No one had actually witnessed McDonald pressing the money into Justice Woodman's hand, nor did Woodman say anything about it two nights later when McDonald made a return visit.

Mike did all of the talking in this second clandestine meeting and provided the names of two judges, Edward F. Glennon, a Republican, and George H. Kettelle, a Democrat, who were "alright," meaning that they were in on the "fix." Woodman listened politely but offered no guarantees. He remained coy and never once flashed the righteous indignation he would exhibit in his courtroom the next day, and for the moment McDonald was left with the optimistic view that Garfield would remain open for the duration.

The veteran jurist was enmeshed in the upcoming fall election campaign. Sensing an opportunity to embarrass and discredit Altgeld with this damaging story, and savoring the chance to drive the final nail into the coffin of the Garfield Park gamblers, Woodman dashed over to the home of John J. Badenoch, chairman of the Republican Central Committee of Cook County, and later met with Superintendent McLaughry, soliciting their advice on how best to play up this situation. It was decided to make political hay with a dramatic and sudden gesture—and it worked to perfection. Woodman's courtroom theatrics triggered a barrage of adverse publicity on a statewide level that compromised Altgeld's chances and left McDonald vulnerable to a grand jury indictment.

Downstate newspapers vigorously condemned the Altgeld-McDonald alliance, based on this latest bribery scandal. "It would be a humiliation and a disgrace to the State of Illinois if Joseph W. Fifer would have to give way to a man who would have to wear the collar of Mike McDonald the law breaker and thug," editorialized the *Decatur Weekly Republican*.[18] The *Bloomington Pantograph* took credit for exposing McDonald's shady manipulations on behalf of Altgeld during the state convention held earlier that summer. "Altgeld was McDonald's candidate . . . and was a thoroughly unfit man for the office of governor."[19]

Backed into a dangerous corner not of his choosing, McDonald denied contacting Woodman. "It is all nonsense to talk about a bribe. I have paid lots of money out for bail bonds, but I didn't pay any of it to Woodman. No one who knows me would think that I am so foolish as to throw away $300 to try to bribe a Justice of the Peace. It seems to me that those people didn't want to have a monopoly of the bribery business," he said of the Republicans, "so they got up this $300 yarn to off-set the $50,000 Hawthorne bribe. This game Woodman has sprung isn't worrying me any."[20]

From his office in the Marine Building, McDonald was informed of his arrest two days later. The mayor had ordered George Dupuy in Corporation Counsel John S. Miller's office to swear out the warrant after expressing strong displeasure that the case had not been brought up for judicial review. Of course, the steady drumbeat of Carter Harrison's newspaper accusing Washburne of shirking his duty by not pushing the prosecution sooner likely influenced the mayor to act.

Hearing the news, McDonald registered little emotion. He appeared before Justice George P. Foster in the magistrate's court. Alfred Trude and another old friend of McDonald, ex-county judge and former mayoral aspirant Richard Prendergast, supplied Mike's bond and asked for a hearing without delay. The defense strategy was to turn this into a political spectacle. Trude accused Woodman and his backers of trying to negatively influence voters in the downstate rural districts by insinuating that McDonald and Altgeld were silent partners conspiring to take over the state. Reporters were subpoenaed to testify to the inconsistencies and embellishments of Woodman's public statements.

The location of the hearing was an amusing irony—Justice Foster's improvised courtroom was convened in the former downtown gambling parlor that once belonged to George Hankins. With biting sarcasm characteristic of his demeanor, Trude said he hoped the "Goddess of Chance" would smile favorably on his client before launching into Woodman. "Now we desire to put this trembling, shrinking putrid piece of humanity on the stand and wring from him the fact that he is not entitled to the slightest consideration of this community. McDonald should be discharged on account of the frail nature of the testimony which has been adduced."[21]

Justice Foster, nervously fiddling with a scrap of paper and speaking in a hesitant voice in the presence of the intimidating veteran attorneys, sustained Trude's motion for dismissal with the feeble explanation that Woodman and Badenoch had conspired to turn this into a campaign issue. McDonald received congratulations from his supporters and disappeared into the street. When questioned by a reporter as to why he freed the defendant on Trude's motion, Foster heaved a sigh and said, "I am a Democrat."

～ 15 ～

Electing Altgeld

THE STATE WAS NOT THROUGH WITH MCDONALD. ALTHOUGH HE had been acquitted by a partisan justice of the peace in a rigged trial, the Cook County grand jury voted a four-count indictment against the old gambling boss, charging him with an act of bribery. As his term of office wound down, Mayor Washburne was frustrated and angered by the outcome of the Woodman affair. His attempt to bring McDonald before the bar a second time was nothing less than political payback. "I'm not going to talk about it," Mike snapped. "My attorney Mr. Trude will do all the talking, but I reckon they've accomplished what they wanted by having me indicted and I suppose the case will be *nolle prossed*."

State's Attorney Joel Longnecker was in no particular hurry to go to trial and was going through the motions. Few people believed McDonald would be prosecuted a second time, and he wasn't. A new Democratic governor would see to that.

The national election was at hand, and McDonald was back at his old desk at Democratic headquarters at 137 West Monroe Street, holding hourly consultations with his henchmen, gamblers, saloon men, and grocery keepers in the interest of promoting John Peter Altgeld's candidacy—and looking ahead to 1893, the mayoral contest. The Eagle was relentless in his editorial attacks against "Mike the Briber." The rant was venomous, but stripping away the tumult and the shouting, Harrison's burning ambition to become the "World's Fair mayor" was exposed. It would be the perfect capstone to a long career in public life. Visiting Joseph Medill in Pasadena, California, weeks before the primary scuffles were set to begin, Harrison, who never pretended to be humble or modest, remarked, "You know Medill, that I am the best qualified man for that position in Chicago, and that I will fulfill its duties better than anyone else that can be had out of either party and there isn't anybody in the city that can beat me if I am nominated for the office."[1]

But logic dictated that Harrison could not hope to accomplish such a thing without the backing of the "King Blackleg" who thrust himself offensively into political activities. Even as he blistered McDonald in print, Harrison could not shake off rumors and published reports of a budding political alliance that would return the mayoralty to him and the license to operate the Garfield racetrack to Mike. In the early going, McDonald favored Altgeld's candidate, Washington Hesing, a cultivated and polished man who was a stakeholder in the Garfield track, a former Harrison supporter, and publisher of the *Staats-Zeitung* newspaper (the most influential foreign-language newspaper west of New York) inherited from his father, Anton C. Hesing.

The newspaper war between Carter Harrison's *Chicago Times* and Mike McDonald's *Chicago Globe* escalated. Bitter words were exchanged. Hesing chaffed when Harrison demanded that he withdraw from the race and give up the chance to become Chicago's first German mayor, and he lashed out against the *Times* as a propaganda tool dispensing lies and half-truths—but with a hidden agenda. Hesing accused his rival Democrat of buying the paper from the Storey estate in order to promote his two sons (and *Times* editors), Carter and Preston, and provide them with a launching stage to further their own future political ambitions. "Harrison bought it so he could give his boys some personality, more than can gain be gained from a real estate sign."[2]

Mike's grasp on power was still strong, even in these changing times when increasingly his influence was significantly challenged by younger party men coming up through the ranks of the ward organizations. It seemed to follow that Harrison's best interests would be served by reaching an accord with the old gambler, because when the *Globe* "sneezed," as the *Tribune* ruefully observed, "certain Democratic organs in the interior followed suit. Their editorial action was based on the stuff printed in the Chicago organ of Mike and John [Altgeld]."[3]

The Eagle faced opposition in the volatile First Ward where "Bathhouse" Coughlin, a "Cregierite" loyal to McDonald, had seized control of the political apparatus following the barroom murder of Billy "Mockingbird" Whelan.[4] The bellicose Alderman Coughlin did much of his talking to the *Chicago Globe* as he publicly sparred with the Harrison forces.

The *Globe* was an important campaign tool—but never a serious news journal. The Chicago Globe Company was organized as a Democratic sheet on March 16, 1888, with $50,000 in working capital—much of it supplied by Charles Dennett and Horace Hurlbut of the Iroquois Club and by Austin Patterson and Andre Matteson, *Chicago Times* editors who had defected to the startup venture. The *Globe* was one of nine dailies vying for circulation in a tough, competitive newspaper town. Although it had the financial backing of the Democratic Party, the paper struggled to meet payroll and operating expenses and was reorganized in November 1890. Mike McDonald, a minority investor in 1888, put up $109,000 of his own money, secured through a mortgage. McDonald took in new partners, including Judge Adlai Ewing, a cousin of Adlai Stevenson (future vice president in the second Grover Cleveland administration), and assumed the assets and debts of the old company. The four-page, eight-column *Chicago Daily Globe* resumed publication with a new mandate and a firm pledge: "A STRAIGHT OUT Democratic journal, it will fight for the men and the principles of the party, unbiased by personal feelings," the editors promised. "The editorial and reportorial staff is being rapidly recruited from the most active workers and brightest writers to be found."[5]

The newspaper ran on a shoestring budget. Harry Wilkinson penned the editorials according to the directives of McDonald and the party regulars. A sodden group of whiskey-soaked veterans of the news world ridden out on a rail from better-paying jobs with more prestigious papers formed the nucleus of a broken-down, cynically detached editorial staff. Young men, callow in the ways of big-city papers but showing promise, were recruited from the streets to learn the ropes. Early in 1892, one of them—a spindly, thick-lipped, twenty-one-year-old Hoosier lad fresh up from Terre Haute—turned up at the back door of the *Globe's* office at 118 Fifth Avenue (now Wells Street) hunting up work. The young man was coldly received by copy editor John Maxwell in a "large, bare, colorless, smoke-colored room filled with a few rows of tables end-to-end," but after much coaxing was put to work exposing mock auction shops and their assorted scams—a criminal enterprise carried on by tricksters outside of the purview of McDonald's operations.

The young stripling looking to break into print was Theodore Dreiser, future author of *Sister Carrie* and a pioneer in the emerging school of realism challenging stodgy Victorian-era literary conventions. In his autobiography, published long after achieving prominence in the world of arts and letters, Dreiser erroneously described McDonald as a keeper of brothels.

The paper as I now soon learned was controlled by one Michael C. McDonald, a celebrated local politician, gambler, racer of horses, and the owner and manager of a string of local houses of prostitution, saloons and gambling houses, all of which combined netted him a handsome income and made him one of the most influential men politically in the city. Some administration attacks were made upon him, or rather his privileges, whereupon, not finding suitable support in the papers of the city which were of his own persuasion, they having axes of their own to grind, he started a paper of his own. This was the *Globe*—the one with which I was connected. He had brought on a capable newspaper man from New York, so I understood, who was doing his best to make an interesting paper which would satisfy Mr. McDonald's desire for influence and circulation in this respect the while he lined his own pockets as best he could against a rainy day. For this reason, perhaps, our general staff, though fairly capable, was underpaid.[6]

Any pretense of journalistic objectivity completely melted away after Mc-Donald stepped in to prop up a faltering enterprise. The principal aims were to publish a paper articulating the views of the McDonald-Fitzgerald faction, to refute the hostile opinions of the *Times,* to vigorously promote the social benefits of the Garfield Park Club and the necessity of a Lake Street "L," and to elect candidates to office who were favorable to these interests.

One day, a reporter new to the job, approached McDonald with trepidation. He had been assigned to cover city politics and was anxious to find out the political policy and editorial stance of the paper. "The political policy?" McDonald repeated. "My boy, the political policy of the paper is this: the meanest convict in the penitentiary at Joliet, if he is on the Democratic ticket is, better than the best Republican out of jail!"[7] And that policy was, of course, articulated to the public.

Managing editor Harry Wilkinson was a member of the Cook County Democratic Party inner circle. He was voted in as a full vice president of the Garfield Park Club. City editor Charles Almy, a whiskey-tippling *bon vivant* who launched Chicago's famed "White Chapel Club" of writers and imbibers, took his cue from McDonald and the partisans. Almy's eventual successor, John T. McEnnis, another hard-bitten old souse, spied a glimmer of talent in the budding genius in his office and dispatched Dreiser and the other young "cubs" to scour the hotel lobbies, train stations, saloons, and restaurants to jot down all the gossip of the day and report back. Much of what was overheard in the corridors had to do with the comings and goings of politicians in Chicago.

Although Wilkinson was the editor, the *Globe* was constantly assailed by the *Tribune* and the *Herald* as the voice of Mike McDonald. They accused the scandal sheet of being the "chief agent" in the "secret manipulations" to push Judge Altgeld into the statehouse. "Those persons had the active cooperation of certain members of the General Assembly of 1891 and of certain members of the State Committee, who were the aiders and abettors of John P. Altgeld in his attempted 'downright treachery' against John M. Palmer."[8]

Palmer, a former Illinois governor born in Alton, was looked up to as a conservative elder statesman of the party, a "gold standard" Democrat, and an impediment to Altgeld's ambition to leapfrog from an obscure judgeship in Chicago to the chief executive of the state. General Palmer was elected to the U.S. Senate in 1891—but Altgeld coveted the Illinois congressional seat and was unenthusiastic about supporting the aging Palmer in the campaign. Vain and ambitious, Palmer was miffed by Altgeld's intraparty challenge, but he was just as easily seduced by McDonald's promise that Cook County would be with him all the way if he declared his candidacy for president in 1892.

Electing Altgeld would require tapping into the judge's considerable fortune—he was a millionaire and owned six Chicago buildings, including the sixteen-story Unity Building—but it would take much more than that to put across a German politician among the powerful Irish ward bosses and office holders. One's ethnicity was the prime consideration in the electoral process of the nineteenth century, and as the largest voting block in the city of Chicago, Germans were a vocal force in politics. Palmer's loyal supporters in Chicago were at best lukewarm to Altgeld's candidacy. The judge enjoyed strong statewide support in the German communities, but elsewhere he was vilified for his liberal sympathies toward the convicted Haymarket men, his alliance with the Iroquois Club of Chicago, and his association with McDonald.

The *Richmond Gazette* predicted that "Altgeld will get the vote of every socialist, anarchist, and tough in the City of Chicago. Do the respectable law-abiding Democrats of McHenry County propose to train with that crowd?"[9] The minister of the Grace Methodist Church in Jersey Heights, New Jersey, stated, "Illinois stands discredited with the threefold A's—Altgeld, Aliens and Anarchists!"[10] Among Democrats, the agreed-upon strategy to overcome the tide of negative press was to build alliances by neutralizing the other announced candidates and winning over Palmer and his supporters prior to the nominating caucuses in Springfield. The campaign to manipulate public opinion was brilliantly executed by Wilkinson in the pages of the *Globe.* The editor printed unsubstantiated but potent gossip that Altgeld, the virtual unknown, was the "coming man" in 1892.

"Democratic leaders are agreed that with Palmer for president and some such man as Judge John P. Altgeld or Brigadier General John C. Black for Governor, Illinois will be placed within the Democratic column."[11] Gradually the names of other potential candidates were winnowed out: State Representative James Cockerell was talked out of an independent run for governor by Clarence Darrow, Altgeld's future law partner who shared office space with him at 115 Monroe Street—a few doors down from McDonald's Store.[12] Darrow's tactic was bitterly criticized. Then the *Globe* reported on February 23 that "there is considerable talk of General Black withdrawing from the contest. He might win the nomination for Congressman-at-large. Judge Altgeld is now the only man mentioned in connection with the Governorship."[13]

Apart from McDonald's *Globe,* no other Chicago newspaper expressed any degree of sympathy for Judge Altgeld. He was reviled by many as a dangerous radical and a grave threat to the business and commercial interests of the state. Among the members of the Chicago judiciary, he had a surly reputation as a peevish, often vindictive, litigator who took every courtroom setback as a personal affront to his character and integrity. Darrow admitted that Altgeld, his friend and closest ally, was "a hater and this was his really great weakness."[14]

The Democratic sheets pleaded for the nomination of General Black, a "respectable Democrat," a Civil War hero, and the former U.S. attorney in Chicago. However, the downstate journals, following the lead of the *Chicago Globe,* spoke favorably about the dark horse from Chicago as a compassionate, reliable man. Delegates from Hardin, Hamilton, LaSalle, Wabash, Gallatin, and Perry Counties arrived in Springfield and were already won over. They had come to the state convention solidly behind Altgeld, a man they dubbed "the poor man's friend." By the same token, they were less inclined to endorse Palmer, who was shelved as a presidential candidate by the delegates. McDonald's assurances had no merit and were merely uttered to neutralize Palmer's opposition to the "Dutchman," as Mike referred to his friend Altgeld.

Judge Altgeld was nominated on the first ballot amid the cacophony of the brass instruments of "Captain" James H. Farrell's Cook County Democratic Marching Club and the war whoops of the raucous First Ward bosses who marched into the hall in their Prince Albert coats, high silk hats, and colorful badges signifying party status and the wards they represented. Sol van Praag, Bathhouse Coughlin, Hinky Dink Kenna, and their ilk were all on hand to stampede the convention, leaving the supporters of the gallant old soldier General Black and Senator Palmer to scratch their heads in wonderment.[15] The Chicago press corps called the rejection of Palmer "an overt act of betrayal" engineered by McDonald, Altgeld, and the *Globe.* "The campaign was run on the same lines that the chief agent [McDonald] runs a portion of his business in Chicago," groused the *Tribune.* "The granger Democrats were confidenced by his political agents, as granger visitors used to be confidenced in the long ago by his gambling agents."[16]

With the nomination in hand, a more difficult challenge loomed for Altgeld: to become the first foreign-born candidate to win the state's highest office by defeating a popular incumbent governor, Joseph Fifer—"Private Joe," remembered for crossing party lines to parole "Oyster Joe" Mackin. Before his surprising success in the 1892 electoral season, Altgeld was neither prominent in public service nor was he a gifted orator and wordsmith, although he earned guarded praise for his cool-headed logic and for making earnest pronouncements. A man of melancholy temperament, Altgeld often appeared rumpled and ill at ease before the public, but he threw himself into the race with great zeal and covered nearly every inch of the state in an exhaustive speaking tour. He attacked Fifer for using convict labor for state projects and assailed his school reform record. Fifer did not answer the charges, and the accusations were accepted as fact by voters.

Assessing the public leader not long after his death in 1902, the *Tribune* described to its readers the essence of an absolute moralist, a man intolerant and vengeful of his Republican foes and their dissenting opinions. "Mr. Altgeld could not concede that his political opponents were 'clean-hearted.' To him they were bad through and through. The man who did not see everything as he saw it was his enemy. He did not know how to conciliate, to consult expediency, or to forgive."[17]

Altgeld was out to wrest control of the national party from Grover Cleveland and the gold-standard Eastern Democrats. Gaining influence in Washington was one of Mike's most powerful motivations, of course.[18] To do so, he took extreme measures and risked his standing in the party to elect this "Dutchman." Fearing that the Woodman bribery scandal would discourage rural downstaters from voting for Altgeld because of the candidate's known association with the hardened sinner from Chicago, Mike announced his resignation as Eleventh Ward representative from the Cook County Central Committee a month ahead of the election. The tender was peremptory and would take effect at once.

A chastened McDonald said he would have no further role to play in the management of the Altgeld campaign or Carter Harrison's opening move to reclaim the mayoralty in the spring. Interestingly, the county executive committee did not rush to fill the vacancy. Trude denied that the Woodman affair factored in McDonald's decision to step down, but the denials did not ring true. "Because his business affairs demanded his entire attention I urged McDonald more than a year ago to withdraw from politics," the lawyer told the *Daily News.* "If anything wrong was done by his party the blame was laid at his door. He worked hard for his party at all times. If success followed he got no credit for it. If failure, he received unlimited abuse. At all times he was the bait of the Republican Party. The Woodman case had not the slightest influence directing McDonald's course. Testimony such as Woodman gave, infected with the vice of admitted falsehood on his part, would be as harmless to McDonald as a bread-pill."[19]

For the next five weeks, McDonald steered clear of Democratic headquarters and kept away from his favored old haunts: Chapin and Gore's Restaurant, 137 West Monroe; Charley Rector's at Monroe and LaSalle; Matt Hogan's at State and Congress; and Billy Boyle's Chophouse at 5 Calhoun Place in Gambler's Alley where, for many years, it was his custom to drop in "on the boys" once a week to feast on his favorite culinary delight—breaded fried salt pork, a baked potato, and a pitcher of buttermilk.

"If his eyes are red, it is not from liquor or into games at poker," jested the *Tribune,* "but from penitential tears at his chance of being jugged. It is understood that he spends much of his time on his knees. Should Altgeld be elected, Mike would throw off his emblems of woe, leave his penitential cell and resume his membership in the various committees and be the Democratic boss once more. Mike would be the same old Mike, but a little more bossy, perhaps because he had a faithful henchman in high office at Springfield."[20]

His resignation lasted up until November 8. The voters went to the polls that day, and there they found McDonald stationed at his familiar post behind a long table at Democratic headquarters, standing opposite his old place of business at Clark and Monroe. His spirits soared—the exile was over. Victory hung in the air. He was certain of it—after all, Mike McDonald was never known to back losers.

Flanked by compatriots on either side, Mike received delegations from the press throughout the day and monitored the returns as they came in. By 10:00 that evening, Republican defeat seemed certain. Bottles of beer—"Milwaukee champagne"—and cigars were passed out to the workers. "Let joy be unconfined!" McDonald gushed. The beaming Alfred Trude, who was also mentioned as a mayoral candidate, circulated through the room collecting payoffs from the doubters who had wagered that Altgeld's plurality would fall below 5,000 votes. "I've been thinkin' about it," chimed in the perpetual hanger-on, Colonel Thomas Jefferson Dolan, as he quaffed a mug of hard cider—one of McDonald's preferred elixirs. "I'm not tootin' my own trombone when I say I did as much as anyone in my own way!"[21]

Every leading Chicago Democrat caught up in the Altgeld euphoria claimed credit for the victory of this political dark horse—a victory orchestrated end to end by Colonel McDonald and his patronage army, with a strident appeal to the public from the *Chicago Globe*. This pivotal alliance of saloon Democrats and gamblers has been all but erased from the historical record by biographers and subsequent generations of historians who, in their rush to canonize Altgeld as the first Progressive and a man without flaws—a saint eulogized by the poet Vachel Lindsay as the "Eagle Forgotten" for pardoning Oscar Neebe, Samuel Fielden, and Michael Schwab, the imprisoned Haymarket men—ignore the less savory aspects of his political associations and the record of his administration.

Concerning the Haymarket pardon, the governor concluded that there had been a serious miscarriage of justice in their prosecutions. In his message to the state following the pardon on June 26, 1893, Altgeld said, "The deed of sentencing the Haymarket men was wrong, a miscarriage of justice. And the truth is that the great multitudes annually arrested are poor, the unfortunate, the young and the neglected. In short, our penal machinery seems to recruit its victims from among those who are fighting an unequal fight in the struggle for existence. The right of the people to assemble in a peaceable manner to consult for the common good being a constitutional right, it can be exercised and enjoyed within the scope and spirit of that provision of the Constitution, independently of every other power of the state government." However, Governor Altgeld had a self-serving motive for freeing these men.

While serving on the bench of the superior court in 1888, Altgeld represented himself in civil matter concerning a dispute over a parcel of land he owned in Cook County. After Altgeld made one hysterical outburst over a technicality, the presiding judge in the case found him guilty of contempt and fined him $100 for conduct unbecoming. Altgeld appealed the decision to the higher court, but the decision was sustained by Judge Joseph E. Gary.

The author of the opinion had presided over the infamous Haymarket trial and had condemned eight of the nine convicted socialists to death. To add insult to injury, Gary wrote an inflammatory article for the *Century Magazine*, ridiculing the Haymarket men and their attorneys. Kevin Tierney, author of a 1979 biography of Clarence Darrow, argues that Altgeld's anger toward Gary festered. Never one to let go of an old grudge, Altgeld's desire to extract revenge and humiliate an old adversary outweighed (in importance) the larger issue of restoring justice and humanity in his decision to pardon the remaining three Haymarket men in 1893. "The truth was . . . he hated Gary. His feeling on this whole matter . . . was very intense," Darrow would later recall.[22]

In other cases involving capital murder and other heinous crimes, Altgeld was inconsistent and capricious in exercising his power to deny or grant clemency. In a January 1894 case, he issued a temporary stay of execution for one George H. Painter, convicted of murdering a prostitute in a downtown Chicago hotel. Sufficient doubt was cast on the verdict based on strong physical evidence that another man drenched in blood at the time of his arrest was the actual murderer. It was shown that the new suspect had both motive and opportunity—Altgeld conceded as much—but he declined to issue a second stay and refused to stand in the way of Painter's execution.

Mostly, the governor showed a dangerous tendency throughout his term to ignore manifest evidence of guilt as he routinely set aside the verdicts of juries and the sentences of Illinois judges. With careless disregard and reckless abandon, he emptied the penitentiaries, and this inflamed public opinion. In one instance, an Altgeld pardon sparked mob violence. In May 1895, opposition to his liberal policies precipitated a mob action in Vermillion County when farmers removed two accused rapists from a Danville jail and lynched them from the bridge spanning the Kankakee River. The leader of the lynch mob laid the blame for their actions on Altgeld, citing his contempt for the law. "Yes we know the jury will convict and give them a severe sentence but Governor Altgeld will pardon them out. He recently pardoned three men you sent up from Champaign County for twenty years and he will pardon these men. If any other man than Altgeld were Governor we would not lynch these men."[23] Between March 1893 and May 1895, as table 15.1 illustrates, the governor wielded the power of pardon to excessive lengths.

By the end of 1895, he had freed eighty-one Illinois prisoners. The newspapers raised a hue and cry and dubbed the governor John "Pardon" Altgeld. Then on his last day in office, January 2, 1897, the "Dutchman" released twenty-six offenders convicted of serious crimes, including seven more murderers. One of them was Maimie Starr, a domestic servant who had fed rat poison

Table 15.1 Governor Altgeld's Pardons and Commutations, 1893–1897

Crime	Sentences Pardoned or Commuted by Altgeld
Murder	19
Rape/Assault/Incest	8
Armed Robbery/Arson	5
Forgery/Embezzlement/Manslaughter/Burglary/Larceny	75

Source: Published accounts in the *Chicago Tribune*, March 1893 to January 1897, including the year-end wrap-up of crime statistics, mortality, and judicial records for each
calendar year.

to a Chicago family of four, killing them all. She too was freed by a stroke of
Altgeld's pen. "I am surprised Governor Altgeld [has] finished out his term and
not turned out *all* criminals in the penitentiary," smirked Chicago attorney
Edward C. Nichols.[24]

It has not been easy for sympathetic historians to reconcile Altgeld's com-
passion for the laboring classes and the political courage he showed facing a
firestorm of criticism following the pardon of the anarchists with his penchant
for freeing violent criminals and linking his administration to an oily Chicago
political machine that elected him; one ruled by a boss gambler and his First
Ward lieutenants who provided recognizance to Levee whorehouse proprietors
and ran racing handbooks and notorious concert saloons.

Altgeld has earned considerable praise from Illinois historians for the high
road he traveled during his one term of office. His willful opposition to President Cleveland's call-up of army regulars to quell the destruction of railroad
and government property and suppress labor unrest during a strike of Pullman
sleeping car workers in 1894 has been called an act of bravery, but the governor's
dilatory actions and the strictures he placed upon Judge Gary threatened the
investment of Eastern capital in Chicago markets. Apprehensive Wall Street
speculators immediately withdrew $2 million in loans to local real estate devel-
opers, fearing that a dangerous and irresponsible demagogue was in control of
the affairs of the state. The city's credit and financial ranking suffered greatly
as a result.

Altgeld was filled with resentment toward the mercantile interests and adapted an effective slogan that played well among the laboring classes, "Equal rights
for all, privileges for none!" But the new governor was still a loyal party man who
imagined political plots everywhere, and with the unchecked force of a prairie
fire he purged Republican office holders in state and municipal agencies. In a
letter to Carter Harrison a week before the mayor was assassinated by a crank,
Altgeld revealed a streak of political paranoia when he accused several Chicago

police officers in the Des Plaines Street Station of spreading false rumors of an anarchist bomb plot on election eve in order to improve the Republican chances. "If you will send word that any such discovery before election will cost them their heads, then you will find the matter will never be heard of again."[25]

Competent men administering the Cook County Asylum and the boards of the city parks were discharged by Altgeld. After he ordered the resignations of three commissioners from the administration of Lincoln Park, the *Tribune* commented, "The superintendent of a charitable institution may be a poor physician, but he is alright if he is an Altgeld man. Altgeld's course has been a consistent one from the beginning."[26]

McDonald had not invested this much time, energy, and money without receiving some early assurance from Altgeld of political payoff and the right to dictate appointments in Cook County. And so it was not surprising that Governor Altgeld found few defenders in the press or among the reform Democrats when he appointed Mike's newspaper editor, Harry Wilkinson, as secretary of the West Side Board of Park Commissioners. The appointment was spurious. Wilkinson was exposed as an incompetent and forced to step down a year later.

Altgeld appointed another McDonald associate, Chicago banker Edward S. Dreyer, to take Wilkinson's place, but Dreyer embezzled $318,169 from the West Park board and was convicted of criminal fraud in June 1898. The press was incensed. "No man in the gubernatorial office of Illinois ever so prostituted his place to his selfish interest as Altgeld. Other men have used the place for political advancement, but his scheme was to take care of himself in all respects no matter what woe came upon others."[27]

The addition of Edward Uihlein of the Schlitz Brewing Company and Charles Vopicka, president of the Bohemian Brewing Company, to the West Park board assured McDonald that sympathetic liquor interests would support his bid to restore the racetrack license and the beer concession at Garfield Park. Finding such a pliant, sympathetic ally—another Altgeld—to lead the Democratic ticket in Chicago presented a more delicate challenge for McDonald, but this time he badly miscalculated the mood and sentiment within his party.

In the spring, as preparations for the world's fair accelerated and as the new governor settled into office, Mike's opponents plotted the "restoration" of Carter Harrison. Early on, Captain Farrell and John Powers were declared Harrison boosters. Others coming from a bewildering array of ward clubs and splinter factions from the three geographic divisions of the city rallied behind Harrison. Meanwhile, McDonald, Coughlin, and John Hopkins were among the dwindling Hesing supporters in the party's ruling cadre.

Washington Hesing coveted the mayoralty as badly as Harrison, but he was to be spurned by the party regulars of Irish background and American-born nativists who harbored seething resentments against the foreign-born Germans, perceived as Altgeld-anarchists and socialists—even after Mike's pleadings to the faithful that they reconsider the wisdom of their actions. As the tide turned against him, Hesing leveled serious accusations of vote fraud against the Harrison loyalists and stormed out of the Democratic City Convention at Central Music Hall in an angry huff. He cited a *Staats-Zeitung* report that "in Wards five, six, fifteen, and eighteen nobody with a German name was allowed to vote and that many votes were thrown away."[28] "Boss" Jim Farrell, grand marshal of the Democratic Marching Club, allegedly warned his Twenty-second Ward "heelers" that it must be won for Harrison "regardless of cost"—and they had taken the "usual" steps."[29]

Disgusted, Hesing denounced the Harrisonites as a "packed mob of unprincipled men." There were certainly enough of them to go around. Wild disorder reigned inside the Music Hall.[30] German delegates from the Fifth Ward accused the Irish of attempting to bar them from entering the hall to vote for Hesing, their spokesman. But the Harrisonites controlled the party apparatus throughout the proceedings, in the same fashion the former mayor had intrigued through sneak tactics to nominate Grover Cleveland in Chicago in 1884.

Carter Harrison was put up for mayor through the "corrupt use of money," according to the embittered German editor who charged Harrison with accepting $30,000 from the railroads in return for a promise that he would not enforce pending city council ordinances that would require them to take the costly step of elevating the tracks to reduce the escalating number of fatalities at grade crossings.[31]

It was a tough intraparty fight although, as the campaign wore on, the Eagle was fast becoming the man of the hour—the next Democratic standard-bearer. With no other recourse, McDonald realized his political survival was in jeopardy. Whether he liked it or not, he would have to go all-out for Harrison and cling to the slim hope for reconciliation, or suffer the consequences. As a first step, he invited leading Democrats and the public to his headquarters to encourage a Harrison turnout. On official party stationary, McDonald penned his message and launched a direct mail campaign.

Dear Sir:
I wish you would please come up to 137 Monroe Street to see me as soon as possible on important business.

Very truly yours,
M. C. McDonald[32]

Harrison refused to soften. He disavowed any connection to Mike and set himself up as an implacable foe of the gamblers and ward bosses, whom he accused of aligning with the "disreputable elements." It was further evidence of cracks in McDonald's previously "bullet-proof" armor. "The exposure of my connection with the campaign," McDonald declared, "will bring 5,000 votes to Harrison!"[33] It didn't matter one way or the other to Carter Harrison at this point.

Cregier was never considered. Among the gamblers and saloon politicians, there was no other choice *but* Harrison. "Harrison may give us the double cross. He may throw us down, but we've got to take our chances. We've got to show with the other people," said one.[34] Remembering McDonald's early support for Hesing and a *Globe* editorial from a year earlier calling Harrison a hindrance to the "far-seeing" Altgeld, Carter Harrison lashed out at Mike and renounced his offer of support. Harrison pledged to defeat Samuel Allerton, his reluctant Republican opponent, honestly. Allerton was one of the large beef and pork packers in the city, but he lacked the support of "gangs and combinations" and had little chance of success.

"Then they go on and say Mike is running my campaign, and that I have made an agreement to open Garfield Park," Harrison exclaimed, defending his position as a reform-minded Democrat.

> [They say] that George Hankins gave me $5,000 in consideration of that. Why $5,000? They have forgotten that last summer the price supposed to be sufficient to buy a mayor was $50,000 from Garfield Park. Now, therefore they say I have made my peace with the gamblers; I am run by Mike; he and the gamblers are going to run me. Now the facts are that Mr. McDonald is not a member of the executive committee. He is not a member of the campaign committee. He is a member of the County committee, and elected himself by barring up the window at the primaries on the 27th day of last February. Mr. McDonald may have some good qualities, and I would not overlook the good qualities of even a gambler, but Mike McDonald has been a loadstone on the neck of the Democratic Party for years.[35]

An April 5, a smug and satisfied Harrison was swept in with a 20,000-vote plurality, minus much of the city's German vote. He made history as Chicago's first five-term mayor and looked upon the next two years as an opportunity to cement in place his public legacy—divorced from the very class of men who made his bones fourteen years earlier. Alfred Trude's younger brother George was elected city attorney, and for McDonald there was a consolation prize: the Woodman indictment conveniently went away. Mike was no longer troubled by the anxieties of a looming prison sentence—that was the good news, but it was a small reward in the larger scheme of things.

The election results seemed to validate and affirm the prophetic boasts of sweeping Democratic success McDonald uttered to Justice Woodman, but for all the successes he helped achieve for his candidates, it turned out to be a zero-sum game for Mike personally.

In what must have come as a bitter blow to McDonald, who stood to lose upwards of $50,000, that neither Mayor Harrison nor Governor Altgeld directly intervened on his behalf in the Garfield Park matter, despite Altgeld's packing the West Side Board of Commissioners with McDonald men. The license was never restored, and Judge Lambert Tree, now a respected former European ambassador, sued McDonald and George Hankins for $35,000 of back rent. "When the police began to raid the place and arrest the bookmakers, Hankins and [John] Condon and the other boys came to me and asked me to go to Judge Tree and I did so," Mike told a jury. He said that the conversation with Tree had occurred between January and September 1892. "Judge Tree said he would see the Mayor but he wanted to do it in such a way that he would be kept in the background. Judge Tree said he didn't want any notoriety in connection with the track but would do all he could to see that the boys were protected."[36] Tree branded McDonald a liar and explained that he was out of town at the time and couldn't have possibly met with Mayor Washburne. When the mayor refused to "protect the boys" and the track closed, the Garfield syndicate stopped paying rent and the suit went forward.

It was pointed out by the defense lawyers that the Garfield club had spent $200,000 to build a spacious grandstand and another $70,000 for a three-year lease. But the jury came back with a decision favorable to the judge. McDonald and his partners were out $35,000. Said George Hankins with a heavy sigh, "We have been laboring against difficult circumstances from the start. Our license was taken from us and disaster has necessarily followed. It is hardly possible that any arrangement can or will be made by which the course will ever be used again."[37]

In January 1895, Judge Tree, whose family had owned the land for over fifty years, transferred the eighty-acre tract to realtor William D. Kerfoot to subdivide for residential and commercial redevelopment. Water, sewer, and gas pipes were installed. New streets were plotted and paved with asphalt, and a building line of fifteen to twenty feet was established. All vestiges of a racetrack were obliterated as the appearance of a modern West Side neighborhood began to take shape. The newspaper became the next financial casualty.

Serving no other useful purpose and bleeding red ink, the *Chicago Daily Globe* was transferred to a court-appointed receiver—who else but Harry Wilkinson?—on March 21, 1893. The publishing company admitted in court that it was in arrears to Mike McDonald for the sum of $109,097. "This matter will in no way affect the publication of the paper," Mike assured the public. It was a lie, but he was anxious to soothe the jitters of the small editorial staff and the Democratic readership it faithfully served. "We simply wish to straighten out matters for money advanced. The management will not be affected by it."[38]

With Democrats occupying the White House, the state house, and city hall for the first time since 1856, the crippled *Globe* served no further useful purpose in promoting McDonald or furthering the Democratic Campaign Committee. Financial support was withdrawn in November, leaving the beleaguered staff writers and the pressmen to ponder a bleak future in hard times. By the time the World's Columbian Exposition ended in October, an economic depression had descended upon the land. The *Globe* employees had not been paid their wages in three weeks. Then the final word came down: the doors of the office were to be padlocked, and no provisions would be made for the staff.

On December 28, a public auction was held at the offices of the *Globe*. Everything was to be sold—the desks, the letter files, stereotyper's outfit—even the steam boilers and the pictures on the wall. Hearing of the plight of former colleagues, Theodore Dreiser, now a well-paid reporter attached to the *St. Louis Globe Democrat* and enjoying the fruits of his success, said he would see what he could do for them, after hearing how McDonald had welched on his promises. "How much better I had done indeed, than my friends thus far—these men who had been in the business longer than I had. Certainly I would see what I can do. They should write me. Incidentally I was at such and such a hotel. The sweets of success!"[39]

～ 16 ～

That Little Feldman Girl

THE WORLD'S FAIR OF 1893 REPRESENTED THE STELLAR TRIUMPH of commerce, industry, the arts and sciences, and humanity's progress as it marched toward the dawn of a new century. For six glorious months that year, the magnificence of the white alabaster buildings in all their splendor revealed Chicago to the world as much more than a clogged metropolis of smokestacks, slaughterhouses, and odious politicians. And that was the hope of the exposition planners, the clubmen, and the *grandes dames* of Chicago society looking to reshape a city in the muck into a "White City," one that would astound the world's visitors and transcend the ages in their memory.

Not even this delightful interlude, played out along this stretch of south lakefront in Jackson Park, could entirely erase thoughts of the omnipresent crime, political corruption, and filth of the city streets existing outside the dreamlike idyll of the fairgrounds. The horror of urban living and the malignant nature of gaslight-era Chicago politics brought these issues into sharper focus and would forever silence the pageantry, the brass bands, and the fireworks overhead, with the sharp crack of the assassin's bullet echoing across the city on Saturday evening, October 28, 1893.

Earlier that morning, Carter Harrison delivered the most memorable oration of his long career to several hundred U.S. mayors seated inside the Jackson Park Music Hall. Pacing the stage for added dramatic effect, he extolled the accomplishments of his city. Looking ahead prophetically, and tragically, to the future, he said, "Genius is audacity and the audacity of Chicago has chosen a star." The mayor beamed, speaking the very words etched upon the base of his statue that would one day be erected in Union Park.

"It has looked upward to it, and knows nothing that it fears to attempt, and thus far has found nothing that it can't accomplish. I intend to live for half a century yet," he added, undoubtedly a sly reference to his upcoming nuptials with Miss Annie Howard, a twenty-five-year-old heiress from New Orleans who was making final preparations to exchange vows with the mayor in less than thirty days. "I myself have taken a new lease on life. I shall live to see the day when even London shall be looking to its laurels."[1]

Turning to Alderman John McGillen and other machine men, John Powers whispered, "The old man is at his best this morning!" Alderman Coughlin agreed. "See how straight the old man holds himself!" Then the mayor of Philadelphia arose from his chair and proposed, "Three cheers for Mayor Carter Harrison!" The assembled dignitaries arose from their chairs and gave him a thunderous ovation. Wearing a new red necktie and a gray suit, Harrison exited the stage, his face smiling broadly. It was Chicago Day, one of the important closing events of the fair.

The mayor spent the entire afternoon enjoying the sites and sounds of the world's fair, before returning to his Ashland Boulevard residence, exhausted but otherwise satisfied by the day's events. After dinner, Harrison settled into his study, asking not to be disturbed unless the matter was of importance. Around 8:00 P.M. the mayor was summoned to the vestibule of the home to receive a visitor—a disheveled, ragged looking youth of twenty-five, named Patrick Eugene Prendergast, who said he had a "scheme to elevate the railroad tracks" of Chicago. It was one of the most bitterly contested issues of the day. Prendergast, who read law books despite the lack of a formal education and a menial job—he was employed as a newspaper distributor for the *Inter-Ocean* and *Post* by day—spoke endlessly about the subject to his immigrant mother in their dismal little hovel on Jane Street.

Like Charles Guiteau, the delusional psychotic who assassinated President James A. Garfield in 1881 because he believed he was entitled to a position in the cabinet, Prendergast was convinced that Harrison had already guaranteed him an appointment as corporation counsel in order for him to see his "scheme" through. Prendergast circulated among the ward characters, office seekers, and politicians in city hall but was ridiculed and dismissed as a crank. Likely he had made contact with Harrison and badgered the mayor for a meeting to present his plan.

At 2:00 that fateful afternoon, Prendergast purchased a .32 caliber Harrington-Richardson six-shooter from a shoemaker on Milwaukee Avenue for four dollars. He spent the next few hours loitering inside a YMCA building, knowing that the mayor would be occupied at the fair for much of the day. At around 8:00 the unkempt young man presented himself to the Harrison maid, Mary Hansen, who summoned the mayor from his study where he was taking a nap following dinner with his son, William Preston.

Prendergast asked Harrison whether or not he intended to appoint him corporation counsel. "He would do nothing I wished and what he had promised," the assassin later told police, and I drew my revolver and shot him."[2] Three shots tore into Harrison's side. Upstairs William Preston Harrison was relaxing with a book when he heard the crack of a pistol and a loud crash. "I realized at once that someone was shooting in the house and I was downstairs as quickly as I could go," he related to police.[3] "I instinctively pulled the patrol alarm as I passed it, and then I turned into the dining room." There he found his father lying in the passageway to the kitchen. "Willie, I'm shot. This is death. Bring Annie," Harrison gasped, asking for his fiancée, Annie Howard, a young New Orleans heiress said to be worth $3 million. "Bring a doctor!"[4] The mayor remained conscious for less than ten minutes, calling for Annie repeatedly. Meanwhile, the family houseman chased Prendergast down the block, firing several errant shots at the assassin, who retreated south on Ashland Boulevard past William Chalmers, who had heard the shots from across the street.

"I know nothing of the man who killed my father. We had no reason to think anyone was such a bitter enemy of my father," Preston Harrison sobbed. A few minutes later, the son fainted, overcome by shock and strain.[5] Carter Henry Harrison expired at 8:27 P.M. The news went out, and the city reacted with horror and disbelief. On the streets, groups of men gathered to discuss the day's event and damn the soul of Eugene Prendergast, who had meekly surrendered to police at the Des Plaines Street Station. The prisoner was transferred to the Cook County Jail, where he shared space in the infamous cell number 11 with a Chinaman and a canal laborer charged with murdering his superintendent. Just six years earlier, Haymarket bomb-maker Louis Lingg committed suicide inside this same prison cell by exploding a fulminating cap in his mouth, cheating the hangman by twenty-four hours.[6] The inmates of the jail scorned Prendergast and volunteered to save the state the cost of execution by meting out their own brand of punishment in the bullpen.

On Sunday morning, as the church bells tolled, the world's fair planners gathered inside the administration building in Jackson Park, where it was decided to call off the gorgeous closing spectacle scheduled for later that day. A small flotilla of ships was to be greeted by triumphant music performed on the grand plaza. Instead of a burst of light, color, and fireworks cascading down from the skies of Chicago, workmen draped long folds of black cashmere over the city hall entrance and cornices. Emblems of mourning were seen everywhere, and heavily veiled women were escorted to the city churches to offer prayer. The assassination was a dark stain on Chicago, its reputation, and its history.

Annie Howard was stricken with illness, it was said, after receiving the news of her fiancé's death. She was not strong enough to attend the funeral procession following the solemn services held at the Epiphany Church across the street from Mike McDonald's residence.[7] Condolences poured in from around the world. The magnates of Chicago commerce and industry who reviled Harrison as a tool of gamblers and saloon brawlers now lined up to sing his praises.

Businessmen-philanthropists Marshall Field, Philip Armour, John B. Drake, and Martin Ryerson extolled Harrison as a great mayor, a civic leader, and a cordial old friend. Joseph Medill, however, hedged on bestowing *too much* of this sentimental high-minded praise. The martyred mayor was narrowly viewed by the silk-stocking element as a Democrat tainted by sympathies for the "socialistic foreign born element."

"The people liked him. While they disliked his actions in a good many respects, and thought that he hadn't enough conscience— that high moral motives in him were too feeble—at the same time, while they regretted it, they liked Harrison. He was a man you couldn't very well dislike," said the publisher. It was a supreme irony that Medill, one of Harrison's most implacable foes, would be asked to serve as an honorary pallbearer.[8]

Eugene Patrick Joseph Prendergast, one of society's angry outcasts—a man of reduced economic circumstances but grandiose ambitions—was defiant. "I knew a large number of people and because of my influence, Harrison promised me a position," he boasted to his police inquisitors. He said he knew the mayor well and that Harrison once referred to him as "his son." It was later shown that Prendergast had paid a call on Governor Altgeld at his office and had scribbled personal messages to half a dozen U.S. senators, offering advice on the nation's monetary system, his belief in Henry George's "single tax" theories, and how the distinguished gentlemen should conduct themselves while in office.

"I was asked what I wanted and I said that I had a scheme for the elevation of the railroad tracks. I wanted to be Corporation Counsel so I could push this scheme," Prendergast explained. "I was told that I might have the position. Since election I have asked for the place again and again. I have been put off repeatedly. The office was given to another. The Mayor had betrayed me and I resolved to have revenge. I have it."

Adolph Kraus, Harrison's corporation counsel designate, would live out the remainder of his days knowing that he bore partial responsibility for the tragedy by egging Prendergast on. Kraus, who regarded Prendergast as a harmless oddball, had taunted him when he came down to the city hall office two weeks before the assassination to unveil his "railroad scheme" and plead for an appointment. In a moment of cruel jest, Kraus presented the disheveled job seeker to his staff. "I took him around the office and introduced him to my colleagues as my successor in office," Kraus said. "I noticed that he kept his hand on his hip. And he may possibly have carried a revolver but he has never troubled me since." Prendergast was shown the door as the sound of sarcasm and laughter rang in his ears.[9]

In a strange reversal of roles, Alfred Trude, who had defended scores of criminals and gamblers in his day, led for the prosecution. Clarence Darrow was the junior member of the defense team, but his closing speech to the jurors was vigorous and full of passion. Darrow provided an early glimpse of the brilliant courtroom oratory that was to come; flashing a style and substance that would mark him as one of the twentieth century's greatest and most gifted trial lawyers.

Spurred by duty, Darrow fought hard for Prendergast, a man he genuinely pitied. He carried a petition for clemency down to his friend John Altgeld after the sentence of death was pronounced on December 29, 1893, but Altgeld refused to intervene, and the Supreme Court of Illinois declined to grant a writ of error to stay the execution. The savage media criticism against Altgeld for pardoning the anarchists weighed heavily on his mind. Politically, he could not risk a repeat of the troubles. A commutation for Prendergast would be career suicide for a politician already in trouble with the voting public.

Efforts to save the life of the cross-eyed assassin, under the claim that he was rendered insane by a serious blow to the head in childhood that left him in a coma for a month, fizzled. It was revealed that Prendergast's grandfather was violently insane, and mental illness was relatively common in his family, but the alienists (psychiatrists) were unanimous in the opinion that the accused possessed all his faculties at the time of the murder. In jail, the condemned man's erratic behavior seemed consistent with symptoms of insanity—in one bizarre instance in his cell, Prendergast jumped on Darrow's neck and planted a kiss. Prendergast showed no contrition, at least not until the final moments of his life ticked away. As the hangman draped the white robe over his head and secured the noose tightly around his neck, the killer's last words were, "I have no malice against anyone."[10]

For Mike McDonald, who marched behind Captain Farrell and the Democratic marching band in the solemn procession to Graceland Cemetery (but otherwise was excluded from the funerary events and tributes honoring his onetime friend and ally), the death of Harrison did not necessarily foretell the death of *Harrisonism*. The martyred mayor's strongest supporters kept firm control of the party, even as the sullen Democratic "bolters" within the city council helped elect Republican businessman George B. Swift mayor pro tem on November 7. It was understood that Swift, the former commissioner of public works in the Roche administration and a man of methodical habits and sober temperament, would serve just five weeks—until the party caucuses could marshal their resources and decide upon candidates for citywide election.

Out of respect to the slain mayor, Harrison office holders were retained—the new leadership of the Democratic Party had come to the fore. City Sealer Robert Emmet "Bobby" Burke, a squat, pudgy little man with twinkling eyes and a persistent chuckle, directed the late mayor's 1893 election campaign with skill and precision. He had emerged as "boss" of the Harrison faction in the days and weeks following the assassination. The signature "O.K. Burke" scrawled on an application for a job, or a letter of favor, was as good as a certified check—he was the new point man. And suddenly, Mike McDonald was a leader of diminished stature—forced to retreat into the shadows; a figure from another age whose time had come and gone.

With Roger C. Sullivan, the former probate clerk, and James Aloysius Quinn, infamously known around town as "Hot Stove Jimmy," because he would steal whatever he could wrap his arms around if it was there for the taking, Burke formed one-third of a ruling triumvirate from the North Side that would control slate-making and dominate ward patronage for the next two decades.

These three picturesque figures of long standing were not always in accord with one another. For years, Burke feuded with Sullivan over the latter's opposition to perennial presidential candidate William Jennings Bryan—the "Boy Orator of the Platte." It would be Sullivan who would emerge as "the strong man" of city politics in the early 1900s. Cook County Sealer Jimmy Quinn, boss of the Twenty-first Ward and the owner of a hat shop at Clark and Erie Streets that became as famous in its day as Mike McDonald's Store for the political shenanigans transpiring behind the drawn shades, fought Bobby Burke tooth and nail, but he wisely made accommodations with the Sullivan faction of the party. "New York politicians in their rottenest days that city ever knew, never stooped to pick up the kind of money he took!" said Quinn about Burke.[11]

The up-and-comers of the post-Harrison era were ambitious and eager to squeeze out the old guard if the slightest weakness or vulnerability was detected. They were young, but they came up through the old school and perfected their mastery of the "insider's game" by studying the techniques of Mackin, McDonald, "Black Bill" Fitzgerald, the county boodlers. and the city council's long-reigning "Big Four"— James Hildreth, Frank Lawler, James Colvin, and Ed Cullerton—and waited for their turn at the public trough. Quinn later bragged that in the rough and tumble days of old when he was a young sport squeezing his way into McDonald's legerdemain, "a fist like a ham was as good as a box full of ballots."[12]

"Asa" Trude, the sly old barrister who flirted with a run for the mayoralty in 1892 and again in 1893, urged McDonald in the gentlest of terms to withdraw from the field and retire to private life. Mike could no longer effectively dictate a slate of citywide candidates to the party—and Burke's Harrison Democrats still viewed him as the late mayor's Judas. His ability to influence the outcome of elections was mostly confined to the West Side District where he resided.

By the 1890s, the city of Chicago was carved up into precise geographic spheres—each with its own boss and agenda. Although Johnny Powers was the acknowledged leader of the faction, McDonald was named vice chairman of the West Side Cook County Democratic Central Committee in December 1894, with a mission to advance West Side candidates and issues, although he still managed to hang on to the prestigious, albeit mostly ceremonial, vice presidency of the nationally recognized Cook County Democratic Marching Club.

His opinions were voiced, and the ward heelers were smart to listen. When he saw an opportunity to articulate his views to opposing factions and draw upon his long years of experience, he took it. In a speech to the county Democracy inside their LaSalle Street clubroom on December 16, 1894, McDonald acknowledged the vulnerabilities of his advancing age and the inevitable changing of the guard. "I don't know as I can say anything to the old battle-scarred war veterans in regard to the Democratic Party, for they too have fought for democracy just the same as me. They haven't died exactly—not them that's here. I am glad to see the young element coming to the front to take the place of us old fellows that's retiring. Most of you have a good education. Most of you can be gentlemen when you want to be—so my advice to you is, don't hanker after political jobs."[13]

His words occasionally provoked hot anger among splinter factions. The legendary saloon brawls of the 1870s and 1880s were reprised inside the Democratic clubrooms in the 1890s when disagreements between the gin-soaked bosses exploded into fistfights. Parliamentary procedures would be cast to the wind as chairs flew across the room and the leaders of the Democracy landed sucker punches on each other's jaws. Such was the state of affairs on December 2, 1895, after McDonald launched into an unexpected tirade against Mayor John P. Hopkins, the former Pullman storekeeper who bested George Swift by the narrowest of margins in the December 1893 runoff election to complete Harrison's unexpired term.[14]

The air was charged with the stench of tobacco smoke, profanity, and high expectations as McDonald arose from his chair to register his deep displeasure with the gentleman from Pullman. Blunt and to the point, he accused Hopkins and his cohorts of absconding with $750,000 of campaign funds belonging to the central committee. "I am going to tell you fellows who have been robbing the Democratic Party and blackmailing candidates for two years some strange facts!" McDonald thundered. Hopkins refused to help reopen Garfield Park in 1894, and Mike was unforgiving. "You men who have been candidates and assessed—where did your money go? Certainly not to benefit the Democratic Party, nor to pay the rent on any of these rooms. Get it and keep it has been the policy of this Hopkins rule! I have been on this committee for 19 years and with men who did not stain their hands by letting the dirty stuff taken from candidates stick to them."[15]

"That's right Mike! Give it to 'em!" a chorus of West Siders shouted back. With these words of provocation uttered, the meeting exploded into a no-holds-barred melee—a "pier-six" donnybrook. Twenty-five men, civic leaders all, were in the center of the room fighting, kicking, and gouging, and Mike was in the thick of it, while Powers stood off to the side, unwilling to ruffle his Prince Albert coat or scuff his patent leather shoes. The *Tribune* reported that McDonald was hit, but not seriously hurt, and managed to land a few telling blows of his own against "Hot Stove" Quinn and several North Siders as he stood his ground alongside Illinois state senator Billy O'Brien (a staunch Powers man) and Captain Farrell.

"McDonald set the pace and the others endeavored to keep up with him in words and actions," the *Chicago Evening Post* reported the next day, "which was sure to be very trying for anyone of [Chairman F. Stuyvesant] Peabody's limited command of stockyards English. Add to this the fact that McDonald tripped over some of his words, was rambling in his ideas except in regards to Hopkins and was then usually at fault in pronunciation and grammatical construction. There was no lack of excitement, oaths and ill feeling. Chairs were used for arguments and fists were plentifully displayed. It was a regular old time Democratic meeting with all the frills and furbelows that rightfully belong to it."[16]

In his reply to McDonald's charges of corruption, Hopkins derided Mike as a "political nuisance," but there was no denying the accusations against the ex-mayor carried a ring of truth: seven members of Hopkins's administration were arrested earlier that year and charged with conspiracy to defraud the city treasury of $175,000 by means of "stuffed" payrolls. The worst excesses of the Gray Wolves and their "boodle ordinances" benefiting their bank accounts, Charles Yerkes, Roger Sullivan and his Ogden "gas trust," and other pirates in business suits occurred during the two disastrous years the dandified Hopkins occupied an office in city hall.

McDonald sounded suspiciously like a Baptist reformer when he urged the central committee in January 1895 to get behind the Civic Federation (every shady Chicago politician's common enemy) when it proposed to set the mayor's term of office in cities with a population over 200,000 at four years, not two, as it had stood since 1837, when the city was incorporated. The bosses said that such a measure would benefit the Republicans and thought that their old comrade had gone daft in advancing years, but McDonald challenged his brethren to elect the "right" candidate, a veiled reference to the disgraceful Hopkins's scandals resulting in voter backlash and the return of the Republican George Swift into office in the city election of 1895. It would take another decade before the practical measure to extend the mayor's term to four years would be enacted in Springfield.

Politics was always uppermost in his mind, but outside business interests commanded much of his attention and energies as a new century approached. McDonald owned land all over the city and sold properties to developers at a fat profit. He was a very shrewd real estate and sporting man, but his interest in business ventures independent of what he knew best yielded disappointing results.

After the Globe Newspaper Company foundered and collapsed, he entered into a partnership with West Town assessor Al Hofmann, his old courthouse bondsman; George Hofmann, Al's brother and a well-known Chicago distiller and Democratic partisan; attorney Edward Maher; Alderman Powers; and James Bowlan in the management of the Brewer and Hofmann Brewing Company. The large West Side plant at 41–53 South Green Street bottled and distributed Bests Premium Milwaukee Beer—an old Chicago elixir enjoyed by the city's burgeoning German immigrant community. McDonald was appointed company president in 1898 and was tasked with ensuring the smooth sailing of the family business and oversight of saloon licensing matters in the treacherous political waters of Chicago.

There were no "sure things" or safeguards against rank stupidity however, and McDonald was powerless to circumvent the downward spiral of the company that began around the time George Hofmann unveiled an absurd scheme to pump the suds into every Chicago household through a system of underground pipes. The City of Chicago took a dim view of the matter and refused a request for a permit. As laughable as it was, the city government found nothing amusing after investigators turned up evidence of a massive tax fraud engineered by Collector Hofmann, who had accepted bribes from the many taverns buying barrels of the company beer in exchange for Hofmann's agreement to cancel their personal taxes. The brewery was thrown into receivership in 1903, and the building with all of its fixtures and equipment was sold at auction to a Milwaukee man on January 1, 1904.

In 1897, McDonald deposited $10,000 into the account of A. J. Murphy, another businessman with a "can't miss scheme" out on the prowl for rich investors. Murphy won a bid for the citywide garbage collection contract but could not come up with the required $200,000 surety bond. The contract was lost, and McDonald sued to recover his money and to enjoin the city from letting the contract to a competitor firm until Murphy's financial affairs could be put in proper order. A March 1897 measure granted the city council absolute power to award contracts—in other words, there was "no abuse of discretion," and McDonald's injunction failed.[17]

Another scheme caught his attention a year later. In February 1898, McDonald and a syndicate of investors with a capitalization of $2 million purchased Fire Island, a 1,500-acre slip of land opposite LaSalle, Ontario, in the Detroit River. As the main stockholder, it was McDonald's intention to turn the island into a resort area with a racetrack and casino—an "American Monte Carlo," or at the very least an extension of Coney Island for Chicago and Detroit junketeers.

The initial plan was to run excursion boats from downtown Detroit out to the island, allowing patrons to gamble at the tables and witness prize fights and other attractions of a similar character. It was hoped that America's reigning champion, "Gentleman" Jim Corbett, would agree to fight a title match at the club.[18] In terms of practicality, the plan was shortsighted and doomed to failure because Edward Gilman of Detroit, charged with establishing regular boat service to and from the island, could not carry out his mission. Visitors to Fire Island complained of sporadic service. It would often require four hours to negotiate passage back to Detroit or to Windsor on the Canadian side. In 1918, the land was sold to John Ford of the Michigan Alkaline Company, who used much of the eight-mile-long island for a dumping ground of alkaline byproducts.[19] A large hotel and billiard hall that once stood on the island were razed, and McDonald's dream of emulating Richard Canfield by establishing a Saratoga Springs–style resort in Canadian waters fizzled.

The plotting of treacherous new political rivals, intraparty scraps among the partisans, numerous business reversals, and a succession of unfavorable judgments stemming from civil lawsuits filed by and against McDonald foreshadowed the final, defining tragedy of his sinuous life. An error of judgment, a fatal weakness of character—whatever the root cause may have been, the lethal consequences of his poorly thought out decision to remarry at age fifty-six seemed to mirror the plot of some classic Greek tragedy. The philosopher Aristotle observed that tragedy involves the fall of a noble man caused by *hamartia*, some excess or mistake in behavior—not because of a willful violation of the gods' laws." And tragedy was to be his final destiny.[20]

Mike was a religious man despite the shady nature of his business and the character of his associates—at least to the extent that he generously supported the Catholic Church both financially and socially—and his home was a way-station for panhandling priests trading moral absolution for a place at his dinner table and a comfortable bed to sleep in, at least while Mary was still around and had a say in the matter. Mike portrayed himself as a family man—he believed in the strength of the family unit, marital fidelity, and respect for elders, although he was physically abusive when drunk and easily provoked into tirades by the words and deeds of others. As a father, he was firm to the point of being occasionally tyrannical, but among his friends in the gambling fraternity and politics he was looked up to as a "square shooter"—the highest compliment bestowed upon a man whose real sense of place is the world of dice and cards. His downfall, as Aristotle observed in men of similar wealth and influence, was traceable to the foibles of human nature—vanity and self-deception.

On the last day of 1894, Mike McDonald checked into Milwaukee's elegant Pfister Hotel, accompanied by George Hofmann and a "woman to whom McDonald was noticeably attentive."[21] Inside the hotel cafe, Mike was spotted by an acquaintance endeavoring to secure an introduction to the radiant, blonde-haired young woman with a pleasant oval face, large eyes, and dark lashes, noticeably younger than her famous companion from Ashland Boulevard standing by her side. McDonald was uncomfortable and agitated by the chance encounter. Anxious to shun gossip and publicity, he refused to disclose the mystery woman's identity and moved away quickly.

Later, rumors of Mike's elopement filtered back to Chicago and crossed the *Tribune* city editor's desk. It was hastily reported in the papers. Two days later, rumors were confirmed by the Reverend A. A. Kiehle of the Calvary Presbyterian Church on 10th Street in downtown Milwaukee as he finished filing a marriage certificate with the local Register of Deeds office. It was true, Reverend Kiehle revealed. He had performed a quiet ceremony in the presence of just two people: George Hofmann and the minister's wife, while joining the famous ex-gambling boss in marriage to twenty-five-year-old Dora Feldman, daughter of Rabbi Fogel "Frank" Feldman and his wife, Frances Shaffner Feldman (or "Fanny"), Jewish immigrants from Prussia. Reverend Kiehle said that the group from Chicago had been exceptionally "liberal" in the amount of fee money they forked over, and the groom presented himself as a real estate man. He did not know until later that this was the famous Mike McDonald of gambling and political fame. The bride was exceptionally beautiful, but he said he knew nothing of her circumstances.

Born in Memphis, Tennessee, "Flora" Feldman (throughout her life she insisted upon being addressed as Dora) endured a series of psychotic episodes as a child.[22] Her erratic behavior is better understood today as borderline personality disorder. Frank and Fanny believed that as she grew older, Dora would shed her unpredictable ways. The family relocated to the West Side of Chicago where it was hoped that their only daughter would progress into adulthood without further incident. In her new surroundings, the frequency of her psychotic episodes indeed dwindled.

Reporting on the marriage of Mike McDonald, the press did not mix metaphors, nor were they particularly sensitive to cruel ethnic stereotypes when they branded Dora a "ghetto girl"—the family settled into the Jewish quarter on Peoria Street for a short time, before moving up to 406 Ashland Boulevard, where they were to become friendly with Mike McDonald and his sons.[23]

The reporters began poking around and discovered that wife number two was a minor celebrity in her own right. Dora Feldman, quick-witted, rebellious, and imperious, appeared in *Aladdin Jr.* and a number of other amateur theatricals. She went by the stage name "Madame Alberta," and although she was never destined for starring roles in the national Orpheum circuit, Dora was a passable actress, and she possessed a remarkable ability to whistle light arias and Irish folk tunes. "Double-tongued" whistling was her special talent.

Not long after the close of the World's Columbian Exposition, McDonald attended a benefit dance for the city firemen at the Clark Street Theater. Among the entertainments scheduled for that evening was a short theatrical sketch. Dora Feldman, attired in a clinging Grecian gown, was cast as the heroine of the play. Enchanted by her unusual beauty, he ventured backstage and summoned her from the dressing room. "Are you that little Feldman girl?" he inquired pleasantly, remembering this enchanting actress as the clever little girl living directly across the street from his mansion and playing with his adopted son Harley years earlier. McDonald often brought home a fistful of candy tucked into his coat pocket to distribute among the children. She said she remembered his kindness very well and was flattered by his attention.

The "little Feldman girl" was now a grown-up, married woman and the mother of a one-year-old boy—although, as McDonald was made to understand, her lot was not a happy one. At the age of eighteen, she suffered a romantic obsession and ran away from home to steal the heart of Sam Barkley, a professional base-ball player who logged five years in the American Association and the National League, with stopovers in St. Louis, Kansas City, Toledo, and Pittsburgh. He played second base for Charles Comiskey's 1885 champion St. Louis Browns, and while not a great star, he was a steady, dependable hitter, a fair glove man, and fan favorite, drawing a large salary. Dora pushed the idea of marriage hard, but with good reason Barkley hesitated. He said that he believed she was "always a little crazy."

"When I first met her, I was playing with the Kansas City team," Barkley recalled. "She was a Chicago girl living at 619 W. Harrison. She followed me to Kansas City and cried and said I did not intend to marry her. That night she went to her room and took poison. She was not expected to live but when she did recover I married her, as I had intended all along."[24]

Sam and Dora's was a romance of the streets; the young couple relished the high life, the late-night hours, the music halls and theaters of the city. Dora was better suited for the role of gay companion and *bon vivant* than a stay-at-home wife—that was soon apparent to Barkley. Her game was money and celebrity, and with Sam's big paychecks, the bride was living large. She spoke wistfully of a theatrical career in Chicago and believed it would be possible, with her husband on the road for much of the time. Sam was opposed to the idea, and his troubles began.

Then Sam's career abruptly ended following a serious knee injury, and with it, his $1,100-a-month salary evaporated. With a modest nest egg he had man-aged to save, Barkley opened a cigar store in Pittsburgh, but the grit and smoky haze from the steel factories hung low over the city. It was not a place of gaiety, excitement, or color for the ambitious Dora, who was in constant high dudgeon, but spending her husband's money without worry where the next dollar was coming from. In February 1891, the sheriff closed Sam's cigar store on execu-tions aggregating $3,500. Bankrupted, the Barkleys returned to Chicago and resumed the living arrangements in a small flat near Fanny Feldman's apart-ment on Ashland Boulevard.

Back in the city, Sam Barkley seemed to catch his second wind. He opened a saloon at 202 West Madison—an old-fashioned resort for ballplayers, railbirds, and gamblers. The respectable element bitterly complained of the noise and the presence of "disreputable" people spilling into the neighborhood late at night. The police kept the place under surveillance, but it was not enough to soothe the meanish tendencies of the businessmen whose tactics suddenly turned co-ercive. The saloon was made the target of tomato-throwing thugs who hurled their rotten fruit missiles from the Madison streetcar line trundling past the establishment. With his partner, "Mississippi Slim," Barkley was driven out of downtown and forced to relocate to 15 North Clark Street in the North Side red-light district—the bailiwick of "Hot Stove" Quinn, where vice merchants and barkeeps kept their doors open until dawn. Barkley's new place was informally known as the "rag shop," because this is where ragtime, as a musical art form, gained currency in Chicago.

It was at this time that Dora began to appear in light comedy and musical roles, capturing Mike McDonald's undivided attention. Sam Barkley, traversing with the "lower element" in his rag shop, seemed less and less the ideal partner for life than the unattached millionaire from Ashland Boulevard in a fine suit of clothes and residing in an expensive house with servants and coachmen. There was after all, her own little boy to think of—Harold Barkley, soon to be Harold McDonald. "I did not want to cause her any trouble, so I did not start a suit against the man who had ruined my life by alienating my wife's affections," Sam Barkley said. "I worried a lot and maybe neglected my business and gradually got poorer."[25]

The day of reckoning came. "Bunk" Allen, an old-time circus man, con-artist, and the owner of the Alhambra Hotel and Theater at State Street and Archer Avenue in the South Side Levee District, was keeping tabs on Barkley and looking to spring a trap on the ballplayer in order to provide an opening for his good friend Mike McDonald.[26] One night Allen enticed Barkley into a "low den" on the South Side where married men had no business. "Bunk" plied him with drugs, booze, and the company of women. When Barkley was in his cups, Allen tipped McDonald to the all-night debauch. Mike, in turn, alerted a private detective he knew to personally convey the information to Dora that Sam was besotted by liquor and drugs and was rolling around with slatterns and dope fiends.

Playing the role of the emotionally outraged wife, Dora was driven to the building in a closed carriage to confront her waylaid husband. It was all the evidence—and motivation—needed to begin a divorce proceeding in chancery court. Money was another matter, however; Dora Barkley had drained her husband's bank account and was flat broke, but Mike was most obliging. It was believed that he put up $30,000 and the personal services of Alfred Trude to see it through—a sum large enough to nudge Barkley out of her life. Some suggested Sam was brokenhearted and suicidal after hearing the news of his wife's impending marriage to the aging gambler. Others would say that Barkley got over it very quickly and could barely contain his glee as he counted his cash. A mischievous smile was telling. So who, pray tell, was the cat, and who was the canary?

"It is enough to say that M. C. McDonald is a married man and let it go at that," beamed the bridegroom, making his first public appearance at Hooley's Theater upon his return to Chicago. "It is my own affair. The public is not interested."[27]

Pearls before Swine: Poetry, Murder, and the McDonalds

THE MATURE, GOLDEN YEARS OF MCDONALD'S LIFE WERE AT hand—he was healthy, robust, and going about his business in the usual ways. Dora provided him with marital pleasures he had not known in many a year; the period of loneliness was over, and now came a redemption of spirit and the chance to feel young, vigorous, and alive again. Grandpa McDonald passed away in 1895. Unlike Mary, who traced the downfall of her marriage to the old man's meddling, the young bride was fortunate not to have to put up with Grandpa's intolerable habits and persistent demands year after year.

The difference in age between Mike and Dora never seemed to be a problem to the love-struck McDonald; it was his personal triumph—the opinions of others were of no consequence. He refused to listen to the malicious gossip of the Ashland Boulevard mainliners who saw in this union a foolish old man embarrassing himself with a West Side Jewess divorcee from amateur vaudeville. The new Mrs. McDonald pretended not to hear the opinions of snobs either as she put on fine airs of her own.

A daily parade of delivery men from the Carson, Pirie, Scott department store and the other fashionable downtown boutiques carted boxes loaded with expensive gowns, fur coats, and accessories to her front door. Rich, spoiled, and pampered, money was her god. Her African American maid, Mary Magruder, who dressed her each morning, said she doubted that her mistress even knew how to lace up her high-buttoned shoes if she had to. Most evenings, the husband and wife drove about the city in their handsome brougham; their carriage excursions and the soothing sound of hooves on cobblestone were a part of the simple, unadulterated joys of daily living McDonald had denied himself for far too long.

They attended the city's annual horse show and opera performances at McVicker's and were first-nighters at all of the major theatrical performances. The couple proudly rode in the 1901 Derby Day procession to Washington Park—the gala event of the season reserved for the highest order of old-line wealth, the elegant men in high silk hats and beautiful women in dazzling gowns. They earned respectful praise in the society pages for the exquisite appearance of their eight-spring victoria carriage.

The mansion was abuzz with gaiety and chatter. The McDonalds entertained lavishly. Performers and politicians sipped cordials before the fireplace and enjoyed the formal dinners and evening soirees. Edna Coblentz, the amazing "child elocutionist" and vaudeville prodigy who, as an adult, was to gain worldwide renown as "Jacques Marchais," a collector of Tibetan works of art and the founder of a museum on Staten Island dedicated to the art and culture of Tibet, was invited to the McDonald home to entertain and delight Mike's dinner guests.

"My mother brought me down to Chicago for a weekend to entertain a big party of people at the home of Mike McDonald, the millionaire gambler of Chicago," she wrote in her memoirs. "He and his second wife 'Dora the Jewess' became so fond of me that they had me down weekends from school as often as they could secure permission for me to leave."[1]

Dora supported all of the major Jewish charities and balls, and with her husband, the devout Catholic, at her side, she made a grand appearance at a retinue of social functions connected to her synagogue and various causes. The society columns reported that Dora wore a white flannel dress with "Bertha of Holly" and made a stunning appearance at the 1895 Rex Masked Ball at the Auditorium Theater benefiting the Jewish Manual Training School. It has long been alleged that Mike converted to the Jewish faith to demonstrate his devotion to Dora, but it seems more likely that the reverse was true. Dora had received convent training at some point in her early life, and she was very impressed by Irish Catholic traditions, the ancient Celtic music, and the rituals of the High Mass.

McDonald catered to Dora's every whim and obliged her parents, son, and siblings. He formally adopted little Harold and secured a position for his new brother-in-law, Harry Feldman, in the office of City Clerk William Loeffler. Harry was in the middle of a number of controversies and constantly under a shadow of suspicion as an employee in a municipal agency steeped in graft and corruption. Richard Vaughn, the husband of Dora's sister, was rewarded with a job as a city building inspector.

Mike glimpsed the odd eccentricities of this quirky family when Emil Feldman charged his wife with desertion in September 1900. She had left Emil in order to run off with his brother, Joseph Feldman—whom she had married and divorced seventeen years earlier. McDonald was helpful and indulgent to Fogel

Feldman, Dora's doddering, eighty-five-year-old father, offering him comfort and shelter in the mansion during his final days. He died there on January 27, 1902, and Mike attended to the funeral arrangements and burial at Jewish Graceland Cemetery. "His loyalties and his charities for his friends or those who had been in his employ during the old halcyon days—the days when the fat purses came out of the West on stagecoach, canal boat and cattle train, and which returned to the setting sun sadly depleted of their wallets—are legend," the *Inter-Ocean* said of McDonald.[2]

Domestic relations between Mike and his two sons, Guy and Cassius, from the first marriage was a different matter. The boys had little empathy for the new woman in their father's life and were united in their dislike. She was an unwelcome intruder into their exclusive little world, and it was hard to reconcile the giddy teenage girl they remembered living down the street from the cagey actress they now believed was bent on robbing them of their future inheritance. Mike sided with his new wife against his sons, leading to a terrible estrangement.

Guy, in particular, nursed a deep and simmering grudge. At age nineteen, desperate to strike out on his own if only to escape his father's oppressive rule, the constant quarrels, and Dora's silly chatter at the breakfast table, he announced his intention to wed his childhood sweetheart, Mary Ann Flowers, the niece of Major General Lloyd Wheaton, a hero of the Spanish-American War.

McDonald was violently opposed to the union, and his famous temper exploded into a blind fury. Guy was threatened that if he went through with this ill-suited marriage, he would be disowned, and it didn't matter a wit to McDonald that the young woman came from Prairie Avenue stock or aristocratic lineage. Mike and Mary's eldest son was warned many times to establish himself in life—but he did not heed the warning and was married in St. James Roman Catholic Church on February 5, 1900. The parents of the groom boycotted the wedding and in response to reporters' questions Mike issued a terse statement to the press expressing his extreme displeasure:

"I have disinherited my son and he is a law unto himself from now on. I did not hesitate a moment, on learning that he had taken out a marriage license, to run a blue pencil through his name in my will. I shall never relent. He is no longer welcome in my house. We will see how the young pair can live on $10 a week! The statement that he is going to Denver on a wedding trip is interesting. He has no money."[3] Guy was employed by the Chicago Sign and Painting Company and lived with his wife and mother-in-law on Prairie Avenue. In time he would attempt to emulate his father's ways and pursue a similar career path—with less than spectacular results.

Guy C. McDonald was arrested on August 1, 1902, after Dora filed a formal complaint against her stepson. Taken before a federal grand jury and charged with writing "improper letters" to his stepmother, the estranged son was hardpressed to explain his peculiar behavior. In the interest of protecting the identity of the person who dictated the letters, young McDonald stoically held out—but the presence of a grand jury and the threat of a stretch in a federal prison for abuse of the postal system finally loosened his lips.

He explained that the slanderous words defaming the morals of Dora Mc-Donald contained in the letters were not his own, but those of his mother, Mary Noonan McDonald, now back in Chicago and operating a rooming house at 1285 Wabash Avenue, south of Roosevelt Road. She hired no domestic help to clean the rooms and do the laundry, but performed all of the manual chores by herself, fighting her way through years of scorn and humiliation. But this "pillar of martyrdom" doing her penance near the South Side red-light district could not keep her name out of the papers for long. Stories circulated that Mary was romantically linked to one Mike Coleman, alias "Charles Wilson," a notorious fiend and convicted safe-blower who was sent away to an Iowa penitentiary. Indignant, Mary accused McDonald of defaming and sullying her reputation by spreading a pack of lies. The remainder of her time spent in Chicago was given to keeping a reproachful eye on her ex-husband and his new bride. Mary's hatred and jealousy of Dora had driven her to commit this pathetic, desperate act, Guy explained, evoking sympathy from the jurors, who took pity on him and his mother and refused to return an indictment. Guy McDonald was freed but still not welcome in the family home.

However, by this time McDonald had grown weary of life on the West Side. The renewal of troubles with Mary, old and painful memories of past times, the estrangement from his kin, and a noticeable neighborhood deterioration just beginning to take root in the Eleventh Ward convinced him that the time was right to abandon the area. The expanding Cook County Hospital complex was swallowing the southern exposure of once elegant Ashland Boulevard. The old millionaires were dying off or fleeing the neighborhood.

As much as it may have pained him to do so, McDonald moved out of the West Side and conveyed the family homestead to his younger son Cassius and Wesley Schimmel, an old-line Chicago gambler who agreed to look after the property until the boy attained his majority. Their three-story, eighteen-room property was leased to Mrs. Joel Connor, who converted the residence into a lodging house for medical students interning at the hospital. It was a sad, but familiar, ending. The stately old buildings of the 1870s and 1880s would serve more utilitarian purposes as transient hotels as the nineteenth century rolled over into the twentieth, but by the 1920s and 1930s what was left of old Ashland Boulevard would be reduced to rubble by the wrecking company.

In December 1897, Mike acquired from Charles Head Smith a fifteen-room, turreted Tudor and Gothic–style mansion of granite and marble at 4501 Drexel Boulevard on the South Side for the sum of $125,000. The new home at the southeast corner of Drexel and 45th Street was a magnificent showplace among the many mansions lining the boulevard at that time. It easily eclipsed in majesty every dwelling along Ashland Boulevard. A lavish use of marble on the floor and in the main staircase drew attention from home decorators and architects.

Charles Smith, a legendary and reckless Board of Trade "plunger" had accumulated and lost multiple fortunes trading futures in the grain pit with his sidekick C. S. "Plunger" Partridge. Smith completed his Drexel Boulevard castle in time for the opening of the 1893 world's fair but would not hold onto it very long. Smith's cohort in the field of real estate speculation, George Hollenbeck Rozet—a big name in his day, but one that has disappeared from the historical record—engineered the purchase of a large tract of ground for the Washington Park racetrack crowd and developed Drexel Boulevard as the next Prairie Avenue for an emerging class of Chicago millionaires who made their fortunes after the Fire.[4]

Illustrating the interconnectivity between men of high finance, commerce, the sporting world, and gambling, Smith owned prizewinning thoroughbreds at Washington Park, including Chicago's pride and joy, the famed 1900 Kentucky Derby winner, "Lieutenant Gibson." Smith was a clubhouse regular who captivated the lesser railbirds with thrilling tales of cornering the market and of speculative fortunes won and lost. Within the commodious surroundings of the clubrooms, McDonald heard these stories and was happy to make Smith's acquaintance. He coveted a Drexel Boulevard address and cut a shrewd deal for the purchase of his mansion, which he saw as the pinnacle of attainment. The disposition of 308 Ashland Boulevard—Mary Noonan's precious "love token," lost forever because of a careless indiscretion—was made final not long after.

John G. Shedd, who lent his name to Chicago's lakefront aquarium as president of Marshall Field and Company, lived two doors down the street from McDonald on Drexel. Alfred Trude and his brother George, never very far from McDonald's orbit, resided four blocks south. The Chauncey Blairs—blue-blooded aristocrats down to the bone—and Annie Oakley, the crack-shot headliner of Buffalo Bill's Wild West Show, lived among the colony of Drexel Boulevard social climbers during the world's fair.[5]

Neither money, nor social ranking, nor the collected works of Shakespeare resting on Mike's bookshelf (the gambler fancied the "Immortal Bard of Avon" and was an amateur scholar of the canon), nor genteel living in a magnificent palace could buy this troubled family a measure of happiness or social acceptance. Days after the McDonalds moved into the neighborhood, a social blue-blood building a new home for his family down the street cancelled his plans after learning the identify of the occupiers at 4501 Drexel.

Dora was a restless spirit with a temperament and personality not unlike the Irish firebrand who formerly occupied her husband's bedchamber. McDonald passed his sixtieth birthday in 1899 and was slowing down. His hair turned gray, and he found it hard to keep up with his vigorous and robust young wife who was becoming increasingly bored and alienated from her husband after only five years of marriage. McDonald's grooming habits were becoming questionable; Dora called him a "slob" behind his back. In his presence, she addressed him as "Dad" or "Papa," terms of endearment suggesting that she now regarded her husband more as a father figure and no longer as a devoted love mate.

The seeds of the final tragedy of Michael McDonald's checkered life were sewn on the West Side at least three years before the family relocated to the South Side. The tawdry circumstances are no less shocking today than when the details first came to light with the sharp crack of a pistol behind the locked doors of a downtown office. Victorian standards were violated, and although some Chicagoans were titillated, many more were appalled. The lingering mystery is how Mike failed to unravel the tangled private life of his out-of-control wife. There is no definitive answer to this question.

He did not pay attention to what Dora was doing while still on Ashland Boulevard or notice that she had become secretly enchanted with Webster Guerin, a thirteen-year-old schoolboy still in knickerbockers living with his mother, his aunt, and his brother across the street from the McDonalds. Had Mike been alerted to this budding "friendship," the very idea of it would have seemed unbelievable. As a practical man of business, he would likely have rejected it as more slanderous gossip engineered by his political enemies to defame his wife's reputation.

The boy's aunt, Nellie Fitzgibbons, became aware that something was not quite right when she observed a small photograph button pinned to the boy's suspenders as he was changing into his clothes one morning. The photo was instantly recognized as that of Dora Feldman McDonald, whose obsession with Webster was apparently kindled from the window of her drawing room as she watched the Guerin brothers skip off to school each day. Archie Guerin remembered the emboldened Dora inviting his brother into her home after school. Then a series of mysterious phone calls to Webster from a woman identifying herself only as "Marian" aroused further suspicions. Months and then years passed, and the friendship between the tall, slender red-headed boy and the married woman deepened. It had evolved into a full-blown romantic and sexual affair.

The dalliance between Guerin and Dora was never confided to the police or juvenile authorities. The mother and the aunt just let it go, believing it was a passing phase; but when it didn't end, and their patience finally wore out, they called upon Mrs. McDonald to plead with her to cease at once the abnormal attention she was showing Webster. The women were admitted to the McDonalds' drawing room, and when confronted, Dora expressed disgust and outrage at their presumptuous accusations.

Recalling the conversation in a packed courtroom two years later, Nellie Fitzgibbons told an astonished jury that "Mrs. McDonald said my sister was mistaken in her charges and Guy McDonald helped her to spread them. 'I am going to have Web kill Guy when he comes back,'" she threatened. Out of a sense of duty, Mike's eldest son confided his suspicions to the old man, and Dora was full of vengeance and threatening murder—but McDonald refused to listen. He must have had his own suspicions at this point, but until he could figure out an appropriate course of action he did not want to hear this news from anyone, let alone his own kin. McDonald ordered his son out of the house. To protect the family honor and to restore a measure of sanity to a household torn asunder, Guy tracked Webster Guerin down and assaulted him outside of Munsey's Poolroom on Madison Street. It was not enough to discourage Guerin. Hearing the news that her beloved boy had been brutally assaulted by her stepson, Dora fired a shot at Guy, but her aim was bad.

In her final plea to Dora, Webster's mother dropped to her knees on the rug and clasped her hands. In tears she beseeched the woman to end the affair immediately. "Won't you let my boy alone?" the mother wailed. "He was a good boy until he met you. You have cast a spell over him. You have your husband and child! I have only my boys! For God's sake let him alone!"

"I am not running around with him!" Dora retorted, laughing like a lunatic and pacing the floor nervously.

"Aren't you ashamed? And you a married woman too?"

Dora reached for the back of her dress as if she were about to extract a concealed dagger. There was no weapon, but in hot anger she threatened the lives of both women. "I'll kill you!" Dora screamed, repeating the threat over and over.

"She was still crying this when we left the house. After this we could do no more for Web," the Fitzgibbons woman said.[6]

Cagey and manipulative, Web Guerin was not so callow, shy, and inexperienced as his mother and aunt wanted to believe. After exchanging his knickerbockers for long pants and leaving the schoolyard behind, Guerin happily accepted his role as Dora's "kept man," if only for the monetary incentive. Webster demanded $700 to pay off the mortgage on his mother's house, and Dora supplied the funds. He accompanied Dora to downtown department stores where she purchased gifts of expensive suits of clothes and jewelry and treated him to theater and dinner. Reservations were always made under the names of "Mr. and Mrs. Fisher," although the downtown maître d's knew the real identity of the couple.

Guerin's ambition to own a business was encouraged and financed by Dora. He opened a haberdashery at 561 West Madison Street but, as might be expected, the shop failed. Guerin was persuaded by his aunt to move to California to start anew, but his dealings with Dora continued despite the separation. It was alleged by Dora McDonald's attorneys that Guerin and his business partner, Homer Smith, stole a packet of Dora's monogrammed notepaper and forged love letters to use in a blackmail scheme aimed at extorting $10,000 from her under the threat of exposing the affair to Mike. In addition, they had a set of studio-made photographs and others taken in hotels showing Dora *in flagrante delicto* and a collection of "love poetry" written in her own hand. One poem read:

> Pull down the curtain, bring in the lights;
> Put from my memory horrible sights
> Of treachery where there should have been love;
> Of blood red where should have been the whiteness of doves
> The past, the present, the future are done;
> How different Oh God had it been had I won
> Have you heard the old saying "Pearls before swine"?
> I gave every pearl that was once mine.
> I've nothing more now to live for,
> And it's hardly worthwhile for me to live.

In another version of Dora's story, Guerin followed her out to Los Angeles (and not the other way around) to push the blackmail scheme. In this account, Dora misleads her husband, or conceals the more incriminating facts, by telling Mike that Guerin was hounding her and threatening blackmail, in a variation of the old "badger game." Dora said she was one of many innocent women who had fallen prey to Guerin's dangerous schemes; the young blackmailer would station himself inside the Beulah House, an out-of-the-way downtown hostelry patronized by Chicago's high rollers, strike up friendships with the wealthy wives—then threaten to confess a real or imagined sexual tryst to their wealthy husbands unless a "consideration" was paid.

Wiring McDonald from California, the panicky Dora allegedly said, "Web Guerin is coming; fear I shall be compromised! Shall I come back?" McDonald answered back: "Stick. Don't let anyone bluff you."[7] The veracity of the story is dubious, although Trude would later state in Dora's defense that he was in possession of a long list of married women who had paid the Guerin boy "hush money."

However, it was shown that the Guerin and McDonald families frequently socialized and were better acquainted with one another than what was previously thought. Dora, perhaps as a means to cloak the affair through deliberate subterfuge, introduced Guerin to her niece, Minnie Salinger, at a family picnic. An attraction developed, and Guerin proposed marriage, but the engagement was called off two years later after Salinger discovered that her fiancé was blackmailing her aunt.

Despite accusations of extortion, Dora maintained a strong affection—in fact, a dangerous obsession—for Webster Guerin. When he returned to Chicago, announcing his intention to open the Harrison Art Studio in partnership with his brother Archibald, Dora was inveigled to become an "investor" in the business in exchange for putting up the startup money for an office suite in the Omaha Building at LaSalle and Van Buren Streets, across the road from the Rock Island train depot. Curiously, Guerin leased the property under his pseudonym, "Louis Fisher."

The office boy, Herman Hanson, recalled that Mrs. McDonald was a frequent visitor and appeared to be a woman of "violent disposition." She and Webster had frequently quarreled to the point where they rearranged the furniture, making it necessary for Hanson to pick up overturned items and papers strewn across the floor after they had both gone.[8]

Dora's wild jealousy knew no limits. Webster Guerin was forced to account for every moment of his time apart from her. She called him in the middle of the night to see if he was home in bed, and if not, or if he stammered an unsatisfactory reply, or was vague in his recollections of where he might have been, Dora accused him of consorting with other women. When she showed him an article from a magazine, photographs or drawings of attractive women would be cut out by Dora because she feared he might comment on their beauty.

Dora was also convinced that Archie Guerin's eighteen-year-old fiancée, Avis Dargan, a tall, slender beauty with a haunting smile, from St. Jarlath's Parish, was attempting to "steal" Webster from her. When she found Avis conversing with him inside the art studio at the Omaha Building one afternoon, wild accusations flew. Dora's paranoid jealousy overtook all logic and reason. In front of a room full of diners at the Bismarck Restaurant not long after, Dora lunged at Dargan and had to be restrained. "You are trying to steal him and I love him!" she screeched at the shaken young woman. "Why can't you let him alone? Just think, after all these years Webster is going to throw me down. Would you blame me if I killed him?"[9]

By now Guerin had grown weary of his role as the "kept man" in this relationship, the repeated public embarrassments, and Dora's recent threats of physical violence. Archie advised his brother to leave Chicago on the next train and wait to see if there was a chance that a cooling off period might help, if such a thing were still possible, but Webster was hesitant. He said he had a business to run and getting away from it all was impossible. In the strongest of words, Archie reminded his brother that Dora was in possession of a pearl-handled .38-caliber revolver, and that he should be more careful in his dealings. There was no telling what this lunatic woman might do. The weapon had been a *Christmas gift* from Webster to Dora a month earlier. "I told him he was foolish to give her anything like that but he had a way of doing his own will, regardless of advice from others."[10]

The final act played out on February 21, 1907. Dora's chambermaid, Mary Magruder, remembered that her mistress was highly agitated and in a state of "intense nervousness" that morning as she dressed. Mrs. McDonald entrusted Mary with her set of house keys—an unusual thing for her to do in hindsight—but at the time, the maid didn't give it a second thought. Mike was nearly finished dressing. He had kept his real estate investment business going and was preparing to head into the city and his office in the Fort Dearborn Building.

"Today will settle it all," Dora told her husband.

"What do you mean?" he asked.

In telling reporters about his wife's agitated state of mind as she left the house that morning, McDonald said, "My wife appeared very nervous and her actions were unusual. She said 'I am tired of being blackmailed and I am going to stop it. Today will settle it.' While the language was strange I did not take it seriously and laughed. 'Let me attend to it if anyone is trying to blackmail you,' I said. 'Put the matter in my hands. I know how to deal with such things, for I have been blackmailed myself in my life.'" McDonald was aware that Guerin had been harassing his wife and threatening blackmail but had either underestimated the seriousness of the problem, or was resolved to the fact that his pretty young wife was enchanted by a younger man and no longer cared.[11]

Dora arrived at the Guerin brothers' seventh-floor office in the Omaha Building shortly after 10:00 A.M. There she found Webster, the office boy Hanson, and Archie Guerin (the former head usher at the Iroquois Theater at the time of the 1903 fire that killed hundreds). In the presence of his brother, Webster coldly and definitively broke it off with Dora.

"Well I'm not through with you by any means!" she hissed, taking a step closer. "Do you think I am going to put a bullet through my head without taking you with me? I've told that old slob of a husband of mine all about it—he knows everything now!"[12] She said she was filing for divorce and was going to New York the following day, but Guerin remained calm and unmoved after hearing these words. He asked his brother and the Hanson boy to please give them both a moment of privacy. "Alright Arch, you go and let me take care of this. I can calm her." With that, they exited the room, and Webster locked the door behind them. The violent quarrel that ensued stemmed from the misplaced jealousy of Dora against Avis Dargan.

Archie left the building to attend to other matters in the city. Down the hall, anxious workers from the American Coatmakers Company overheard the terrible row and a woman's hysterical screams, but the door glass was opaque and the door locked. A shot was fired, but there were no eyewitnesses. Three tailors from the coat shop and seventeen-year-old Lorenz Blasi, a worker on the sixth floor, rushed toward the locked studio to see what the commotion was all about. They froze in their tracks, as a screaming, incoherent Dora McDonald stood before them in the aperture of shattered glass. She had smashed the pane with her fists in an effort to escape the art studio.[13]

Abraham Wolinski and Ruben Lewis from the tailor shop spotted Guerin lying face down in a widening pool of blood, and one of them reached inside to unlock the door. Dora's pearl-handed revolver rested on the floor a few feet away. "Oh get a doctor quick, quick! He shot himself! He shot himself!" she screamed, her delicately coiffed hair in disarray and blood streaks from the broken shards of glass soiling her gown. Dora lapsed into a shrieking fit and could not be quieted down.

In an odd coincidence, Chicago police detective Sergeant Clifton Rodman Wooldridge, a publicity-hound soliciting fame and after newspaper headlines, was on his way to the Harrison Art studio with partner John F. Dougherty to investigate a fraud complaint leveled against the Guerin brothers for deceptive business practices, when they stumbled into the crime scene. They were joined by policeman John Peterson, but Wooldridge took control of the chaotic crime scene and called for the wagon. Dora was taken into police custody. "Oh God, tell me if he is dead!" she wailed, tearing at her hair.

Dora was delivered to the women's annex of the imposing Armory Station at Harrison and Clark Streets, where she was booked as "Mary Jones" after refusing to give her name. "I killed him. Will they have to hang me?" she wailed. In an unguarded moment, she tried to throw herself out the window but police matron Elizabeth McNulty pulled her back. There was no stopping her incessant crying and hysterical rant. McNulty never forgot the ordeal. "For three days she was alternately stubbornly silent or talking wildly. I had a terrible time with her."[14] The alienist was summoned, and an order was issued to transfer her to the Cook County Jail hospital. Her mind had snapped, it was plain to see.

Mike McDonald was notified of the shooting at his office at 2:00 that afternoon by Dora's brother, attorney Ben Shaffner, as he was finishing his lunch. Whatever thoughts churned through his mind at that particular moment can only be surmised, but he displayed outward composure in this dreadful situation he found himself in. Mike's first impulse was to rush to his wife's side to offer comfort and support, but he kept his wits about him. Before proceeding to the jail, he placed a discreet telephone call to police superintendent John M. Collins, a friendly Democrat who had recently appointed Frank D. Comerford to the newly created post of police attorney. Comerford supervised the gathering and preparation of evidence in police cases and would be an important person for Mike to "reach."[15]

The McDonald influence in Chicago politics and policing was still strong. At his request, news of the investigation was "bottled up" by Collins, press leaks sealed, and Dora's admission of guilt during her processing hushed up. Detective Wooldridge, whose self-aggrandizing memoir was published in book form as *Hands Up in the World of Crime*, pledged his support to Mike in whatever shape or form it would take. One Chicago newspaper, the *Evening Post,* devoted less than four paragraphs to the story and buried the mention inside the paper.

Dr. Hugh Patrick, an alienist retained by the state to watch Dora, accompanied Mike to the jail hospital. Dora did not know she was sleeping in a lockup. She imagined she was resting safely in a mental institution and alternated between periods of violent delirium and lucidity. "You know you would be better off if I were dead," she sighed, wrapping her arms around Mike and begging his forgiveness. "I want to go home papa. I want to go to my beautiful pink room with the canary bird and my cat. I don't like it here. They are mean to me."[16]

His health in decline, McDonald wore spectacles, and his posture was no longer erect. In the weeks to come, his closest friends and advisers, observing the gradual deterioration, begged him to slow down, rest comfortably in his mansion, and leave the cheating murderess to suffer her just fate. But that was not Mike McDonald's personal style.

Those first few days after the shooting, he never left Dora's side. Under the most trying, humiliating circumstances a man could experience in a lifetime, he went without sleep and gave Dora every benefit of the doubt. Alfred Trude was summoned out of retirement to organize the legal team and use every trick of his profession, honed from years of experience rescuing the likes of Jere Dunn from the gallows, to quash a likely murder indictment.

Trude was instructed to secure bond and provide for Dora's living arrangements at the Windsor-Clifton Hotel after the coroner's jury submitted a ruling. As much as Mike *wanted* to believe in Dora's innocence, he refused to allow his wife back into the South Side mansion until he was satisfied in his own mind that she was the innocent victim of a cruel blackmail scandal hatched by a cad.

Mike's faint hope that his wife was the victim and not a perpetrator was dashed at the inquest. Archie Guerin and a parade of witnesses went before municipal judge John Newcomer (who convened court in the hospital annex near Dora's bedside), repeating essentially the same story. All eyes were on McDonald as Guerin recited the damning words spoken by Dora to Webster moments before the shooting. "I am through with that old slob," he repeated. "I'm going to New York or somewhere else. You needn't think though that I will put a bullet through my brain without taking you with me."[17]

Hearing her words of betrayal for the first time, McDonald sank into his chair. His eyes were red and moist. Here was a broken, defeated man. Money, power, and influence meant little to him now. "Where is the sunshine of life for Mike McDonald now?" the *Chicago Journal* wondered.

Do the ghosts of the men who lost their all at the old Store on Clark Street haunt McDonald now that the hour of his great sorrow has come upon him? Do the specters of the slain policemen shot by Jim Brown at Mike McDonald's raided track laugh as they circle round the stricken gambler today? Does the Texas horseman Brown, he who slew and died, stand behind his one-time patron now? There was a gambling house and there was a racetrack; there were the janglings of politics in the old days of coarse work; there was the cracking of bullets, many, many bullets, who lost their all at Mike McDonald's green cloth and passed to the payless dark, as Jere Dunn, gambler and friend of Mike McDonald sent Jim Elliott dying to the floor, as Billy Whelan, alderman and friend of Mike McDonald and dead, pierced through and through; and as Jim Brown, riddled with lead. The ghosts that lurk around the Store on Clark Street must squeak and gibber in their glee today and the ghosts that stalk across the long-dead course at Garfield Park are laughing spectrally this morning . . . and the great blackness has come upon the life of Mike McDonald.[18]

~ 18 ~

Betrayal and Death

EXHAUSTED BY HIS LABORS, MIKE MCDONALD WAS A LIVING POR-
trait of despair. Looking careworn and deeply troubled, he sat at Dora's side
every day following the tragedy in the Omaha Building. The sight of his wife
thrashing about violently on her bed and muttering nonsense deeply affected
him. The jailhouse cynics chuckled and said that she was either the greatest
actress in the world or completely insane. There was little sympathy shown for
Dora among the prisoners or staff. They believed her raving was all an act.

Driven, and ultimately defeated, by a tragic destiny, McDonald said he was
"heartbroken. I am overwhelmed by the frightful things being brought to light,"
he added, in a barely audible tone. "It is a mighty tough proposition but I shall
stand by my wife to the end. I believe it is my duty to do so."[1] In old age, Mike
tried to convey the image of honor and integrity even if all else was lost. He clung
to the faint hope that Guerin shot himself in the studio because of despondency
and a failed blackmail scheme, but his common sense must have told him that
Dora was neither the heroine of the melodrama nor the victim.

"McDonald's on the verge of collapse," opined Alfred Trude. "He is well-ad-
vanced in years and the strain he has been under is enough to kill an ordinary
man. He may break down at any time."[2]

On March 5, the coroner's jury returned an open verdict in the manner of
death. After eight hours of deliberation, they reported a deadlock, unable to
determine if the fatal shot to the chest was fired by a suicidal Guerin or a scorned
Mrs. McDonald. However, Assistant Police Chief Herman Schuettler sent word
to Judge John R. Newcomer of the department's intention to detain her until
a grand jury could be called, and a mittimus for her arrest was granted. Dora
Feldman McDonald was bound over to the grand jury. With the posting of a
$50,000 bond, the accused murderess would enjoy the comforts of an elegant

hotel room—and not a dank cell in the county stir, where she would have been unmercifully mocked and tormented by the people of the streets.

McDonald exited the courtroom accompanied and comforted by his son Guy, who approached his father in a spirit of reconciliation born from the seeds of this tragedy. "Take me home, son," he said with a heavy sigh. Home was to be his last refuge.

Owing to the infirmities of old age and nervous collapse, McDonald was admitted to St. Anthony de Padua Hospital on the West Side on May 26. His condition was diagnosed as uremic poisoning and a weakening heart, but as Dr. Leonard St. John, his friend and medical adviser for many years, ruefully observed, "Plainly speaking it is a broken heart. It is sorrow that brought the old man to [the edge of the] grave."

As his condition worsened, the team of physicians abandoned all hope for a recovery. On July 10, Mike dictated his last will and testament to Alexander Sullivan, with the one-armed gambler Wesley Schimmel, his old faro dealer Charles Winship, and William Pinkerton—three loyal friends from bygone days—standing by as witnesses and executors of an estate valued at $2 million. It was decided that two-thirds of it was to be divided among the two sons, Guy and Cassius, equally, with the provision that they would not receive their shares until they passed their thirty-fifth birthday.

Dora, confined to the Laura C. Buck Sanitarium at 5042 Washington Boulevard on the West Side as she awaited a trial date, was to receive a widow's dower of one-third. The will specified that Harold McDonald, Dora's fourteen-year-old son, would split $50,000 with Mike's brother Ed, living in quiet retirement, and a significant retainer of $25,000 was to be paid to James Hamilton Lewis, a criminal defense attorney, former mayoral aspirant, and a future U.S. senator, hired to represent Dora when her case was finally called before the bar. McDonald bequeathed generous sums to the hospital, the Catholic archdiocese, and other charitable institutions.

To his former wife, Mary Noonan, who hurried home from New York where she had been working for the Board of Charities and the Destitute Old Ladies Home in Paterson, New Jersey (an institution she claimed to have founded), under the name of Mary Grasshoff, after giving up the rooming-house business on Wabash Avenue, he left nothing. And yet it was Mary (and not Dora) who maintained a bedside vigil, soliciting his forgiveness, offering contrition and prayer, and professing eternal love to her dying ex-husband.

McDonald had been providing for her in small ways ever since the divorce went through, but he could not see his way clear to bestow upon her a final forgiveness expressed in dollars and cents—the only kind of forgiveness she could truly understand and fully appreciate. By failing to reconcile his bitterness toward the mother of his children, the old gambler unintentionally kindled a long and bitter probate battle between Mary, her daughter-in-law

Mary O'Shaughnessy McDonald, and the executors of the estate that would drag on in the courts for *the next twenty-five years.*

Before his death, McDonald was reminded by his priest that in the eyes of the Catholic Church there was no such thing as divorce, and he would have to formally repudiate his marriage to Dora in order to receive penance, the Holy Eucharist, and extreme unction. Only by doing so would he be permitted to rest comfortably in Mount Olivet Cemetery as a Roman Catholic in good stead. Mike said he was very sorry for his sins and asked to receive the sacraments. In his final waking hours, the old gambler made his final confession, renounced his marriage to Dora, and was welcomed back into the embrace of the Church.

For the next two days, the old man drifted in and out of consciousness, unable to acknowledge the presence of family members gathered around him. The end came shortly before noon on August 9, 1907. With him at the final roll of the dice were brother Ed, Mary Noonan McDonald Grasshoff, sons Cassius and Guy and Guy's wife, his sister Jennie McDonald Miller from Montana, and attorney Sullivan.

A dramatic scene played out earlier in the morning when a heavily veiled Dora McDonald, accompanied by one of her attorneys, Colin C. Fyffe, and a trained nurse from the sanitarium, arrived at the hospital so that she could say her farewell. After a two-hour wait she was finally allowed to visit with the man she had betrayed so cruelly, but there was no glimmer of recognition from Mike. In a mental fog, he looked up at her vacantly, saying nothing. In tears, Dora was driven back to the hospital to await the final word.

Respecting his stated intentions, McDonald's remains were transferred to the home of his brother and sister-in-law at 311 Central Park Avenue, where he would lie in state until the funeral mass at the Church of Our Lady of Sorrows on August 12. A floral piece sculpted in the shape of a broken heart was delivered to Ed McDonald's residence and placed beside the coffin. It had been sent over by Dora, who was permitted only a few moments to mourn her husband beside the funeral bier. She was forbidden by the family to attend the mass.

The pews of the church were filled to capacity with rows of politicians, business people, and weeping women who came to pay their last respects and hear the funeral discourse of Reverend Maurice Dorney, pastor of St. Gabriel's Roman Catholic Church, who put the life of the old gambling king and politician into its proper perspective with the hope that the world would remember Mike as one of Chicago's notable citizens who had contributed to the common good—and not as a gambler, a boodler, a jury fixer, a common thief or man of the town complicit in ancient swindles and old, long-forgotten murders. The priest urged the congregation:

> Ask Lyman Gage, a great factor in one of the largest financial institutions in Chicago, for his estimate of Mike McDonald. Doubtless he will tell

you that Mike's word and his paper [were] good. Who was it who gave to the City of Chicago one of its best health commissioners [Dr. Swayne Wickersham] at a time when the city needed a good man for the position? Mike McDonald.

Who was instrumental in placing Murray F. Tuley in the common council of the City of Chicago? While it is true that Mike McDonald has been the associate of gamblers whose operations are not approved by the Church and gave scandal in various ways, yet I have found in this complex character many qualities really commendable. Before his death he was heartily sorry for it and he died a true Christian.[3]

Reverend Robert McGuire of the Church of Our Lady of Sorrows delivered the mass, and afterward a large throng of people boarded a special funeral train at the Polk Street Station to accompany the casket out to the cemetery where it would be placed in a mausoleum beside his mother and father and stepchildren.[4] Among the long procession of mourners were some of the old familiar faces: "Black Bill" Fitzgerald; Joseph Chesterfield Mackin; William McGarigle; party boss Roger C. Sullivan; ex-alderman James Hildreth's son Harry; brewer George Hofmann; Police Captain Martin Hayes, who looked after Mike's racetrack interests in his war with Ed Corrigan; Captain James Farrell and the members of the Democratic marching band; Billy O'Brien, alderman John Powers's sidekick and city hall point man; Michael Corcoran, the old Hatch House head-knocker; "Bunk" Allen; gamblers Harry Romaine, "One Arm" Wesley Schimmel, and Johnny Dorgan; and Dan Trude, the son of Mike's longtime friend Alfred S. Trude, who was vacationing at his Idaho ranch and did not learn of his old friend's passing until after he had returned to Chicago.

Also conspicuous by his absence was former mayor Carter Harrison II, whose mean-spiritedness and abiding dislike of the man who more than anyone made it possible for his father to lead the city through five stormy terms of office (paving the way for a continuation of the family dynasty beginning in 1897). In each of their lifetimes, neither the father or the son would own up to the fact that *pater* Harrison's success in public life was attributable to McDonald's tactics as he helped his former West Side neighbor get elected in a crowded field of political contenders. They refused to acknowledge Mike's passion for developing Democratic candidates on both the local and national levels. To give thanks or assign credit to a rogue gambler would have made them look bad in the eyes of the public and was a risk not worth taking, or so they believed.

With Mike in the ground, public attention shifted to the pending trial of Dora Feldman McDonald for capital murder. The city was fascinated by the three-cornered May-December romance, and there was a furious scramble for seating in the courtroom. For weeks it was discussed, analyzed, and likened to the concurrent trial in New York City of Pittsburgh millionaire Harry K. Thaw for the murder of his wife's lover, the famed architect Stanford White on the rooftop theater of Madison Square Garden. Evelyn Nesbit, the ravishing, but faithless young wife was already a national celebrity, destined for the Vaudeville stage and starring roles in silent movies. Dora's trial was one packed with eerie similarities, but unlike the vivacious and scheming Nesbit, Mrs. McDonald's sanity was the central issue of this trial as it unfolded in the courtroom of Judge Theodore Brentano on January 20, 1908.[5]

Attorney J. Hamilton Lewis, known as "Old Pink Whiskers" because of the curious pinkish tint to his beard, said in a prepared statement that "Mrs. McDonald is suffering from a profound case of neurodementia, and is apparently unable to coordinate either thought or expression.[6] Her memory of past events, of either recent or long-past occurrences, is practically a blank. She is at the present time unable to discuss the ordinary topics of the day or the most common and well-known current events. Notwithstanding the fact that she is about to be put on trial for her life, she does not feel the enormity of the situation or any of the surrounding circumstances."[7]

Dora failed in three suicide attempts, but she succeeded in delaying the start of the trial by three months. First she ingested pills at the sanitarium, but at the threshold of death was revived. Relocated from the hospital to her mother's home at 8680 South Calumet Avenue, she tried to end her sufferings *twice* in one day. She pirouetted on the second floor windowsill one afternoon in late November, but was pulled back to safety by her brother Emil. Her screams were so frightfully loud and unending that a riot call had to be placed to the 35th Street Police Station by the neighbors. A patrol wagon was summoned, and a detachment of bluecoats dispersed a large contingent of spectators gathered outside the home. Later the same day, she turned on the gas jet inside her bedroom and threw herself across the bed, prepared to die, but she was revived before the deadly fumes sent her to an appointment in the Great Beyond. Dora complained that the McDonald sons and the executors of the estate were depriving her of her most essential needs.

In September, Dora moved her things into her old room inside the Drexel Boulevard mansion. Citing the terms of his father's last will and testament, Guy McDonald ordered her eviction from the premises. "She is not welcome here and she knows it," he said. "It was my father's wish that she should never again set foot inside the place which she has brought so much trouble to. As a matter of fact she is legally entitled only to her dower of one-third of the income from the estate."[8]

"Those who have everything which my husband left me have even taken the shelter from my head. They will not give me so much as the bread necessary to keep me alive!" she wailed. "I have not even a dress to wear!"[9]

Attorney Lewis expressed the fear that she would not survive a prolonged trial in her weakened physical and mental state. The court agreed to allow her nurse, Amanda K. Beck, and the attending physician, Dr. James Whitney Hall, to sit by her side throughout the proceedings.

From the selection of the venire men right up to the closing arguments, the trial was laden with drama and intrigue. Assistant State's Attorneys Edward S. Day and William A. Rittenhouse, leading for the prosecution, discovered evidence of bribes being paid to jurors and witnesses. Emil Feldman had slipped Lorenz Blasi a ten-dollar bill to change his testimony. Probing further, Rittenhouse revealed that Detective Wooldridge, the self-styled "Incorruptible Sherlock Holmes of America," had been secretly aiding and abetting the defense by communicating prosecution strategy passed on to him by Frank Comerford to "Jumbo" Frank Cantwell, a hired detective in the employ of attorney Lewis at clandestine meetings on the South Side.

The new police superintendent, George Shippy (a Republican who had no sympathies or prior dealings with McDonald), ordered Wooldridge's immediate suspension and his star confiscated. Rittenhouse charged that the full machinery of the police department had been used to deliberately withhold evidence of the crime—McDonald's long shadow, it seemed, extended from beyond the grave. The State demanded to know why Officer John Meany of the Harrison Street Station had not been ordered to testify at the murder inquest. Meany would later state that he heard it straight from Dora—she had admitted to shooting Webster Guerin. "The case was handled by Chief Collins and the detective bureau and was entirely out of my hands," alibied Inspector John Wheeler unconvincingly. Wheeler was known to be a personal friend of McDonald and now stood accused of silencing his subordinates in the Harrison Street lockup for Mike's benefit.[10]

J. "Ham" Lewis was a mesmerizing courtroom presence; a singular force who attacked prosecution witnesses with the fury of a pit bull. Abandoning his courtly manner, Lewis blistered Archie Guerin relentlessly. During jury selection, he physically shoved the young man away from the jury box, accusing him in loud terms of attempting to converse with one of the venire men. "I've been watching you sir! If you do so again I shall notify his honor and have you dealt with severely!"[11]

Under cross-examination, Guerin's face turned white as a sheet while Lewis paced the floor, gesticulating wildly and hurling accusations at the young man in a furious staccato as he attempted to impeach Guerin's earlier testimony on behalf of the State. "Is it not true that you are a thief, that you were discharged from the Colonial Theater for stealing $400 from your chief, and did you not have to take your wife's savings from the bank to keep yourself out of jail? Did you not promise to pay the money back and fail to pay a cent of it? Did you not present diamond rings to women in a resort [house of ill repute] with that money and afterward go there with George Cohan and George Silver and endeavor to get the rings back?"[12]

Guerin denied the accusation, and Lewis flew into an unbridled rage. At one point he doubled his fists and made a threatening move toward the witness box. Judge Brentano banged the gavel and called for order. Lewis did not pursue the insanity defense. Rather, he said, "The shooting was done in self-defense of the life and body of this woman not by her hand but by his own while she was endeavoring to turn his deadly hand from her," portraying her as an object of pity.

Time and again, Dora fainted in the courtroom and had to be taken out. The bloodstained coat of Webster Guerin and a hospital skeleton brought into court by Lewis to use in the cross-examination of an expert witness for the prosecution caused frightful shrieks. "It's the skeleton of Webster Guerin!" Dora screamed. "It's Web's skeleton that they've brought here to testify against me!"[13]

At other times she appeared to be dozing peacefully. Nearby, Avis Dargan and Archie Guerin glared at Dora with cold fury, attempting to rattle her nerves. The defense expressed fears that Dora might pass away from the stress of the ordeal—the trial hurried along for these reasons. Closing arguments were heard on February 10.

In a dramatic flourish, Lewis summed it all up: "Punished—punished? Oh heaven! How can we punish this helpless, homeless woman against the door of tomorrow if closed forever? Where is the death, where the imprisonment that can be greater punishment than she is suffering before your eyes? You are not called upon gentlemen to pass judgment upon the imperfections of this miserable and unfortunate woman. You are assembled to say how far her transgressions may be forgiven and a new life and hope held out to her."[14]

Rittenhouse could never hope to match the theatrical eloquence of his famous adversary. His reply was straightforward and vigorous, but he erred badly by attacking the credibility of Lewis, and mimicking his gestures in a poor attempt at humor instead of focusing on the essential facts of the case or the statements of witnesses. "Such is his power that Colonel Lewis could hold before you a slimy serpent and picture it in terms that would make you believe you beheld a fairy!"[15]

Great crowds had gathered in the street to await the verdict as the jury retired to deliberate. Bookmakers were observed clocking bets with spectators. Guilty or innocent? What was it going to be? Dora was half carried to the custodian's office to await a decision. She was highly nervous and could only manage a bite of toast and some tea. To ease the tension, Dora whistled some of Mike's favorite Irish tunes.

The jury deliberated for five hours. Four of the jurors voted to convict, but the majority prevailed, and the verdict was "not guilty." A hush fell over the courtroom for a brief moment, then a low murmur was heard, and suddenly reporters were clamoring for the telephones to file their story. Nurse Beck broke down in tears, but for the first time in the trial, Dora appeared composed and perfectly at ease. "There, there, don't cry Nursie," she said, wrapping an arm around Beck. Attorney Gabriel J. Norden, one of the phalanx of defense attorneys, assisted Dora to the jury box, where she personally thanked each of the eight men who spared her.

Spectators swarmed around Dora, offering their congratulations and encouragement as the Guerin family hurried from the courtroom, brushing past reporters. "I am pleased," said Dora, her sanity and composure now miraculously restored. "Do you want me to tell you the five reasons why? Because no Jewish woman could ever do a deed like that of which I have been accused. Because it removes the stigma from Dad's name. Because of my boy. Because of my darling old mother. Please believe it last and least—absolutely least of these—because of myself. The only real disappointment to me is that dad did not live to hear that verdict and it is a bitter disappointment. But he knows, so what is the difference?" she added, staring off into the distance wistfully.[16]

Emotions ran high throughout the trial, and the public's sympathy was clearly with Dora in the closing days, but consistent with nearly every incident in Mike McDonald's world, the outcome was tempered by the politics of influence. "It was a subversion of justice," charged Prosecutor Day. "In the face of the perjury, treachery and bribery shown in the testimony it does not seem possible that such a verdict could have been reached."[17] There seemed little doubt that Lewis, a man with important political connections, carried out McDonald's wishes to the letter and had dispensed monies from the defense fund to the detectives and others to do "all that was necessary."

Accusations of jury fixing and bribery notwithstanding, it is highly unlikely that Dora Feldman McDonald would have been convicted of capital murder. Between 1904 and 1918, twenty-six women indicted for murder were set free in Cook County, even with overwhelming evidence of guilt. The leading lights of the criminal justice field weighed in on the subject. "Any kind of woman can kill at her pleasure. She can go into court after killing, shed a few tears, and cast a few wistful glances at the jury and she will be acquitted," complained attorney Stephen Malato in 1914.[18] Cook County State's Attorney John E. W. Wayman concurred. "A woman cannot be convicted of murder in Cook County, especially if she is pretty."[19]

The McDonald jurors explained that they could not be sure whether the fatal shot was self-inflicted, the result of an accidental discharge of the weapon during Dora's struggle with Guerin, or willful murder. They could not convict based on the testimony of the witnesses.

Interviewed in her suite of rooms at the Sherman House where she had been staying through the duration of the trial, Dora caressed a spray of roses that had been delivered to her room and said that she would devote the remainder of her life to philanthropic causes. She said she would build a hospital or perform charitable work for children, but first she would accompany her mother to Palestine to visit the Holy land, or go to a place that was warm and pleasant.

"I am going away somewhere. I don't know where yet. Just back with the grass and trees and the music and away from the trolley cars and noise here," she said as she rested her head on the shoulder of her devoted nurse and confidante Amanda Beck. "There are so many places but they're all brighter than here. I'm going where it's bright and I can rest."

"To Florida where your son is [going to school]?" asked a reporter.

"Why Florida of course, I never thought of that."

Asked if she was ever afraid of the jury sending back a guilty verdict, Dora was coy in her response. She replied that she was dreaming most of the time and didn't give it a passing thought, but was quite sure that the newspapers were wrong about her so-called raving in court. Dora's features, which had been without expression throughout the interview, suddenly lit up. Looking up at the reporter, she smiled in a sly kind of way, recalling Mike McDonald's pet saying.

"What was it that Dad used to say? You can't always sometimes very often tell. Yes, that's it. *You can't always sometimes very often tell . . .*"[20]

Postscript

Dramatis Personae

THE WOES OF DORA FELDMAN DID NOT END WITH THE CLOSE OF the trial. The widow never made it to Palestine or Florida, nor did she fulfill a promise to build a hospital, aid sickly children, or erect a monument to the eternal memory of her late husband. Rather, Dora chose to remain in Chicago for the next eighteen years contesting the will and battling Mary Noonan and her two sons from the first marriage for a larger share of Mike's estate. Her complicated and tortured life took many strange twists and turns. In 1908, Dora ran off to Mexico with business executive Benjamin Briggs Goodrich, a married man and the court-appointed guardian of her teenage son, Harold. While traveling south of the border, the new lovers had a serious falling out. Dora indignantly returned to Chicago to file a criminal complaint charging Goodrich with the embezzlement of $5,000 and for conspiring to seize control of her trust deed. "Briggs spoiled a trip I had planned," complained Mrs. McDonald. "I was going to Honolulu, Japan, and Hong Kong and a lot of places. Now that the story is out I am afraid he will get away."[1]

Then Myrtle Briggs Goodrich, the estranged wife of the accused, sued Dora for alienation of affection after divorcing her husband. In the midst of the proceeding, Wesley Schimmel went before the court and stated for the record that he would "not believe anything Dora said under oath." Mrs. Goodrich testified that Mrs. McDonald became friendly with her estranged husband when he was "only a boy of eighteen or nineteen." Goodrich was eventually convicted of embezzlement.[2]

In 1911, Dora was back in the news after filing a lawsuit against the Wells-Fargo Company and Guy McDonald for negligence after she discovered that $10,000 worth of gems had mysteriously disappeared (or had been stolen) from a safety deposit box in a downtown vault. The gems were eventually found and returned to Dora. Mrs. McDonald was herself sued for nonpayment of fees by Frank Cantwell, the private detective employed by the defense team during the murder trial. "I worked 300 days for her, and put in a bill for $3,500," Cantwell said.[3]

After many pratfalls and nuisance lawsuits against the trustees of Mike's estate for maladministration, the gas company, and other parties, Dora left Chicago for good in 1925. Settling in Los Angeles, she married Dr. Carmen A. Newcomb and quietly lived out the remainder of her days at 2032 East Sorrano Street. She died of carcinoma complicated by pneumonia on July 1, 1930, and was laid to rest in a mausoleum at the Hollywood Forever Cemetery. She was sixty years old.

Dora's only son, Harold Barkley McDonald, attended school in Florida but returned to Chicago, where he married actress Evelyn Marie Yould before attaining his nineteenth birthday. The union was strongly opposed by Dora, who did everything in her power to sabotage relations between the young couple. Evelyn deeply resented the meddling of her mother-in-law and her fat husband's lazy habits. Harold's weight ballooned to over 230 pounds, and he was in the habit of sleeping in rather than going off to work. Brandishing a revolver, Evelyn rousted him from his bed one morning and demanded that he make himself useful. "You big fat slob! Get up and go to work! Who the hell was your father anyway? Nothing but a Goddam old gambler!"[4] Harold arose, got dressed, left the residence, and never came back. In July 1912, he was convicted on a charge of wife abandonment and assessed a $500 fine. However, with the help of Dora's attorneys and a large sum of cash from his inheritance, the marriage was annulled on April 7, 1913. Harold would be married three more times before his death in Daytona Beach, Florida, in 1968.

Within three days of Mike's passing, Mary Noonan McDonald filed a lawsuit to set aside the divorce decree obtained by her husband in 1889, calling it an illegal "star chamber" proceeding, carried out without her prior consent or knowledge. "Even if I was lawfully divorced I still owned the property Mr. McDonald gave me of his own free will. He made me a present of the house and grounds at 308 Ashland Boulevard as he would have given me a diamond ring. It was a love gift. For he loved me in those days and I loved him. It was worth fully $400,000. It was taken away from me by violent and dishonest means," she sobbed to the court on August 13, 1907.[5] However, attorneys for the estate produced letters written in her own hand to a friend named "Mrs. Handy," clearly showing that she had full knowledge of the divorce action at the time of her second departure to Europe. She had in fact obtained $50,000 from McDonald as a cash settlement, which partly explains why Mike did not name her in his will at the time of his death. Interestingly, the incriminating letter produced in probate court was signed "Mrs. J. Moysant." It was further revealed that the name Grasshoff was not a pseudonym, but in fact her married name. She was betrothed to Hugo Grasshoff in Lockport, New York, long before she returned to Chicago in 1907 to plead for Mike's forgiveness and stake a claim to a share of his fortune.

Mary lived out the remainder of her days with the widow of her first son, Harley Goudy McDonald (who had passed away at age forty in 1905) in suburban LaGrange, Illinois. Late in life, she became a social worker for the Florence Crittenden Rescue Home for Unfortunate Girls on the South Side of Chicago. Mary passed away on May 11, 1917, at age sixty-seven. She was interred beside Mike in the McDonald family mausoleum at Mount Olivet.

Lacking stable, mature parental supervision and guidance and growing up in an unpredictable and often menacing home environment, it is not surprising that the two sons from Mary's tempestuous union with Mike McDonald each ran afoul of the law to some degree. Guy C. McDonald lived at 3542 Grand Boulevard on the South Side with his wife, Mary Ellen, and seemed to be getting along fine as an adjuster for the Maurer and Jackson Insurance Company—that is, until May 31, 1910, when his employer had him arrested on a charge of embezzling $210 from a customer. McDonald said he was a partner in the firm and therefore was entitled to do with the money as he pleased. The firm denied that he had any such privilege or that he had any role to play in the management and ownership of the business. In June 1919, Guy was back in the criminal justice system, this time charged with the assault and battery of a married woman he was seeing up on Sheridan Road along the Chicago lakefront. Although he was arrested three times in one year for assaulting this same woman, Mrs. Donna Stere-Langley, McDonald was discharged—to no one's great surprise, since the judge in the proceedings was Samuel Trude, the son of Mike's old friend and defender. He was last employed as a timekeeper for the federal Works Progress Administration (WPA). Guy Cassius McDonald died of pneumonia at age fifty-six, two days before Christmas, 1936.

Of the four young men who called Mike McDonald "dad" and lived under his roof, Cassius McDonald was closest to his father in temperament, occupation, choice of companions, and criminal inclination. A hot-headed and furious young lion when provoked, Cassius struck old Wes Schimmel in the face and then swore out a warrant for his arrest after a heated disagreement over the monthly $100 stipend he was being paid from the estate. There were many others who experienced young McDonald's wrath. Inside the bar of the Sherman House one night in 1917, Cassius thrashed a gambler attempting to rope a friend of his into a crooked dice game. There was amusement in the criminal court that afternoon as lawyers reflected on the irony of Mike's younger son busting up the face of a gambler's shill trying to rope a sucker into a crooked crap game. Less amusing were his associations with underworld criminals, including the notorious conman Joseph "Yellow Kid" Weil, who was provided recognizance by Cassius McDonald—a licensed bondsman whose shady dealings resulted in his name and the name of his brother Guy being added to the Cook County "blacklist" by Chief Judge Harry Olson of the Municipal Court.

Cassius and his young wife, Marie, eventually purchased a hunting lodge in Gogebic, Watersmeet Township, in Michigan's Upper Peninsula, where he lived the life of a young prince with his queen consort, a servant, and two hired men. The inheritance had finally kicked in. In later years, he grew wealthy running a log-cutting business in the Upper Peninsula and working as a consulting engineer for the city of Detroit. On the surface of things, Cassius McDonald appeared to be "legit"—a respectable man of property and wealth who owned a pricey mansion in Grosse Pointe, an elite Detroit suburb. Successful and established, he still could not see his way clear to avoid the lure of the under- world. McDonald was the financial brain behind the kidnapping of wealthy St. Paul, Minnesota, brewer Edward G. Bremer by members of the Alvin "Creepy" Karpis–Doc Barker holdup gang. With cold-blooded efficiency, Bremer was snatched up after he had dropped off his daughter at school on January 18, 1934, taken to a safe house in Bensenville, Illinois, and held for a $200,000 ransom. The blood money was paid, Bremer released, and Cassius McDonald, known to the gang as "Cash" McDonald, was tasked with laundering the marked bills in Havana, Cuba, where he held an interest in a racetrack. In return for a 25 percent cut, Cassius exchanged the money twice—in foreign and domestic cur- rency—and then dispersed the funds via banks in Mexico and Venezuela. The laundering cost, including McDonald's 15 percent commission, was $34,000, leaving $166,000 for the gang to divvy up. Arrested, charged with the crime, tried, and finally convicted in a federal court in St. Paul on January 31, 1936, Mike's son was sentenced to fifteen years in Leavenworth. He served nearly the entire term before his release back into society—an incredible but true story. Cassius McDonald's death from natural causes was reported by the *Detroit News* on March 26, 1952.

Gambler's Ruin

As the Chicago media pondered the deeper significance of Mike McDonald and the ultimate tragedy that drove him into the grave, they paused to recall the unhappy circumstances of some of his closest cohorts from the world of gambling and politics, reflecting the prevailing belief that no good can come from a lifetime engaged in what was considered to be an evil and wicked en- terprise. If such a curse exists, it must have surely touched the lives of each of the McDonald family members and many other individuals closely associated with Mike during his lifetime.

In his colorful and extravagant life, George V. Hankins opened racetracks and operated dinner-pail gambling dens all over the city. Driven out of the city in the late 1890s, he operated a saloon in Gary, Indiana, until he was stricken with paralysis in May 1911. By that time, he had run through all of his money and died destitute on the South Side of Chicago on August 19, 1912.

George's brother Al Hankins suffered a horrible death on August 19, 1897, in one of the rooms inside his gambling house at 3908 Cottage Grove Avenue. The heavy cherry case of a folding bed toppled over and crushed him. The massive iron weights of the bed pinned Hankins to the floor, choking off his supply of oxygen. The efforts of a young boy to pry him loose failed, and the official cause of death was listed as strangulation. The *Tribune* noted with grim irony that he died in the same manner as a condemned prisoner dropped to eternity in a hangman's noose.

County boodler "Prince Hal" Varnell was only forty-six years of age when he unexpectedly passed away at his home from a stomach ailment on September 12, 1898. Varnell's deluxe gambling emporium and saloon valued at $100,000 was closed down by Mayor Hopkins in 1894 during a reform drive engineered by the Civic Federation, and with it a collection of handsome tapestries, furniture, and paintings grew mildewed and were finally auctioned off at a fraction of their original value or simply given away.

Pat Sheedy, one of the most famous Clark Street gamblers of old and the great John L. Sullivan's fight promoter, sat down at a faro table in Charleston, South Carolina, on January 22, 1902, and lost his entire fortune—a sum conservatively pegged at $50,000. He died in 1909.

John Dowling, an early partner in the Store, died a pauper somewhere in the East.

William McGarigle, the "loyal Mac" who ran off to Canada rather than expose Mike's secrets in return for a promise of leniency from the courts, lost two of his young children to diphtheria in 1891. McGarigle's "Round Bar" saloon at 122–124 North Clark Street, a famous Chicago watering hole since 1872, was forced to close its doors in February 1899, after a catering business he ran in partnership with Ike Lansing went bankrupt. McGarigle retired to private life and died on April 29, 1917.

Racetrack owner John Condon, a man of exceptional business ability and Mike's partner in the failed Garfield Park venture, was one of the ringleaders of the "Gambler's Trust" of the 1890s. Condon is credited with dividing up the city into precise geographic "spheres of influence" as a means of preserving order among the various rival bookmaking syndicates fighting for hegemony after McDonald's retirement from the gambling business in the mid-1890s. He opened the Harlem Racetrack in July 1897, but in that same year, he lost his eyesight. Thereafter the veteran gambler was known to the denizens of the sporting world as "Blind" John Condon. He died of paralysis on August 9, 1915.

Alfred S. Trude—the penniless young city prosecutor McDonald befriended aboard an express wagon in 1871—became wealthy utilizing McDonald's great real estate acumen and purchased properties on LaSalle Street and the land beneath City Hall Square and the Peoples Gas, Light and Coke Company. A lifelong Democrat and liberal idealist who defended gamblers, vice mongers, murderers, and bunco men, Trude lived to see his son Dan elevated to the circuit court. He died of natural causes at home in his mansion at 4960 Drexel Boulevard on December 12, 1933. He was eighty-seven years old and worth $2 million at the time of his passing. Politically, Daniel P. Trude was nothing like his father. He championed a conservative Republican agenda and was a member of the Vice Commission organized to drive out the proprietors of houses of ill repute and the very same gamblers his father once protected.

Joseph Chesterfield Mackin, a.k.a. "Oyster Joe," a great power in state politics during the 1880s and Mike's second in command, lost his mind and was committed to the Dunning sanitarium in February 1914—the same state hospital "Prince Hal" Varnell plundered during the heyday of the county boodlers. Joe died there broke and alone on March 10, 1914, but his funeral expenses were paid through the generosity of Alderman Michael "Hinky Dink" Kenna. "Joe Mackin was a big politician in the days before women voters and 'Bull Moosers' were heard of," Kenna said, and "we'll give Joe his last great sendoff with tears as an accompaniment."[6] Mackin is buried less than five hundred feet from McDonald's mausoleum.

Colonel J. Hamilton Lewis rode roughshod over Archie Guerin throughout the murder trial of Dora McDonald. He berated the young man as a liar, a four-flusher, and a schemer. At one point, Lewis hurled even more vile insults at Guerin as the young man attempted to respond to the brutal cross-examination in a dignified manner. However, when Lewis found out after the trial had concluded that the death of Webster left Archie, the state's principal witness, broken in spirit and without gainful employment, Lewis encouraged him to study law and found him a job with the City Railway to tide him over. In 1912, the year before "Ham" Lewis was elected to the U.S. Senate from Illinois, Archie Guerin passed the bar. In his first case before a jury, he successfully defended another accused "crime of passion" murderess—Mrs. Jane Quinn—with his former cross-examiner *acting as co-counsel*. Archie received high praise from his onetime adversary for showing great promise. Then, in the prime of young manhood, he contracted a deadly case of typhoid fever. Guerin passed away January 17, 1913, making a widow of Avis Dargan—the woman Dora McDonald wrongly accused of trying to steal her beau, Webster.

Police inspector John Wheeler, who aided and abetted Mike McDonald's request to cover up Dora's incriminating statements after she was taken into the Armory Station women's annex, was fired from the department in 1912 for neglect of duty and for protecting the 22nd Street prostitution rackets. On May 21, 1918, he shot himself through the heart. The thirty-four-year police veteran was said to be sickly and despondent at the time of death.

Justice Charles Walhart Woodman, who failed to make his accusation of bribery against Mike McDonald stick, was removed from the bench in disgrace. He was declared legally insane in October 1897 and committed to the Elgin State Mental Hospital. The press reported that he had suffered a "brain hemorrhage," although the symptoms sound suspiciously like untreated syphilis.

Epilogue: A Legacy of Corruption

THE PREVAILING VIEW OF CHICAGO AS A METROPOLIS RULED BY political mischief makers, wire-pullers, and underworld figures operating in the shadows was engrained in the public mind decades before the bloody reign of Al Capone—the name most often equated with organized criminality in the Windy City. Arguably, it was Mike McDonald, and not Capone, who was the first to integrate the "rackets" into the electoral and legislative process and thus influence the governance of Chicago.

Twenty-five years before Capone glimpsed the light of day in a Brooklyn slum, McDonald was building the structural framework of the modern Chicago Democratic "machine" by marshaling control and suborning a bewildering maze of precinct workers, ward and county bosses, justices of the peace, police captains, contractors, suppliers, and spoilsmen. He anointed the untrustworthy, and with his connivance, they achieved the unacceptable—positions of importance in local government. Saloon-bred politicians and corrupt police exploited the ills of the system in the belief that it was their natural right to do so. Because elected officials were paid notoriously low wages, bribery, kickbacks, and other forms of graft were seen as the normal perquisites of the job in nineteenth-century Chicago and in other big cities.

As the party of "good government" and reform, the Republicans vociferously protested the ills of the patronage "system" but abandoned the immigrant poor in the short-sighted belief that the new arrivals with too many vowels in their last names comprised the "dangerous classes" and were likely to become criminals, anarchists, and social malcontents. Such ethnic intolerance resulted in a political vacuum and the creation of urban "machines" controlled by saloon bosses tied to the large breweries and liquor associations. The bosses filled a widening chasm in society by exploiting public resentment against Protestant

Republican "high hats" preaching sobriety and opposing the right of working-men to drink and gamble as they pleased. In Chicago, the press began referring to McDonald's organization as the "Machine" not long after Carter Harrison's election in 1879, and Mike freely admitted he was a "Machine man" to the bone. He ran this coalition of Democratic Party bosses and county potentates with machinelike efficiency for nearly two decades, until personal setbacks and the hardships of old age took their toll.

With McDonald in retirement, leadership of the fractious ward organizations, mostly dominated by the Irish, passed to Robert Emmet "Bobby" Burke, a Carter Harrison man. Roger C. Sullivan, an implacable foe of Burke, wrested control of the party apparatus after Burke was indicted and cast adrift by the organization. At the turn of the twentieth century, Sullivan enlisted and mentored Anton Cermak, future mayor of Chicago, into the Democratic fold through his capable lieutenant, George "Boss" Brennan, a former school teacher who took over the reins of party leadership after Sullivan died in 1920. Although Brennan held only one *official* title during his career—that of national committeeman—"Boss" was an *unofficial* designation that he never objected to and in fact relished. Brennan died in 1928. Anton Cermak (by now a potent force on the Cook County Board of Commissioners) and his successors, Jacob Arvey, Ed Kelly, and Pat Nash, a friend and neighbor of Roger Sullivan, were poised to guide the monolithic machine through the Great Depression and war.

The city was bold and "wide open"—gambling, sleaze, and vice everywhere, as it had been in the heyday of 1880s parlor gambling on Clark Street. "Organized, commercialized gangster-controlled gambling in Chicago is inextricably tangled with the Democratic political machine of the city," the *Tribune* bitterly noted on July 17, 1942. "The gambling franchises are an article of commerce dealt in by the Democratic ward committeemen." The organization approached the apex of its power in the postwar world with Chicago's organized crime group—known colloquially as the "Outfit." Crime figures from the West Side "River Wards" found they could do business with the lords of the Chicago machine and their allies in the Illinois General Assembly.

The Republican Party of Cook County, dominated by William "the Blond Boss" Lorimer and his able lieutenant, Thomas N. "Doc" Jamieson in the 1890s and 1900s, atrophied in the 1930s, once Cermak and the Kelly-Nash-Arvey triumvirate swayed the large and influential African American vote from the South Side Republicans through two powerful politicians, Arthur W. Mitchell, the first black man to be elected to the U.S. Congress as a Democrat, and Second Ward alderman William Levi Dawson. William Hale Thompson, the city's last Republican mayor, left office in disgrace in 1931 after his aborted attempt at machine-style control collapsed under the weight of lawlessness and scandal. By 1934 the Republicans had lost control of all state and federal patronage. One by one, the old-time Republican bosses fell. "Thomponism" as a political movement was a distant echo during the time the Richard J. Daley "dynasty" ran full throttle in the 1950s, 1960s, and 1970s. "Under Daley, the aldermen acted like a bunch of trained seals," recalled John Hoellen, one of the last of the Republican aldermen and a challenger to Daley for the mayoralty in 1975.[1] That sense of invincibility eroded in the 1970s as Daley's old age, deep racial divisions among the party elders, and declining patronage seemed to foretell the collapse of Democratic boss rule. However, expectations that the machine would roll over and die with Daley proved premature.

Chicago is still a one-party machine town under the rule of the son, Richard M. Daley, who, with great irony, advocates legalized casino gambling for downtown Chicago. In the absence of an effective two-party system, political differences and ideology boil down to intraparty squabbles crafted along racial and ethnic lines—although the city's minority groups lack the cohesion and political unity necessary to garner control of the city.

Chicago has paid a high price to maintain machine rule. Since the early 1980s, the city's reputation for dishonesty, crookedness, and collusion with the criminal element has been reinforced in wave after wave of indictments accompanying major U.S. Justice Department anticorruption initiatives. There has been a common thread running through Operation "Greylord" (1983), Operation "Safebet" (1984), Operation "Phocus" (1985), Operation "Incubator" (1986), Operation "Gambat" (1990), Operation "Haunted Hall" (1997), Operation "Silver Shovel" (1999), and Operation "Safe Road" (1998): the exchange of money for influence., "Safe Road," a statewide scandal, even ensnared a Republican governor, George Ryan, and a score of his operatives. Holding public office in Chicago has been tantamount to a license to steal.

Chicagoans pay the highest sales tax in the nation—owing to the mismanagement of Cook County budgets, the public transit system, the board of education, and the county hospital; and the hiring of a profusion of relatives, friends, and family of politically connected people tied to the Cook County Board of Commissioners and rewarding them with generous pay raises is an echo of the 1887 "Boodle Board," It is an old and unacceptable practice recalling Mike McDonald's tactics. Ask the politicians their justification for such egregious nepotism, and they are likely to repeat the words of the late Fred Roti, defiant alderman of the First Ward, when he snapped back: "So what's wrong with that? They're all well qualified!"[2]

Voter complacency perpetuates the system and allows machine sachems such as Roti, residing in a handful of "political wards" where minidynasties still flourish, to hire a percentage of patronage workers, some for nonexistent jobs—called "ghost pay-rollers."

Corruption is systemic. Since 1972, twenty-seven aldermen (twenty-six of them Democrats) were indicted for various bribery schemes and malfeasance. Five of the fifty aldermen elected in 1983 were either imprisoned or indicted before the next city election rolled around. At that time, a proposal to establish an inspector generalship to monitor the city council was met with derision and scorn. Former alderman Robert Shaw reminded the public that the city politicians "are not the only crooks in town."[3]

Shaw was right. There are crooks working in *many* agencies of municipal and county government, not all of them elected officials. Every year, contractors, suppliers, clerks, and public employees replicating the methods of McDonald's gang perpetuate this "culture of corruption." A recent example occurred in 2008, when seven employees of the Building and Zoning Departments and eight others were indicted for giving and receiving cash bribes.

One-party control fosters official misconduct and breeds public indifference. In such a climate, malfeasance reigns supreme and reinforces the prophetic words of the late Everett McKinley Dirksen, former U.S. senator from Illinois, in October 1950: "The vitality of our country rests upon two vigorous political parties. One party is therefore the party of responsibility when in office and the other is the party which helps people obtain an accounting of political stewardship. If this system should be destroyed it will mean one party government, which in turn will mean political dictatorship and control."[4]

The name Michael C. McDonald is no longer familiar to modern-day Chicagoans. His reputation as the political-gambler boss of the city faded as incidents of nineteenth-century living retreated into history, although from time to time the dusty window into the past opened and Chicagoans were once again reminded. Edna Ferber, the Pulitzer prizewinning author of *So Big,* penned her famous novel while residing in Chicago's Windemere Hotel, not far from Mike's fifteen-room turreted Drexel Boulevard mansion. Ferber places her fictional character "Simeon Peake" playing faro inside the "red plush and mirrored gambling houses" belonging to Jeff Hankins and Mike McDonald. Although William Wellman's cinematic adaptation of the Ferber novel in 1932 has Simeon Peake being slain in one of McDonald's gambling rooms, in her book the crime occurs in a Hankins resort by a vengeful woman wielding a horsewhip and a pistol. In Ferber's memorable 1926 novel *Showboat,* later a hit Broadway musical choreographed by Jerome Kern and Oscar Hammerstein, the author's inspiration for the flashy Mississippi riverboat gambler Gaylord Ravenal was Mike McDonald.

Recollections of the man and his era resurface sporadically. In the midst of the brutal Prohibition gang wars of the lawless 1920s, Cook County state's attorney Robert Emmet Crowe attempted to defend the shoddy record of the city's crime-fighting agencies by drawing attention to conditions in McDonald's era. "I remember when I was a young fellow, right opposite the courthouse there was wide-open gambling on Clark Street. Not the back room with the curtain drawn, but right on the main floor with the doors open and the capper standing outside inviting people to come in," he told the press on May 16, 1928. "You remember

Harry Varnell's place, Mike McDonald's place and Gambler's Alley where Billy
Boyle had his chop house? That gambling ran south on Clark Street until you
got to Carrie Watson's house, where unmolested prostitution began."⁵

In the *Chicago Tribune's* long-running *Line O' Type* column—a collection
of nostalgic tidbits of living memory submitted by readers, the writer painted
a more idealized portrait. There were many passing references to the Store and
the other Clark Street gambling dens romanticized by veteran news columnists,
authors, and street characters with traces of gray showing up around the temples
as they evoked strong and visceral recollections of "Gambler's Alley." They
spoke of the colorful decadence of old Clark Street before the arrival of the
impersonal commercial office towers and banks built along the thoroughfare.
The modest little commercial structure at 79 West Monroe that was once Mike
McDonald's Store was demolished around 1926, before construction began on
the 130,976 square-foot, twenty-two-story commercial office building occupying
the northwest corner of Clark and Monroe today.

The passing of the Store and old Clark Street, as they were remembered by
the old-timers still around after World War I, was tinged with nostalgia and
a surprisingly wistful longing for a lost era—captured in the words of Lloyd
Wendt and Herman Kogan, from their 1948 book *Bet a Million!*

> Chicago was bold and gamey . . . its business leaders were lusty, breezy men,
> fellows who worked hard all day and wanted fun at night, who winked
> at the faults of a government and drank well at Kinsley's, Vogelsaang's or
> Billy Boyle's Chophouse and when their office doors were shut they sur-
> rounded themselves with their elegant wives or bedizened mistresses at
> the Palmer House or Grand Pacific. They cavorted with the nymphs at the
> Everleigh Club or Carrie Watson's or they crowded around the faro and
> poker tables at "King" Mike McDonald's place, Harry Varnell's marble
> gambling palace, or in any of the dozen gambling hells on Hairtrigger
> Block and Gambler's Alley within the shadows of the new City Hall.

~

Appendixes

Notes

Bibliography

Index

Appendix 1

Organized Gambling in Chicago during the Reign of Mike McDonald, 1868–1888

The following table is derived from various published newspaper accounts that listed the addresses of gambling raids in the period 1870–88. See, for example, the two-week-long *Chicago Inter-Ocean* exposé of public gambling in Chicago, February 18–March 3, 1882. It was common practice in those less litigious times for newspapers to publish the names and addresses of keepers of gaming houses as a public service to the community, without undue fear of lawsuits. It is doubtful however, that this type of sensational coverage did much to stir the public outrage; instead, it proved to be a valuable publicity tool and a useful roadmap for the patrons of gambling dens.

The *Inter-Ocean* reported on February 20, 1882, that there were "3,562 places licensed to sell liquor and not less than 1,500 more unlicensed." Tracing the root of the gambling scourge and the moral downfall of the city to the liquor trade, the paper went on to say that "Many of these saloons have all the accessories of the darker vices that pollute the very fountain of society. They are fitted up with the most skillful appliances and contrivances for the perpetration of crimes so dark that they cannot be named."

It is interesting to note that some of Chicago's most influential citizens and WASPish business leaders of the day, including hotel magnate Potter Palmer and the prominent local real estate developer William D. Kerfoot, leased their property holdings to gamblers. When indictments were handed down following the February 1882 press exposure, Cook County commissioner John Mattocks and Kerfoot both threatened lawsuits and pleaded ignorance while Palmer stoically answered the grand jury summons without comment.

Keeper of the Gaming House	Recorded Owner of the Property	Address of Gaming House
Michael C. McDonald	Edwin Walker, president of the Chicago & Lemont Stone Co.; George Snydecker, agent	176 Clark Street (the "Store")
George Norris		
Cliff Dougherty		
Charles Winship		
John Ferguson		
Charles "Parson" Davies		
Harry Perry		
Michael C. McDonald	John M. Durand, Commission Merchant, 160 Washington St.	91 Clark St.
Al Smith		
John Walpole		
William Skakel (aka "the Clock")		
George Martin		
James Crowe		
Hugh Brady		
Tom Brewer		83 Clark St.
Michael C. McDonald	Heirs of Thomas J. Shreeve of Louisville, KY; W.D. Kerfoot, agent. Sold to Charles Matthews in 1890	85 & 134 Clark St.
George Hankins		
William P. Wightman		
Benjamin Metzger		
David Johnson		
George Guyon		
John Belknap	Henry, Joseph, David & Julius Kohn, clothiers, 88 Wabash Ave.; John Strong, Proprietor of St. James Hotel	119 Clark St. & St. James Hotel
Eddie Belknap		
James Crowe	Henry, Joseph, David & Julius Kohn, clothiers, 88 Wabash Ave.	119 Clark St.
John Condon		
Albert Hankins		
Jeff Hankins		
William Mell Fitts		
John Gibbons		

Curt Gunn (aka Kirk Gunn)	James Todd, Louisville, Ky.; William D. Kerfoot, agent	124 Clark St.
Patrick "Patsy" King		75 S. Halsted
Frank Kiernan		
Sy Jaynes (aka Si James)		
John Smith		
John Dowling		
William Walters		126 Clark St.
Edward Wilson (aka James Ferris)	John Borden, attorney, Borden Block, Randolph & Dearborn	148 Clark St.
Frank "Kid" Leonard	Edward Mendel, 2321 Wabash Ave.	168 Clark St.
Harvey Taylor		
"Matinee" Charley Simpson		
Sig Cohn	Joseph H. Andrews, Clifton House hotel, agent; Joseph E. Otis	192 Clark St.
George Train (aka "Jule Train")		
Hugh Brady		
William Johnson		
A. J. Scott	Zebulon G. Simmons, Kenosha, Wisc.	295 Clark St.
Michael C. McDonald	N/A	72 & 89 Randolph St.
William T. Swift	N/A	72 Randolph St.
Lyman Page	N/A	72 Randolph St.
Curt Gunn (aka Kirk Gunn)	Liela Bryant; Gardner S. Chapin & James J. Gore, restaurateurs	98 Randolph St.
Cy Jaynes (aka Si James)		
Robert Jaynes (aka Bob James)		
John Tiernan		
"Soap" Gunn		
James Crawford		
Thomas Howe		
John Graves	N/A	42 Randolph St.
"Colonel" James Blass	Rudolph Wehril	155 Randolph St.
Tom Hines	Estate of ex-county commissioner John Jones	119 Dearborn St. (Arcade Club)
Pat Sheedy		
Charles Bush (took over for Sheedy)		
James Conlisk Sr.	James Fitzgerald, John B. Porter	5 Calhoun Place

Marcus Warren		
George Powell		
George Saviers		
Johnny Corcoran[1]	Billy Mead, Henry Green, & George Smith	71 Monroe St. (Hotel Frankfurt)
Billy Mead	Edward W. Morrison, 113 Madison St.	13 Calhoun Place (House of David)
Charles Barbour		
George Holt		
Billy Whitman	George Holt	136 Madison St.
Michael C. McDonald	Levi Rosenfeld, lessor to A.G. Nutting & Co., clothiers	104 & 106 Madison
Sam Dahl (aka Sam Doll)		
Joe Martin		
John Brown (aka Dirty Shirt)		
E. F. McQuaid		355 Madison St.
Tom Wallace	Catherine Boomer, 89 Thirty-seventh St.	2 Theatre Court
John Powers		
Wallace Warner		
Isaac Marks (aka Chinaman)		
George Smith	Potter Palmer, hotelier; Benjamin Grossman, 3734 Ellis Ave.	178 State St.
John Lawler		
James Smith		
Joseph H. Suits	N/A	348 State St.
Peter E. McGuire	Joseph O. Rutter, president, Trader's National Bank, and Cook County Commissioner John Mattocks	2137 Wabash Ave.
"Handsome" Harry Romaine		
Dyer Smith	George Reichold, 360 State St. & 179 Madison St.	179 Madison St.
Hugh Dunn		
Ed Shawcross		
John Dowling	H.C. Morcy; Cornelia A. Cole, Cole & Co., 188 W. Madison St.	189 Madison St.
Lyman Page		
Charles Atwood		
George Ryder	Andrew Ortmayer; no deed filed for 10 years	77 Halsted St.

Dave Oakes	N/A	Madison & LaSalle, (St. Mark Hotel)
Dan Scott[2]	N/A	Harrison & Clark
Matt Hogan	N/A	37–39 Congress
Charley Wicks	N/A	115 Randolph St.
Frank Turner	N/A	23 Madison St.
Morris Martin	N/A	118 Madison St.
Tom Daniels	N/A	177 Madison St.
Andy Daniels	N/A	(The Peruvian), 23 Madison St.
Dan Hazelborn	N/A	(The Peruvian), 23 Madison St.
Barney Campbell	N/A	73 Halsted St.
Dan Kellogg	N/A	85 Halsted St.
"Italian John"	N/A	87 Halsted St.
Bill Swift	N/A	519 State St.
"Dutch" Charley	N/A	148 Clark St.
Watt Robbins	N/A	179 Clark St.
John Bull	N/A	Barnes House
Bill Singleton	N/A	Kentucky Block
"Jew" Abe	N/A	118 Wabash Ave.
George Noyes	N/A	Washington St.

Note: In 1909, the City of Chicago changed its street numbering system. Addresses shown in the table predate the change.

1. Corcoran was an elected official, an alderman.
2. Scott was a black man who ran a game in the "Custom House" levee district catering exclusively to an African American clientele. When his resort was "pulled" and his gambling paraphernalia seized by a Chicago Police raiding party on September 27, 1878, and the keeper subsequently fined $25 by Justice Summerfield Reed, the *Inter-Ocean* ruefully noted that "it is a pity that this court cannot try some of the gangs from the downtown dens."

Appendix 2

Organized Gambling and Horse Racing Poolrooms in Chicago, Post-McDonald Period, 1889–1900

During the administration of DeWitt Clinton Cregier, a Democratic mayor in league with the gambling syndicates that elevated him to office in 1889, the resorts concentrated along Clark Street north from Randolph and south to Harrison Street through the heart of downtown Chicago cautiously reopened after a two-year hiatus, with many new places being added (see "Gambling in Full Swing," *Chicago Tribune*, May 2 and 3, 1889). However, by the mid-1890s, the downtown parlor-house era was expiring. Clark Street ceased being a gambler's mecca, as George Ade reported in one of his "Stories of the Street and of the Town" columns. "In the swift changes since then [1889] some of the old places have been torn away to make room for new buildings and others have been converted to staid business establishments. With the demolition of 'Old 134' the best known landmark of the old region will disappear" (*Chicago Record-Herald*, April 4, 1895).

With city boundaries constantly expanding, increased social mobility, better roads, transportation, and the relentless pressure of the Civic Federation to cleanse the Loop of its "gambling hells," the keepers of the traditional card and dice rooms were relocating away from downtown in favor of the South and North Sides and outlying areas of the county where law enforcement presence and media attention were less intrusive. The nature of public gambling was undergoing profound change during this period as well. With the increasing popularity of horse racing, bets could now be "taken on the fly" by a traveling handbook operator carrying with him little more than a notepad, a pencil, and an odds sheet in his vest pocket. A mobile bookie was much harder for police to identify and capture than the storefront gamblers in their fixed locations who were periodically rounded up. Moreover, the cost of police protection was far less than the typical weekly or monthly payoff to keep a downtown den open and free from raiding parties.

In 1894, a Chicago Civic Federation investigation confirmed what the newspaper editorialists had been reporting for years: that several of Chicago's most prominent and distinguished business leaders owned or leased notorious "gambling hells" in the city. The keepers of the gaming houses listed in the following table were the immediate heirs and successors of Mike McDonald and generally well-known to the press as "sharps" and members of the "sporting class" gentry, but unless they owned the questionable property outright, criminal penalties were likely to be less severe for them: grand juries were reluctant to prosecute the "better element," even when their names were revealed to the press and indisputably linked to the operation of a card room or pool-selling operation. For example, Levi Z. Leiter, business partner of dry goods magnate Marshall Field, was the recorded owner of a gambling den at 331 State Street (see the *Chicago Tribune*, September 30, 1894).

Back in the 1880s, hotel magnate Potter Palmer, husband of Bertha Honore Palmer, grand matriarch of Chicago's Gilded Age high society, frequently rented the upper floors of his hostelry to McDonald and lesser gamblers like W. H. Taylor, who ran a faro bank that "fleeced" a "sucker" from Boston named R. Brooks who brought suit against the proprietor, charging that he fell victim to a "skin game." The young man, a student, lost $120 (see the *Chicago Inter-Ocean*, March 13, 1882). Police raids were infrequent, but on one ignoble occasion in 1882, Palmer was arrested inside his hotel for keeping a gaming house and detained in a cell with McDonald. Traction magnate Charles Tyson Yerkes, who tried and failed to establish an absolute street railway monopoly in Chicago before being driven out of the city in 1900, invested in the Pacific Garden, a gambling resort located at 625 Milwaukee Avenue. His silent partner was Mike McDonald. Meanwhile, Edward J. Lehmann, a business rival of Field and the founder of the "Fair," a famous State Street department store that continued in business until the mid-1960s, owned the den at 14 Quincy Street, where John Condon, a onetime partner of Mike McDonald fronted the operation. In 1883, Lehmann was revealed to be the true owner of the Berlin at 298 State Street, a disreputable saloon fronted to Tom McGinnis and populated by streetwalkers and the worst dregs of "Whiskey Row"—less than three blocks south of the Fair Store.

Ethnicity is another important theme. The table shows that Chicago's gambling fraternity consisted for the most part of men of Irish or Anglo-Saxon extraction rooted in the liquor trade and connected to city politicians to varying degrees. Bob Mott and John V. "Mushmouth" Johnson on the other hand, were African Americans acknowledged by police as the "bosses" of the city's lucrative policy rackets catering to the city's growing black population concentrated on the South Side. They operated their saloons side-by-side with the State St. resorts owned by white saloon-politicians in a spirit of surprising cooperation, equanimity, and mutual protection.

George Hankins, an "old-time" gambler, occasional partner, and later archrival of Mike McDonald during the "parlor house era" of the 1870s, organized the Roby Fair Racing Association in February 1894 for the "purpose of conducting race meetings in an orderly manner" across the Illinois state line in Roby, Indiana (*Chicago Tribune*, June 9, 1895). With the cooperation of the Chicago National Bank who helped finance the venture, Hankins partnered with Charles "Social" Smith, Harry Perry, Sam Dahl, James O'Leary, and John Condon in this

Indiana racetrack venture designed to challenge McDonald's ill-fated Garfield Park foray in a locale less conducive to raids from police and private constables. Each man contributed $27,000 and articles of partnership were drawn up. It was an important shift away from the more traditional downtown gaming rooms operated for decades along Clark Street ("Gambler's Row"), and it marked the genesis of the first territorial alignments and geographic "spheres of influence" agreed to by Chicago's previously "decentralized" criminal associations. Smith, Perry, and Condon formed a Downtown–South Side bookmaking syndicate that was destined to wage continuous warfare during a twelve-year period (1900-1912) with Jim O'Leary, who broke away from the Hankins combine, and Mont Tennes, who rose from obscurity to "open up" and rule the up-and-coming North Side after 1900. After 1895, West Side interests were controlled by Alderman John A. Rogers of the Eighteenth Ward, who ran a saloon and an upstairs gambling den at 343 West Madison Street but was rarely harassed by the police. While many of the gambling operations shown on the table were closed down, driven out of town (or into hiding), or shut their doors when their proprietors retired by 1905, the Smith-Perry-Condon "gambler's trust" floated the *City of Traverse* gambling cruise ship and managed to thrive and prosper against the two major handbook competitors organized by Tennes and O'Leary. By 1920, all of these gambling consortiums were absorbed into the vortex of the modern Chicago organized crime syndicate.

Keeper of the Gaming House	Address of the Gaming House/or Poolroom	Neighborhood Location
John Dowling	74 Adams St., 2nd floor	Downtown
Curt Gunn (aka Kirk Gunn)	98 Randolph St. (Leonitis Club)	Downtown
Cy Jaynes (aka Si James)		
George Reichwold	115 W. Madison St.	Downtown
Wesley "One Arm" Schimmel		
Patrick "Patsy" King		
Sol Van Praag *	392 State St.	Downtown
"Long Shorty" (aka Barton)	170 Madison St.	Downtown
Mickey Conlon *	207 Madison St.	Downtown
William Skakel (aka "the Clock") *	170 Madison St. & 125 Clark St.; 73 & 78 W. Jackson	Downtown
A.H. Mayer		
George Alloway	78 W. Jackson	Downtown
Edward Schimmel		
William "Silver Bill" Riley		
Michael "Hinky Dink" Kenna *	19 Plymouth Place & Van Buren & Clark St. (The Workingman's Exchange)	Downtown
John Ryan *	120 Van Buren St.	Downtown
"Tug" Wilson		
Gus Hoffman		
Patrick Guerin		
William McGarigle (dba "Peter Crumby") *	124 Clark St. (Lansing & McGarigle Saloon)	Downtown
William Wightman		
John Gregory (aka "Dago" John)	134 Clark St. (The "Old 134")	Downtown
Charles Edwards		
Charles "Social" Smith	134 & 174 Clark St.	Downtown
Byron E. Pritchmore	164 Clark St.	Downtown
George Fegley	174 Clark St.	Downtown
Richard Morgan		
Charles Winship	176 Clark St. (The Club, formerly McDonald's "Store")	Downtown
Harry Perry		
George Norris		
William Fagan	162 Clark St. (The House of David)	Downtown
Charles Barber		
John Morris *	168 Clark St.	

Jerry Driscoll		
Ed Johnson		
Edward Jones		
Samuel Dahl (aka Sam Doll)	119 Clark St. & 14 Quincy St.	Downtown
Harry "Prince Hal" Varnell	119 Clark St.	Downtown
John Davis		
Ed Ehrman		
Joseph Raitch		
Harry Perry		
Rod Laverty	126 Clark St.	Downtown
Ben Dix		
"Little Barney" Simons	153 Clark St. (Chicago Opera House Building)	Downtown
Sid McHie (dba "Peck & Kelly")	153 Clark St. & 264 Clark St.	Downtown
A. W. Davis	264 Clark St.	Downtown
James McHie		
Harry Brown		
Walter Corrigan	267 Clark St. (The Columbia)	Downtown
Jacob Connors		
George Cadore		
Patrick "Pat" O'Malley	421 Clark St.	Downtown
Fred Wells	121 Dearborn St. (chartered club)	Downtown
William G. Gibbons	100 Madison St., rear of Saloon	Downtown
J. A. Webb	146 Madison St., above Saloon	Downtown
Frank Hicks		
"Bunk" Allen	151 W. Madison St., above Saloon	Downtown
William Wagner	177 W. Madison St.	Downtown
Bill Carpenter	335 W. Madison St., above Saloon	Downtown
Dave Cromelin	169 Wabash Ave., 3rd & 4th floors	Downtown
Dave Hutchinson	206 Wabash Ave., 2nd Floor	Downtown
Abe Silver	233 Wabash Ave.	Downtown
Joe Ullman	233 Wabash Ave. & West Side Driving Park	Downtown/ West Side
Max Blumenthal	West Side Driving Park	West Side
George Saulsbury	246 Wabash Ave., 3rd floor & 47 Congress St.	Downtown & Custom House Levee

Mike Mallory	305 Wabash Ave., above Saloon	Downtown
Bob Rose		
Louis Betts	1266 Wabash Ave., rear of Saloon	Downtown
James T. "Jimmy D'Apps" Appleton *	1626 Wabash Ave.	Downtown
Frank Williams	71 Monroe St.	Downtown
A. J. Levy		
Samuel Phillips		
John O'Neil	73 Monroe St. (The Newport Club)	Downtown
William Mell Fitts		
Thomas Howe		
"Figg" Leo Mayer		
A. Levi		
Tom Howe		
Phil Schaffner	169 Monroe St., 3rd & 4th floors	Downtown
"Doc" Green	118 State St.	Downtown/ Whiskey Row
Jerome Daley	298 State St. (The Berlin Cafe)	Downtown/ Whiskey Row
Tom M. McGinnis		
Sam Abrahams	368 State St., 2nd floor	Downtown/ Whiskey Row
Fenton Marsh	438 State St., rear of Saloon	Downtown/ Whiskey Row
Ed Tague	448 State St., rear of Saloon	Downtown/ Whiskey Row
John Wells	120 Washington St. (Gaiety Theater)	Downtown
William McLean	14–19 Quincy St., entire building	Downtown
Patrick "Paddy" Ryan	14–19 Quincy St. & 162 Clark St., 2nd floor	Downtown
John Condon	14–19 Quincy St.	Downtown
Charley Green		
Ed Bradley		
Dan Stewart		
L. Epstean *	20 Quincy St.	Downtown
Horace Argo	10 Calhoun Place	Downtown
Dave Shephard		
Peter Bliss		

Dan McCarthy		
M.H. Crawford		
Frank Lawler *	174 Clark St. & 329 Halsted St.	Downtown/West Side
Joe Lawler		
Mike Lawler		
Matt Hogan	47 Congress St.	Downtown/Custom House Place Levee
George Hathaway		
Tommy Major	Harrison St. & Fourth Ave.	Downtown/Custom House Place Levee
George V. Hankins	134, 174 184, Clark St. & 3858 Cottage Grove Ave.	Downtown/South Side
John V. "Mushmouth" Johnson	464 State St. & 311 Clark St.	Downtown/South Side
Ed Wagner	170 Madison St. & Cottage Grove Ave. & Thirty-fifth St.	Downtown/South Side
Harry Romaine	134, 174 Clark St. & 3858 Cottage Grove Ave.	Downtown/South Side
Albert Hankins	162 Clark St. & 3008 Cottage Grove Ave.	Downtown/South Side
James Hunter	2036 Wabash Ave.	South Side Levee District
J. Thomas Hinch	1871 Wabash Ave. (Rossmore Hotel)	South Side Levee District
Tommy Danforth	Twentieth St. & State St. (Rialto Saloon)	South Side Levee District
Joseph H. Suits	Twenty-second St. & the Elevated Line	South Side Levee District
William Johnson	Twenty-second St., west of State St., 2nd floor	South Side Levee District
"Stockyards" Sam	2846 State St.	South Side Levee District
Billy Bryant	Twenty-ninth St. & State St., rear of Saloon	South Side Levee District
Tim McKeough	194 Twenty-second St., 2nd floor	South Side Levee District
Peter M. Samey	Fifty-seventh St. & State St.	South Side
Bob Mott	2700 S. State St.	South Side
Sam Cohen		
"Major" Blakely		
John McCarthy	3533 S. Halsted St.	South Side Stockyards District
James "Big Jim" O'Leary		

Edward O'Leary		
William Burns	42nd St. & Halsted, above U.S. Post Office	South Side Stockyards District
Frank McWhorter	3846 & 3854 S. State St. & DuPage County	South Side & Western Suburbs
John O'Malley *	Clark St. & Kinzie	North Side
"Pudd" Malcolm	Madison St. & Loomis & 153 Clark St. (Chicago Opera House Building)	Downtown/Near West Side
"Kid" Royal	Madison St. & Halsted, basement	Near West Side
Jack Dwyer		
A. L. Morris	93 Clinton St.	Near West Side
John Rogers *	May & Madison St., rear of Saloon	Near West Side
John Hoey	Madison St. & Halsted, basement	Near West Side

Sources: Civic Federation of Chicago, "The Work of the Civic Federation of Chicago: Report of the Secretary Ralph M. Easley Read at the 5th Annual Meeting, April 26, 1899," Municipal Reference Collection, Chicago Public Library. Also, various newspaper accounts of gambling raids conducted 1885-1900.

Note: In 1909, the City of Chicago changed its street numbering system. Addresses shown in the table predate the change.

* Elected public official, i.e., Chicago alderman or Illinois state representative. Frank Lawler was a U.S. congressman and an alderman.

~

Notes

Introduction: The Dark City on the Edge of Civilization

1. Farwell, *Reminiscences of John V. Farwell*, 51.

2. "Chicago in the Thirties: Stories of the Times When Pelicans Were Shot within Corporate Limits," *Chicago Inter-Ocean*, April 18, 1884.

3. "Foul Ewing Street," *Chicago Inter-Ocean*, March 30, 1893.

4. "The Party of Revolution and Robbery," *Chicago Inter-Ocean*, March 26, 1879. "Democratic leaders of Chicago confidently expect to carry the forthcoming municipal election. They insist that on a full vote . . . the city is largely Democratic; this false assumption paves the way for the repeaters and the ballot-box stuffers brigade. It means frauds are necessary to success."

5. "The Wages of Sin," *Chicago Times*, August 5, 1877.

6. Karabell, *Chester Alan Arthur*, 5–6.

7. Quoted in the *Chicago Tribune*, August 23, 1883. See also "Party Hardy," by Tom Chalkley, online at www.citypaperonline.com for a historical review of the Gorman machine.

8. *Chicago Daily Times*, December 27, 1936.

9. William Marcy Tweed (1823–78) was the first "boss" of Tammany Hall, the Democratic organization of New York. From 1860 to 1871 he controlled all city patronage. His rise to power culminated in the election of Abraham Oakey Hall as mayor—who was subsequently indicted on a charge of neglect of duty in 1872.

10. Chicago Common Council, *Journal of the Proceedings*, December 4, 1871, 1–9.

11. Facing the grimy railroad freight yards, "Biler Avenue" sprung up almost immediately after the Chicago Fire, proving that not even a conflagration of that magnitude could block the relentless expansion of vice. Historians are not sure of just how Pacific Avenue (now LaSalle Street) acquired its dubious nickname, but with the construction of a Jewish synagogue in 1879 in the middle of the block and the determination of the Temple to rid the district of lewd women and objectionable saloons, vice operations shifted eastward to Clark Street where the notorious Custom House Place levee was taking shape. See the *Chicago Tribune*, October 8, 1879, for a further account of "Biler Avenue."

12. Others have since staked their claim to the famous phrase, notably the famous 1920s Broadway show lounge maven and speakeasy owner, Mary Louise "Texas" Guinan (1884–1933). Guinan greeted patrons at the door of her 300 Club in New York with a

cheerfully familiar "Hello, Suckers! Come on in and leave your wallet on the bar." In another version, historians credit Syracuse, N.Y., banker and promoter David Hannum who unveiled the "Cardiff Giant," a 12-foot stone carving manufactured by hoaxer George Hull in 1868 at Fort Dodge, Iowa, and transported to Cardiff, N.Y., where it was retouched, put on display, and advertised as the remains of an ancient man. Hannum had purchased the object for $30,000 and looked forward to doubling his investment by capitalizing on the gullibility of the ticket-buying public who believed such nonsense. Phineas T. Barnum exposed the fraud and supposedly quoted Hannum's exact words, to the effect that "There's a sucker born every minute." For further information, see R. J. Brown, "P. T. Barnum Never Did Say 'There's a Sucker Born Every Minute,'" *History Buff.com,* http://www.historybuff.com/library/refbarnum.html; and Asbury, *Sucker's Progress,* 305.

13. "A Despicable Wretch," *Chicago Herald,* October 27, 1882.

1. A Train Butcher Raising the Wind

1. A short biographical sketch of Mike McDonald's father appears in the *Chicago Tribune,* March 26, 1895. Genealogical information about the McDonald family in Chicago, New York, and Ireland (while very fragmented and sometimes unverifiable) was obtained through the Mormon databases at their Family Research Center in Wilmette, Ill.; also the Population Census Schedules for Niagara County, N.Y., 1840–50, in the National Archives, Washington, D.C.; the Office of the Cook County Clerk; Mount Olivet Cemetery, Chicago; Latter Day Saints Genealogy Data Base; the generous assistance of Dorman Nelson of Granada Hills, Calif.; and Brenda Mason of Kincardine, Ontario.

2. For further information about this obscure incident of American history, see Robert Kostoff, "Patriot's War Affected Niagara Area," *Niagara Falls Reporter,* July 22, 2003.

3. *Chicago Tribune,* March 26, 1895.

4. Saint Rafael became the Parish of the Sacred Heart in 1854 with 617 registered families. The parish church is located at South Avenue and 11th Street. *Niagara Falls Gazette,* March 11, 2008. See also *Steele's Book of Niagara Falls,* 7th ed. (Buffalo, N.Y.: Oliver G. Steele, 1840), and *Burke's Descriptive Guide to Niagara Falls* (Buffalo, N.Y.: Andrew Burke, 1851).

5. For a short biographical sketch, see Ahern, *Political History of Chicago,* 375–76. There are lingering questions as to the actual name and location of White's Academy in the Niagara Falls region and the time frame when McDonald supposedly was enrolled as a student. Another source of information reported in the "Chicago Irish Families, 1875–1925" page of Ancestry.com states that the school's name was "Hoyt's College." However, this name could not be found in any Niagara Falls history or directory.

6. *Chicago Herald,* October 27, 1882. See also the *Chicago Tribune,* October 27, 1882.

7. *Chicago Herald,* October 27, 1882.

8. *Baltimore American,* November 5, 1842. For many years, food services were provided by trackside vendors to hungry, disembarking passengers during brief refueling stops. See also the reminiscences of a 40-year train butcher, "Trade of the Train Butcher," *Chicago Tribune,* December 10, 1905.

9. "Trade of the Train Butcher."

10. Bennett, *Politics and Politicians of Chicago,* 526. Marvin was killed in a train accident on June 5, 1855, and was buried by McDonald and his friends. James Fehan went on to become secretary to Chief Silas McBride of the Chicago Fire Department, no doubt an appointment brokered by McDonald.

11. In later years, McDonald was selected to serve as "Grand Marshal" of the New Orleans Fire Department grand parade, his past doings in the Crescent City long remembered.

12. *Chicago Times*, August 21, 1889. This is just one theory as to the origin of the famous phrase. See the introduction, note 12, above.

13. *Blackleg* was a Southern term in vogue from the end of the eighteenth century through the latter half of the nineteenth century to describe a crooked gambler or particular type of card cheat or confidence man.

14. *Chicago Herald*, October 27, 1882.

15. These table-top devices were used to view 3-D images, typically famous buildings and natural wonders.

16. Asbury, *Sucker's Progress*, 229–34.

17. *New Orleans Bee*, February 8, 1860.

18. For a discussion of gambling in antebellum New Orleans, see Abbye A. Gorin, "Gambling in Louisiana: It's a Tradition!" at http://www.tulane.edu/~rivgate/appendix/appendix3.html. Another source worth mentioning is Roger Busbice and John Keeling, "Fortune Favored Few: A History of Gambling in Early Louisiana," *Louisiana Political Review*, no. 14 (July 1993). In 1840, New Orleans had an estimated 500 gambling establishments employing over 4,000 people. The nation's earliest casinos were in operation but generating little or no revenue to the benefit of the city despite the enabling legislation.

19. Bennett, *Politics and Politicians of Chicago*, 526; *Chicago Tribune*, December 15, 1892. It wasn't until 1884, during a return visit to New Orleans, that McDonald found out that his compatriot Sherman had escaped a firing squad.

20. Keno, similar to bingo, involves a set of five winning numbers drawn in a lottery. Faro, otherwise known as the "Tiger" from the common image of a Bengal Tiger often portrayed on the façades of big-city gambling dens, was played with a dealing box, cards placed faceup. Players who bet on a card equal in numerical value to the second are losers; those wagering on cards equal in value to the card on top are winners. See DeArment, "Gambling on the Frontier," 39–50. See also Sante, *Low Life*, 158–59.

21. Dexter Park opened in the Stockyards District at 42nd and Halsted Streets in 1866. Nationally known in racing circles, the namesake horse was the most famous trotter of his day, worth a cool $17,000. Trussell paid $7,000 for a half-ownership in the steed from A. F. Fawcett, Esq., a Baltimore breeder who reacquired Dexter after George's murder and doubled his investment.

22. *Chicago Times*, September 5, 1866. Gunplay among gamblers cohabitating in the brothel districts of Chicago was common. A Cook County constable was shot and killed by Annie Stewart, keeper of a bordello at 441 South Clark Street on July 11, 1868, after accusing the woman of cheating him out of $10 during a game of euchre. The *Times* believed the incident was "possibly the result of the practical teachings of the verdict rendered in the Mollie Trussell and other similar affairs."

23. *Chicago Times*, February 9, 1867.

24. *Chicago Times*, November 4, 1873.

25. Ibid. See also Dedmon, *Fabulous Chicago*, 79–82, for an anecdotal review of Cap Hyman's doings along the Hairtrigger Block.

26. See appendixes 1 and 2 for a listing of the principal keepers of gambling houses in Chicago, 1868–1900. More than two-thirds have Irish surnames.

27. Not to be confused with the Black Star Line chartered by the African American nationalist Marcus Garvey in 1919. See the *Chicago Tribune*, June 19, 1887.

2. Brace Games and Bunko Men

1. Asbury, *French Quarter*, 155–65, 223.

2. See Asbury, *Sucker's Progress*, 260.

3. *Chicago Herald*, October 28, 1882. See also *Chicago Inter-Ocean*, October 28, 1882.

4. Hewitt, *Roster of Union Soldiers*, 319. From Kane's Brewery on Polk Street in Chicago, the regiment moved south to Quincy, Ill.; then, after a few days encampment, to the arsenal at St. Louis. On July 21, the Irish Brigade was located at Jefferson City, Mo., where they launched initial excursions to engage the enemy. Within the month, the brigade was forced to surrender to a Confederate regiment near Lexington, Mo. The name of Michael C. McDonald does not appear anywhere in the complete regimental roster contained in the adjutant general's report. Frederick Francis Cook was a reporter for the *Chicago Times* during the Civil War, filing local dispatches for Wilbur Storey.

5. *Chicago Tribune*, December 18, 1864.

6. Ibid.

7. "Dodging the Enrollment," *Chicago Tribune*, December 20–21, 1863; "Alien Voters," *Chicago Tribune*, April 16, 1864. "Michael McDonald, Irish" is listed as a shirker.

8. *Chicago Tribune*, April 17, 1864.

9. *Chicago Tribune*, November 5, 1864. Broken down by the city wards they resided in, the published names reflect the ethnic composition of Chicago during the war. The tide of immigration from Eastern Europe into Chicago would not reach its peak for another ten to fifteen years. The majority of draft evaders were men with Anglo or Irish surnames with a handful of Germans sprinkled in, suggesting that many of these individuals were claiming Canadian citizenship as a means to avoid military service. It is likely that McDonald managed to convince the draft board that he was born on the Canadian side of Niagara Falls, which of course would have been a deliberate deception.

10. Calvin Paige often went by the pseudonym "Peter Page," confusing the press and causing embarrassment to builder, developer, Republican alderman, and Internal Revenue assessor Peter Page (1814–80), one of the city's "Old Settlers" remembered in death as a "good, substantial citizen." Ironically, the famous antebellum Richmond House Hotel was named after Thomas Richmond, Chicago resident, abolitionist, and friend of Abraham Lincoln.

11. *Bunko,* or *bunco,* is a derivation of *Banco,* or "Eight-Dice Cloth," an old English dice-and-card game that gained popularity in San Francisco in the 1850s, and spread across the country during the Civil War. The game was crooked and unwinable; the corruption of the name entered the language to mean any crooked or fraudulent scheme involving the swindle of the unsuspecting. Banco faded from the public scene in the 1890s, but police fraud details were ever afterward known as "bunko squads." See Sante, *Low Life*, 166–67. See also Asbury, *Sucker's Paradise*, 56–58.

12. Pierce, *History of Chicago*, 476. See also *Chicago Tribune*, September 16, 20, and 21, 1882.

13. See the 1862–64 *Lakeside Directory of Chicago*. Mike McDonald is listed with Paige as the co-owner of the Richmond House Saloon but is misidentified as "Michael C. McDonnell."

14. Gilbert and Bryson, *Chicago and Its Makers*, 125.

15. See John C. W. Bailey, *Lakeside Annual Chicago City Directory, 1866–1867* (Chicago: Williams, Donnelley, 1867) for commercial listings and residential addresses. *Steerers, ropers,* and *cappers* were nineteenth-century designations commonly applied to sociable young men drumming up business for the gambling house. Nineteenth-century

gambling houses were sharply segregated by social rank and privilege. As the popularity of draw poker spread northward in the 1860s, high stakes "gentlemen's games" for professional men in the clubrooms and first-class hotels of the city were left unmolested by police, while a plethora of storefront "dinner pail" resorts for the small tradesmen to wager their nickels and dimes while on the way home from the lumberyard, factory, or streetcar catered to a less-affluent clientele.

16. Built in 1857 on Madison Street near State, the theater was a famous temple of the performing arts, featuring drama and lighter musical fare under the management of James H. McVicker (1822–96), an actor and former employee of the postwar mayor, John Blake Rice. It was destroyed in the Chicago Fire of 1871 and rebuilt a year later.

17. Jack Haverly (1837–1901), nationally known theater promoter, racetrack owner, compulsive gambler, and business entrepreneur, gained fame with his burlesque opera and traveling minstrel shows showcasing African American performers. Haverly, hotelier Potter Palmer, and dry goods merchant E. J. Lehmann were three business and civic leaders from Chicago's "upper world" who seemed to enjoy slumming with the "sports" of the city in defiance of the admonitions of the Republican press. On September 30, 1879, Haverly purchased controlling interest in the Chicago Jockey and Trotting Club from Harry Lawrence and Morris Martin, two of Mike McDonald's better-known henchmen from the early days. They constructed the oval and buildings on the West Side in 1878 in order to give Chicagoans a "first class race-track" with "commendable enterprise." *Chicago Tribune*, August 2, 1878.

18. "Attacks Divorce, Will and Deed," *Chicago Tribune*, August 14, 1907. Belle Jewel's name is listed in the 1870 census records as a resident of McDonald's household. The society page of the March 24, 1907, *Washington Post* reports that a Mrs. Burton Gay was visiting her mother, Mrs. George Mayo, in the capital. Mrs. John Gay was the sister of the late Isabella Jewel, who passed away c. 1889 in the St. Louis convent. John E. Gay was a Chicago jailer and, ironically, the turnkey who locked up Dora Feldman McDonald for murder in 1907.

19. Address of Bernard Caulfield to the Seventh Ward Irish, *Chicago Times*, June 16, 1868. Such sentiments struck a respondent chord among the immigrant Irish, who feared that the enfranchised former slave population would pour into Chicago and deprive them of their livelihoods. Caulfield (1828–87), fled to Mexico with a contingent of Southerners and lived in exile until 1867 when he returned to Chicago that year to resume his law practice and oppose the Radical Republican Reconstructionists in the ward caucuses and political campaigning. He was appointed to Congress in 1873 and reelected in 1875. Concise information about the Camp Douglas conspiracy can be found in "The Great North-Western Conspiracy in All Its Startling Details," by I. Windslow Ayer, an out-of-print text republished online in *Authorama*, http://www.authorama.com/north-western-conspiracy-1.html. See also the *Chicago Inter-Ocean*, October 31, 1874, and a recent reexamination of events by Levy, *To Die in Chicago*.

20. Ayer, "Great North-Western Conspiracy," chapter 17.

21. *Chicago Tribune*, January 9, 1865. See also Lindberg, *To Serve and Collect*.

22. *Chicago Herald*, October 28, 1882.

23. The reconstructed conversation is reported in the May 29, 1875, edition of the *Chicago Tribune* in a letter of concern and admonishment from a disgusted "Spectator," along with similar accounts of frauds perpetrated by members of the McDonald bunko syndicate against unsuspecting "Grangers."

24. See Farr, *Chicago*.

25. Tom Foley was arguably the "dean" of nineteenth-century American billiards. He dabbled in professional sports, gambling, and politics—the three avocations were almost interchangeable in the big cities at this time. In 1869, he assembled and managed the original Chicago White Stockings baseball team. Two years later, he was a delegate to the Democratic State Nominating Convention, and two years after that (January 1873) he opened the largest, costliest, and most magnificent billiard parlor in the Western world amid the ruins of the downtown burnt district. McDonald was a close friend and ally who clocked bets on all of the big championship matches.

26. *Chicago Inter-Ocean*, April 28, 1870.

27. The *Lakeside Directory of Chicago for 1872* lists McDonald's employment with Young's Omnibus Line.

28. *Chicago Inter-Ocean*, November 13–15, 1868.

29. *Chicago Tribune*, January 28 and February 23, 1870. Citing statistics published in the *New Englander* of February 1870, the *Tribune* suggested that worldwide crime rates were proportionately higher among nations where the Roman Catholic faith was predominant, than in the Western and Northern European bastions of Protestantism.

3. A Department Store of Gambling

1. "Moral Support," *Chicago Tribune*, October 11, 1872. S. B. Gookins (1809–80), outspoken proponent of liquor probation and former judge of the Indiana Supreme Court in the early 1850s, was another in a lengthy roster of New England patricians (Gookins was born in Bennington County, Vt.) attempting to apply temperance and the moral standards of the Puritans to the liberal-minded citizens of the post-Fire period. For many years, following his term on the bench, he was a practicing attorney in Chicago.

2. Interview with Donald L. Miller, *CNN Saturday*, September 17, 2005. Miller, a MacCracken Professor of History at Lafayette College in Easton, Pa., is the author of *City of the Century: The Epic of Chicago and the Making of America* (New York: Simon & Schuster, 1996).

3. It was fortunate for McDonald that he sold this saloon within the year, because it burned down in an 1874 fire that decimated Cheyenne.

4. *Town Talker*, February 21, 1872.

5. *Chicago Times*, February 24, 1872.

6. Foss was accused by the *Times* of instigating this bill after his business partner had lost a considerable sum to Chicago gambler John Lyons. "The damned old fool hadn't sense enough to do his own writing and he hired a lawyer" to draft the bill, one gambler was quoted as saying. See *Chicago Times*, February 18, 1872.

7. Ibid.

8. Ibid.

9. Massachusetts native Elmer Washburn (1834–1918) held many jobs in the public and private sectors. At various times, he was a banker, civil engineer, supervisor for the Town of Lake (the South Side Stockyards neighborhood), president of the livestock exchange, chief of the Secret Service under President Ulysses S. Grant, and a Chicago mayoral candidate (in 1891) in addition to the two-year term he served as police superintendent in the 1870s. Long identified with reform efforts in Chicago, Washburn was the first "outsider" appointed to lead the Chicago Police Department. In the long history of the CPD, only three other men ascended to this position that did not come up through the rank and file. See the *Chicago Evening Post*, January 29, 1873, for an overview of Washburn's career.

10. *Chicago Tribune*, January 29, 1873.

11. "Eleven Houses Pulled and 68 Persons Arrested," *Chicago Tribune*, December 1, 1872. See also *Chicago Tribune*, August 20, 1873.

12. *Chicago Tribune*, February 2, 1873. Other published reports accused Washburn's bluecoats of accepting bribes.

13. Flinn and Wilkie, *History of the Chicago Police*, 139. This is hardly an unimpeachable source. Publication costs for the book were paid by subscription, and editorial direction was provided by the various police fraternal societies and supervisory cadre.

14. "Some Facts about Gage's Defalcation," *Chicago Tribune*, April 4, 1885. See also October 29, 1873, and August 23, 1877. Gage served as city treasurer from 1869 to 1873, when he fled to France. He was eventually extradited back to Chicago and deeded monies received from the sale of his home to the city in order to pay off more than half a million dollars in absconded funds

15. The *Staats-Zeitung* was an influential journal of the German working class constantly at odds with the pro-business, reform-minded bluebloods like Joseph Medill and a sympathetic ally of McDonald.

16. Richard A. Canfield (1855–1914), America's "casino king," opened the Madison Square Club in New York City in 1888. The top floors were living quarters. Poker wasn't offered; only house-banked games like faro and roulette were featured. In 1894 Canfield launched the Saratoga Club House, complete with art gallery, in Saratoga Springs, N.Y., the Las Vegas of its day. Here the potato chip and quite possibly the club sandwich were first popularized.

17. Edwin Walker (1838–1910) was born in Leeds, Yorkshire, England. The exterior walls of the Chicago Water Tower and pumping station on Michigan Avenue and the Illinois State Capitol building in Springfield (750,000 square-feet of stone, completed in 1888) were supplied by Walker's firm. In 1892, he opened the Illinois Pure Aluminum Company in Lemont, a company that continued in business under the direction of his son George until 1947. See Wiss and Eistener Associates, "Will County Rural Historical Survey."

18. Chicago Recorder of Deeds tract records for Lot 20, Block 118, of the School Addition to Chicago. In 1873, the recorded lessor was the heirs of Benjamin Lawrence, conceivably a relative of gambler Harry Lawrence.

19. Ibid. Between April 1873 and April 1877, twenty different people were recorded as lessees in this building. Walker was both lessee and lessor four different times during this period.

20. *Chicago Tribune* retrospective, June 18, 1899.

21. See *Chicago Tribune*, January 7, 1896, for a look back at Casey's career.

22. *Chicago Tribune*, August 1, 1875. Conversation reported verbatim by an eavesdropping reporter, from inside the store.

23. Ibid. The same reporter suggested to *Tribune* readers that the only viable way to rid Chicago of this "real-life Fagin and his gang of 'Artful Dodgers'" was to flog them to death. Justice Summerfield, who caused much consternation to the gamblers until he could be replaced, presided over night court at the Armory Police Station.

24. "In the Wake of the News," *Chicago Tribune*, February 23, 1931.

25. *Chicago Tribune*, October 30, 1887. Sir Charles Russell, Baron Russell of Killowen (1832–1900), was a British statesman and member of Parliament born in County Down. He was appointed lord chief justice of England in 1894, becoming the first Catholic to attain that office for centuries. In 1910, Russell's brother, the Reverend Matthew Russell, S.J., posthumously published *A Diary of a Visit to the United States,* issued by the

U.S. Catholic Historical Society. Mike McDonald passively supported the cause of Irish independence, but was not aligned with the Clan-na-Gael or other extremist movements committed to carrying out armed violence in Ireland.

26. *Chicago Tribune*, June 18, 1899. Senator James Graham Fair (1831–94) was part-owner of Nevada's lucrative Comstock Lode. He served one term in Congress, 1881–86, promoting silver issues against the gold standard. The Fairmont Hotel in San Francisco, begun by his daughters in 1902, is a monument to his memory.

27. *Chicago Tribune*, "Earlier Chicago," July 26, 1935.

28. *Chicago Tribune*, "Mike McDonald's Store," May 26, 1921; and *Chicago Inter-Ocean*, October 15, 1878.

29. Marital Record of the Clerk of the Circuit Court of Cook County. The date of the Noonan-McDonald union is recorded in the county clerk's office with the date December 5, 1871.

30. *Chicago Times*, August 22, 1889.

31. *Chicago Tribune*, November 24, 1878.

32. *Chicago Tribune*, March 30, 1890.

33. *Chicago Herald*, March 25, 1883.

34. Obituary, *Chicago Times*, October 30, 1888. William King McAllister (1818–88) was elected to the Illinois Supreme Court on August 8, 1870, but resigned in protest on November 26, 1875, because of low compensation and a four-year backlog of cases he found intolerable. His election to the Cook County Circuit Court that same year actually increased his salary by $2,000 a year. See Stephen Anderson, "Wisdom and Deliberation," *Illinois State Bar Association News*, June 1, 2001.

35. "Recollections of an Old Grand Jury and the Peculiarities regarding Mike Mc-Donald," *Chicago Inter-Ocean*, February 28, 1882.

36. *Chicago Tribune*, February 28, 1882.

37. *Chicago Tribune*, August 13, 1907.

38. Ibid. The incident was reported on August 20, 1873, about a month before the Store formally opened for business. It seems highly unlikely that McDonald was on the verge of financial ruin because of one night spent wagering inside a rival's gambling house.

39. *Chicago Tribune*, December 12, 1875. Arlington performed at Hooley's Theater in October–December 1875.

40. Biographical sketch in Rice, *Monarchs of the Minstrelsy*, 115. Billy Arlington (1835–1913) died of a heart attack in Los Angeles, on May 23, 1913.

41. *Chicago Times*, May 3, 1876.

42. Interview with Mary McDonald Grasshoff, *Chicago Daily News*, August 13, 1907.

43. *Chicago Times*, May 3, 1876. Trading in scandal, Storey justified publication thus: "But like Banquo's ghost, the rumors would not [die] down and at length the *Times* deemed them of sufficient interest to warrant a thorough investigation."

44. Ibid.

45. Edith Harrison, *Strange to Say*, 54.

46. *Lakeside Directory of Chicago, 1882*. Mary was still listed as the proprietress of the Palace European Hotel at 176 South Clark. Mike's other property holdings at this time included 660 West Van Buren Street, where M. C. McDonald & Co.—the liquor distribution business—was headquartered, and a satellite office at 9 Calhoun Place in Gambler's Alley. The various gambling dens and faro banks under his control were unlisted.

47. Harrison, *Strange to Say*, 58.

48. *Chicago Tribune*, April 21, 1895. See also Henry Justin Smith, *Chicago*, 168–70.

4. Tammany by the Lake

1. Bennett, *Politics and Politicians of Chicago*, 533.

2. *Chicago Tribune*, May 3, 1890.

3. *Chicago Tribune*, November 27, 1875.

4. The immigrant people of Europe who occupied "Little Hell" in the era of McDonald were mostly gone by the 1950s as poor Southern blacks poured into the neighborhood, and a more modern kind of urban horror took shape: gang violence and drug dealing. Harvey Warren Zorbaugh's seminal 1929 account, *The Gold Coast and the Slum*, profiles the evolution of this North Side enclave and how it remained a crime-ridden slum for nearly 80 years.

5. Bennett, *Politics and Politicians of Chicago*, 533–34.

6. *Chicago Tribune*, October 10, 1880.

7. Andreas, *History of Chicago*, 2:501. With borrowed capital, John R. Walsh opened his downtown news agency in 1861. He foresaw the great westward expansion and recognized that papers and magazines could be distributed to the outlying states faster and cheaper than through the mails. Walsh's company revolutionized circulation by delivering the news via rail 24 hours ahead of the competition.

8. *Chicago Tribune*, June 30, 1868, and November 14, 1877.

9. *Chicago Tribune*, March 3, 1877.

10. *Chicago Times*, May 25, 1878; *Chicago Tribune*, May 25–26, 1878. Dowling was one of scores of gamblers who squandered a fortune and died a pauper.

11. *Chicago Tribune*, May 25–26, 1878.

12. *Chicago Tribune*, January 28, 1870. "When the Justices found that an appeal was equivalent to a discharge, they frequently fined and then suspended execution on condition that the parties leave town. Of course but a few left."

13. *Chicago Tribune*, September 25, 1873.

14. Hugh Garrity was eventually convicted of bank robbery in Galesburg, Ill., and sent to the penitentiary. He died in Minneapolis on February 1, 1891, after being pulled out of the gutter by a local gendarme.

15. Dunne's character was originally "McNeary," but the real McGarry disliked the name, saying it was uncomfortably close to his own and demanded a change. Dunne obliged, and soon the fictional "Martin Dooley" was born. The barkeep died without funds in the Cook County Hospital on October 29, 1901.

16. "In the Wake of the News," *Chicago Tribune*, March 26, 1921.

17. *Chicago Tribune*, December 27, 1874. The *Tribune* derided Mayor Harvey Colvin and his cabinet as frauds and "actors"—playing the role of statesmen.

18. Charles Edward "Parson" Davies (1851–1920) was born in Antrim, Ireland. He arrived in Chicago in 1868.

19. *Chicago Herald*, May 12, 1883.

20. *Chicago Herald*, March 3, 1883.

21. Ibid.

22. Emery Storrs (1835–85) was a delegate at large to Republican nominating conventions in 1868, 1872, and 1880 and was instrumental in shaping the party platform. A few months before his death, he accepted a large retainer to defend the Mormons in Utah.

23. *Chicago Herald*, May 17, 1883.

24. *Chicago Herald*, May 19, 1883.

25. Dunn drifted west, reveling in his reputation as the notorious gunsel who killed Elliott, telling anyone who cared to listen, the "real inside story." He died from the complications of cancer in San Francisco not long after surviving the great earthquake of 1906.

5. The People's Party and the Overturn of Puritan Rule

1. While McDonald desired a stable home life and a household full of children despite his shady street associations, George Hankins married a notorious brothel keeper who operated her vice den at 2131 South Dearborn Street—the future home of the world-famous Everleigh Club from 1900 to 1911. Effie H. Hankins was an extravagant madam who covered herself in diamonds and furs and was a frequenter of New Orleans and other locales favored by nineteenth-century pleasure seekers.

2. *Chicago Tribune*, August 31, 1873.

3. These nuggets were loose pieces of gold mixed in with the rocks, gravel, and dirt commonly found in mountain streams. See Rosen, "*Gold!*"

4. *Chicago Tribune*, February 14, 1875. The brothers set up business in Blackfoot City in 1865. George, the least experienced of the trio, was assigned bartender duties, while Jeff and Al worked the tables, engaging the miners in "brace" (crooked) faro.

5. *Chicago Inter-Ocean*, August 7, 1876.

6. *Chicago Morning News*, November 5, 1884.

7. *Chicago Tribune*, July 15, 1880. Portuguese by birth, Jack Yattaw (1848–93) always maintained his operation was perfectly legal because he ran it well outside city and state limits. Law enforcement argued that its jurisdiction extended three miles offshore and therefore it could raid the bumboats with impunity; but the courts upheld Yattaw's right to operate in the neutral waters of Lake Michigan. The hull of his most famous craft, *El Tempo*, was riddled with bullets—the historic record of years of shootings and other assorted mayhem on board.

8. For further accounts of Yattaw's battles with the city, see *Chicago Tribune*, July 13, 1879, November 5, 1884, and July 21, 1887; and *Chicago Daily Mail*, March 15, 1891.

9. William Skakel (1843–1925) opened eight gambling dens and several more "bucket shops" at 130 West Van Buren Street, 170 West Madison, and 73 West Jackson Boulevard, buying and selling shares of mining stocks on margin with his sidekick and business partner Hugh Maher. Author Dorman Nelson of Granada Hills, Calif., has established that Skakel was the great uncle of Ethyl Skakel Kennedy (widow of the late Senator Robert Kennedy), her grandfather's brother.

10. *Chicago Times*, March 12, 1883.

11. *Chicago Tribune*, November 5, 1873.

12. By 1873, 15 percent of the Chicago City Council members were engaged in the liquor trade as saloon keepers, suppliers, or manufacturers of intoxicants. John Corcoran, leader of the Hatch House contingent, passed away on May 22, 1878. The *Times* likened him to New York gambling boss John Morrissey—"but on a small scale"—and mixed their partisan praise of the deceased with surprising criticism. McDonald served as a pallbearer at the funeral. See the *Chicago Times* and the *Chicago Inter-Ocean*, May 23, 1878.

13. Anton Hesing (1823–95) rose from the obscurity of brick manufacturer to become the recognized leader of Chicago's German community in the span of a few years.

14. *Chicago Tribune*, October 27, 1873.

15. *Chicago Tribune*, November 5, 1873. See also: Skilnick, *Beer and Brewing in Chicago*, 45–46.

16. Wendt, *The Chicago Tribune*, 258–59. See also the *Chicago Times*, November 4, 1873.

17. *Chicago Tribune*, October 31, 1873.

18. *Chicago Times*, November 4, 1873. Once allies, Hickey and McDonald became bitter enemies after the 1876 election when Mike refused to support Hickey's man, the Republican candidate Monroe Heath, for mayor. In retaliation, Hickey sanctioned gambling raids against the store, including the 1878 "pull" that nearly resulted in the shooting deaths of the two officers by Mary Noonan McDonald's hand.

19. Mayor Colvin and the city council acting in accord eliminated the police commission by executive decree on June 30, 1875. The office of "police marshal" was created but was subordinate to departmental fiat.

20. *Chicago Tribune*, November 15, 1874.

6. Bummers, Gutter-Rats, Whiskey Soakers, and Saloon Loafers

1. "The Temperance War," *Chicago Journal*, March 20, 1874.

2. Ibid.

3. Tenth Ward alderman George E. White to a *Journal* reporter in "Temperance War." On a national level, the rise of the United States Brewer's Association (USBA), a trade organization representing the interests of distillers, vigorously fought prohibition efforts at the state level and carried their fight to Washington, D.C. See Blocker, Fahey, and Tyrrell, *Alcohol and Temperance*.

4. Letter to the editor, *Chicago Tribune*, November 21, 1874.

5. *Chicago Tribune*, November 3, 1873. The "redress" refers to McDonald's desire to punish Washburn's police cadre, who carried out the objectionable raids against the Store in 1872–73.

6. *Chicago Times*, May 16, 1876.

7. *Chicago Tribune*, June 5, 1877.

8. *Chicago Tribune*, May 13, 1876.

9. See White, *Republican Era*. See also H. V. Boynton, "The Whiskey Ring," *North American Review* 73 (1876): 299.

10. *Chicago Tribune*, May 17, 1876. Robert Green Ingersoll (1833–99), noted political orator and former Illinois attorney general, was defending Daniel W. Munn, local supervisor of the Internal Revenue Service and others caught up in the scheme to embezzle federal tax revenue. Ingersoll was trying to absolve his clients of responsibility for wrongdoing and shift the blame to Rehm.

11. *Chicago Tribune*, July 8, 1876.

12. Anton Hesing would remain a popular and sympathetic figure to much of the German working class up until his death at age 73 on March 31, 1895. Hesing, whose forebears were brewers and distillers from Vechta, Oldenburg, lived long enough to see his son Washington elevated to the office of postmaster of Chicago.

13. Henry "Buffalo" Miller (1819–89) was associated with Storey in a newspaper venture in Niles, Mich. Resettled in New York, he was an early promoter of the Erie Canal and a two-term member of the New York legislature. Elected as city treasurer on the People's Party ticket, Chicagoans knew him as "Buffalo" Miller because he mounted the large head of a stuffed buffalo over the transom of his Chicago saloon and spoke with warm affection for the western New York metropolis. At the time of his death, he left behind a sizeable $200,000 estate.

14. Thomas Hoyne (1817–83), another New Yorker, made his way west to Chicago, where he served as city clerk, probate justice of the peace, U.S. district attorney, U.S.

marshal, Democratic congressman, and president of the Chicago Library Board, before winning the disputed mayoral election.

15. Bennett, *Politics and Politicians of Chicago*, 527.

16. *Chicago Tribune*, June 27, 1876. See also *Official Proceedings of the National Democratic Convention, Held in St. Louis, Mo., June 27th, 28th and 29th, 1876*. St. Louis: Woodward, Tiernan & Hale, printers, 1876.

17. Born in rural New Hampshire, Monroe Heath (1828–94) was an early associate of President Franklin Pierce in Concord, before relocating to Chicago in 1851, where he opened a paint and dry goods store on the North Side. He was elected alderman on Medill's "Fireproof" ticket in 1871 and served a second term before being recommended to the city's highest office by the Republicans.

18. Michael Carroll Hickey (1830–1900) was promoted to a captaincy in 1866, but resigned after the Chicago Fire, only to be brought back by Colvin in 1875. Generally liked by the rank and file, Hickey was accused of conspiring with criminal fences and brothel madams.

19. *Chicago Tribune*, October 24, 1876. See also City Law Department letter to Monroe Heath with transcript of hearings, November 27, 1876, Municipal Archives of Chicago.

20. *Chicago Tribune* , October 24, 1876.

21. *Chicago Tribune*, January 17, 1877.

22. *Chicago Tribune*, November 26, 1876.

23. *Chicago Tribune*, April 1, 1877.

24. *Chicago Tribune*, March 25, 1877.

25. "The Democracy Routed Horse, Foot, Artillery and Horn Blowers," *Chicago Tribune*, April 4, 1877.

26. Kirkland, *Chicago Yesterdays*, 266.

27. *Chicago Tribune*, January 26, 1879.

28. Following a reduction of wages, the firemen and brakemen of the Baltimore & Ohio Railroad in Baltimore launched a strike resulting in the call-up of federal troops by President Rutherford B. Hayes. Wild scenes of bloodshed and violence ensued in Pittsburgh and Chicago, where millions of dollars of railroad property were destroyed. For a description of the events, see *Harper's Weekly*, August 18, 1877.

29. Flinn and Wilkie, *History of the Chicago Police*, 165.

30. Edward F. Cullerton (1842–1920) was elected from the old Seventh Ward in 1871. Since that time, a Cullerton family member has occupied a chair in the city council or the Illinois General Assembly for 119 of the next 136 years. With the redrawing of ward boundary lines, the Seventh Ward became the Sixth, the Ninth, and the Eleventh. Cullerton represented the ward for nearly 45 years—he was forced out by reformers for a few years in the 1890s after he moved out of the district, but was elected again in 1898 and held office until his death in 1920.

31. *Chicago Journal*, July 10, 1878. See also *Chicago Tribune*, July 10 and 12, 1878.

32. *Chicago Times*, July 10, 1878.

7. The City Hall Swindle

1. Between 1871 and 1885, encompassing the some of the worst years of unchecked graft in Cook County, its bonded indebtedness rose from $3.1 million to $4.9 million.

2. *Chicago Tribune*, July 8, 1887, and November 8, 1877. "The Republican Party. . . . in defeating and routing the Colvin bummers who had seized the City Government has

also inspired confidence that the County thieves can be best defeated and scattered in the same manner."

3. *Chicago Tribune*, January 3, 1875. The *Tribune* estimated that under the contracting system in place in 1875, the city was losing upwards of $100,000 a year purchasing goods and services at above-market prices from the friends and cronies of the Cook County board "ring."

4. Clemmens F. Periolat (1839–1926) was born in his father's general store, a one-story brick building at Lake and Franklin Streets. As a boy, he trapped muskrats and mink in the Chicago River—the catalyst for his future avocation as Chicago's first commercial furrier. Periolat was a boyhood friend of George Pullman and had charge of the first Pullman sleeping car on its initial run from Chicago to Alton, Ill., in 1857.

5. "Highway and Byway," *Chicago Tribune*, May 4, 1890.

6. *Chicago Tribune*, June 26, 1881.

7. Gambler Harry Lawrence was born and raised in Birmingham, England. He changed his name after immigrating to the United States.

8. *Chicago Tribune*, July 1, 1877.

9. *Chicago Tribune*, May 13, 1877. The change from limestone to granite was estimated to cost Cook County taxpayers $125,000 to $175,000 in 1877 dollars—about $30 million today.

10. Andreas, *History of Chicago*, 3:106. See also Lowe, *Lost Chicago*, 107.

11. Harry L Holland, slavishly and devoted to McDonald through their many business ventures spanning 25 years, administered the financial ledgers of the Lake Street elevated line and the Garfield racetrack, Mike's two pet projects in the 1880s and 1890s. Holland was also a wagering man. In March 1902, he was indicted in Lake County, Ill., for running an illegal poolroom and "keeping a common gaming house" near Highwood with "Bud" White, a horse-race gambler clocking bets on out-of-town races via the telegraph lines installed in remote suburban "wire-rooms." Harley Cassius McDonald, Mike's adopted son would later christen his third child Harry Holland McDonald (1890–1963).

12. *Chicago Tribune*, February 18, 1887. Brainerd's original estimate was $80,000. He submitted a final bill for $180,000 after claiming that he found wider, unseen crevices in the building that had to be repaired.

13. *Chicago Tribune*, April 10, 1908. Summoned to testify in a civil suit filed by Holland more than 20 years later, William J. McGarigle revealed the inside story in open court of how the "Paint and Putty" job really went down.

14. Lindberg, *Chicago Ragtime*, 52–53.

15. *Chicago Tribune*, January 25, 1905, and November 2, 1887. See also Charles Johnson, *Growth of Cook County*.

8. Our Carter

1. *Chicago Tribune*, November 26–28, 1875.

2. *Chicago Tribune*, November 27, 1875.

3. Edward R. Kantowicz, "Carter Harrison II: The Politics of Balance," in Green and Holli, *Mayors*, 17.

4. *Chicago Inter-Ocean*, March 29, 1879. Harrison signed the vouchers, and the men received their money. The fraud was exposed by the doorkeeper of the House of Representatives—a Democrat—who was summarily fired for his whistle-blowing. There was talk of a grand jury indictment, but the matter quietly died.

5. *Chicago Times*, April 3, 1879.

6. "Genial" Dave Thornton (1847–81), a County Cork man, entered the saloon business in 1866. After his tavern was destroyed in the Chicago Fire, Thornton regrouped and opened his famous House of David restaurant, saloon, and gambling den at Clark Street and Arcade Court in 1874.

7. "Mobocracy," *Chicago Inter-Ocean*, April 2, 1879.

8. *Chicago Tribune*, September 26, 1879. Accusations flew that Mackin was "doctoring" the liquor in his saloon, but before the matter could be fully investigated, he filed for bankruptcy, and James McGarry of "Martin Dooley" fame took over the business. Pending the proceedings, Mackin opened another tavern with Mike McDonald's financial backing, until giving up the business for politics.

9. *Chicago Daily News*, April 3–4, 1879.

10. *Chicago Tribune*, August 4, 1880.

11. *Chicago Tribune*, August 4–5, 1880. Prindiville, a wealthy yachtsman and party stalwart frequently criticized for his lenient decisions, served as a police court justice from 1878 until December 1, 1906, the final day of the old Cook County judicial system. The municipal court system, inaugurated that morning, stripped away layers of institutional graft in the county "justice shops," a parasitical system of fee collection benefiting the bailiffs, the judges, and the bondsmen. Prindiville was one of 50 justices and 28 bailiffs forced to step down.

12. The Farmer's and Mechanic's Bank was robbed of $9,050 on July 3, 1879. Jimmy Carroll was a New Yorker who settled on the West Side of Chicago. The Carroll gang committed robberies all across the Midwest and in Canada. Carroll also frequented McDonald's Store, and on an earlier occasion had an arrest warrant served on him while playing the faro table by Henry Greenebaum, a prominent Chicago banker. McDonald provided the bond and secured his release from the Central Station.

13. *Chicago Tribune*, January 8 and 19, 1880.

14. *Chicago Tribune*, January 9, 1880. Carroll served out his term, was arrested multiple times, and ended up in the Joliet Penitentiary in the 1890s.

15. Flinn and Wilkie, *History of the Chicago Police*, 358–59. Eager was called the "solid man," because he was "solid" with the South Side police justices. When a Biler Avenue prostitute named Lizzie Meyer confessed to O'Donnell that she was in possession of $1,400, stolen from a Mississippi man inside a bagnio, Eager was "cut in" for $200. "The Captain's [O'Donnell] good nature was never again mistaken for a sign of accessibility with corrupt propositions." Ibid., 359.

16. *Chicago Tribune*, June 28, 1878.

17. *Chicago Tribune*, November 30, 1880.

18. *Chicago Tribune*, December 1, 1880.

19. *Chicago Tribune*, March 2, 1882.

20. *Chicago Tribune*, December 16, 1881.

21. *Chicago Inter-Ocean*, October 3, 1882. Brevet Brig. Gen. Israel Newton Stiles was a highly regarded Civil War hero whose army won the battle of Franklin, Tenn., in November 1864. He settled in Chicago after the war and launched a successful law practice.

22. Ibid.

23. *Chicago Inter-Ocean*, October 29, 1882.

24. *Chicago Times*, November 4, 1882.

25. *Chicago Daily News*, November 9, 1882.

26. *Chicago Tribune*, November 4, 1882.

9. Oyster on the Half Shell

1. Lang and Platt, *Autobiography*, 225. Senator Platt was a three-term senator from New York and a powerful Republican Party boss, 1881–1909. See also Karabell, *Chester Alan Arthur*, 16.

2. *Chicago Tribune*, February 28, 1885, for an in-depth, wrap-up account of the "Fund W" caper.

3. Claudius Johnson, *Carter Henry Harrison*, 187.

4. *Kansas City Times*, July 20, 1881.

5. *Chicago Tribune*, February 28 and March 1, 1885.

6. *Chicago Tribune*, January 30, 1884.

7. *Chicago Times*, June 18, 1884.

8. *Chicago Herald*, April 1, 1884. "Harrison went to McDonald today and said: 'If you don't pull Mackin off, I will make it hot for you and the other gamblers.' What could be done under the circumstances, but for Mackin to resign the nomination though the boys offered to stand by him and fight the Mayor."

9. *Chicago Tribune*, June 27, 1884.

10. Ibid.

11. *Chicago Tribune*, June 21, 1884.

12. *Chicago Herald*, June 26, 1884; *Chicago Tribune*, June 21, 1884.

13. Claudius Johnson, *Carter Henry Harrison* , 145–46; Abbot, *Carter Henry Harrison*, 129–36.

14. "The Machine at Peoria," *Chicago Tribune*, July 3–4, 1884.

15. "The Boys Come Back," *Chicago Tribune*, July 4, 1884.

10. Boodle for the Gang

1. Andreas, *History of Chicago*, 3:872.

2. "Honest" John Kelly (1822–86) was an original Tammany Hall chieftain—a "proud brave"—during the time William Marcy Tweed was its grand sachem and plundering the New York City treasury. A devout Catholic and uncompromising in his faith, Kelly refused to support Grover Cleveland or any fusion candidate perceived to be against the best interests of the immigrant Irish or the Fenian movement.

3. *Chicago Tribune*, July 11, 1884.

4. *Chicago Inter-Ocean*, July 10, 1884.

5. *Chicago Inter-Ocean*, July 11, 1884; Nevins, *Grover Cleveland*, 152.

6. *Chicago Times*, November 6, 1884.

7. Ibid.

8. "The Political Situation as Viewed by an Eminent Democrat," *Chicago Tribune*, October 4, 1884.

9. *Chicago Tribune*, March 11, 1885. Daniel Manning (1831–87) was chairman of the New York Democratic Committee, 1881–84, an unsuccessful candidate for the 1884 presidential nomination, and Cleveland's secretary of the treasury until his death in 1887.

10. Ibid.

11. "The Gang in Bad Odor: Ex-Alderman Comiskey and County Clerk Ryan at Washington Fighting McGarigle," *Chicago Tribune*, April 30, 1885.

12. Frederick Marsh later served as superintendent of the Chicago police, 1890–91, under the Republican mayor, Hempstead Washburne.

13. "Gang in Bad Odor."

14. Blodgett, "Ethno-Cultural Realities." See also Nevins, *Grover Cleveland*, 237.

15. See the *Chicago Times*, February 6–21, 1885, for daily coverage of the trial. Emery Storrs died under mysterious circumstances in St. Paul, Minn., in the fall of 1886. Rumors swirled that McDonald agents had poisoned him because he had acquired inside knowledge of the "machine" and was preparing to go to the authorities. McDonald laughed it off and called Storrs a drunk and his own worst enemy. See the interview with McDonald in the *Chicago Tribune*, October 3, 1886.

16. *Chicago Globe*, July 3, 1889.

17. Ibid.

18. *Chicago Tribune*, February 15, 1914.

19. *Chicago Daily News*, July 2, 1889.

20. *Chicago Daily News*, September 4, 1883. In a February 13, 1887, editorial, "A Chamber of Horrors," the *Chicago Tribune* called the county hospital an "eyesore" and the grounds "a disgrace." Years of institutionalized graft and plunder practiced by succeeding county boards had diverted funding for maintenance and repairs into the pockets of the politicians.

21. Republican Lennington Small (1862–1936) was governor in 1921–29. He went to prison for allegedly running a money-laundering scheme during the time he was state treasurer. Otto Kerner (1908–76), governor from 1961 to 1968, accepted bribes in the form of racing stocks in exchange for the awarding of choice racing dates. He was sentenced to three years in prison. Dan Walker (1922–), served from 1972 to 1976, but was convicted of financial improprieties in connection with a troubled savings and loan in 1987. Then, on April 17, 2006, former governor George Ryan was convicted on eighteen counts of steering state government business to influential firms and campaign supporters and misusing state resources for personal gain. He was sentenced to six and a half years in the federal penitentiary at Oxford, Wisc.

22. The Civic Federation formally organized on December 10, 1893, at the Palmer House to work on the "social betterment of the city and the economic, moral, and political climate." Lyman Gage, Bertha Palmer, Jane Addams, William Penn Nixon, and Anton Hesing drew up the charter, based on recommendations of English reformer William P. Stead. See *Chicago Tribune*, December 10, 1893. The Cook County Institutions at Dunning opened in 1851 as a poor farm on the Northwest Side. The insane asylum was added in 1858. The poorhouse was relocated to Oak Forest, Ill., in 1910, and two years later the state bought the mental hospital and property for one dollar. After 1912, the mental hospital was known as the Chicago State Hospital; however, many continued to refer to the institution simply as Dunning. See Richard Vachula's article, "Canst thou not minister to a mind disease" at: http://www.abandonedasylum.com/dunning1.html.

23. "The Lordly Payrolls," *Chicago Tribune*, February 5, 1887. The extravagance of Varnell and the commissioners was appalling. "These are the ones who live on oysters, bananas and strawberries and drink liquors. They are tenants of the apartments for whose costly furnishing the County has had to pay." Harry Varnell (1852–1900) routinely padded his payroll and submitted a wage expense report for $4,431 for 133 employees in the month of December 1886. Varnell and four other administrators drew salaries of more than $100 per month; laborers averaged $28. These were the cumulative salaries

for maintenance people, attendants, and cooks and did not include salaries for the professional administrative staff, carpenters, or skilled tradesmen. The bill for their salaries that same month was $5,442.81.

24. Review of *The Don Quixote of Psychiatry*, by Victor Robinson, *Chicago Tribune*, July 13, 1919. Robinson was a writer of medical history books. Clevenger goes on to describe his battle to reform Dunning and in its sister facility located in Kankakee.

25. *Chicago Tribune*, March 4, 1887.

26. *Chicago Daily News*, October 5, 1876, quoted in Roberts, "Businessmen in Revolt," 71–72. See also Lindberg, *Chicago Ragtime*, 54–55, and the J. Frank Aldrich papers in the collection of the Union League Club Civic and Arts Foundation.

27. Roberts, "Businessmen in Revolt," 73.

28. *Chicago Tribune*, March 12, 1887.

29. *Chicago Tribune*, July 5, 1887.

30. Lindberg, *Chicago Ragtime*, 57.

31. Ibid.

32. After retiring from the bench, Shephard was general counsel to Charles Tyson Yerkes, the city railway magnate.

33. Ginger, *Altgeld's America*, 68–71.

34. *Chicago Tribune*, June 11, 1887.

35. *Chicago Tribune*, July 5, 1887.

36. Leonard St. John was indicted for complicity in the plot to spring McGarigle, but the charge was "nolle prossed" on December 22, 1887, due to lack of evidence and the inability to pry loose information from known informants.

37. *Chicago Tribune*, June 30, 1887.

11. Is He Not a Typical Democrat?

1. Phillip Kinsley, "Tells How Ring of Boodlers Was Smashed in 1887," *Chicago Tribune*, April 20, 1930.

2. *Chicago Tribune*, April 15, 1889, and August 4, 1890.

3. *Chicago Tribune*, July 11, 1897; Nelson quote cited in *Chicago Tribune*, October 13, 1932.

4. *Chicago Tribune*, November 17, 1888.

5. William McGarigle was an unsuccessful candidate for alderman of the 26th Ward in 1891. That same year he lost his eldest son George and youngest daughter Isabel to diphtheria—a deadly killer in those days.

6. *Chicago Tribune*, October 25, 1890.

7. William Davies, the "Parson's" father, was one of the Pinkerton detectives who foiled the plot to kill Abraham Lincoln in Baltimore as the president made his way to Washington for the inauguration in 1861. Davies is best remembered for promoting every important prize fighter, including John L. Sullivan, from 1878 to 1895. Interview with Mark Dunn, general counsel of Northeastern Illinois University and a research historian.

8. The Store became the Hotel Ross, and the upper floors were converted to overnight lodging in 1895. During renovation, a workman uncovered trap doors in a dozen rooms and a cache of money and jewels hidden in a rusted tin box inside one such hiding place, a testament to bygone days. *Chicago Tribune*, June 18, 1899.

9. *Chicago Tribune*, July 20, 1890.

10. Nevins, *Grover Cleveland*, 394; *Chicago Daily News*, April 4, 1887.

11. "Democrats for Roche," *Chicago Tribune*, April 3, 1887.

12. Carter Harrison II, *Growing Up with Chicago*, 261–62. Harrison's chapter is titled "Honest Man, Politician, Administrator," a self-conscious admission on the author's part that there were many in Chicago who did not view the Eagle in quite those same generous terms.

13. William Fitzgerald (1842–1913) was a local political power in the 1880s. A native of Skaneateles, N.Y., he ran a hardware store before entering politics and casting his lot with the McDonald faction of the Democratic Party. It was said that he could be counted on to carry his ward in every election.

14. John Powers (1852–1930) was a native of Brannon, in County Kilkenny, Ireland. He arrived in Chicago just after the Chicago Fire. After closing his grocery store, he opened a saloon at Madison and LaSalle Streets with Billy O'Brien and began to gain political exposure. Despite his notorious reputation for collecting bribes from wealthy traction magnates looking to operate street railways in Chicago, Powers was also known as a friend to his constituents who dispensed turkeys to the needy at Christmas and found jobs in city government for the unemployed.

15. *Chicago Herald*, March 28, 1890.

12. A Flighty and Excitable Woman

1. Carter Harrison, *Growing Up with Chicago*, 270–71.

2. "A Friendly Call Made on Mike McDonald by a Brace of Burglars," *Chicago Tribune*, April 5, 1884.

3. *Chicago Times*, August 22, 1889.

4. The rectory was finished in 1886. Construction of the Notre Dame de Chicago Church began March 19, 1887, and was completed in 1888. The octagonal-shaped structure, costing $100,000, was formally dedicated by Archbishop Feehan on May 1, 1892. The parish served the needs of some 18,000 French Canadians living in the surrounding neighborhood. It took until June 1912 to retire the debt, by which time the French Canadian parishioners had abandoned the area—supplanted by immigrant Italians.

5. *Chicago Daily News*, August 22, 1889.

6. The Sisters of Charity of St. Joseph's was founded in 1809 by Elizabeth Bayley Seton (Mother Seton, 1774–1821) near Emmetsburg, Md. Their mission in the church continued the original charisms of Saint Vincent de Paul (1581–1660) and Elizabeth Seton.

7. *Chicago Daily News*, August 22, 1889.

8. *Chicago Times*, August 23, 1889. Mary McDonald's mental state was called to question not only by the neighbors, but by guests at a hotel in Hot Springs, Ark., where she vacationed in 1888. Her conduct was noted as "peculiar," and guests at the hotel were afraid to be near her.

9. Père Hyacinth (1827–1912), French priest, was a Sulpician, a Dominican, and a Carmelite. In 1869, he declared his opposition to the calling of the Vatican Council. He opposed enunciation of the doctrine of the infallibility of the pope and left the Church in 1871. In 1878, he founded a Gallican church at Paris where Mary and Father Moysant were thought to be headed. This church joined the Jansenists of Utrecht in 1893.

10. *Chicago Times*, August 22, 1889.

11. *Chicago Inter-Ocean*, August 21, 1889.

12. *Chicago Times*, August 22, 1889.

13. *Chicago Herald*, October 12, 1889.

14. *Chicago Daily Journal*, February 22, 1907.

13. Bribing the Gray Wolves for an "Upstairs" Railway

1. Josiah Vincent Meigs of Tennessee invented the nation's first monorail system in 1886. With the patronage of former Civil War general Benjamin Butler, he built a 227-foot demonstration line in Cambridge, Mass., crossing over into Boston. But the Meigs monorail failed to catch on anywhere in the country and was scrapped in 1894. Conventional elevated trains dwarfed the Meigs cars and were more efficient. See the *Boston Globe*, February 23, 1992; and "Meigs Elevated Railway," *Scientific American*, July 16, 1886.

2. *Chicago Times*, January 9, 1891.

3. Dedmon, *Fabulous Chicago*, 260.

4. Franch, *Robber Baron*, 119; and *Chicago Tribune*, July 8, 1886.

5. *Chicago Mail*, July 11, 1886.

6. *Chicago Tribune*, January 29, 1890.

7. Franch, *Robber Baron*, 180.

8. *Chicago Daily News*, September 12, 1889.

9. *Chicago Tribune*, June 25, 1890.

10. *Chicago Tribune*, June 29, 1890.

11. *Chicago Tribune*, June 27, 1890.

12. Thomas Jefferson Dolan (1856–96) held inconsequential jobs in the city Water Department and Special Assessments Bureau. He was not a man of any great importance, nor was he at any time a military "colonel." He was however, a bona fide member of the Democratic inner circle for nearly 15 years—a mascot. "All the politicians in town knew Dolan. No Democratic convention, no Democratic mass meeting could be considered ready for business until he appeared." On September 10, 1894, police officers found Dolan lying in the gutter at 47th and Lake, dazed, and babbling incoherently. He was diagnosed with untreated syphilis and was dispatched to the Elgin Mental Hospital, where he died two years later. "Col. Dolan Believed to Be Insane," *Chicago Tribune*, September 11, 1894.

13. *Niagara Falls Gazette*, July 26, 1890.

14. *Chicago Tribune*, May 20, 1892.

15. *Chicago Tribune*, January 11, 1893.

16. Ibid.

17. *Chicago Tribune*, July 9, 1891.

18. Borzo, *Chicago "L,"* 39.

19. Young, *Chicago Transit*, 30–35.

20. *Chicago Tribune*, January 9, 1895.

21. Cudahy, "Chicago's Early Elevated Lines," 198–203.

14. The Garfield Park Racetrack War

1. "Ed Corrigan's Chances," *Chicago Tribune*, July 31, 1890.

2. "In Aid of Gamblers," *Chicago Tribune*, February 19, 1892; Richard Lindberg, "The Evolution of an Evil Business," *Chicago History* 12, no. 2 (July 1993): 47.

3. "Stories of the Street and Town," *Chicago Record Herald*, April 4, 1895.

4. Chicago's 185-acre Central Park was renamed Garfield Park to honor the slain president, James A. Garfield (1831–81). Humboldt, Garfield, and Douglas parks were the handiwork and inspiration of William Le Baron Jenney, the famed Chicago architect remembered today as the father of the modern steel-frame skyscraper. In 1934, Garfield

Park became part of the Chicago Park District when the city's 22 independent park commissions merged into a single, citywide agency.

5. *Chicago Tribune*, June 27, 1891.

6. *Chicago Times*, September 18, 1892.

7. *Chicago Tribune*, July 20, 1891.

8. *Chicago Tribune*, August 10, 1891.

9. *Chicago Tribune*, September 4, 1892.

10. *Chicago Tribune*, September 7, 1892.

11. Ibid. See also Wendt and Kogan, *Lords of the Levee*, 49–58, for an amusing, anecdotal overview of the affray and Alderman Coughlin's role as one of the staunch Garfield Park backers on the council.

12. *Chicago Globe*, September 7, 1892.

13. *Chicago Tribune*, September 13, 1892.

14. *Chicago Inter-Ocean*, September 23, 1892. Charles Walhart Woodman (1844–98) was a Chicago lawyer and a Ninth Ward Republican politician appointed assistant city prosecutor in 1877 and justice of the peace in 1881, before winning a congressional seat in 1894.

15. *Chicago Inter-Ocean*, September 18, 1892.

16. Ibid.

17. Ibid.

18. *Decatur Weekly Republican*, September 22 and 29, 1892.

19. *Bloomington Pantograph*, September 29, 1892. See also Keiser, *Building for the Centuries*, 105.

20. *Chicago Tribune*, September 18, 1892.

21. *Chicago Tribune*, September 25, 1892.

15. Electing Altgeld

1. *Chicago Tribune*, November 8, 1893.

2. *Chicago Tribune*, November 27, 1893.

3. *Chicago Tribune*, September 30, 1892.

4. *Chicago Tribune*, October 27–30, 1890. Gambler George H. Hathaway shot Whelan inside "Appetite" Bill Langdon's place, now owned by Matt Hogan. The murder accompanied a drunken disagreement inside a notorious political saloon. Whelan was hopelessly intoxicated when the itinerant blackleg Hathaway apparently uttered words of provocation, and a melee ensued. It was later charged that Lt. Max Kipley of the Chicago Police Department deliberately suppressed evidence showing that Hathaway had acted in self-defense. Hathaway was tried twice for murder and twice convicted. He was sentenced to life in prison. It was the second time in less than six years an alderman had been slain inside a saloon. In May 1884, Alderman Michael Gaynor was shot dead on Election Day by James Dacey, a political rival, in Frank McIntyre's saloon at Madison and Halsted Streets.

5. *Chicago Globe*, November 24, 1890.

6. Dreiser, *Newspaper Days*, 91–92.

7. *Chicago Journal*, February 22, 1907.

8. *Chicago Herald*, April 25, 1891.

9. *Richmond Gazette*, September 23, 1892.

10. *Staats-Zeitung*, July 4, 1893; Hofmeister, *Germans of Chicago*, 110.

11. *Chicago Globe*, January 10, 1892.

12. Barnard, *Eagle Forgotten*, 145.

13. *Chicago Globe*, February 23–25, 1892.

14. Tierney, *Darrow*, 69.

15. The Cook County Marching Club, organized in the 1870s, was quite a spectacle. In full regalia, they marched in support of Democratic rallies and initiatives in St. Louis, New Orleans, New York, and Cincinnati; the inauguration of Iowa governor Horace Boies in Des Moines; and expositions in South Carolina and Atlanta.

16. *Chicago Tribune*, October 1, 1892.

17. *Chicago Tribune*, March 13, 1902.

18. Ginger, *Altgeld's America*, 168–69.

19. *Chicago Daily News*, October 1, 1892.

20. *Chicago Tribune*, October 2, 1892.

21. Dolan quoted in *Chicago Tribune*, November 9, 1892.

22. Tierney, *Darrow*, 43. See also Howard, *Mostly Good and Competent Men*, 194.

23. *Chicago Tribune*, May 26, 1895.

24. *Chicago Tribune*, January 3, 1897.

25. John Altgeld to Carter H. Harrison, October 17, 1893, Carter Harrison IV Papers, Midwest Manuscript Collection, the Newberry Library, Chicago.

26. *Chicago Tribune*, March 18, 1894.

27. *Chicago Tribune*, January 7, 1897.

28. *Staats-Zeitung*, February 28, 1893.

29. Hofmeister, *Germans of Chicago*, 97.

30. "By Force and Fraud," *Chicago Tribune*, March 9, 1893. Central Music Hall stood at the corner of State and Randolph—the present-day location of Macy's (Marshall Field's Department Store). The popular theater was razed in 1903 to make way for Field's planned expansion, doubling the size of his existing store on State Street so that it would occupy the entire block.

31. *Staats-Zeitung*, March 1, 1893. Outraged and defiant, Washington Hesing (1849–97) swore he was through with politics and would resume his duties as a humble newspaper editor, nothing more. His vow lasted only until November 25, 1893, when President Grover Cleveland appointed him postmaster of Chicago. It was a political sop to Chicago's large German community, which the president badly needed to shore up faltering support in the city.

32. "McDonald Runs It," *Chicago Tribune*, March 26, 1893.

33. *Chicago Tribune*, March 28, 1893; *Chicago Globe*, January 9, 1892.

34. *Chicago Globe*, January 9, 1892.

35. Willis, *Carter Henry Harrison*, 214–15.

36. *Chicago Tribune*, February 21, 1896.

37. *Chicago Tribune*, September 23, 1893.

38. *Chicago Tribune*, March 22, 1893.

39. Dreiser, *Newspaper Days*, 317.

16. That Little Feldman Girl

1. McNamara, "Drama in the Death House."

2. *Chicago Tribune*, October 29, 1893.

3. *Chicago Herald*, October 29, 1893.

4. Ibid.

5. Ibid.

6. David, *History of the Haymarket Affair*, 379.

7. Annie Howard, a frail and sickly young woman, was a friend of Carter Harrison's daughter-in-law, Edith Ogden. She married a London stockbroker on November 12, 1896.

8. *Chicago Tribune*, November 8, 1893.

9. *Chicago Herald*, November 1, 1893.

10. At his trial, Prendergast said that he "thought he was sane." The jurors concurred that his aspiration to become corporation counsel was neither delusional nor the actions of an insane man. He was hanged in the Cook County Jail on Friday, July 13, 1894. The condemned man made the comment that Friday the thirteenth was always "unlucky."

11. *Chicago Tribune*, May 26, 1902.

12. *Chicago Tribune*, June 5, 1924.

13. *Chicago Tribune*, December 17, 1894.

14. At age 36, John P. Hopkins (1858–1918) was the youngest candidate to be elected mayor of Chicago. His rise in politics was meteoric, and he enjoyed the strong backing of the silk-stocking Iroquois Club, who credited him with delivering a solid block of Pullman Republicans into the Democratic camp. In 1892, he spearheaded Altgeld's election campaign and was boosted for the mayoralty by his close friend and sponsor Roger Sullivan, but his term was marred by rampant corruption, battles with the Civic Federation over wide-open public gambling, and his indecisive stance during the 1894 Pullman strike, which was assailed by the Republican press. Hopkins's misappropriation of vast sums of campaign contributions drove a wedge in the party and alienated McDonald and the former "Harrisonites." See "Disaffection in Democratic Ranks," *Chicago Tribune*, October 9, 1894; and *Chicago Inter-Ocean*, January 16, 1895.

15. *Chicago Tribune*, December 3, 1895.

16. *Chicago Evening Post*, December 3, 1895.

17. *Chicago Tribune*, December 10, 14, and 16, 1897.

18. *New York Times*, February 6, 1898; *Chicago Tribune*, February 6, 1898.

19. Fire Island was later acquired by the Wyandotte Chemical Corporation. It is now owned by BASF. The company recently launched an extensive environmental cleanup.

20. See Montreat College, Asheville, N.C.: http://www.montreat.edu/ humanities/ english/ King/TRAGEDY.HTM, November 18, 1987.

21. *Chicago Tribune*, January 17, 1895.

22. Genealogist Michael Karsen investigated Dora Feldman's family background for the Jewish Historical Society of Chicago and discovered probate records in Los Angeles pertaining to the settlement of her estate. Karsen established that her real name was Flora Feldman, one of four children. Dora had four brothers—David, Harris (Harry), Emil, and Joseph.

23. *Chicago Inter-Ocean*, February 22, 1907.

24. *Chicago Daily Journal*, February 22, 1907.

25. Ibid.

26. For nearly 30 years, Henry E. Allott (a.k.a. "Bunk" Allen; died September 16, 1912), was a well-known Chicago saloon owner, circus promoter, and sponsor of Wild West shows. Allen is credited with inventing pink lemonade—after he accidentally dropped red-

coated cinnamon into a batch of lemonade he was stirring for a circus concession stand. The mix was a popular hit, and a coloring powder was added for mass production.

27. *Chicago Tribune*, January 16, 1895.

17. Pearls before Swine: Poetry, Murder, and the McDonalds

1. Undated journal entry of Jacques Marchais, author's interview with Sarah Johnson, October 12, 2006. Johnson, the curator of the Jacques Marchais Museum of Tibetan Art at Staten Island, N.Y., has a biography of Marchais in development.

2. *Chicago Inter-Ocean*, February 22, 1907.

3. *Chicago Tribune*, February 6, 1900.

4. George Rozet (1829–1900) brokered millions of dollars in lucrative land sales after the Chicago Fire, including tracts along Lake Shore Boulevard and the property where the archbishop's mansion was built. Drexel Boulevard was named after George Rozet's sister, married to A. J. Drexel of Philadelphia, where Rozet was born.

5. *Chicago Blue Book, 1893*, 94–96.

6. *Chicago Inter-Ocean*, January 28, 1908; *Chicago Tribune*, January 28, 1908.

7. *Chicago American*, February 13, 1908.

8. *Chicago Inter-Ocean*, February 22, 1907.

9. *Chicago Tribune*, March 2, 1907.

10. *Chicago Daily Journal*, February 22, 1907.

11. *Chicago Inter-Ocean*, February 23, 1907.

12. *Chicago Tribune*, January 28, 1908.

13. Published newspaper accounts are contradictory. The *Inter-Ocean* reported that Dora was clutching the gun when Blasi found her and apparently had used the butt handle of the weapon to break the glass.

14. *Chicago Tribune*, February 6, 1926.

15. Lindberg, *To Serve and Collect*, 114.

16. *Chicago Inter-Ocean*, February 22, 1907. See also *Chicago Tribune*, February 25, 1907.

17. *Chicago Tribune*, March 6, 1907.

18. *Chicago Daily Journal*, February 22, 1907.

18. Betrayal and Death

1. *Chicago Herald*, February 27, 1907.

2. *Chicago Record-Herald*, February 27, 1907.

3. *Chicago Record-Herald*, August 13, 1907; *Chicago Tribune*, August 13, 1907.

4. The Italian Renaissance church located at 1321 West Jackson Boulevard on the West Side was designed by Henry Engelbert and John Pope in 1892. It was formally designated as a basilica by the Vatican in 1956.

5. Theodore Brentano (1854–1940) served as judge of the Superior Court, 1890–1922. He was appointed minister to Hungary in 1923 by President Warren G. Harding.

6. James Hamilton Lewis (1866–1939), born in Danville, Ill., was City of Chicago corporation counsel, 1905–7; a U.S. senator, 1913–19, and 1930–39; and the first U.S. senate whip, serving under President Woodrow Wilson.

7. *Chicago Tribune*, January 19, 1908.

8. *Chicago Tribune*, September 3, 1907.

9. *Chicago Tribune*, November 29, 1907.

10. *Chicago Record-Herald*, January 31, 1908.

11. *Chicago Record-Herald*, January 23, 1908.

12. George Silver was the owner of a notorious concert saloon called the Maxim. The name George Cohan is a mystery. It doesn't seem possible that this could be the famous Broadway composer. See the January 28, 1908, *Record-Herald* for a transcript.

13. *Chicago American*, February 3, 1908.

14. Avery, "Dora Goes Free!"

15. *Chicago American*, February 12, 1908.

16. Ibid.

17. Ibid.

18. *Chicago Tribune*, October 3, 1914.

19. Quoted posthumously, *Chicago Tribune*, March 12, 1914. No woman has ever been executed in Cook County. In Illinois, however, there have been two women paying the ultimate price: Elizabeth Reed, who poisoned her husband, in Lawrenceville in April 1845, and Marie Porter, a St. Louis woman and mother of four who murdered her brother outside of Belleville over an insurance policy in 1936. Porter was electrocuted on January 27, 1938, at the Menard Penitentiary.

20. *Chicago Record-Herald*, February 11, 1908.

Postscript

1. *Chicago Tribune*, December 6, 1908.

2. *Chicago Tribune*, March 2, 1909.

3. *Chicago Tribune*, September 2, 1908.

4. *Chicago Tribune*, June 29, 1912.

5. *Chicago Tribune*, August 13, 1907.

6. *Chicago Tribune*, March 11, 1914.

Epilogue: A Legacy of Corruption

1. Fremon, "Chicago City Council," 29.

2. Lindberg, "No More Greylords?" 23.

3. Fremon, "Chicago City Council," 28.

4. *Chicago Tribune*, October 31, 1950.

5. *Chicago Tribune*, May 16, 1928.

Bibliography

Books

Abbot, Willis John. *Carter Henry Harrison: A Memoir.* New York: Dodd, Mead, 1895.

Adler, Jeffrey S. *First in Violence, Deepest in Dirt: Homicide in Chicago, 1875–1920.* Cambridge, Mass.: Harvard University Press, 2006.

Ahern, M. L. *Political History of Chicago, 1837–1887.* Chicago: Donohue and Henneberry, 1886.

Andreas, Alfred T. *History of Chicago.* Vol. 2. Chicago A. T. Andreas, 1885.

———. *History of Chicago.* Vol. 3. Chicago A. T. Andreas, 1886.

Andrews, Wayne. *Battle for Chicago.* New York: Harcourt, Brace, 1946.

Asbury, Herbert. *The French Quarter: An Informal History of the New Orleans Underworld.* New York: Alfred Knopf, 1936.

———. *Gem of the Prairie.* New York: Alfred Knopf, 1940.

———. *Sucker's Progress: An Informal History of Gambling in America from the Colonies to Canfield.* New York: Dodd, Mead, 1938.

Barnard, Harry. *Eagle Forgotten: The Turbulent Life of John Peter Altgeld .* New York: Bobbs-Merrill, *1938.*

Beer, Thomas. *The Mauve Decade: American Life at the End of the Nineteenth Century.* New York: Alfred Knopf, 1926

Bell, Rev. Ernest A., ed. *Fighting the Traffic in Young Girls; or, The War on the White Slave Trade.* Chicago: G. S. Ball, 1910.

Bennett, Fremont O. *Politics and Politicians of Chicago, Cook County and Illinois, 1787–1887.* Chicago: Blakely, 1887.

Bernstein, Arnie. *The Hoofs and Guns of the Storm: Chicago's Civil War Connections.* Chicago: Lake Claremont, 2003.

Blocker, Jack, Jr., David M. Fahey, and Ian R.. Tyrrell, eds. *Alcohol and Temperance in Modern History: An International History.* Santa Barbara, Calif.: ABC-CLIO, 2003.

Borzo, Greg. *The Chicago "L."* Charleston, S.C.: Arcadia, 2007.

Carlin, Christopher J. *Protecting Niagara: A History of the Niagara County Sheriff's Office.* Ransomville, N.Y.: Aegis, 1995.

Chafetz, Henry. *Play the Devil: A History of Gambling in the United States from 1492–1950.* New York: Clarkson N. Potter, 1960.

Chicago Blue Book of Selected Names, 1893. Chicago: Chicago Directory, 1893.

Chicago Directory and Merchants Census Report. Chicago: Edwards City Directories, 1861–1871.

Cook, Frederick Francis. *Bygone Days in Chicago: Recollections of the Garden City of the Sixties.* Chicago: A. C. McClurg, 1910.

Currey, Seymour S. *Chicago: Its History, Its Builders: A Century of Marvelous Growth.* Vol. 2. Chicago: S. J. Clarke, 1912.

David, Henry. *The History of the Haymarket Affair.* New York: Russell & Russell, 1936.

Dedmon, Emmett. *Fabulous Chicago: A Great City's History and People.* New York: Atheneum, 1981.

Dreiser, Theodore. *Newspaper Days: An Autobiography.* Philadelphia: University of Pennsylvania Press, Black Sparrow Press, 1991.

English, T. J. *Paddy Whacked: The Untold Story of the Irish-American Gangster.* New York: Regan Books, 2005.

Farr, Finis. *Chicago: A Personal History of America's Most American City.* New Rochelle, N.Y.: Arlington House, 1973.

Farwell, Abby. *Reminiscences of John V. Farwell by His Elder Daughter.* Chicago: Ralph Fletcher Seymour, 1928.

Fehrenbacher, Don E. *Chicago Giant: A Biography of Long John Wentworth.* Washington, D.C.: American Historical Research Center, 1957.

Ferber, Edna. *So Big.* New York: Doubleday & Page, 1924.

Flinn, John J., with John E. Wilkie. *History of the Chicago Police from the Settlement of the Community to the Present Time.* Chicago: Police Book Fund, 1887.

Franch, John. *Robber Baron: The Life of Charles Tyson Yerkes.* Urbana: University of Illinois Press, 2006.

Gilbert, Paul, and Charles Lee Bryson. *Chicago and Its Makers: A Narrative of Events from the Day of the First White Man to the Inception of the Second World's Fair.* Chicago: Felix Mendelsohn, 1929.

Ginger, Ray. *Altgeld's America: The Lincoln Ideal versus Changing Realities.* New York: Funk & Wagnals, 1958

Gosnell, Harold F. *Machine Politics: Chicago Model.* Chicago: University of Chicago Press, 1937.

Green, Paul, and Melvin Holli, eds. *The Mayors: The Chicago Political Tradition.* Carbondale: Southern Illinois University Press, 1995.

Harrison, Carter, II. *Growing Up with Chicago: A Sequel to the Stormy Years.* New York: Ralph Fletcher Seymour, 1944.

———. *The Stormy Years.* Indianapolis: Bobbs-Merrill, 1935.

Harrison, Edith. *Strange to Say: Recollections of Persons and Events in New Orleans and Chicago.* Chicago: A. Kroch & Sons, 1949.

Hewitt, Janet E., ed. *Roster of Union Soldiers, 1861–1865, Illinois.* Wilmington, Del.: Broadfoot, 1999.

History of Chicago and Souvenir of the Liquor Interests. Chicago: Belgravia, 1891.

Hofmeister, Rudolf. *The Germans of Chicago.* Champaign, Ill.: Stipes, 1976.

Howard, Robert P. *Mostly Good and Competent Men: Illinois Governors, 1818–1988.* Springfield: Illinois Issues; Illinois State Historical Society, 1988.

Johnson, Charles. *Growth of Cook County.* Vol. 1. Chicago: Board of Commissioners of Cook County, Northwestern Printing House, 1910.

Johnson, Claudius O. *Carter Henry Harrison.* Chicago: University of Chicago Press, 1928.

Karabell, Zachary. *Chester Alan Arthur.* New York: Times Books, Henry Holt, 2004.

Kee, Robert. *The Green Flag*. 5th ed. New York: Penguin, 2001.

Keiser, John H. *Building for the Centuries: Illinois, 1865–1898*. Urbana: University of Illinois Press for the Illinois Sesquicentennial Commission and the Illinois State Historical Society, 1977.

Kirkland, Caroline. *Chicago Yesterdays: A Sheaf of Reminiscences*. Chicago: Daughaday, 1919.

Lakeside Directory of Chicago. Chicago: Chicago Directory, 1871–1900.

Lang, Louis J., and Thomas Platt. *The Autobiography of Thomas J. Platt: The Ordeal of Self Government in America*. New York: B. W. Dodge, 1910.

Larson, Henrietta. *Jay Cooke: Private Banker*. New York: Greenwood, 1968.

Levy, George. *To Die in Chicago: Confederate Prisoners at Camp Douglas, 1862–1865*. Gretna, La.: Pelican, 1999.

Lewis, Lloyd, and Henry Justin Smith. *Chicago: The History of Its Reputation*. New York: Harcourt, Brace, 1929.

Lindberg, Richard. *Chicago Ragtime: Another Look at Chicago, 1880–1920*. South Bend, Ind.: Icarus, 1985.

———. *To Serve and Collect: Chicago Politics and Police Corruption from the Lager Beer Riot to the Summerdale Scandal, 1855–1960*. Westport, Conn.: Praeger, 1990.

Longstreet, Stephen. *Chicago, 1860–1919*. New York: David McKay, 1973.

Lowe, David. *Lost Chicago*. New York: Houghton-Mifflin, 1975.

Marrow, Raphael N., and Harriet Carter. *In Pursuit of Crime: The Police of Chicago; Chronicle of a Hundred Years*. Sunbury, Ohio: Flats, 1996.

Merriner, James L. *Grafters and Goo-Goos: Corruption and Reform in Chicago, 1833–2003*. Carbondale: Southern Illinois University Press, 2003.

Morton, James. *Gangland International: The Mafia and Other Mobs*. New York: Warner Books, 1999.

Nevins, Allan. *Grover Cleveland: A Study in Courage*. New York: Dodd, Mead, 1948.

Pierce, Bessie Louise. *A History of Chicago: The Rise of the Modern City, 1871–1893*. New York: Alfred Knopf, 1952.

Poole, Ernest. *Giants Gone: The Men Who Made Chicago*. New York: McGraw Hill, 1943.

Quinn, John Philip. *Fools of Fortune; or, Gambling and Gamblers*, Chicago: Quinn, 1890.

Report of the Adjutant General of the State of Illinois. Vol. 2, 1861–1866. Springfield, Ill.: H. W. Rokker, 1886.

Rice, Edward LeRoy. *Monarchs of the Minstrelsy: From "Daddy" Rice to Date*. New York: Kenny, 1911.

Rose, I. Nelson. *Gambling and the Law*. Secaucus, N.J.: L. Stuart, 1986.

Rosen, Fred. *"Gold!": The Story of the 1848 Gold Rush and How It Shaped a Nation*. New York: Thunder's Mouth, 2005.

Roth, Walter. *Looking Backward: True Stories from Chicago's Jewish Past*. Chicago: Academy Chicago, 2006.

Sante, Luc. *Low Life of Old New York*. New York: Farrar, Straus and Giroux, 1991.

Sautter, R. Craig, and Edward M. Burke. *Inside the Wigwam: Chicago Presidential Conventions, 1860–1996*. Chicago: Loyola Press, 1996.

Schlereth, Thomas J. *Victorian America: Transformations in Everyday Life*. New York: HarperPerennial, 1991.

Schroeder, H. L., and C. W. Forbrich. *Men Who Have Made the Fifth Ward*. Chicago: Schroeder & Forbrich, 1895.

Simpson, Dick. *Rogues, Rebels and Rubber Stamps: The Politics of the Chicago City Council from 1863 to the Present*. Boulder, Colo.: Westview, 2001.

Skilnick, Bob. *Beer and Brewing in Chicago, 1833–1878.* Chicago: Pogo, 1999.

Smith, Henry Justin. *Chicago: A Portrait.* New York: Century, 1931.

Smith, Henry Nash, ed. *Popular Culture and Industrialism, 1865–1890.* New York: Anchor Books, 1967.

Sutherland, Douglas. *Fifty Years on the Civic Front: A History of the Civic Federation's Dynamic Activities.* Chicago: Civic Federation of Chicago, 1943.

Tarr, Joel A. *A Study in Boss Politics: William Lorimer of Chicago.* Champaign: University of Illinois Press, 1971.

Tierney, Kevin. *Darrow: A Biography,* New York: Thomas Y. Crowell, 1979.

Townsend, Walter A. *Illinois Democracy: A History of the Party and Its Representative Members Past and Present.* Vol. 1. Springfield, Ill.: Democratic Historical Association, 1935.

Wagenknecht, Edward. *Chicago: Centers of Civilization Series.* Norman: University of Oklahoma Press, 1964.

Wendt, Lloyd. *The Chicago Tribune: The Rise of a Great American Newspaper.* Chicago: Rand McNally, 1979.

Wendt, Lloyd, and Herman Kogan. *Lords of the Levee: The Story of Bathhouse John and Hinky Dink.* New York: Bobbs-Merrill, 1943.

White, Leonard D. *The Republican Era: A Study in Administrative History, 1869–1901.* New York: Free Press, 1958.

Witcover, James. *Party of the People: A History of the Democrats.* New York: Random House, 2003.

Young, David M. *Chicago Transit: An Illustrated History.* DeKalb, Ill.: Northern Illinois University Press, 1988.

Articles and Pamphlets

Avery, Delos. "Dora Goes Free!" *Chicago Tribune,* May 23, 1943.

Blodgett, Geoffrey. "Ethno-Cultural Realities in Presidential Patronage: Grover Cleveland's Choices." *New York History* 81, no. 2 (2000): 189–210.

Cudahy, John J. "Chicago's Early Elevated Lines and the Construction of the Union Loop." *Chicago History* 8, no. 4 (Winter 1979–80).

Davis, Allen F. "Jane Addams vs. the Ward Boss." *Journal of the Illinois Historical Society* 53 (Autumn 1960).

DeArment, Robert K. "Gambling on the Frontier." *Wild West: Chronicle of the American Frontier,* April 2005.

Dick, David B. "Resurgence of the Chicago Democracy, April–November 1861." *Journal of the Illinois Historical Society* 56 (Summer 1963).

Fremon, David. "Chicago City Council: Wolves or Sheep?" *Illinois Issues* 28 (August–September 1991).

Fullerton, Hugh S., "American Gambling and Gamblers: Preying upon the Wage Earners." *American Magazine* 47 (February–April 1914).

Kehoe, John E. "Trial Lawyers I Have Known." *Journal of the Illinois Historical Society* 39 (June 1946).

Kinsley, Phillip. "Tells How Ring of Boodlers Was Smashed in 1887." *Chicago Tribune,* April 20, 1930.

Lindberg, Richard. "No More Greylords?" *Illinois Police and Sheriff's News* 22, no. 2 (Summer 1994).

Matthews, Franklin. "Wide Open Chicago." *Harper's Magazine,* January 22, 1898.

May, Stephen. "The Object at Hand." *Smithsonian Magazine,* September 1996.

McNamara, Dr. Francis W. "Drama in the Death House." *Chicago Tribune Magazine,* December 6, 1936.

Morton, Richard Allen. "Public Transportation and the Failure of Municipal Socialism in Chicago, 1905–1907." *Illinois History Teacher* 9, no. 1 (2002). Published by the Illinois Historic Preservation Agency, Springfield. Available from Illinois Periodicals Online, http://www.lib.niu.edu/ipo/index.html.

Nord, David Paul. "Read All about It." *Chicago History* 31, no. 1 (Summer 2002).

Powers, Charles I. "The Harrison Dynasty: Carter and Graft." *Chicago Tribune,* May 7, 1911.

Roberts, Sidney I. "The Municipal Voters' League and Chicago's Boodlers." *Journal of the Illinois Historical Society* 53 (Summer 1960).

Smith, Harold F. "Mulligan and the Irish Brigade." *Journal of the Illinois Historical Society* 56 (Summer 1963).

Sporting Club House Directory: Containing a Full and Complete List of All Strictly First Class Clubs and Sporting Houses, 1889. Chicago: Ross & St. Clair, 1889.

Tabscott, Robert. "Profile in Courage: John Peter Altgeld and the Haymarket Pardons." *St. Louis Post-Dispatch,* May 5, 2000.

Uzdanovich, William J., ed. "On the Fast Track." *Newsletter of the Hammond Historical Society,* May–August, 2005.

Vachula, Richard. *"Canst Thou Not Minister to a Mind Disease."* http://www.abandone-dasylum.com/dunning1.html

Wiss, Janney, and Eistener Associates, Inc. "The Will County Rural Historical Survey, Homer Township, Appendix C." http://www.willcountydata.com.

Manuscripts, Papers, and Municipal and Federal Reports

"Blue Book of the Cook County Democracy 1902, with a History and Record of Organization." Chicago: R. F. Petibone, 1902.

Chicago Common Council. *Journal of the Proceedings,* December 4, 1871, 1–9. Municipal Reference Collection, Chicago Public Library.

Easley, Ralph M. "The Work of the Civic Federation of Chicago." Report of the Secretary Read at the 5th Meeting, April 26, 1899.

Harrison, Carter, IV. Papers. Midwest Manuscript Collection, the Newberry Library, Chicago.

Roberts, Sidney I. "Businessmen in Revolt: Chicago, 1874–1900." Ph.D. diss., Northwestern University, 1960.

Tree, Lambert. Papers. Midwest Manuscript Collection, the Newberry Library, Chicago.

U.S. Bureau of the Census. Annual Census Reports, 1830–1920.

Newspapers

Bloomington Pantograph
Boston Globe
Chicago American
Chicago Daily Globe
Chicago Daily Mail

Chicago Daily News
Chicago Evening Post
Chicago Herald
Chicago Inter-Ocean
Chicago Journal
Chicago Record-Herald
Chicago Staats-Zeitung
Chicago Times
Chicago Tribune
Decatur Weekly Republican
Detroit News
Kansas City Times
New Orleans Bee
New York Times
Niagara Falls Gazette
Niagara Falls Reporter
Richmond (Ill.) Gazette
St. Louis Post-Dispatch
Washington Post

Index

Richard C. Lindberg is a noted Chicago historian and the author of twelve earlier books, including *Shattered Sense of Innocence: The 1955 Murders of Three Chicago Children*; *To Serve and Collect: Chicago Politics and Police Corruption from the Lager Beer Riot to the Summerdale Scandal*; *Return to the Scene of the Crime: A Guide to Infamous Places in Chicago*; *Passport's Guide to Ethnic Chicago*; *Total White Sox*; and *Chicago Ragtime: Another Look at Chicago, 1880–1920*. He is a past president of the Society of Midland Authors and a 2008 recipient of the Morris Wexler Award from the Illinois Academy of Criminology.